Making Waves

7⁰⁰

D0963846

Editorial Board for the Asian Women United Anthology

Diane Yen-Mei Wong
Chief Editor

Emilya Cachapero
Creative Editor

Chung Hoang Chuong

Elaine H. Kim

Sucheta Mazumdar
Social Sciences Editor

Janice Mirikitani
Creative Editor

Jane Singh

Judy Yung
Project Director

Nancy Hom
Artistic Director

Making Waves

An Anthology
of Writings
By and About
Asian American
Women

EDITED BY

Asian Women United
of California

BEACON PRESS

Boston

Beacon Press
25 Beacon Street
Boston, Massachusetts 02108

Beacon Press books
are published under the auspices of
the Unitarian Universalist Association of Congregations.

© 1989 by Asian Women United of California
All rights reserved
Printed in the United States of America

96 95 94 93 92 91   4 5 6 7 8

Text design by Ann H. Stewart

Library of Congress Cataloging-in-Publication Data
Making waves.
1. Asian American women.   I. Wong, Diane Yen-Mei.
E184.06M24   1989   305.4'8895073   88-47661
ISBN 0-8070-5904-8
ISBN 0-8070-5905-6 (pbk.)

Contents

Preface   ix

Acknowledgments   xiii

General Introduction: A Woman-Centered Perspective
on Asian American History / *Sucheta Mazumdar*   I

Part One / From Shore to Shore: Immigration

INTRODUCTION   25
POEM BY THE WELLSIDE / *Meena Alexander*   27
OKASAN/MOTHER / *Sakae S. Roberson*   29
A GIRL ON THE SWING / *Chungmi Kim*   30
THE PEOPLE HERE: A LETTER / *Myrna Peña-Reyes*   31
MAGIC ISLAND / *Cathy Song*   32
THE WORLD OF OUR GRANDMOTHERS /
    Connie Young Yu   33
VOICES FROM THE PAST: WHY THEY CAME /
    Dorothy Cordova   42
KOREAN IMMIGRANT WOMEN IN EARLY
    TWENTIETH-CENTURY AMERICA / *Sun Bin Yim*   50
THE HARDSHIPS OF ESCAPE FOR VIETNAMESE
    WOMEN / *Van Luu*   60

Part Two / Crashing Waves: War

INTRODUCTION   75
SHADOW IN STONE / *Janice Mirikitani*   76
WE THE EXILED / *Brenda Paik Sunoo*   79

WAR STORY / *Elaine H. Kim*   80

THE HOPELAND / *K. Kam*   92

MY MOTHER'S PURPLE DRESS / *Evelyn Lee and Gloria Oberst*   99

NISEI WOMEN AND RESETTLEMENT DURING WORLD WAR II / *Valerie Matsumoto*   115

Part Three / Moving Currents: Work

INTRODUCTION   129

AND ALL THE GIRLS CRIED / *Kathy Wong*   130

CHINATOWN TALKING STORY / *Kitty Tsui*   132

ISSEI WORKING WOMEN IN HAWAII / *Gail M. Nomura*   135

LADIES ON THE LINE: PUNJABI CANNERY WORKERS IN CENTRAL CALIFORNIA / *Marcelle Williams*   148

BEHIND UNMARKED DOORS: DEVELOPMENTS IN THE GARMENT INDUSTRY / *Diane Yen-Mei Wong with Dennis Hayashi*   159

WOMEN IN THE SILICON VALLEY / *Rebecca Villones*   172

ASIAN AMERICAN WOMEN IN BROADCASTING / *Felicia Lowe*   176

THE GAP BETWEEN STRIVING AND ACHIEVING: THE CASE OF ASIAN AMERICAN WOMEN / *Deborah Woo*   185

Part Four / Where Rivers Merge: Generations

INTRODUCTION   197

MOTHER / *Beheroze F. Shroff*   198

THE LOOM / *R. A. Sasaki*   199

THE PARROT'S BEAK / *Kartar Dhillon*   214

WAITING FOR PAPA'S RETURN / *Cecilia Manguerra Brainard*   223

DREAMS OF MANONG FRANKIE / *Virginia Cerenio*   228

Part Five / Clearing the Mist: Identity

INTRODUCTION 239

BEHIND THE SHADOW / *Angela Lobo-Cobb* 240

DOUBLE DOORS / *Jonny Sullivan Price* 241

GROWING UP ASIAN IN AMERICA / *Kesaya E. Noda* 243

MAKAPUU BAY / *Wakako Yamauchi* 251

BROAD SHOULDERS / *Nellie Wong* 260

YOU'RE SHORT, BESIDES! / *Sucheng Chan* 265

MESTIZA GIRLHOOD: INTERRACIAL FAMILIES IN
CHICAGO'S FILIPINO AMERICAN COMMUNITY
SINCE 1925 / *Barbara M. Posadas* 273

ASIAN AMERICAN LESBIANS: AN EMERGING VOICE
IN THE ASIAN AMERICAN COMMUNITY / *Pamela H.* 282

Part Six / Thunderstorms: Injustice

INTRODUCTION 293

FACTORY GIRLS / *Chea Villanueva* 295

MOSQUITOES IN THE MAIN ROOM / *Meena Alexander* 296

TWO DESERTS / *Valerie Matsumoto* 299

LOTUS BLOSSOMS DON'T BLEED: IMAGES OF ASIAN
WOMEN / *Renee E. Tajima* 308

THE BUSINESS OF SELLING MAIL-ORDER BRIDES /
Venny Villapando 318

DOMESTIC VIOLENCE AMONG PACIFIC ASIANS /
Nilda Rimonte 327

MATCHMAKING IN THE CLASSIFIEDS OF THE
IMMIGRANT INDIAN PRESS / *Rashmi Luthra* 337

Part Seven / Making Waves: Activism

INTRODUCTION 347

IN REMEMBRANCE / *Janice Mirikitani* 349

viii

FOR THE POETS OF "FIRETREE" ON THE SECOND
ANNIVERSARY OF THE DEATH OF BENIGNO
AQUINO / *Valorie Bejarano*   352

GROWING UP, 1968–1985 / *Juanita Tamayo Lott*   353

THE FEMINIST MOVEMENT: WHERE ARE ALL THE
ASIAN AMERICAN WOMEN? / *Esther Ngan-Ling Chow*   362

FROM HOMEMAKER TO HOUSING ADVOCATE:
AN INTERVIEW WITH MRS. CHANG JOK LEE /
Nancy Diao   377

DUST AND DISHES: ORGANIZING WORKERS /
Yoichi Shimatsu and Patricia Lee   386

SEEKING A VOICE: SOUTH ASIAN WOMEN'S GROUPS
IN NORTH AMERICA / *Jyotsna Vaid*   395

ASIAN PACIFIC AMERICAN WOMEN IN MAINSTREAM
POLITICS / *Judy Chu*   405

Appendix: A Chronology of Asian American History /
Judy Yung   423

About the Contributors   433

Notes   445

Preface

This anthology is the first major compilation of primarily unpublished works by and about Asian American women since the early 1970s. During the past decade and a half, many people have been recording the experiences and history of those women in America who can trace their roots to Asia—China, Japan, Korea, the Philippines, South Asia, and Southeast Asia. The works collected here reflect our heterogeneity. They range from pieces by writers whose first published piece is in this book to those whose names are already familiar in Asian American literature; from essays to poems, short stories, and memoirs; from selections about older immigrant groups—such as the Chinese, Japanese, Korean, and Filipino—to those about newer arrivals—such as South Asians and Southeast Asians.

We used many avenues to reach all the communities and received a tremendous response. We contacted ethnic media, college programs, friends, and colleagues, and made special efforts to include works of the Korean, Southeast Asian, Filipino, and South Asian American communities. After several months we finally collected over three times the amount of written materials you see here!

We had aimed to have equal representation of all ethnic groups and of all written forms of expression. However, because of the complexity of the different cultures, this was not to be. We found it difficult to obtain written materials from some of the groups, especially the new and emerging ones.

Most of the ethnic groups we write about are familiar—Chinese, Filipino, Japanese, and Korean Americans. Others, however, may need some explanation. By South Asian women, we mean those whose roots extend to India, Pakistan, Bangladesh, and the other countries in that area. The term Southeast Asian refers to women from the Indochinese

Peninsula—Vietnam, Cambodia, and Laos—as well as women from Burma and Thailand. Though our search for works on Asian American women was open to both women and men writers, most of the pieces submitted to and selected for the anthology were written by women.

The seven sections of the book provide a general context for all the individual pieces. We struggled over this division because although we wanted to group the works in a relevant and connected manner, we discovered that sometimes the themes overlapped. These themes, however, help organize the diversity of subjects which range from memories of Asian American women in their homelands to current issues in the United States, from personal relationships to those in the workplace, from introspection to war. The water image found throughout was suggested by writer Janice Mirikitani, who also served as one of the creative editors for the book.

As we worked hard to achieve a fair and balanced representation, tensions arose when we had to sacrifice a piece because of length or when we tried to convince an author to treat a topic more accessibly or when we had to make more effort to reach a particular writer or community. We agreed, however, to retain as much as possible of the individual writers' styles and cultural integrity, and have respected their choices in a variety of ethnic designations (such as Filipino or Pilipino) and romanization (such as the modern pinyin system or the Cantonese dialect familiar to most earlier immigrants from China).

In all, the making of this anthology involved many long hours of work—soliciting, editing, selecting, negotiating, designing, and publishing. It was especially trying for the editorial board. Because of space limitations, we could not be absolutely inclusive, but we could provide at least a representative collection of writers and works. So we fought for pieces; we fought against pieces; we even fought each other. Sometimes we felt the selections were too academic; at other times not substantive enough. The disagreements were good and creative for all of us, though. They forced each of us to examine what was important to include in our history as Asian American women; they taught us to work together and make collective decisions that reflected our diverse board of poets, historians, educators, and community workers. Finally, the conflicts helped us realize—with elation—that there are many creative and thoughtful people across this country recording the experiences of Asian women in America, and they were willing to share their works with us. We have grown from this process, and we are proud of our work.

Contrary to the erroneous stereotype that Asian American women are passive and submissive, this anthology shows that we are not afraid to rock the boat. Making waves. This is what Asian American women have done and will continue to do.

Acknowledgments

Making Waves would not have been possible without the generous support and help of many people and organizations. The editorial board of this anthology is greatly indebted to the board and members of Asian Women United of California for their guidance. Special recognition should also go to Elaine Kim, who not only served as one of the editors but also generated the idea for the anthology and actively sought funding for its fruition. We also received computer assistance from Gary Kawaguchi and legal advice from Dale Minami.

The community advisory board was particularly helpful in reaching out to the Asian American community and reviewing an earlier draft of the book. Members included Manuela Albuquerque, Madge Bello, Suzy Chung, Wendy Horikoshi, Usha Jain, Ruthanne Lum McCunn, Sandra Uyeunten, Caridad Vallangca, and Henry Woon.

The U.S. Department of Education Women's Educational Equity Act Program provided much of the funding for the compilation, editing, and production of this book.

Other acknowledgments include:

Meena Alexander's "Poem by the Wellside" appeared in *The Toronto South Asian Review* 1:2 (Summer 1982); "Mosquitoes in the Main Room" appeared in *Ikon* Second Series 4 (Winter/Summer 1985). These works are also in Alexander's own collection of poems and short prose pieces, *House of a Thousand Doors* (Washington, D.C.: Three Continents Press, 1986).

Virginia Cerenio's "Dreams of Manong Frankie" appeared in the University of California's *Berkeley Fiction Review* (1983).

Esther Chow presented an earlier version of "The Feminist Movement: Where Are All the Asian American Women?" at the Tenth World Congress of Sociology, sponsored by the International Sociological Association in Mexico City in 1982.

xiv

Dorothy Cordova's "Voices from the Past: Why They Came" is based on oral histories collected in 1985 for Cordova's exhibit and book project on Filipina Americans.

Chungmi Kim's "A Girl on the Swing" appeared in her collection entitled *Chungmi* (Los Angeles: Pioneer Press).

Angela Lobo-Cobb's "Behind the Shadow" appeared in a collection called "A Confluence of Colors" from the *First Anthology of Wisconsin Minority Poets* (Madison: Blue Reed Arts, 1984).

Valerie Matsumoto's article "Nisei Women and Resettlement during World War II" is revised from a longer piece, "Japanese American Women during World War II," which appeared in *Frontiers* 8 : 1 (1984).

Sakae Roberson's "Okasan/Mother" appeared in *Prisma* (Oakland: Mills College, 1983).

Brenda Sunoo's "We the Exiled" appeared in *Time to Greez: Incantations from the Third World,* eds. Third World Communication (San Francisco: Glide Publications, 1975).

An earlier version of Renee Tajima's "Lotus Blossoms Don't Bleed: Images of Asian Women" appeared in the catalogues *In Color* (New York: Third World Newsreel, 1982) and *Anthology: Asian American Film and Video* (New York: Association of Independent Video and Filmmakers, Inc., 1985); and the National Asian American Telecommunications Association newsletter (1985).

Chea Villanueva's "Factory Girls" appeared in *Asian Lesbians of the East Coast,* newsletter (New York City, August 1984); *Feminary Magazine* 15 (San Francisco, Summer 1985); and *Ang Katipunan,* newspaper (July 1985).

Wakako Yamauchi's "Makapuu Bay" appeared in *The Bamboo Ridge* (Honolulu, June-August 1979); and in the San Francisco newspaper *Rafu Shimpo* (Holiday Edition, December 1978).

General Introduction: A Woman-Centered Perspective on Asian American History

SUCHETA MAZUMDAR

What did it mean to be a Chinese woman in nineteenth-century California? Or a Japanese woman on the sugar plantations in early twentieth-century Hawaii? Or a Filipina on today's electronic assembly lines in the Silicon Valley; a Korean garment worker in New York? If society has ever thought about these women, it has often been in clichés: the depraved prostitute in nineteenth-century San Francisco; the quiet, courteous, and efficient Asian female office worker today. Asian women in America have emerged not as individuals but as nameless and faceless members of an alien community. Their identity has been formed by the lore of the majority community, not by their own history, their own stories. In an attempt to hear those muted voices, to provide a woman-centered perspective of the Asian American experience, this chronological overview explores the lines along which women have shaped, and been shaped by, the history of Asian America.[1]

The Early Years: A Thousand Pieces of Gold[2]

On 24 January 1848, gold was discovered in the California Sierra Nevada foothills. At about the same time across the Pacific, China was also experiencing momentous events. The ravages of the Opium War (1839–42) had colored the long emigration history of the coastal districts of Guangdong with a particular urgency. Jobs had been lost after the war, land laid waste, and there was unrest everywhere. They were the first group of immigrants from Asia. Then came the news from California; first hundreds and then thousands of Chinese were touched by gold fever. After arriving, however, most of them found that the legendary gold was not easy to obtain; through the 1850s and 1860s, many worked at railroad construction sites in the West.

By 1870, 58,625 Chinese men and 4,574 Chinese women (of whom 3,881 were in San Francisco) had arrived in the United States.[3] This skewed male-female ratio was not unique to the Chinese immigrants. In 1850 there were twelve men for every woman in San Francisco regardless of race; in 1880 men outnumbered women in California three to one.[4] In the raucous and heady frontier atmosphere of gold digging and overnight riches, San Francisco was transformed from a village of 812 people in 1848, into a city of 40,000 within just one year.[5] Bars and brothels were an inevitable consequence. Substandard wages and the uncertainty of frontier life prevented many men from bringing their families; thereby they provided a potential clientele. The lack of work options and low wages for women, and the absence of support systems when they were unemployed, contributed to the pool of potential employees.[6]

Madames and prostitutes of every nationality—French, Chilean and Mexican—came to San Francisco. And there was Ah-Choi, "the girl in the green silk pantaloons."[7] Ah-Choi, along with a handful of other Chinese women, was an entrepreneur who arrived in 1849, and a few years later set up her own brothel.[8] But the majority of Chinese women who worked as prostitutes in the alleys and back streets of San Francisco from the 1850s to the 1870s were not free agents. They were bonded women who had been sold, kidnapped, and enticed under false pretenses by brothel owners; and they had scant control over their lives and incomes. In Hawaii too, the other Pacific frontier which developed during the 1860s and 1870s, somewhat similar circumstances prevailed. The islands yielded a different kind of gold—tons of sugar produced by Asian and other workers. Thousands of Chinese and then Japanese laborers were recruited to work the cane fields and, because of an unbalanced ratio of men to women and the dismal wages paid to female plantation workers, Japanese prostitution emerged.[9]

In the 1860s and early 1870s, however, neither the press nor the public on the mainland was willing to see Chinese prostitution as a reflection of the same situation facing many other women. The unusually detailed information available on the lives of Chinese prostitutes in San Francisco was not inspired by purely humanitarian concerns. Rather, the publicity about "debauched" Chinese women who only came to work as prostitutes fueled the fears and hostility held by many California residents against the "unassimilable Chinese."

Racial Oppression and Asian Exclusion

Racism in the California mines and in every other economic sector in which the Chinese competed assumed virulent proportions by the 1870s. The completion of the transcontinental railroad had put many out of work. The depression of the 1870s and the large-scale migration of white workers from the East Coast into California whipped anti-Chinese sentiments into a frenzy, often ending in lynchings and beatings of Chinese.[10] The much publicized hearings regarding Chinese prostitution dovetailed with the rise of anti-Chinese hysteria. Singling out Chinese prostitution in an era of widespread general prostitution served to produce many clichés: the depravity of the Orientals; the sexually subservient Asian female.

Sexual practice has been used repeatedly to enforce hierarchies of gender, race, and class. The assumption that blacks are oversexed has served to justify their subordination and control by white people, who have more "civilized" values;[11] similarly, the sexuality of "Oriental" women, depicted as somehow immoral and different, underlined the "heathen" values of the Chinese and became yet another reason for advocating the exclusion of Asians. The myth of the "erotic Oriental" and her objectification as a sexual mannequin, born of the 1870s racist environment, continues to haunt portrayals of Asian women: from Ah-Choi to Suzie Wong to sultry Indian princesses in the movie *Far Pavillions*.[12]

The 1870 hearings on Chinese prostitution helped to pass "An Act to Prevent the Kidnapping and Importation of Mongolian, Chinese, and Japanese Females for Criminal and Demoralizing Purposes," which, in essence, assumed that all "Oriental" females seeking to immigrate to California were doing so in order to engage in "criminal and demoralizing purposes." This act gave the immigration commissioner the right to determine whether the incoming woman was "a person of correct habits and good character."[13]

The hostility behind this act and a myriad of other legislation aimed against the Chinese, culminated in the Chinese Exclusion Act of 1882, the first federal exclusion law directed at a specific nationality. The law suspended Chinese labor immigration and excluded all Chinese, other than merchants, students, diplomats, and visitors. Additional restrictive legislation prohibited the return of about twenty-two thousand Chinese laborers who had gone back to visit China, thereby nullifying reentry certificates given to them upon leaving the United States.[14]

Thus began a most regressive and racist phase in U.S. immigration history, when people—particularly laborers seeking a better livelihood—from one nonwhite nation after another were denied entry. Time and time again when industrialists and growers needed cheap labor, they welcomed Asians; yet time and time again, when their demands ceased or when the economy stagnated, they sought to exclude them. The sequence of legislation tells the story. The 1907 Gentlemen's Agreement curtailed Japanese and Korean labor immigration; then came the 1917 act restricting Asian Indian immigration, the 1924 Oriental Exclusion Act terminating labor immigration from all mainland Asia, and the 1934 Tydings-McDuffie Act restricting Filipino immigration.

Citizenship through naturalization was denied to all Asians from 1924 until 1943, when over the next ten years the laws were changed on a country-by-country basis. After 1943, with the exception of war brides and family members of U.S. citizens, immigration was permitted only on a quota system which allowed between 100 and 150 Asians annually from each country. Then on 3 October 1965, the forty-four-year-old "national origins" immigration system of the United States was terminated. An amendment established a worldwide limit of 290,000 immigrants per year, with 20,000 new immigrants permitted entry from each Asian country.

These periods of restrictive and exclusionary immigration laws had profound implications on the development of the family in Asian communities in America. Asian women married to immigrant men could not join their husbands—sometimes for years, sometimes for decades.

The Waiting Years [15]

"One moonless night in a little village in Guangdong, Aunt No Name threw herself and her newborn into the well. Her child was illegitimate. Her husband had left for California to search for gold many summers ago." [16]

Almost half the Chinese men who emigrated were married, but only a handful could bring their spouses. According to the 1900 census, although 38 percent of Chinese males over the age of fifteen were married, there was only one Chinese female to every twenty-six Chinese males in the United States. [17] The wives left behind in Taishan (Toisan) district poured out their sorrows and frustrations in folksongs:

> I am still young, with a husband, yet a widow.
> The pillow is cold, so frightening.
>
> O, don't ever marry a daughter to a man from Gold Mountain,
> Lonely and sad, her only companion is her cooking pot. [18]

Filipino immigration to the United States, which started in 1906 with recruitment by Hawaiian Sugar Planters, fared no differently; plantation owners simply saw little advantage in having female immigrants. "Plantations have to view laborers primarily as instruments of production. Their business interest[s] require cheap, not too intelligent, docile, unmarried men," reported the labor commissioner. [19] Among Filipino immigrants for every one woman there were eight to ten men in Hawaii, fourteen men in California, thirty-three men in Washington, and forty-seven men in New York. [20]

Farmworkers from the Punjab province in South Asia who came to California between 1904 and 1924 shared a similar fate. A 1909 Immigration Commission survey of 474 male "Hindoo" farmworkers found that 215 were married but that all 215 of the wives had remained in India. [21] One such young husband, nurturing memories of his teenage bride, was not able to send for her for forty years. As she got off the plane in San Francisco, in pained bewilderment he gasped, "But she is such an old woman." [22]

6

For thousands of women in the 1910s and 1920s, the sequence of events shaping their lives differed dramatically from those married and left behind. These were the women who came as picture brides, the women who waited on the docksides of ports in Honolulu, San Francisco, and Seattle for husbands they had married by proxy in Japan or Korea.

Picture Brides

"It was on the day that the Weaver Maiden met the Cowherd."[23] So began a poem carved by an immigrant on the walls of Angel Island, the immigration processing center on the West Coast between 1910 and 1940. The poem recalled the popular Chinese story of the Celestial Weaver Maiden doomed to see her true love only once a year, after crossing the breadth of the heavens to do so. To the women in the detention wards waiting to be processed for immigration, crossing the Pacific Ocean seemed no less arduous. The initial phase of Japanese immigration (1885–1900) did not include very many women. In 1900 for example, out of a total population of 24,326 Japanese on the U.S. mainland, only 985 were women.[24] Even in Hawaii, where the Japanese government had stipulated that 30 percent of the laborers recruited had to be women, the immigrant sex ratio in Hawaii was only slightly better.[25]

Hawaii's skewed gender distribution existed also in the Korean community, which had begun to develop between 1902 and 1907. Korean workers were brought in to break the dominance of increasingly militant Japanese workers, to "drive the Japs out," as one plantation owner put it.[26] The sex ratio in the Korean community was ten men to one woman. Though several of the Korean men were married, the policies of the plantation association precluded actively seeking women for immigration. Of the 7,296 Korean immigrants in Hawaii during this period, only 613 were women.[27]

The so-called Gentlemen's Agreement of 1907 barred further immigration of Japanese and Korean laborers but permitted wives to rejoin Japanese and Korean husbands domiciled in the United States. Thus, bringing over picture brides became a lifeline to survival for the Japanese and Korean communities. Arranged by the families of the potential bride and groom, marriage was not so much for individual fulfillment as for societal and familial responsibility. In early twentieth-century Japan and Korea, picture brides were often found through the village match-makers and selected by the groom's family. As negotiations ended, photographs were exchanged and the bride's name written into the family register to legalize the union. The bride then set sail for the United States to meet her mate. On one hand, traditional Asian social customs made this arrangement possible; on the other, immigration restrictions preventing the reentry of male laborers necessitated such arrangements even among those who may have had the money to go back and select brides themselves.

Almost 40 percent of the immigrants from Japan over the next decade were women; the majority came as brides of men they had seen only in a photo. Socialized to be uncomplaining and stoical, and with few options in a strange land, thousands of picture brides set up homes and stayed with their husbands, who sometimes bore little resemblance to their handsome photos.

For many women, though, becoming a picture bride provided choices denied them in their home countries. Sometimes the motivating factor was a straightforward desire for travel and excitement.[28] In other cases it was a direct protest against and circumvention of social restrictions on women. As one seventy-eight-year-old Korean grandmother who had essentially run away from home exclaimed, "Ah, marriage! Then I could get to America! That land of freedom with streets paved of gold! . . . Since I became ten, I've been forbidden to step outside our gates, just like all the rest of the girls of my day. . . . Becoming a picture bride, whatever that was, would be my answer and release."[29]

Through Harsh Winters in a Land of Sunshine[30]

For most immigrant women, however, the United States was far from a "land paved of gold." Hard work began soon after landing, and one worked not for gold but for copper pennies.

Except for the wives of rich merchants—who formed less than 1 percent of the Chinese immigrant population—all the other women worked; sometimes outside the home, but, because of limited opportunities for wage work, more often within the home. From taking in laundry or keeping boarders and sewing and cooking for bachelors, to raising beansprouts in bathtubs and cabbages and chickens in the backyard, domestic skills were vital work in terms of the family economy. Even among the 753 Chinese women in the 1870 Census who identified themselves as "keeping house," at least 20 percent had several boarders and lodgers, sometimes as many as thirty-eight additional people within the home.[31]

This work became a major form of self-employment for immigrant women on the mainland and in Hawaii from the late nineteenth to the middle of the twentieth century. For example Mrs. Tai Yoo Kim, who had just turned eighteen in 1905, ran a plantation boarding house at Honokaa and prepared three meals a day for twenty-one men, including her husband.[32] Another woman recalled, "My mother and sister-in-law took in laundry. They scrubbed, ironed and mended shirts for a nickle a piece. It was pitiful. Their knuckles became swollen and raw from using the harsh yellow laundry soap."[33]

Household skills often enabled immigrant women to enter the urban labor force. In 1940 one-fourth of all employed issei Japanese women in Oakland and over one-half of all employed issei women in San Francisco worked as domestic maids.[34] That story continues even now as thousands of Filipino, Korean, and Chinese hotel room cleaners don uniforms in tourist spots across the country each day. The necessity of a paycheck still forces many immigrant women to postpone efforts to learn English and attempts to transfer old job skills to positions in the highly competitive work environment of urban America. Many never manage to leave their entry-level jobs.

Down on the Farm[35]

After the grape pruning season . . . we would go to the asparagus camps in Stockton's Cannery Ranch. . . . [Then] pear picking started

in Walnut Grove. . . . After pears came peach packing in Marysville. . . . Apple packing came next in Watsonville. . . . From Watsonville we moved on to Pismo. . . . We worked for Masuoka-san
picking peas.[36]

Michiko Kikumura, recalling her life in the 1920s in California, vividly
describes the farm labor cycle that thousands of agricultural workers still
follow today.

The development of California and other Western states in the late
nineteenth century occasionally provided some atypical avenues of employment. There were some Chinese and Japanese women in the mining
districts of California, Nevada, and Idaho; others in the fishing industry
off the coast of Monterey, California; some Chinese women even did
railroad construction work.[37] But by far the largest percentage of Asian
women working outside the home prior to World War II were in the
agricultural sector: plantation workers in Hawaii; farmers, farm laborers, and tenant farmers on the West Coast. By 1920, 14 percent of all
Oahu plantation laborers were women, about 80 percent of whom were
of Japanese origin, the others of Chinese, Korean, Portuguese, and Nor-
wegian descent.[38] In 1915 Japanese women formed 38 percent of all cane
loaders. Though given the same assignments as men, including the
particularly strenuous tasks of cutting and loading cane, women received wages about 30 percent lower. Anna Choi, a Korean woman who
came to Hawaii as a picture bride, remembered:

I arose at four o'clock in the morning and we took a truck to the sugar
cane fields, eating breakfast on the way. Work in the sugar plantations
was back breaking. It involved cutting canes, watering and pulling
out weeds. . . . The sugar cane fields were endless and twice the
height of myself. Now that I look back, I *thank goodness* for the height
for if I had seen how far the fields stretched I probably would have
fainted from knowing how much work was ahead.[39]

During the first four decades of the twentieth century thousands of
Japanese women also worked alongside their husbands on farms in California, Oregon, Washington, Colorado, Utah, and Idaho. Many Japa-

nese had hoped to buy their own farms, but the Alien Land Law of 1923 ended those dreams for all but a few. Promulgated in all the states in which the Japanese and other Asians were active as farmers, this law forbade land purchases by "aliens ineligible for citizenship."[40] Those with U.S.-born children managed to buy land in the name of the children; others worked as tenants on farms they actually owned, but which they registered in the name of an eligible white neighbor or friend.

To set up farms and homes where there had been nothing but desert—often the only land they could afford—pioneering issei women had much to do: haul well water, collect firewood, tend fields, and help harvest, as well as cook, clean, sew, and raise families. And on these isolated farms, they rarely had other women to turn to for friendship or comfort. Teiko Tomita, an issei woman striving to maintain her farm in Washington's Yakima Valley, wrote:

> Neighbors are five miles away.
> Many days without seeing anyone.
> Today, too, without seeing anyone.
> The sun sets.[41]

On 7 December 1941, Pearl Harbor was bombed by Japan. Then in 1942 neither luck nor hard work nor accommodation of the law was enough to save Japanese families their hard earned farms. Federal Executive Order 9066 signed by President Roosevelt ordered the forced relocation and internment of 120,000 people of Japanese origin residing on the West Coast. Allowed only a week to ten days to prepare for the move, women, men, and children abandoned possessions, jobs, homes, and fields to live behind barbed wire for the next three years. Eighty percent of those who returned home after the war found that their property had been "rifled, stolen or sold during their absence."[42] While some Japanese families continued to work in the agricultural sector after their return from the camps, most of the first-generation Asian women and men moved away from the farms in the 1950s.

Changes in the Asian World

<pre>
birds
living in the cage
human spirit
    Gensui   thorns of the iron fence
                              pointed inward
                              toward camp
                              Kyokusui[43]
</pre>

In 1943, while most of the Japanese community lived in internment camps, the War Manpower Commission undertook a massive campaign to get women from other communities out to work. Newspaper ads, radio spots, film shorts, and billboards ran the message: "What job is mine on the Victory Line" and "If you've followed recipes exactly in making cakes, you can learn to load shell."[44] Like other women across the nation, second- and third-generation Asian American women joined the urban labor force. While some Chinese American women found war-related production jobs in the defense industry, the majority took clerical positions in the government.[45]

Though social and economic racial barriers proved resistant to change, institutional racism was forced to make certain accommodations during the war years. Thousands of nonwhite servicemen fought side by side with white soldiers, but upon returning home found they were still treated like second-class citizens. Blacks and Asian Americans challenged housing segregation in the late forties, and many states repealed their antimiscegenation laws.[46] While the Supreme Court did not rule against antimiscegenation laws until 1967, the number of white American servicemen marrying and bringing back Asian wives tested the validity of the discriminatory laws.

Other changes occurred in the U.S. immigration laws. The quota system established in the early 1940s partially lifted the ban on Asian immigration and allowed between 105 and 150 immigrants to enter from each of the Asian countries. The War Brides Act of 1945 also facilitated immigration of women and children. This legislation thus contributed to a relative normalization of the skewed gender ratios of earlier years and aided the process of regeneration in all the Asian American communities.

Between 1940 and 1960 the political map of Asia changed dramatically, with significant implications for the next generation of Asian immigrants. Struggles for independence gained momentum as the former colony of the Philippines became independent in 1946, and India and Pakistan in 1947.

In Korea, annexed by the Japanese in 1910, the 1945 surrender of the Japanese army was accepted by the Soviet Union in the North and the United States in the South. North and South Korea were divided by the 38th parallel, a fragile border which erupted into war in 1950. Though the Korean Conflict ended in 1953, there are still forty thousand U.S. troops in Korea today, grim reminders of a tenuous peace. Until 1977 U.S. passports were not valid for travel to North Korea, and even now travel to the North is looked upon with suspicion by U.S. federal agencies.

The civil war in China, which ended in 1949 with Nationalist-led Republic of China on Taiwan and a Communist-led government on the mainland, also left a divided legacy for Chinese immigrants. U.S. diplomatic relations only with Taiwan until 1972 made it impossible for Chinese Americans to visit family in China. "Not once have I swept my parents graves. I sent them money, but how can I even think of myself as filial? Now? Now it is too late for me, I'm too old to travel," says Auntie Ling, remembering the long years between 1949 and 1972, when travel to the People's Republic of China was prohibited.[47]

In the 1940s the people of Vietnam were drawn into a war that was to span two generations. First colonized by the French and then occupied by the Japanese during World War II, Vietnam's nationalist, anti-imperialist struggle emerged in 1941, eventually engulfing the country in civil war. When the war finally ended in 1975, the United States enacted the Refugee Resettlement Act of 1975, which permitted the migration of 500,000 people from Vietnam, and which was amended in 1979 to include Laotian, Cambodian, and other ethnic groups from Southeast Asia. Many families, however, remain separated. "Yes, I still have family over in Vietnam—parents and sisters. I haven't seen them in ten years. And now it takes two or three years stay in a refugee camp in the Philippines or Malaysia before even a sponsored brother or sister can come to this country. I don't know if I'll ever see Vietnam again," says a middle-aged Vietnamese laundry owner in Seattle.[48] The U.S. government has neither diplomatic relations nor open travel with Vietnam, Laos, or Cambodia.

From Yellow Peril to Model Minorities: The New Immigrants[49]

The 1952 McCarran-Walter Act enabled Asians to acquire citizenship through naturalization, and changes in the 1965 immigration laws raised the quota of aliens permitted entry to twenty thousand from each Asian country. These liberalized policies meant that the immigrants entering after 1965 typically entered as families or could send for their families soon after arrival. However, the system has not been without biases.

Between the years 1943 and 1965, when the quota system was in effect, 50 percent of the quota was reserved for professionals.[50] This selective process facilitated the immigration of those with post-secondary education, technical training, and specialized experience. It continued even after the 1965 liberalization of immigration laws, which permitted entry based either on occupational skills needed by the United States or on the presence of relatives in this country. Professionals could immigrate under both types of preference categories; most other potential immigrants could apply only under the family reunification category. Without a relative willing to act as a sponsor, those who are unskilled may have to wait five to ten years for a visa. Complicated, time-consuming, and intimidating application procedures also favor the educated.

Though there are now more job opportunities available to these professionals and to second- and third-generation Asian Americans, one must be concerned that the sensationalized "yellow peril" cliché of poverty-stricken Asians not be replaced by yet another cliché, that of the "super successful model minority." This new success myth is dangerous because it does not tell the full story.

Despite various federal affirmative action policies and programs of the 1970s, 10.7 percent of all Asian Pacific families in 1979 had incomes below the poverty level. Statistics suggest that one-fifth of all employed Asian Pacific women work as waitresses, maids, and sewing machine operators.[51] Many Asian Americans, including older immigrants and recent arrivals, live in Manilatowns and Koreatowns and Little Saigons, congested urban ghettoes like San Francisco Chinatown, where 77 percent of the housing does not even meet city codes and only 6 percent has adequate plumbing.[52]

Many of these Asian ethnic ghettoes were on the decline in the 1950s and 1960s; their revival and proliferation in the 1970s and 1980s is not so much due to Chamber of Commerce promotion of tourist exotica as a genuine response to the needs of the new immigrants who live, work, or find support services there. Even highly trained professionals may find the language barrier overwhelming or their foreign credentials unacceptable here and be forced to turn to low-income housing and semi-skilled jobs in ethnic markets, restaurants, and custodial services in order to survive.

Relationships between new arrivals and long-term residents or citizens and between professional and working classes can be complex and tense. The established working class sees new arrivals as competitors for the same scarce resources; the established professionals look askance at their limited English proficient or culturally ill-at-ease immigrant counterparts. Professionals dissociate themselves from the residents of ethnic ghettoes; working-class Asians view the professionals' tendency to be spokespersons for the community with suspicion. The new arrival from the middle class is often more politically conservative and may look to Asia for a frame of reference; the U.S.-born tends to view the world from an American perspective.

Race and ethnic origin are frequently the most cohesive forces in defining identity. Organizers in Chinatown have found, for example, that the paternalistic attitude of garment factory owners for their employees is matched by a sense of obligation and loyalty among the workers.[53] The isolation of workers and their lack of contact with the non-Chinese world make them all the more reluctant to trust outsiders or to challenge their Chinese employers.[54] In times of crisis when an entire racial or national group has undergone severe trauma—such as during the World War II internment of Japanese Americans or the resettlement experience of Southeast Asians—ethnic identity supersedes gender and class. For women of color, concerns arising out of racial identity are an integral aspect of their overall identity.

For first-generation immigrants in particular, class issues can be quite confusing because class boundaries based on occupation can change dramatically with migration. For example, many of the early Japanese and Chinese immigrant women came from relatively wealthy land- and business-owning families.[55] Once here, as wives of immigrant laborers, they often lived difficult and frequently impoverished lives. Similarly, among more recent immigrants, women from middle-class, white-collar backgrounds frequently only find work in semiskilled jobs as waitresses, cooks, shop clerks, or electronics assembly line workers. Their consciousness and aspirations nevertheless remain middle-class.

The impact of gender on Asian women in America varies enormously even within the same class and ethnic group. While the idea that female children are of less value than male children permeates all Asian cultures to greater or lesser degrees, the effect of this value system on an American-born woman is quite different than on an immigrant one. For immigrant women arrival in America can be liberating. Societal norms of the majority community frequently provide greater personal freedom than permitted in Asian societies. The young wife, though dependent on her husband in the unfamiliar environment, often finds she has greater control of her life when living apart from her mother-in-law. The stigma attached to divorce is also somewhat muted in the American setting, thus providing a measure of choice to women with adequate survival skills. In recalling her life in the 1920s, one Filipina echoed a theme found in many Asian American communities then and now: "When I finally ran away from him, it was only because we were far away from my parents and parents-in-law who would have insisted that I accept my fate and stay with him no matter what."[56]

Individual freedom is especially palpable for women from the middle or upper classes, whose lives tend to be much more constricted in Asia.

A Pakistani woman remarked recently: "I like the freedom for the woman in this country. . . . Women back home, they are kept so much inside the house and . . . things were very hard. . . . After living that kind of life . . . I came here and [found] so much freedom."[57] A national survey of college-educated women from India living in the United States showed that 33.3 percent of the women working in technical fields and 50 percent in academic fields described themselves as feminists.[58]

For second-, third-, and fourth-generation Asian American women, the chasm between traditional Asian familial values and mainstream values has often yielded conflict. Though some of this conflict is inter-generational and common to all societies, the disparate cultural values of East and West are a source of particular anguish. On the one hand, the preservation of ethnic identity within an environment often hostile to people of color has meant a closer allegiance to Asian cultural norms; on the other, these same cultural norms and values have been a source of oppression and discrimination, especially for women. Marrying outside the community has served as one way of expressing dissatisfaction with the traditional role. Interracial marriage among the earlier immigrants, such as Japanese Americans, is approaching a level of 50 percent; and among newer immigrants, one survey found that 12 percent of Korean women college students preferred non-Korean Asian Americans as spouses and another 13 percent preferred whites.[59]

It would be inaccurate to talk about a homogeneous Asian American community when discussing class, education, national origin, economic status, or the potential for economic mobility. Similarly it would be erroneous to ascribe one common description to all Asian American women. The experiences of a Southeast Asian working-class woman and what she may perceive as the major causes of her oppression will differ greatly from those of a professional, middle-class Japanese American woman. Because it is difficult to capture the entire experience of Asian American women in this overview, what follows are but glimpses and facets of that experience.

Why Chinatown Restaurants Are Cheaper

"Nearly everyone in the city goes down to Chinatown now and then for a cheap meal out," one San Franciscan explained. He had observed that even tips were lower in Chinatown. "You just look around. Downtown, for any meal, you'll tip fifteen percent. In Chinatown, you tip ten percent. Nobody thinks twice about it. The meal is lower priced, so naturally the tip is lower too."[60]

The ethnic restaurants from Little Tokyos to Little Saigons are cheaper because they draw on not only a largely non-English-speaking labor pool which cannot find employment outside the ethnic sector, but also on the unpaid or underpaid labor of family members. While restaurants and "mom and pop" stores have been romanticized and labeled "a personal American dream . . . the ultimate statement of independence,"[61] the stark reality is that such businesses are built on the back-breaking labor of the family and, most frequently, of women.

The survival of such small businesses depends on the number of hours they can stay open. Florence Hoy, who started a grocery store with her husband in Venice, California, in the early 1930s, did not close the doors of the store until 1961; she worked 7 A.M. to 7 P.M., six and a half days a week, with no time off.[62] Across the country in a small Mississippi Delta town, Mrs. Jong Gen, one of the many Chinese who started grocery stores there in the 1910s and 1920s, remembers, "I don't sleep much, don't need to. I have been used to the long hours when we owned the store, and so my life followed the rising and the setting of the sun."[63] The pattern exists all over the country. In Southern California today, between one-fourth and one-third of all Korean immigrant women operate small businesses.[64]

The story does not change from generation to generation. The competition is so intense that the number of years a business has been in operation does not matter; the number of hours put in by the family cannot be reduced unless business is so profitable that employees can be hired to work the same hours. For the woman operating the family business, there is little opportunity for improving other skills and language facility, or for developing friendships with co-workers as in a factory situation.

The family-owned-and-operated hotel and motel business is perhaps the most extreme example of isolation and dependence in small business. Many South Asians—some of them displaced shopowners from Uganda, Kenya, and South Africa—have pooled their limited capital and invested in labor-intensive businesses such as shops, hotels, and motels. As seems to be the case with Korean Americans, the wife runs the business while the husband works elsewhere at a salaried job. Often located in decrepit downtowns and catering to a transient population, these low-budget hotels and motels encompass a wide range of work— room cleaning, laundry, phone reception, counter work—seven days a week, twenty-four hours a day. Mrs. Patel describes her typical day:

> I get up at 5:30 in the morning, make breakfast for the family, get the two children ready for school. If there is a guest, I check him in. After the kids are gone, I clean the rooms which have just been vacated, and make all the beds, take out the laundry. . . . In the evening the guests start coming and I check them in. Then I cook.[65]

Working and contributing to the family income have changed the balance of power between the sexes. While independent earnings and a pay check may not be as tangible for women operating a family business, managing the cash register nevertheless gives them more voice within the family. However, traditional Asian cultural norms emphasizing the dominant authoritarian role of husbands frequently conflict with the changing roles and expectations of working wives. One man says, "In Korea she used to have breakfast ready for me. . . . She didn't do it anymore because she said she was too busy getting ready to go to work. If I complained she talked back at me, telling me to fix my own breakfast. . . . I was very frustrated about her, started fighting and hit her."[66]

The family and the family business have served as anchors in the lives of many women. The exhaustion of long hours, constant anxiety over financial and physical survival, tedium of routine, and isolation of the self-employed have all been deemed "worth it" by these women for the sake of their children. And because starting a small business requires capital and also gives the self-employed a modicum of control over their lives, it is considered more privileged work than the type of wage labor available to most immigrant women. Mei Wong's experience speaks for many. An immigrant mother of five, she had to find a job straightaway. She took one that did not require much English: sewing.[67]

From Sewing Woman to Corporate Boardroom[68]

Historically located in New York City, the garment industry expanded to California in the 1930s and is now also entrenched in Los Angeles and San Francisco. The industry draws workers from a continuous pool of Asian and Central American immigrants whose limited language and job skills keep them trapped in the low-paying industry. Though often perceived as just a first job, sewing is often their only job. Sui Sim Tom Yee started sewing in 1955, soon after she arrived in San Francisco. At first she earned 75¢ an hour and could only survive by working longer hours; in 1978, after twenty-three years in the industry, her wages were $2.50 an hour, minimum wage.[69] In Hawaii the story is the same: Nora, a Filipina who has worked as a seamstress for twelve years, still has no job security and receives wages just 10¢ above minimum wage.[70] Like her mainland counterparts, she cannot afford to take time off to acquire other job and language skills.

The electronics industry, another major employer of Asian immigrant women, also offers little chance for upward mobility. Whether in the United States or in Asia, the "women's place in the integrated circuit,"[71] is typically on the lowest rung of the pay scale. Women comprise about 90 percent of the workers in semiconductor manufacturing and testing lines in California's Silicon Valley; about half of them are Filipinas, Vietnamese, Koreans, and South Asians. Workers in this largely nonunion industry often find minimum wage, forced overtime, work speedups, health hazards, stress, and plant closures a normal part of their work environment.

But there is another side to the profile of Asian American working women. For professional immigrant women and for second- and third-generation Asian American women who grew up in the expanding economy of post–World War II United States, reaping the benefits of a hard, long struggle by women and people of color, there have indeed been possibilities denied to earlier generations. Yet even this progress must be looked at closely. Though some Asian American women now work in positions of responsibility, visibility, and authority as lawyers, doctors, teachers, and businesswomen,[72] most work "behind the scenes" as file clerks, office machine operators, typists, and cashiers. In 1970 Chinese women with four or more years of college were still concentrated in clerical work, as were about one-third of the native-born, college-educated Filipino women in 1980.[73]

At this point it becomes necessary to question the concept of "success." Success is usually defined in terms of individual achievements—a recognition that one's undaunted spirit somehow beat the odds. But this paean to the individual disguises reality. The success of many women of color now in positions of power and visibility is not a fortuitous coincidence of opportunity and ability. Their individual achievements are founded on many years and many generations of struggle and pathmaking determination.

Immigrants and Survivors

> I eat what you tell me, I swallow my pride . . .
> I've come a long way from home . . .
> Yes, I've changed my look and I've changed my walk . . .
> I mind my manners and I know how to talk . . .
> Yes, you changed me but you know I'm gonna change you . . .[74]

The struggle of women of color for psychological and physical survival extracts a high price, and the cost goes up when the women are immigrants as well. Survival, as a woman and as a minority group member, is in itself a form of resistance. Survival for Asian women in America has taken many forms, from scrubbing floors to picking berries; from suppressing anger and swallowing loneliness to saying it is all right to look the way they do. Yet there has been much more than mere survival; there has been a whole history of resistance. Private forms of resistance pass by unnoticed precisely because myths, such as the passive Asian woman, may cloud our vision. Portraits of resistance, of the struggle to preserve human dignity, abound when one begins to recognize them: mothers in Chinatown who lovingly tended little patches called "gardens" and grew flowers on windowsills as a statement of self instead of growing more "sensible" vegetables; mothers who miraculously found empty cardboard cartons to be used as screens for privacy at the internment camps.[75] Private resistance may extend to refusing to speak English—a personal gesture that negates the world of the majority in which the immigrant woman is powerless and marginalized.

But there have also been individual and collective political forms of resistance, struggles largely unheralded except in the ethnic press. The history of labor union activism is nearly forgotten. Few remember the role of Asian immigrant women in the plantation strikes of turn-of-the-century Hawaii or know about recent struggles in the garment, hotel, and food-packaging industries. Few have heard of Esther Lau, a Chinese American whose 1970 charges of sexual harassment and physical assault by white policemen in Los Angeles brought to light scores of similar incidents perpetrated on other women of color; or Dr. Shymala Rajender, who won a class-action suit charging gender discrimination against the University of Minnesota in 1973; or of fifty-eight-year-old Helen Kim, a Korean American design engineer, who fought and won her seven-year sex discrimination suit against the Los Angeles Department of Transportation in 1980. Few know the names of the hundreds of Japanese American women who, in the 1982 hearings held to investigate the World War II internment of Japanese Americans, publicly spoke about their pain, humiliation, and degradation after forty years of agonizing silence. These Japanese American women broke their silence because they hoped "never again, would such wrong be done to a people, never again." Similarly engineer Kim stated, "It was never my intent to hurt anyone, not my department or the city. I just wanted the system to change. . . . Now, because of what I went through, maybe some other people will have an easier time of it."[76]

Yet this sense of the larger political collective is no stranger to Asian American women, who have been involved in political issues both in the United States and their ancestral homelands. Prior to World War II, women from Asian countries under colonial rule were actively involved in independence struggles, forming support organizations, raising money. Korean women in Hawaii, for instance, raised $200,000 for the patriotic cause by working in the cane fields, doing needlework, and selling candies and Korean rice cakes.[77] The handful of South Asian women in America at the turn of the century donated their gold bangles to finance the 1914–15 Gadhar (Revolution) against the British.[78] And Chinese American women organized public marches and fundraisers and raised thousands of dollars for war relief in Japanese-occupied China.

The civil rights and anti-war movements motivated many younger Asian American women to become politically active over issues of discrimination because of race, sex, or place of origin. Others have become involved in the cause of the homeless and poor—many of whom are elderly immigrants—or in nuclear disarmament efforts. For some younger women the broader perspective of being Asian Americans, born of a dual heritage, has also meant involvement on international issues: Filipinas and Korean women fighting to change political and social conditions in the Philippines and in Korea; women from many different communities working to stop the sex tourism trade in Asian countries.

For all these women, the chosen road is not easy. The political and social climate, in which blatantly racial violence against visible minorities has increased sharply,[79] renders the challenges even more numerous and complex for Asian American women in the 1990s. But the women persevere. Many are taking assertive stances in defining solutions to local, national, and international issues affecting women of color. Working within their own communities or in new coalitions, they are ensuring that the voices of Asian women in America will be heard.

PART ONE

From Shore to Shore:

Immigration

Introduction

Asian women have immigrated to the United States since the mid-1800s. This section includes works about many of the different Asian ethnic groups that have come to America. Asian immigration began with the early arrival of Chinese and Japanese, followed by Koreans, Filipinos, South Asians and, more recently, Southeast Asians.

Regardless of their ethnicity or date of arrival, the women had some striking characteristics in common. In their homelands, they generally found limited social and economic options. For some, emigration seemed the only reasonable alternative to poverty, war, or persecution. Social practices limited young Korean girls' chances to venture beyond the walls around their homes. In Chungmi Kim's "A Girl on the Swing," the girl's only glimpse of the outside world is the view from her swing. The woman in "Poem by the Wellside" by Meena Alexander looks back at the poverty of India that led to her emigration.

The newest arrivals to this country, the Southeast Asians, came as refugees of the wars that plagued their homelands. The women of Van Luu's essay, "The Hardships of Escape for Vietnamese Women," came to America fleeing both the war that had wracked their country for decades and the aftermath of that bloody conflict. As refugees, they faced violence on land and at sea, and many still carry the psychological and physical wounds of the journey.

Some of the early women pioneers, however, came to America in search of adventure and the excitement of living in a new country. These reasons spurred the emigration of many of the women who shared their stories in Dorothy Cordova's "Voices from the Past: Why They Came."

Physical departure did not necessarily mean the severing of emotional ties to the homeland. Myrna Peña-Reyes's "The People Here: A Letter" is evidence of the close family ties that survive a journey across thousands of ocean miles. Her piece responds to the questions asked of a woman who left by one who stayed behind.

Traditional cultural values often made the sea journey with the immigrant women, as evidenced by the women interviewed by Sun Bin Yim in "Korean Immigrant Women in Early Twentieth-Century America." Their roles in the family, community, and new homeland were adapted from the old to fit the demands of living in America.

Upon their arrival, the women often face a hostile society. Values compatible with Western ways help in the adjustment process; others work to alienate women from mainstream America. The early pioneers in Connie Young Yu's "The World of Our Grandmothers" received less than a warm welcome. One woman was detained at Angel Island Immigration Station for over a year while her family and attorney tried to fight the discriminatory laws designed to keep Chinese out of the United States. Even living in America for many decades is no guarantee of fair treatment. The mother in Sakae Roberson's "Okasan/Mother" tries to retain many of the old ways as talismans against ongoing hostility and prejudice.

Financial hardships, violence, and social ostracism made life difficult for the women, but they also forced these pioneers from diverse social classes and cultural backgrounds to learn survival skills and adapt to life in a new country. In many ways, the adaptation process continues today among recent immigrants and even American-born Asians.

Hard as life may have been, however, the women did experience good times as well. The attitude of the family in Cathy Song's "Magic Island" reflects the feelings of many immigrants. The sunny day and prospect of sharing a picnic together bring joy, but just in case of rain, the family brings an umbrella.

Poem by the Wellside

MEENA ALEXANDER

1
Body, you're a stranger here
I dare not touch the scars
of stippled flesh
milk left when it fled,
a dry worn belly,
palms filled with dark water.

Herbs: chamomile, the boxed and sheltered rue
wild heliotrope (did mother
rub it to her cheeks so the sun would kiss and not burn?)
melting, all melting in water.

2
I was seven when I bent the bough
and saw my eyes in well water.
Nightly as the bark cracks
an old hag
with herbs in her teeth
yells "Meena!
Meena, my daughter."

I will not turn to her
I will not perish.
My poem
made in a cold country
is not about death.

3
But the blue of heliotrope is bitter;
rue, its stalks

plucked from my dreams
make a necklace of grief.

Will I kneel in this patch of sunlight?
Will I pray?

4
Severed from my birthplace, I hear my name
(she cried out my name through her black teeth)
shed syllables
in air so tender
the sounds melt, twisting
sunlight in threads.

I cannot stop my tongue.
"Old woman,
will water pour from the well?
Will a stream of water take root,
make a table, a pitcher, a bowl, bread?

"I am hungry old woman.
I must live!"

5
At dawn, her voice turns
in the coil of my ear,
an ancient anonymity
savage as sunlight.

"We are poor"
she whispers,
"women from a poor country.

"By the wellside,
our dreams
drop their clothes
and flee.

"You can ask for nothing.

"As for your belly
let it burn
as wild grass is burnt
at nightfall, in your mother's country."

Okasan/Mother

SAKAE S. ROBERSON

twenty-five years she's been here
and still
    a-me-ri-ka makes her mouth sour tight
    sticks in her mind like spit-wet thread
    caught in the eye of a needle.

twenty-five years of doing christmas
and still
    she saves generation-old
    bamboo mats for wrapping new year osushi/rice cakes
    hums songs of japan
    in the quiet dark of christmas mornings.

every year
for twenty-five years she plans new year
and still
    one more dress to sew. one more bill to pay.
    one more year passes.
    she celebrates
    sewing silk gowns for rich ladies.

twenty-five years
and still
    she tells no stories of war to a daughter
    she saves marriage lace and
    satin baby kimonos in a cedar chest for

a daughter who denies her conversation
watches her sew her life designs
into someone else's wedding day

twenty-five years of city living
people calling her oriental or chinese
sometimes jap
and still
   her eyes, like teardrops turned sideways,
   say nothing.
   with pride, she writes from right to left
   of the greatness of a-me-ri-ka to her people.

twenty-five years
alone.
still
she cries in japanese

A Girl on the Swing

CHUNGMI KIM

She sees the mountain
upside down.
With her long hair
sweeping the fallen leaves
she swings
like a pendulum.

From the lagoon at sunset
a hundred sparrows fly away.

Wishing them back
she whistles softly
and downward
she falls into the sky.

The People Here: A Letter

MYRNA PEÑA-REYES

Dear Manang, thanks for your call.
As for your fears . . .
Americans are friendly and they know some things
about our country.
Old women admire my black hair,
then inquire politely if all the girls are small.
The older men know more:
they say they were in Leyte
but don't remember much,
though one with the navy in Luzon
told me he could still feel
the warm rains that lashed him
as he stood on an open deck
thinking of Joseph Conrad.
A PCV sent home three months into his job
blames Davao water for the fluke in his liver.
A lady just returned on a chartered flight
complains about Manila heat,
the dirt and smell in the open market.
Still they have little malice
(but don't we all?).
Next time, perhaps, I can tell you
how they remember people.
Try not to worry,
and keep those letters coming.
Your sister, Ading.

Magic Island

CATHY SONG

A collar of water
surrounds the park peninsula
at noon.
Voices are lost
in waves of wind
that catches a kite
and keeps it there
in the air above the trees.
If the day has one color,
it is this:
the blue immersion of horizons,
the sea taking the sky like a swimmer.

The picnickers have come
to rest their bicycles
in the sprawling shade.
Under each tree, a stillness
of small pleasures:
a boy, half in sunlight,
naps with his dog;
a woman of forty
squints up from her book
to bite into an apple.

It is a day an immigrant
and his family might remember,
the husband taking off his shirt
to sit like an Indian
before the hot grill.
He would not in his own language
call it work, to cook

the sticks of marinated meat
for his son circling a yarn
of joy around the chosen tree.
A bit of luck has made him generous.
At this moment in his life,
with the sun sifting through
the leaves in panes of light,
he can easily say he loves his wife.
She lifts an infant
onto her left shoulder
as if the child
were a treasured sack of rice.
He cannot see her happiness,
hidden in a thicket of blanket
and shining hair.
On the grass beside their straw mat,
a black umbrella,
blooming like an ancient flower,
betrays their recent arrival.
Suspicious of so much sunshine,
they keep expecting rain.

The World of Our Grandmothers

CONNIE YOUNG YU

In Asian America there are two kinds of history. The first is what is written about us in various old volumes on immigrants and echoed in textbooks, and the second is our own oral history, what we learn in the family chain of generations. We are writing this oral history ourselves. But as we research the factual background of our story, we face the dilemma of finding sources. Worse than burning the books is not being included in the record at all, and in American history—traditionally viewed from the white male perspective—minority women have been virtually ignored. Certainly the accomplishments and struggles of early Chinese immigrants, men as well as women, have been obscured.

Yet for a period in the development of the West, Chinese immigration was a focus of prolonged political and social debate and a subject of daily news. When I first began searching into the background of my people, I read this nineteenth-century material with curious excitement, grateful for any information on Chinese immigration.

Looking for the history of Chinese pioneer women, I began with the first glimpses of Chinese in America—newspaper accounts found in bound volumes of the *Alta California* in the basement of a university library. For Chinese workers, survival in the hostile and chaotic world of Gum San, or Gold Mountain, as California was called by Chinese immigrants, was perilous and a constant struggle, leaving little time or inclination for reflection or diary writing. So for a look into the everyday life of early arrivals from China, we have only the impressions of white reporters on which to depend.

The newspapers told of the comings and goings of "Chinamen," their mining activities, new Chinese settlements, their murders by claim-jumpers, and assaults by whites in the city. An item from 17 August 1855, reported a "disgraceful outrage": Mr. Ho Alum was setting his watch under a street clock when a man called Thomas Field walked up and deliberately dashed the time-piece to the pavement. "Such unprovoked assaults upon unoffending Chinamen are not of rare occurrence. . . ." On the same day the paper also reported the suicide of a Chinese prostitute. In this item no name, details, or commentary were given, only a stark announcement. We can imagine the tragic story behind it: the short miserable life of a young girl sold into slavery by her impoverished parents and taken to Gum San to be a prostitute in a society of single men.

An early history of this period, *Lights and Shades in San Francisco* by B. E. Lloyd (1878), devoted ten chapters to the life of California Chinese, describing in detail "the subjects of the Celestial Kingdom." Chinese women, however, are relegated to a single paragraph:

Females are little better than slaves. They are looked upon as merchantable property, and are bought and sold like any other article of traffic, though their value is not generally great. A Chinese woman never gains any distinction until after death. . . . Considering the humble position the women occupy in China, and the hard life they therefore lead, it would perhaps be better (certainly more merciful) were they all slain in infancy, and better still, were they never born.[1]

Public opinion, inflamed by lurid stories of Chinese slave girls, agreed with this odious commentary. The only Chinese women whose existence American society acknowledged were the prostitutes who lived miserable and usually short lives. Senate hearings on Chinese immigration in 1876 resounded with harangues about prostitutes and slave girls corrupting the morals of young white boys. "The Chinese race is debauched," claimed one lawyer arguing for the passage of the Chinese Exclusion Law: "They bring no decent women with them." This stigma on the Chinese immigrant woman remained for many decades, causing unnecessary hardship for countless wives, daughters, and slave girls.

Chinese American society finally established itself as families appeared, just as they did in the white society of the forty-niners who arrived from the East Coast without bringing "decent women" with them. Despite American laws intended to prevent the "settlement" of Chinese, Chinese women did make the journey and endured the isolation and hostility, braving it for future generations here.

Even though Chinese working men were excluded from most facets of American society and their lives were left unrecorded, their labors bespoke their existence—completed railroads, reclaimed lands, and a myriad of new industries. The evidence of women's lives seems less tangible. Perhaps the record of their struggles to immigrate and overcome discriminatory barriers is their greatest legacy. Tracing that record therefore becomes a means of recovering our history.

Our grandmothers are our historical links. As a fourth-generation Chinese American on my mother's side, and a third-generation on my father's, I grew up hearing stories about ancestors coming from China and going back and returning again. Both of my grandmothers, like so many others, spent a lot of time waiting in China.

My father's parents lived with us when I was growing up, and through them I absorbed a village culture and the heritage of my pioneer

Chinese family. In the kitchen my grandmother told repeated stories of coming to America after waiting for her husband to send for her. (It took sixteen years before Grandfather could attain the status of merchant and only then arrange for her passage to this country.)[2] She also told stories from the village about bandits, festivals, and incidents showing the tyranny of tradition. For example, Grandma was forbidden by her mother-in-law to return to her own village to visit her mother: A married woman belonged solely within the boundaries of her husband's world.

Sometimes I was too young to understand or didn't listen, so my mother—who knew all the stories by heart—told me those stories again later. We heard over and over how lucky Grandpa was to have come to America when he was eleven—just one year before the gate was shut by the exclusion law banning Chinese laborers. Grandpa told of his many jobs washing dishes, making bricks, and working on a strawberry farm. Once, while walking outside Chinatown, he was stoned by a group of whites and ran so fast he lost his cap. Grandma had this story to tell of her anger and frustration: "While I was waiting in the immigration shed,[3] Grandpa sent in a box of *dim sum*.[4] I was still waiting to be released. I would have jumped in the ocean if they decided to deport me." A woman in her position was quite helpless, but she still had her pride and was not easily pacified. "I threw the box of *dim sum* out the window."

Such was the kind of history I absorbed. I regret deeply that I was too young to have asked the questions about the past that I now want answered; all my grandparents are now gone. But I have another chance to recover some history from my mother's side. Family papers, photographs, old trunks that have traveled across the ocean several times filled with clothes, letters, and mementos provide a documentary on our immigration. My mother—and some of my grandmother's younger contemporaries—fill in the narrative.

A year before the Joint Special Committee of Congress to investigate Chinese immigration met in San Francisco in 1876, my great-grandmother, Chin Shee, arrived to join her husband, Lee Wong Sang, who had come to America a decade earlier to work on the transcontinental railroad. Chin Shee arrived with two brides who had never seen their husbands. Like her own, their marriages had been arranged by their families. The voyage on the clipper ship was rough and long. Seasick for weeks, rolling back and forth as she lay in the bunk, Chin Shee lost most of her hair. The two other women laughed, "Some newlywed you'll make!" But the joke was on them as they mistakenly set off with the wrong husbands, the situation realized only when one man looked at his bride's normal-sized feet and exclaimed, "But the letter described my bride as having bound feet!" Chin Shee did not have her feet bound because she came from a peasant family. But her husband did not seem to care about that nor that the back of her head was practically bald. He felt himself fortunate just to be able to bring his wife to Gum San.

Chin Shee bore six children in San Francisco, where her husband assisted in the deliveries. They all lived in the rear of their grocery store, which also exported dried shrimp and seaweed to China. Great-Grandma seldom left home; she could count the number of times she went out. She and other Chinese wives did not appear in the streets even for holidays, lest they be looked upon as prostitutes. She took care of the children, made special cakes to sell on feast days, and helped with her husband's work. A photograph of her shows a middle-aged woman with a kindly, but careworn face, wearing a very regal brocade gown and a long, beaded necklace. As a respectable, well-to-do Chinese wife in America, married to a successful Chinatown merchant, with children who were by birthright American citizens, she was a rarity in her day. (In contrast, in 1884 Mrs. Jew Lim, the wife of a laborer, sued in federal court to be allowed to join her husband, but was denied and deported.)

In 1890 there were only 3,868 Chinese women among 103,620 Chinese males in America. Men such as Lee Yoke Suey, my mother's father, went to China to marry. He was one of Chin Shee's sons born in the rear of the grocery store, and he grew up learning the import and export trade. As a Gum San merchant, he had money and status and was able to build a fine house in Toishan. Not only did he acquire a wife but also two concubines. When his wife became very ill after giving birth to an infant who soon died, Yoke Suey was warned by his father that she was too weak to return to America with him. Reminding Yoke Suey of the harsh life in Gum San, he advised his son to get a new wife.

In the town of Foshan, not far from my grandfather's village, lived a girl who was recommended to him by his father's friend. Extremely capable, bright, and with some education, she was from a once prosperous family that had fallen on hard times. A plague had killed her two older brothers, and her heartbroken mother died soon afterwards. She was an excellent cook and took good care of her father, an herb doctor. Her name was Jeong Hing Tong, and she was pretty, with bound feet only three and a half inches long. Her father rejected the offer of the Lee family at first; he did not want his daughter to be a concubine, even to a wealthy Gum San merchant. But the elder Lee assured him this girl would be the wife, the one who would go to America with her husband.

So my maternal grandmother, bride of sixteen, went with my grandfather, then twenty-six, to live in America. Once in San Francisco, Grandmother lived a life of confinement, as did her mother-in-law before her. When she went out, even in Chinatown, she was ridiculed for her bound feet. People called out mockingly to her, "*Jhat!*" meaning bound. She tried to unbind her feet by soaking them every night and putting a heavy weight on each foot. But she was already a grown woman, and her feet were permanently stunted, the arches bent and the toes crippled. It was hard for her to stand for long periods of time, and she frequently had to sit on the floor to do her chores. My mother comments: "Tradition makes life so hard. My father traveled all over the world. There were stamps all over his passport—London, Paris—and stickers all over his suitcases, but his wife could not go into the street by herself."

Their first child was a girl, and on the morning of her month-old "red eggs and ginger party" the earth shook 8.3 on the Richter scale. Everyone in San Francisco, even Chinese women, poured out into the streets. My grandmother, babe in arms, managed to get a ride to Golden Gate Park on a horse-drawn wagon. Two other Chinese women who survived the earthquake recall the shock of suddenly being out in the street milling with thousands of people. The elderly goldsmith in a dimly lit Chinatown store had a twinkle in his eye when I asked him about the scene after the quake. "We all stared at the women because we so seldom saw them in the streets." The city was soon in flames. "We could feel the fire on our faces," recalls Lily Sung, who was seven at the time, "but my sister and I couldn't walk very fast because we had to escort this lady, our neighbor, who had bound feet." The poor woman kept stumbling and falling on the rubble and debris during their long walk to the Oakland-bound ferry.

That devastating natural disaster forced some modernity on the San Francisco Chinese community. Women had to adjust to the emergency and makeshift living conditions and had to work right alongside the men. Life in America, my grandmother found, was indeed rugged and unpredictable.

As the city began to rebuild itself, she proceeded to raise a large family, bearing four more children. The only school in San Francisco admitting Chinese was the Oriental school in Chinatown. But her husband felt, as did most men of his class, that the only way his children could get a good education was for the family to return to China. So they lived in China and my grandfather traveled back and forth to the United States for his trade business. Then suddenly, at the age of forty-three, he died of an illness on board a ship returning to China. After a long and painful mourning, Grandmother decided to return to America with her brood of now seven children. That decision eventually affected immigration history.

At the Angel Island immigration station in San Francisco Bay, Grandmother went through a physical examination so thorough that even her teeth were checked to determine whether she was the age stated on her passport. The health inspector said she had filariasis, liver fluke, a common ailment of Asian immigrants which caused their deportation by countless numbers. The authorities thereby ordered Grandmother to be deported as well.

While her distraught children had to fend for themselves in San Francisco (my mother, then fifteen, and her older sister had found work in a sewing factory), a lawyer was hired to fight for Grandmother's release from the detention barracks. A letter addressed to her on Angel Island from her attorney, C. M. Fickert, dated 24 March 1924, reads: "Everything I can legitimately do will be done on your behalf. As you say, it seems most inhuman for you to be separated from your children who need your care. I am sorry that the immigration officers will not look at the human side of your case."

Times were tough for Chinese immigrants in 1924. Two years before, the federal government had passed the Cable Act, which provided that any woman born in the United States who married a man "ineligible for citizenship" (including the Chinese, whose naturalization rights had been eliminated by the Chinese Exclusion Act) would lose her own citizenship. So, for example, when American-born Lily Sung, whom I also interviewed, married a Chinese citizen she forfeited her birthright. When she and her four daughters tried to re-enter the United States after a stay in China, they were denied permission. The immigration inspector accused her of "smuggling little girls to sell." The Cable Act was not repealed until 1930.

The year my grandmother was detained on Angel Island, a law had just taken effect that forbade all aliens ineligible for citizenship from landing in America.[5] This constituted a virtual ban on the immigration of all Chinese, including Chinese wives of U.S. citizens.

Waiting month after month in the bleak barracks, Grandmother heard many heart-rending stories from women awaiting deportation. They spoke of the suicides of several despondent women who hanged themselves in the shower stalls. Grandmother could see the calligraphy carved on the walls by other detained immigrants, eloquent poems expressing homesickness, sorrow, and a sense of injustice.

Meanwhile, Fickert was sending telegrams to Washington (a total of ten the bill stated) and building up a case for the circuit court. Mrs. Lee, after all, was the wife of a citizen who was a respected San Francisco merchant, and her children were American citizens. He also consulted a medical authority to see about a cure for liver fluke.

My mother took the ferry from San Francisco twice a week to visit Grandmother and take her Chinese dishes such as salted eggs and steamed pork because Grandmother could not eat the beef stew served in the mess hall. Mother and daughter could not help crying frequently during their short visits in the administration building. They were under close watch of both a guard and an interpreter.

After fifteen months the case was finally won. Grandmother was easily cured of filariasis and was allowed—with nine months probation—to join her children in San Francisco. The legal fees amounted to $782.50, a fortune in those days.

In 1927 Dr. Frederick Lam in Hawaii, moved by the plight of Chinese families deported from the islands because of the liver fluke disease, worked to convince federal health officials that the disease was noncommunicable. He used the case of Mrs. Lee Yoke Suey, my grandmother, as a precedent for allowing an immigrant to land with such an ailment and thus succeeded in breaking down a major barrier to Asian immigration.

My most vivid memory of Grandmother Lee is when she was in her seventies and studying for her citizenship. She had asked me to test her on the three branches of government and how to pronounce them correctly. I was a sophomore in high school and had entered the "What American Democracy Means To Me" speech contest of the Chinese American Citizens Alliance. When I said the words "judicial, executive, and legislative," I looked directly at my grandmother in the audience. She didn't smile, and afterwards, didn't comment much on my patriotic words. She had never told me about being on Angel Island or about her friends losing their citizenship. It wasn't in my textbooks either. I may have thought she wanted to be a citizen because her sons and sons-in-law had fought for this country, and we lived in a land of freedom and opportunity, but my guess now is that she wanted to avoid any possible confrontation—even at her age—with immigration authorities. The bad laws had been repealed, but she wasn't taking any chances.

I think a lot about my grandmother now and can understand why, despite her quiet, elegant dignity, an aura of sadness always surrounded her. She suffered from racism in the new country, as well as from traditional cruelties in the old. We, her grandchildren, remember walking very slowly with her, escorting her to a family banquet in Chinatown, hating the stares of tourists at her tiny feet. Did she, I wonder, ever feel like the victim of a terrible hoax, told as a small weeping girl that if she tried to untie the bandages tightly binding her feet she would grow up ugly, unwanted, and without the comforts and privileges of the wife of a wealthy man?

We seemed so huge and clumsy around her—a small, slim figure always dressed in black. She exclaimed once that the size of my growing feet were "like boats." But she lived to see some of her granddaughters graduate from college and pursue careers and feel that the world she once knew with its feudal customs had begun to crumble. I wonder what she would have said of my own daughter who is now attending a university on an athletic scholarship. Feet like boats travel far?

I keep looking at the artifacts of the past: the photograph of my grandmother when she was an innocent young bride and the sad face in the news photo taken on Angel Island. I visit the immigration barracks from time to time, a weather-beaten wooden building with its walls marked by calligraphy bespeaking the struggles of our history. I see the view of sky and water from the window out of which my grandmother gazed. My mother told me how, after visiting hours, she would walk to the ferry and turn back to see her mother waving to her from this window. This image has been passed on to me like an heirloom of pain and of love. When I leave the building, emerging from the darkness into the glaring sunlight of the island, I too turn back to look at my grandmother's window.

Voices from the Past: Why They Came

DOROTHY CORDOVA

Their numbers are rapidly dwindling—those hardy, adventurous, pioneering Filipino women who came to America from the early 1900s to the 1930s. They came as part of the "Second Wave" of Filipino immigration to this country. [1] Though the largest group of Filipino immigrants during this period was comprised of young single men, a very small minority were married; and a few of the more fortunate ones brought their families with them to the new land. In addition to the few women who accompanied their spouses, other women arrived to seek educational opportunities, employment, and cultural and social freedom. Several women shared their experiences in a series of interviews.

Mercedes Balco came to study. She arrived here in 1930 as a *pensionada,* her living and school expenses paid for by the government or school.

I came by boat in one of those Empress of Russia boats. And then by train through Canada . . . to Toronto and [then] to Washington, D.C. I stayed at the boarding house of the . . . School of Social Work of Catholic University where I had a scholarship for two years. . . . There were several *pensionadas* before I came. They were all women. They all did go to the School of Social Work.

Second Wave Filipinas constituted the first group of professionals who immigrated here in large numbers. In California they became the first teachers of Filipino descent; in New York, the first nurses of Filipino descent; in Washington, the first pharmacist of Filipino descent. Others were the first Filipino Americans to enter office work and other areas of employment previously denied to Filipino men, who had been relegated primarily to jobs in the culinary and custodial industries.

Maria Abastilla Beltran was one of the Filipina professionals who came to the United States. After working in the Philippines as a nurse, she emigrated to obtain further professional education and training.

Those days, you know, you can go to nursing without completing high school. But when I came over here, I've got to take post-graduate work. I have to finish my high school [education] through correspondence because otherwise I cannot get my credits. [In the Philippines] my first job was industrial—in the mining company. Then I was a school nurse, and then I became a Red Cross nurse for four years. . . . I went all over the north and then in the central Philippines, you know, Manila. I . . . wanted to come and finish my B.A. in nursing here [in America], public health nursing, so I could go back again and work for the Red Cross.

Not all those who emigrated from the archipelago nation left with such clear goals in mind, however. A few women came in an attempt to escape the restricted life that they felt they faced in their homeland— lives of family-determined marriages, of poverty and hardship.

Alberta Asis was only ten years old when she arrived in Hawaii with her widowed mother, her brothers, and her sisters. She recalls her family's difficult times in the Philippines and her mother's search for a better life for herself and her children.

I was born in Cebu—Carcar—in 1900. . . . My parents is poor. We have our own land, I think about five acre for sugar cane and two acre for corn. Then one acre my dad plant vegetable. Then [came] that pestilence in 1904. The crop is dry; even the water is dry! We got no water, so my dad suffered too much to look around . . . for food for us—his children. So it happen in 1910 my dad passed away June the thirteenth. My dad left the five acres of land to us, but we cannot do the land, you know, plant something, because we are small. . . . Uncle Lucity only twelve years old, and I am ten. We are seven sister and brother. . . .

So it happen my mother said, "You stay here in Carcar, because I go down to Cebu to look for job." So my grandma said, "No, don't leave your children alone, because I am too old, too. We cannot take care of the children." So my mother bring us to Cebu. And it happen we reach Cebu. For one week . . . we stay in Cebu. My mother found a job for babysitting. Just only one peso—one peso and cincuenta a week. Can you imagine that? She support us on one peso and cincuenta a week!

Asis's family soon met an elderly woman whose job it was to recruit people to go to Hawaii as laborers.

She is agent of immigration. . . . She go around the block looking for even women. "Son," one day my mama said, "I thinks . . . we go to Hawaii." So my brother Ceto said, "What you going to do in Hawaii?" "You should be, got to know, you got lots of work in there," the old woman said, the agent woman. . . . We call our grandmother, you know, to let [her] know that we go to Hawaii. And then my grandmother goes to Cebu to bid us all goodbye. . . . When we leave Cebu, goes to Manila . . . for one week; then they ship us to Hong Kong. . . . Then they put us in the Japanese ship . . . name is *Shumaru*. We arrive in Hawaii, December 25, 1910.

The plantation boss, they give us a house and we are fifty-seven people, include the children. . . . The big boss on the plantation, Mr. Renton, said [we] live near to his house because mother got no husband. And then my mama said, "[When] we are in the Philippines . . . we got no nothing. . . . Babysitting for one peso and fifty centavos . . . not enough for my children, not enough for me. . . . Old lady tell me that, if I want, to come to Hawaii. So, I agreed to come . . . I thought Hawaii is good." Then Mr. Renton [told] my mother, "Okay, I give you work in the plantation store. . . . Just sweep the floor. . . . Twenty-five cents an hour."

In 1924 Ambrosa Marquez left her home in Ilocos Norte and came to the United States—also to escape. What she fled, however, was not poverty, it was an unwanted marriage.

Our neighbors, they like me marry, but I don't like. That's why I like to run away from my house. . . . Not my parents, but the boy's grandpa, [he's] the one who like [me] to marry to the grandson. . . . My mother no like, because the mother of that boy sometimes she fight my mother. I no like, too, because he got a sweetheart in our [town]. . . . My agent come to my house . . . [recruiting] two men and two women. . . . [He] tell, "The workmen need laundry ladies, and you can wash their clothes, because they have no more wife. And [if] you like it, you can take it." My mother said, "You go to Hawaii. If you don't like that man, you go Hawaii."

Marquez left the Philippines with her brother, a girl friend, and another man from the province. She eventually settled on the island of Kauai in Hawaii, the only single Filipina in the entire labor camp.

From 1920 to 1929, 65,618 Filipino men were brought by the Hawaiian Sugar Plantation Association to work on the Hawaii sugar plantations. During that same period, only 5,286 women with their 3,091 children settled there. According to the 1930 U.S. census, there were 42,328 males and 2,940 females—less than seven Pinays (Filipino women) for every one hundred men. On the mainland the disparity in the female to male ratio was even greater.

Many Filipino women saw the treacherous voyage across the Pacific as a necessary step to see husbands, fathers, or fiancés. They came to rejoin loved ones who had come earlier to seek their fortune in the promised land of milk and honey—the United States. Leonora Mangiben, like Alberta Asis who had arrived one decade earlier, was also just a little girl when she came to America in the late 1920s. And like many others, her mother had immigrated with the children to rejoin her husband.

Dad was here first. . . . I was only two and a half when he came here. [I] stayed with mother [in the Philippines], and she was the breadwinner of all my aunties, my grandfather, you know. She did little commercial selling in Baguio. . . . That's how we survived. Mother ran a little grocery store underneath the house. . . . Then mother got mad because dad wouldn't send us any money for support. So she sold all the land we had, and we came here.

When Mangiben's family finally arrived in San Francisco, she was given the responsibility of seeking out her long-absent father.

I had to find my father, and at two-and-a-half you can't remember what your father looked like. I used to look at his pictures. Mother let me out because she had to be checked out [by immigration]. She said, "You go out and see if you can find your father." So I went out and looked at all those Filipinos just standing there, and I went directly to my dad and threw my arms on him. He was shaking like a leaf. That's how I found dad. It was my father.

Though outnumbered by Filipino men, Filipinas still made their presence known and usually were the focal points of the extended family. Regardless of their age or appearance, the few women received special treatment, often finding themselves escorted to social events by a whole group of single Filipino men who were content just to be near a Pinay.

The journeys across the ocean were long and sometimes very rough. Mangiben recalls her trip with vivid memory.

I remember coming over here . . . it was not first class. All Filipinos never came first class. We took third class because of the women. We had cabins . . . maybe six or eight in a cabin. We shared a bathroom. When the ship was in motion . . . most of the women were seasick. I was the youngest one. I used to go in the top of the deck and look at the ocean. I used to get . . . sick [for land]; come down and tell my mother there's no land at all. Used to cry 'cause it was about twenty-eight days coming here. Can you imagine, twenty-eight days on the ship?

The first port of call was China, Hong Kong. We couldn't go down 'cause there was always some wars in China. . . . The next stop was Tokyo. We were able to go down there. . . . Oh, yes, we went on shore. We went out to dinner. Mother was fine then. Soon as the ship stopped she was fine. That was the only time she ate. Then from

Tokyo we went to Hawaii. We stayed there overnight. Then we came here—straight to San Francisco.

Nurse Maria Beltran also describes her trip to the United States in detail.

There were no planes those days. So I came with three hundred Filipinos in the boat. . . . There were many meningitis cases in the boat. I offered my services there, you know, in the boat. And so when we arrived in Seattle, they quarantined everybody [for meningitis], and the women, they took us to Firland [Sanitarium]. There were about three Japanese and me and . . . two Russians. I roomed with the two Russian women, and the Japanese were in the other room.

Despite the confinement of the new arrivals to a health facility, Beltran remembers that her stay at Firland helped her decide to stay in this new country, a decision which paralleled that of many Filipinas.

The immigration people took us there [to Firland], and we were quarantined for ten days. And the head nurse at Firland, when she found out I was a nurse, you know, she told me that [one] school was giving special work for public health nurses. That's the only school in the whole world that was giving that, and I want to do it. I played safe, so I went to apply after I was released. I met Miss DeCano [another Filipino nurse]. So we both went to apply and we were both admitted.

Pensionada Mercedes Balco had planned to return to her homeland, but her plans were diverted.

I didn't quite make it back to the Philippines. . . . I met my husband at the time when I was supposed to go back to the Philippines, and so we decided to get married. . . . A daughter was born to us, and we stayed in Washington, D.C., from then on. [My husband] was a secretary to Senator Claro M. Recto, who was with the Mission of Independence at that time. . . . When the Mission of Independence was finished, my husband stayed in Washington and got a job in the U.S. government . . . assigned to the War Department.

Though the mission on which Balco's husband worked resulted in the end of U.S. colonial rule over the Philippines, it ironically left the Filipino people in a less favorable immigration status. The Tydings-McDuffie Act, which was enacted by Congress on March 24, 1934, granted independence to the Philippines in ten years. At the same time, though, it limited entry of Filipinos to the United States to only fifty per year.

Prior to the new law, Filipinos were considered U.S. nationals and were free to come to America as long as they had the money to buy a boat ticket; now they were aliens and subject to the immigration quota. During the financial boom of the 1920s, Filipino workers were welcome; with the trauma and hardships of the Depression, however, these same workers came to be viewed as a "growing economic and social threat." [2]

Consequently the already small but steady trickle of Filipino women to America dwindled to almost nothing. Over the next seven years, until just before World War II, the only women coming from the Philippines aside from students were those joining husbands or fiancés already settled in the United States. The growth that Filipino communities experienced prior to the mid-1930s virtually ceased until the end of the war.

Filipinas had settled throughout the country—in Hawaii, California, Washington, Oregon, Alaska, Illinois, New York, Louisiana, and Washington, D.C. However, because their numbers were so small, the feeling of loneliness sometimes became unbearable. While the following sentiments of nurse Beltran were expressed before the enactment of the immigration quotas, such feelings of isolation could not help but become much worse.

> I went to Chicago; I work in Chicago; and I didn't like it. I went to Cleveland and I work in Cleveland and I was not happy. I was all alone; there were no Filipinos. They didn't even know what I was in those places, especially in Cleveland. In Philadelphia, they just give me a look. I didn't like it over there, so I go back to Chicago.

Happily, in many areas the loneliness did not last, because after the end of World War II many more Filipinas immigrated to America; they were part of the "Third Wave." Some came as children and grand-children of Spanish-American War veterans who had chosen to remain in the Philippines at the end of that war. Others came as war brides and children of Filipino soldiers who became American citizens by virtue of having fought in the U.S. armed forces; as American citizens and military dependents, they did not fall under the immigration quota limits.[3]

Filipino immigration to the United States reached its zenith in the "Fourth Wave." This influx occurred after the enactment of the 1965 amendment to the Immigration Nationality Act, which abolished the exclusionary regulations of previous immigration laws. The amendment established an annual ceiling of twenty thousand immigrants from each country, including the Philippines.

The arrival and settlement of new groups of Filipinas, coupled with the birth of second- and third-generation Filipino Americans, caused their ethnic communities to become more and more established. As guardians of Filipino culture in America, the women played an important role. They sought to preserve the language, traditions such as folk dance and music, and a sense of family and community.

The women came as war brides, students, plantation workers, teachers, housekeepers, seamstresses, wives, kitchen helpers, labor camp cooks, entertainers, and nurses. Some were small business entrepreneurs who ran pool halls, restaurants, grocery stores, beauty parlors, and gambling concessions. Regardless, they were welcome arrivals to the Filipino men who had immigrated earlier.

> American life was stark for lonely brown men. The women who had joined them in this faraway, hostile society served as symbols of the mothers, sisters and wives those men had left behind in the Philippines. . . .
> The heart and soul of the development of the Filipino American experience were personified in Pinays. . . . [They] have been the yeast that set their men and children rising and the leaven that got their communities producing.[4]

Korean Immigrant Women in
Early Twentieth-Century America

SUN BIN YIM

While women constituted only one-fifth of the nearly eight thousand Koreans who immigrated to Hawaii and the mainland between 1899 and 1924, their impact on the newly formed Korean communities was far greater than could be expected from their small number. Not only were they obviously essential in the formation of families and the propagation of the Korean population in America, but their work in and outside of their homes was an important element in the economic survival of this population.

The major objective of this essay is to document and analyze the multiplicity of roles that Korean women had in America and the contribution of these roles to their communities. The first section will describe the trends and characteristics of Korean immigrant women in America, particularly on the mainland. The second will consider the familial roles of women, especially patterns of marriage and reproduction. The third will be devoted to nonfamilial roles, with an emphasis on the type of work that women did and their contribution to the family income.

Immigration to America

Since there were only three women among the 168 Koreans who immigrated between 1899 and 1902, 1903 marks the first year of substantial female immigration. From that year till 1924, women arrived in two phases, with families and as "picture brides."[1]

The first phase of immigration, family migration, took place from about 1903 to 1910. Korean immigrants in this period were predominantly males, with a sex ratio of 971 men for every 100 women. More particularly, in the period 1903 to 1905, the majority of Korean males came as plantation workers, bachelors recruited by sugar plantation owners in Hawaii. Therefore, the few women who immigrated in this period were likely already married and arrived with—or later joined—their husbands, bringing their children with them. A woman who left Korea with her daughter arrived in Hawaii in 1904 to join her husband, who worked on a sugar plantation. That woman's granddaughter described the pioneer as ambitious and well educated, a woman who came with hopes of continuing her education in America.[2]

Though few of the women who migrated with their children during this early period survive today, they lived long enough to share their stories. One is Mrs. Kim, who arrived in Hawaii with her mother, two brothers, and her sister-in-law in 1905. She was twenty years old when her family left for America.

> I came from Pyongyang, from a decent family with money. My brother and I were well educated. My father had mistresses, and since he spent days and nights with them and didn't take care of my family, my mother was very angry. At forty-three, she decided we would emigrate without letting my father know. My mother said, "It is better for you to study than spend time uselessly here. Let's have a better life in a new world because your father is irresponsible to the family." When the ship arrived in Japan [on its way to America], we were told by the [American] immigration authorities that my brother was too young to work as a [plantation] laborer, but my mother persuaded the immigration officer to let him go.

An important feature of this family migration in the early period is seen in the ratio of children under fourteen years of age to women immigrants. The ratio reached a high of 740 children per one thousand women from 1903 to 1910, and then declined to 130 children per one thousand women from 1911 to 1921.[3] Migration in general declined rapidly after Korea became a Japanese protectorate in 1905.[4] The Japanese government, which annexed Korea in 1910, severely restricted emigration from Korea. Any Korean who wished to come to the United States directly from Korea had to first obtain permission from the Japanese authorities. In order to bypass these restrictions and emigrate, some Koreans went instead to Manchuria and left for the United States from there.

The next phase of women's arrival to America occurred from about

1911 to 1924. Picture brides, that is, Korean women who had marriage contracts with men in the United States, constituted one of the groups for which Japan authorized exit permits. As a consequence, the male to female ratio among Korean immigrants made a spectacular decline from 971 men to 100 women between 1903 and 1910, to 70 to 100 between 1911 and 1924, and then reached a low of 56 men to 100 women between 1915 and 1919.[5] There were even more dramatic declines in the male to female ratios in California and Hawaii,[6] indicating that the immigration of picture brides may have been more significant in these states than in the rest of the country.

While the classification of "picture bride" did not appear on immigration records, starting around 1911, stories about arrivals of Koreans in San Francisco always contained references to them.[7] The immigration procedures for picture brides were clear:

> Picture brides are allowed to arrive and pass the immigration without any certificate, but their present or future husbands have to show some evidence indicating the support of their wives. If these procedures are violated, the picture brides could be sent back.[8]

Many picture brides had go-betweens who handled the exchange of pictures. Usually a prospective husband sent his photograph to a friend, relative, or neighbor of the woman. This person functioned as the agent who in turn contacted the prospective bride and sent her picture to the man.

Korean picture brides were motivated to come because of poverty, or a quest for education or freedom. Economic conditions of a woman's family often influenced her decision to emigrate in search of a prosperous husband. Mrs. Park, who arrived in Seattle in 1916, said that she came to America as a picture bride "in order to help her family financially" because "it was rumored that America [was] a rich country." When her father's small business became unstable and no longer supported the family, she wanted to help. Then her parents received a letter from their friend in California. Enclosed was a picture of a young man whom they liked very much. Her father said, "This man seems to have sufficient money, and if you marry him, you will be able to live the rest of your life very comfortably and to support your family until my business is in better shape." Thus, she came as a picture bride for her parents' sake.

One woman, Mrs. Suh, recounted how she accepted a marriage proposal in order to escape her family's poverty and came to California in 1915 as a picture bride:

> When my neighbor showed me a photograph of a man who had been in America, I decided to marry him right away. Because I was raised in a poor family in Kyungsang province, in the southern part of Korea, honestly speaking, I was more interested in his money than his appearance.

For some women, the status of "picture bride" was used as a disguise to immigrate and study in America. Though plans upon arrival may have included going back to school, many of the brides, including Mrs. Park, found their original schemes thwarted. Mrs. Park asked her sister, who had gone earlier to America as a picture bride, to have someone send her pictures of her future husband. She spoke of her plans to study:

> When I received the picture, I sent mine. The arrangements did not take long. After I arrived I did not want to marry and do housework. I wanted to go East and study. But since my husband was fairly old, he did not want to let me go. Besides, I got pregnant every year. As the Koran saying goes, "Before the sparrow has chicks, she will readily fly when she is shot at; but after she has her chicks, nothing can keep her away from her nest."

Mrs. Lee, another picture bride, was also not able to achieve her educational objective and had to settle for domestic life. Through her brother's friend in Hawaii, she arranged to come to the islands in 1914. She had completed a high school education in Korea and, as a Christian influenced by Western missionaries, was more eager to study abroad than to marry.

> My intention was to leave my prospective husband for study as soon as I arrived and to return to Korea with a higher education, but I did not know anyone who could help me apply for admission [to college]. Moreover, I had no place to stay if I left him. For about ten days, I was seriously confused about choosing him or education.

Many Korean women used the "picture bride" status as a means to flee from the oppression of the Japanese occupation of Korea from 1910 to 1945. (Japan had annexed Korea in 1910 as a result of the Russo-Japanese War of 1904–1905.) Mrs. Park, who came to Seattle in 1916, also in part to help her family's finances, recalls her search for freedom as another motive for emigrating.

After we exchanged photographs through my aunt's friend, who also came as a picture bride, I became determined to come because of Japanese oppression, even though my parents disapproved. I just had no freedom.

Similarly, Mrs. Paik, a teacher who had a high school education from Korea, had to leave for political reasons. In addition to her regular job as an educator, she also worked for the independence movement by secretly distributing documents and leaflets. The Japanese police kept an eye on her, and because she did not want them to disturb her parents, she was forced to leave her country.

Familial Roles

There is no doubt that the roles of wife and mother were the key ones for most Korean women in America. The strong sense of duty a Korean woman felt toward her husband and especially her children took precedence over any other goals she may have had before marriage. For example, even though Mrs. Paik, who was introduced earlier, had wanted to study when she arrived in America, she eventually married the man who helped her immigrate. Out of a sense of obligation rather than love, she bore him five children. After he died, she never remarried but instead devoted the rest of her life to the children. Mrs. Paik sacrificed her wish for an education, but, as she admitted, getting pregnant every year left her little alternative. And besides, she was attached to the children.

Throughout the early 1900s marriage seemed not only universal among the Korean women in America, but it also occurred at a young age. In 1910 half of the Korean women in Hawaii between ages fifteen and nineteen were or had been married. (One decade later, the figure had dropped to 41.7 percent and then in 1930 to only 7.4 percent.) Also in

Hawaii from 1910 to 1920, 97.6 percent of Korean women ages twenty to twenty-four had already been married; by the end of their child-bearing years, *all* Korean women had been married. Though figures for Korean women in California were not as detailed, and are available only since 1930, they show that the percentage of women fifteen and older who were ever married is also high (74.3 percent).[9]

Another striking fact that emerges from the census data and personal histories is the wide discrepancy between the spouses' ages. In Hawaii in 1920, the median age of married Korean men was forty-one; for women twenty-nine.[10] The age at marriage of the six picture brides interviewed for this essay ranged from twelve to twenty-one; their husbands were on the average eighteen years older.[11] Often when a woman met her prospective husband at the port, her disappointment led to second thoughts about the marriage. He looked so much older—sometimes old enough to be her father—and certainly not like the picture he had sent her for the arrangement. One woman remembers: "When I first saw my fiancé, I could not believe my eyes. His hair was grey and I could not see any resemblance to the picture I had. He was a lot older than I had imagined."

Some women approached the first meeting more pragmatically. Mrs. Kim, who was married to her husband for twenty-five years, said that of course she was shocked that her groom looked so old and that his face was so tanned and wrinkled. She wondered what had happened to the handsome young man she saw in the picture, but when he told her in a gentle voice that she "looked tired" and "let's go to eat first," she felt more inclined to accept him.

Another consequence of the age difference was that some Korean women found themselves widowed at a relatively young age. One woman lost her husband when she was only thirty-four. Twelve of the thirty-two widows in Hawaii in 1920 were under forty-five.

Korean marriages in America during the first two decades of the 1900s seldom, if ever, ended in divorce. This near absence of divorce reflected in part the strong traditional Korean value of family stability. The community's disapproval of divorce and desertion, particularly by the wife, also reinforced family unions. The *New Korea* reported that a Korean wife in Sacramento planned to divorce her generous husband and to remarry. "If it is true, they will be forced to leave town, since their behavior is against Korean morality." [12] In another instance, Mrs. Lee was forced to leave her home in Montana after she divorced her husband because the Koreans there viewed her as "an immoral and inconsiderate wife," accusations she said she "could not face." She fled to New York where she worked as a cook. The communities in both cases shared the same moral opposition to divorce that characterized the traditional Korean society of their native homeland.

In 1910 there were no divorced Korean women in Hawaii, and in 1920 there was only one out of the 681 women ever married. On the mainland the divorce rate was a little higher, with two divorces out of 242 ever-married Korean women. The only reference to divorce in *New Korea* between 1906 and 1924 was to a Korean man who had married a Mexican woman and subsequently divorced her. [13]

This lack of divorce does not mean, however, that there were no husbands deserting their families, no wives running away with other men, nor young women trying to break their engagements. [14] The *New Korea* reported a 1915 incident about a broken relationship:

Chun Myung Kang in San Francisco planned to marry his fiancé from Hawaii, but she ran away on the tenth of February. She went to see a Korean man who was studying at a seminary in San Francisco and begged him to help her break her engagement. He took her to an orphanage. One day he took her fiancé to see her and convinced him to break up the engagement. [15]

These few cases of open marital conflict, however, posed no serious challenge to the sanctity of women's familial roles and the stability of the family. In fact, in response to the conflicts, some women embraced even more strongly the traditional Korean values. For example, after Mrs. Ahn's husband ran away, she did not remarry, but instead became the family breadwinner. During the day she worked on the farm as a piece worker; at night she did laundry. Her six young children were dependent on her alone because her husband had left them no money. She said that her only happiness was watching the children grow and giving them food and education. She wanted to raise the children as if they had both parents, and despite the absence of the father, her family remained very cohesive.

Most Korean women in America during the 1900s and 1910s had a large number of children.[16] The eight women in this study bore an average of 5.2 children, most of whom were still living at the time of the interviews. The consistently high fertility of Koreans throughout the years from 1906 to 1924 suggests that there were no significant changes in the reproductive and maternal roles of Korean women. Bearing and rearing children continued to be central in the lives of these women. But this did not prevent them from working alongside their husbands or grown children as well. Mrs. Ahn washed dishes and worked as a waitress in their restaurant while her husband cooked. "I worked all the time while carrying my baby on my back and taking care of the older children," she said. Mrs. Kim, another pioneer woman, had seven children and an aged husband. When he became seriously ill, her grown son took charge as the head of the household and worked on the railroad; she took up washing and ironing for whites.

In spite of the importance of the mother's role in raising children, sometimes the rigor of the early Korean settlements made it difficult for the family to stay physically together. Men often had to go from one farm area to another in search of work. Many of the wives were needed as additional laborers or as cooks and housekeepers. The children, however, were too young to work and had to go to school.

> Sometimes Korean parents take their children from farm to farm, but have difficulties in taking care of them. When they cannot take them along anymore, they put the children in orphanages.[17]

However, placement in these orphanages, which functioned like boarding schools, was not too common among early Korean immigrants. Childcare was taxing but not considered a serious problem. Most often mothers or older siblings took care of the younger children at home.

Nonfamilial Roles

Several problems hinder the study of occupational roles of Korean women. The relevant statistics are not available until for the year 1930, and then only for Hawaii. Also, many Korean women believed that their work was intimately tied to their family roles and not a separate aspect of their lives; this individual viewpoint was shared and reinforced by the community. The closest the *New Korea* came to mentioning women's occupational roles was an item about a Fresno, California, boarding-house operated by a Korean couple. [18] The directories of such cities as Los Angeles and San Francisco provided some additional information, but listed women separately only if no husband was present. [19] Lastly, personal histories reveal that women performed a wide variety of nonfamilial tasks, but were not paid for them because they worked on family-owned businesses or farms. Despite these limitations, however, we can draw a sketch of Korean women as wage workers or entrepreneurs.

Around 1910 there was a very low proportion of women among Korean farmworkers. This was inevitable considering the imbalanced sex ratio of nearly thirteen hundred males per one hundred females in the U.S. Korean community. A California agriculture report stated that there was one Korean woman per sixty Korean male farmworkers, well below the ratio of one to ten for all farmworkers. [20] In Hawaii, the ratio was one Korean female to eighty Korean male farmworkers.

The main reason for the small number of women in the fields was their concentration in helping their husbands in other ways, such as cooking and washing for "work gangs" of Korean men. [21] Mrs. Park described her experience as follows:

> When we were in the citrus orchards in Redlands, I was in the kitchen cooking food, Korean food. I was one of the cooks for Korean farm workers. One hundred workers needed women cooking in the kitchen. . . . In Colusa, there were fifteen to twenty Korean workers working, and I cooked their meals. At the same time I had to raise ten children. Oh, it was pretty hard, but what could you do?

Mrs. Kim said that in Hawaii she too "did all the household chores and cooked all the meals for Korean farm laborers as well."

Women in urban locations, as in rural areas, were engaged in manual labor that seemed compatible with their roles as wife and mother. Mrs. Lee, who resided in Sacramento where her husband had been a laborer, remembered that she took in laundry for eight years while at the same time caring for her husband and their five children.

> I did the laundry for Caucasians and Korean bachelors. I had to wash by hand and iron. I got paid about eighty cents or one dollar per day [in 1916]. . . . I never went to bed before 1:00 A.M. and had to get up at 4:00 A.M. to cook for my husband who had stomach trouble.

Toiling as unpaid but essential workers, wives also helped in the operation of the small family businesses that constituted the bulk of the Korean entrepreneurial community: boarding houses or inns, laundries, barber shops, fruit stands, and restaurants. On a few occasions wives took the initiative to establish the business, as in the case of this woman in Chicago:

> [When her husband could not work] Bokki took it all in stride and calmly set up a roadside stand. At first her Old Man [sic] scoffed at the idea, but eventually success was far beyond their expectations. Soon they set up a regular highway market. They were doing so well that it became necessary for their customers to put in advance orders for their vegetables. Even the retail produce markets were ordering directly from them. . . . Bokki and her old man bought out the vegetables from the neighboring farms to supplement their own produce, and continued in this fashion for nine years.[22]

Of course, when a husband died or was busy outside the home, women had to continue the operation of the farm or business. Mrs. Lee's husband, who was highly educated, lacked the skills for manual labor. With the help of his friend, the Lees started a small boarding house in Sacramento. Even though the husband was the owner, he was rarely home. So until she had had four children, Mrs. Lee took charge of managing the business.

> He traveled around cities in California [Los Angeles, San Francisco, Fresno, and other cities where many Koreans resided] to organize and raise funds for the Korean National Association [Daehan Kukmin-hoe] and participated actively in the Korean Independence Movement. When we made some profit, I persuaded him to buy a hotel. I was, of course, a manager because of his frequent absence for the Movement.

Conclusion

In the early years of the Korean communities in California and Hawaii, women contributed immensely to the rapid growth of these communities and to their stability. Furthermore, without their hard work, many Korean enterprises would have failed, and many families would have been in worse poverty than they sometimes already were.

A few women came with their families, but the majority of Korean immigrant women in the early twentieth century arrived as picture brides who emigrated for economic and educational reasons and to escape oppressive Japanese rule. They were in their teens; their husbands were on the average eighteen years older.

Their arrival in great numbers in the early part of the century carried important implications for their familial and nonfamilial roles. Being wives and mothers dominated their lives, nevertheless, many of them also labored as unpaid family workers and as wage earners and entrepreneurs outside the home. Despite the hardships they endured as immigrant women in a foreign place—balancing their roles as wives, mothers, and workers—Korean women in America made valuable contributions to their families, their communities, and their new country.

The Hardships of Escape for Vietnamese Women

VAN LUU

At present only a limited amount of research is being done on Vietnamese refugee women. In writing this essay, which is based on personal interviews and research, I hope to contribute some knowledge and understanding to the study of these women's lives and experiences in America. In addition to their stressful escape, they are also facing new challenges during their resettlement. What makes these experiences significant is that they have a great impact on the women's mental health. In this essay, I will focus on the external causes of mental health problems rather than their psychological manifestations. Understanding the evacuation and resettlement of Vietnamese women is a necessary prerequisite to understanding their needs and problems. Thus, I will examine the problem from the period of the women's escape to their present situation. And since the majority of problems are experienced by the women who have come to America in recent years, I will concentrate on them in this discussion.

Ever since the Communists took over South Vietnam in 1975, thousands of Vietnamese refugees have left their country in search of freedom. Despite the increasing risks and dangers such as piracy, a majority of people, 575,000 in total, have fled by sea.[1] After arriving at an asylum camp in Hong Kong, Malaysia, the Philippines, or Thailand, they hope they will be able to resettle in new countries—Japan, France, Canada, and especially the United States, the nation most willing to accept refugees. By the end of 1981, over 450,000 refugees had resettled in the United States; approximately 45 percent of these people are women.[2] Only recently have the women been recognized as a vulnerable group that needs special programs and attention. In addition to their poor mental health resulting from the traumatic experiences during their escapes, many Vietnamese women also suffer emotional problems during their adjustment in the United States.

Leaving Their Homes

Vietnamese women—both those who work in the home and those outside the home—experience a great deal of grief and loss.[3] The separation from family, in many ways, causes depression among the Vietnamese women. Because of the high cost of leaving the country—approximately two thousand dollars per person is charged by boat owners—usually only wealthy families can afford to raise enough money to transport the entire family. Other families must decide which member has the most potential in their future endeavors and transport him or her out of the country, leaving the less promising relatives at home. This has created a dilemma because Vietnamese families are traditionally close-knit: name, status, and personal as well as financial support all come from the family.[4] As in other Asian cultures, children are expected to take care of their aged parents to "compensate the gift of birth and upbringing."[5] It is very common to find several generations living together under one roof.

After settling in America, the Vietnamese women, as well as the men, often feel guilty about leaving their relatives behind. According to Dr. Le Tai Rieu, director of Indo-Chinese Mental Health Projects in San Francisco, the Vietnamese refugees are plagued by "survivor's guilt"— they feel that they have run away while their relatives are still suffering.[6] Some women save money from work and often send gifts through the black market such as medicine and, if possible, currency, so their relatives can pay for the passage of the remaining family members. However, many times their dreams of reuniting with their relatives are very difficult to fulfill because the passage to the asylum camp is unsafe. Consequently, the Vietnamese women feel helpless and continue to bear depression and guilt as the years go by in the new land.

The ability to finance an escape to foreign countries does not guarantee admission into asylum camps. Hong Kong, Malaysia, the Philippines, and Thailand were chosen by the refugees as sites for the camps because of their proximity to the escape points, which are located mostly along the southern coast of Vietnam. (Some refugees have also found ways of leaving the country by land route, walking through Laos and Cambodia with paid guides who speak several languages and lead them to safety in Thailand.) In recent years many countries that experienced an early influx of refugees have begun to deny admissions. In 1979 Malaysia refused entry to 55,000 refugees, and Indonesia deployed a twenty-four vessel force to prevent refugees from reaching its soil.[7] Apparently these governments are afraid of the economic problems in feeding and housing the refugees, as well as the interethnic conflict resulting from longstanding tension among these countries' peoples. However, their efforts to stem the migration have not been successful due to the refugees' desperation to find shelter after their long struggle for survival during their exodus.

Robbery and Violence at Sea

The interval between deciding to leave their homes and arriving in a safe camp can be long and very harrowing. The boats in which the refugees escape are small and in poor condition; they can easily be sunk en route to the asylum camps. Sometimes sinking boats have been saved in time by passing vessels; sometimes not. This tragedy resulted in 150,000 refugee deaths in the ocean from May 1975 to mid-1979.[8] The fortunate refugees who survive the exodus still must face the possibility of witnessing the deaths of their family members or other passengers. In one case, Tran Hue Hue, a sixteen-year-old girl, was the only survivor out of fifty people during the escape in 1980. She suffered the traumatic experiences of watching both her brother and aunt pass away and being stranded on a tiny atoll before her rescue. Despite the long years spent resettling in her new country, Tran Hue Hue still suffers from the grief of her lost relatives.

Since 1978 one of the main hindrances to safe passage has been piracy. Many people believe that refugees carry fortunes in gold, jewelry, and U.S. dollars, and that "collectively the wealth could be substantial, especially when in 1978 the boats became larger and started carrying not a few score but as many as 600 to 700 people."[9] With the lure of their potential wealth, these refugees on the rickety boats are brutally attacked by the pirates in the waters joining Vietnam's Mekong Delta, the coasts of southern Thailand, and northeast Malaysia. Some pirates rob but provide food and water in return. However, in recent years the incidence of violent attacks has increased dramatically, with the pirates using a variety of weapons—including guns, daggers, knives, and even hammers—to attack the defenseless refugees. U.S. refugee officials interviewing the victims often write the initials "RPM" in their case histories. "RPM" stands for "rape, pillage, and murder," a summary of the dreadful experiences of these newcomers.[10]

Female Vietnamese refugees are in a particularly vulnerable situation, one that began back in their old country where they were oppressed in the traditional caste system. There these women held an inferior status and had fewer privileges than men. Usually the males were encouraged to get a good education while the females were expected to take care of the household and later become good wives and mothers. In addition, the importance of *noi doi tong duaon,* that is, carrying the family name from one generation to the next through the male heir, led to the increasing practice of bigamy until just recently. Pressure from the society as well as from the family often made women share their husbands with others; it was not surprising to see men with three or four wives living under one roof. Many women had a hard time getting out of this unwanted situation because when a woman married, she became part of the husband's family. To leave their husbands, even in instances of bad marriages, was a great risk because they feared slander, which was very difficult to withstand in the caste society of Vietnam. At present the women are found to be less oppressed than in the past, but problems still exist.

Even after leaving their country, the ordeal of Vietnamese women may continue because they are subjected to risks of sexual abuse. They suffer not only from the terrible journey to the asylum camps, but also from rape and violence at the hands of Thai fishermen, otherwise known as "sea pirates." Nhat Tien, a famous Vietnamese writer and an expert on the Vietnamese refugee issue, says that "these women deserve very special consideration and assistance, much different from that prescribed for ordinary boat people, special materials as well as psychological and emotional support necessary to enable them to stand secure and build a fine new life in the U.S." [11]

In a personal interview [12] Mrs. L., a thirty-three-year-old nurse, described her painful experiences during her escape in 1983:

> Staying on the boat was very uncomfortable, because sixty-six people had been crammed together in a small boat. There was neither food, drinks, nor shelter. We had to wait until the rain came to get fresh water. One day, the boat suddenly stopped moving and a storm arrived. The men teamed up to work on the engine and at the same time they tried to scoop the water out of the boat. No other women helped out, except me. As I was scooping out the water, I had a sudden impulse to smear my face with black oil from the engine. I looked

filthy and disgusting. Up until now, I do not know why I did that, but it surely saved me from the pirates who later attacked our boat.

About twenty pirates from two boats set upon the refugees' vessel. Armed with guns, hammers, and large metal bars, they demanded gold, money, and other valuables. They carefully searched both the boats and the people to make sure Mrs. L. and her fellow escapees had not hidden anything from them. Then the pirates, satisfied with their booty, turned their attention to the women on board.

Everyone felt so helpless since we were unarmed. After searching, the pirates started the rape and abuse of the women. They took all of them, except me, to the back of the boat and raped them. I was so lucky because I looked so ugly and filthy. I fainted and couldn't see anything. . . . I closed my eyes really tight to stop myself from witnessing the horrible scene, but I could not help hearing the moans and groans, and especially the beggings for mercy by those poor women. There were thirteen or fourteen women altogether, whose ages ranged from fifteen to early forties. I really felt sorry for a young girl: she was about fifteen. She was raped continuously by four or five pirates. The whole ordeal lasted for two hours.

The pirates eventually left, but stripped the engine and motor from the boat, and left the refugees stranded in the middle of the ocean. Mrs. L. remembers thinking that "death seemed to approach closer and closer daily," even though the men tried to get the boat moving by using whatever means they could devise. After about seven days and nights adrift at sea, the refugees managed to land on the Malaysian shore where they were finally taken in by the authorities.

One of the most notorious incidents that shocked the Vietnamese community in America took place on Kro-Kra Island, located in southern Thailand, where many Vietnamese refugees were captured in 1980. Due to the isolated location of the island, the Vietnamese refugees could not find ways to escape, and almost every female was raped.

According to a United Nation High Commissioner of Refugees report, a woman was severely burned when pirates set fire to the hillside where she was hiding in an attempt to force her to come out. Another had stayed for days in a cave, waist-deep in water despite the attack of crabs on her legs. [13] One victim who later settled in America explained, "Thai pirates used steel bars to strike any Vietnamese man who struggled against the attacks on the women." [14] Fortunately, some of these women were lucky enough to return to their families. Others were not. And most women were reluctant to press charges against the barbaric pirates in Thailand, because they were afraid that any legal action might delay or jeopardize their departure for resettlement in the new country.

Other problems can plague the women. Some, for instance, suffer from rape-related medical difficulties, such as vaginal disorders, which often interfere with their daily lives. Aside from the physical problems, these women experience long-lasting psychological and emotional problems, including depression and anxiety over unwanted pregnancies and possible reduced chances for a happy marriage. [15]

Most of these Vietnamese women do not want to talk about their experiences with anybody, even their close friends and relatives; they remain silent even after settling in America. Vinh, a rape victim from the Kro-Kra Island incident, says that most people can never understand that what she went through is painful and cannot be described in words. [16] The women are afraid of rejection by their relatives if their experiences became known. But because they are silent about the rapes, no specific report or information is available on the mental health of this group of Vietnamese women. Nevertheless, it is clear to many people that these women do suffer, both physically and mentally, from their trauma. "Perhaps those who suffered silently were more affected by the rape experience than those who spoke more openly," said Eve Burton, a prominent writer on Vietnamese women refugee issues who in recent years sponsored the entry of four Vietnamese rape victims. [17]

Economic Adjustment

Vietnamese women coming to America have experienced fatigue, humiliation, and anger, and continue to face new obstacles here. "Their main problem is feeling helpless and ineffective in coping with reality in this country. They are overwhelmed with the needs of adjustment, especially with their roles in the family," said Dr. Ton That Toai, a psychologist of Prince William County Public School in Virginia, during a personal interview. Thirty percent of his clients are Vietnamese women having psychological problems who have been referred to him by American social workers.

The employment of the Vietnamese wives places these women in a highly stressful situation because the traditional Vietnamese culture is deeply influenced by Confucian doctrine: authority of parent over children, husbands over wives, older children over younger ones. Confucianism also stresses that women have to be submissive: first to their fathers, then later to their husbands.[18] In Vietnam, the women are expected to take care of the household, raise the children, and obey their husbands. Although most women in the past were primarily restricted to the home, some had to take outside jobs due to the continuing war in Vietnam. They had to make a living while their husbands were on the battlefields. "Even though my husband was an officer in the navy, his salary was not enough to support the family. Luckily, I was employed before our marriage so I just continued being a nurse," said Mrs. L., one of the more fortunate women who had skills and a good job. Women with a lower level of education had difficulties in becoming self-sufficient or helping out their families. Even though many became shopkeepers, others were trapped in prostitution.

When Vietnamese women come to America, more of them drift from their traditional roles in order to help the family financially. This has caused additional cultural stress. The employment of women brings out in the open the conflict between the traditional Vietnamese role of wife and mother, and the role of women in modern American society.[19] Now able to contribute money to the family, the women feel they should have more power in the family than before. Moreover, they want to be treated as equals with their husbands. "The women should have an equal partnership in the marriage. This is America, not Vietnam," said Lan Nguyen during an interview with the author. Lan was a Vietnamese housewife who was able to obtain a technical position in a high-tech company after receiving special training.

These drastic changes in the roles of Vietnamese women have disturbed many men. They cannot cope well with the changes in the deeply-rooted Vietnamese customs and traditions; they cannot easily accept their loss of dominance within the family, their declining role as patriarch of the family. "Despite the recent importation of Western-style ways of life and the current feminist movements including the Women's Liberation Movement in the United States, the Vietnamese man in his country is still the boss, [even] if not the big boss anymore," comments Dr. Gia Thuy Vuong, a language and culture specialist.[20] The loss of their home in Vietnam appears to mean also the loss of men's authoritarian role within the family.

The husbands have not found it easy to use their working skills in America and consequently have to accept any available job. Approximately 65 percent of the Vietnamese refugees formerly working in white-collar professions have had to enter blue-collar professions in the United States, and then can no longer support their families as they did in Vietnam. Ironically, whereas many men experience downward mobility, many wives experience upward mobility in their work because they are exposed to more occupational opportunities here than in Vietnam. For instance, many electronics companies have been hiring Vietnamese women for electro-mechanical positions. With this type of job, the women do not need to speak English well, have a high level of education, or do heavy physical work. Other refugee women enter service jobs, such as beauticians, and some open little shops and restaurants to serve the local Vietnamese community.

Marital Status

The man's loss of status and power, coupled with his downward mobility, has placed severe pressure on the traditional marriage relationship. An increase in spousal abuse, which is accepted to some degree in Vietnam, is a direct result of the stress marriage faces in the transition to a new, modern culture.[21] According to Dr. Ton, violence does exist in the homes of the Vietnamese, but it rarely gets reported. Though women are physically abused by their spouses, they do not want to discuss the experience. Therefore, counselors cannot pursue the matter even though they are aware of it.

In a 1979 survey, marital conflict was found to be one of the top four problems of Vietnamese refugees in America.[22] The divorce rate among Vietnamese couples is increasing markedly. "Women in Vietnam are very dependent," says Thang Cao, a young man who is disturbed by the changes he sees in Vietnamese women.[23] "You can be sure your wife will stay with you forever. Husbands feel safe," he adds. However, in the United States where divorce is more common and acceptable, Vietnamese women are able to end their marriages without suffering as much from gossip or humiliation in the community.

Some divorced husbands have blamed their wives' new roles and new freedom for the break-up of their marriages. During a personal interview, Mr. H., recently divorced after ten years of marriage, gave his reaction to the difficulties associated with the changing roles of women:

Back in the country, my role was only to bring home money from work, and my wife would take care of the household. Now everything has changed. My wife had to work as hard as I did to support the family. Soon after, she demanded more power at home. In other words, she wanted equal partnership. I am so disappointed! I realized that things are different now, but I could not help feeling the way I do. It is hard to get rid of or change my principles and beliefs which are deeply rooted in me.

Language and Cultural Differences

In addition to problems within the family, Vietnamese women also face adjustment to the outside community. Women may suffer more than men during the resettlement period because most of the responsibility of survival has traditionally fallen on them: they are expected to take care of the children and do all the same household chores they performed in Vietnam. Unfortunately in the new environment and culture, unfamiliar situations prevent women from doing all these tasks as easily as they once did.

Most of the older women are not literate because they were never encouraged to go to school in Vietnam. This fact combined with an inability to communicate in English presents a major problem. Because they often do not know how to read the labels on merchandise, every day chores are difficult or even risky when women mistakenly use cleaning fluids in cooking. Their lack of formal education and their limited exposure to Western ways make adjustment in the United States both hard and frustrating. "I can imagine life would be difficult without my husband's help since I cannot speak English well. I feel frustrated when I cannot express myself to Americans. Therefore, at home I always try my best to learn the new language through books or television," said Mrs. L. when she was interviewed for this essay.

Inevitably, the women also come face to face with cultural differences. Vietnamese mothers lack familiarity with the new customs and are often misunderstood by the American public. Social workers often conclude inaccurately that these women do not know how to take care of their children properly, because, for example, some women let their children attend school wearing pajamas.[24] The mothers in this case think the attire is quite appropriate, however, because wearing pajamas as street clothes in Vietnam is a common and socially acceptable practice.

Confusion about American values and customs contributes to the mental health problems suffered by Vietnamese immigrant women. This confusion can lead to feelings of rejection and then depression. As Mrs. L. said, "I know that there are cultural differences, so I am very careful when I go out. I try to dress properly because I do not want to be looked down upon by the Americans as they occasionally did with the other Vietnamese women down the block." Mental health problems are most frequent among refugees who have limited experience in Western culture and have little formal education or knowledge of English. And it is clear that the majority of Vietnamese immigrant women fall into this category.

Conclusion

Past harrowing experiences and present difficulties combine to make resettlement a very strenuous process for Vietnamese women. They face a dichotomy between tradition and modernity. The emotional problems caused by the exodus may not have an immediate effect. After settling in, however, the old problems merge with new ones. "The women have been emotionally distressed constantly because their roles change so drastically. In addition, male expectations have not changed. At home, [Vietnamese women] are required to be totally submissive to their husbands, while at work they are respected by co-workers and friends," commented Dr. Ton in our interview. "Many also have problems outside the home in adjusting to the new environment. They are in need of psychological help, but they would not come to see me if they are not constantly pushed by the American social workers," he added. Without help, they usually remain silent and pretend to be fine when they see other Vietnamese.

The Vietnamese culture favors repression of negative or aggressive feelings.[25] Emotional problems are considered a personal matter to be resolved by oneself or within the family. It is very hard to find out exactly how much impact changing roles has on these women's mental health, especially because they are reluctant to reveal their emotional problems. Though the limited studies on Vietnamese women do not emphasize their mental health problems, the phenomenon still remains an issue within the Vietnamese American community, especially among the women.

What can be done to help them? The past cannot be undone, but with appropriate and well-conceived programs, the mental health of these women can be improved. They need encouragement to open up and talk about their problems so they can receive help and support in overcoming their difficulties. A small program with specially trained counselors can be a source of relief and information for the women. The program must be promoted so the Vietnamese people can become acquainted with the service. In time a successful program will have the old members coming back to help the new members overcome their hardships. To alleviate the difficulty of adjusting to a new culture and environment, the program could be expanded to teach Vietnamese women about the American way of life and Vietnamese men about the need to be more understanding and compassionate.

Vietnamese women hope to be more productive and contribute to their new society, and to enjoy their lives after the long struggle for freedom and happiness. And overall there is a positive outlook for the Vietnamese woman. As Lan Nguyen said, "I would not exchange anything for the life that I have now. A woman now has a chance to lead a happy and meaningful life for herself, instead of devoting it only to her husband and family."

PART TWO

Crashing Waves: War

Introduction

The devastation of war touched the lives of Asian women now in America, whether or not they were ever actually on the war front, because war drove them and their families from their homes. Some women came here as brides of U.S. military men; others came as refugees; still others were imprisoned in desolate concentration camps in the United States.

War leaves a legacy of deep emotional, physical, and economic consequences to the women who survive. Janice Mirikitani's "Shadow in Stone" speaks of the horrors of the atomic blasts that rocked Japan at the close of World War II. These cataclysmic events effect all our lives, regardless of our ethnic origin, nationality, religious beliefs, or political leanings.

The effects of war know no time barriers; nor do they touch only those in the war-torn country. As K. Kam points out in "The Hopeland," her *parents'* experiences during World War II have had a profound impact on *her* present life and work. According to Valerie Matsumoto's "Nisei Women and Resettlement during World War II," Japanese American women on the West Coast were directly effected by the war. Panic-stricken and racially motivated forces erroneously equated Japanese Americans with the Japanese enemy, even though there was no evidence of wrongdoing by the American residents. Because of their ethnic background, they found themselves forcibly relocated and detained in desolate camps, surrounded by barbed wire and armed guards for the duration of the war. Family life within the community was changed irrevocably by the experience.

Civil wars that wracked many parts of Asia have also wreaked havoc on the lives of Asian American women. The voice in Brenda Paik Sunoo's "We the Exiled" laments being cut off from ancestral homes and family members in Korea. Similarly, Elaine Kim's "War Story" recounts one woman's attempt to understand her sister's struggle to survive the Korean War.

The experiences of Southeast Asian women provide a contemporary example of the pernicious effects of war. The students in Kam's piece fight to succeed because of the sacrifices made on their behalf; the main character of Evelyn Lee and Gloria Oberst's "My Mother's Purple Dress" is overwhelmed by "survivor's guilt." All the selections in this section remind us that war has profound and long-term effects on Asian women in America.

Shadow in Stone

JANICE MIRIKITANI

Journey to the Hiroshima
International Peace Conference, 1984

We wander in the stifling heat
of August.
Hiroshima,
your museum, peace park,
paper cranes rustling whispers
of hei-wa   peace.
Burning incense
throbbing with white chrysanthemums,
plum blossoms, mounds
of soundless bones.
Hiroshima
how you rise up
in relentless waves of heat.
I come to you late,
when the weather bludgeons and blisters.
        I put my mouth
on your burning sky

on the lips of your murmuring river.
Motoyasu, river of the dead.
      The river speaks:
          I received the bodies
          leaping into my wet arms
          their flesh in flame, and the flies
          that followed
          maggots in the bloated sightless waste,
          skin rotting like wet leaves.
      My rhythm stifled, my movement stilled.
Motoyasu cries with rituals,
bearing a thousand flickering candles
in floating lanterns of yellow, red, blue
to remember the suffering.
I light a lantern for grandmother's sister
whom they never found amidst the ashes
of your cremation.
She floats beside the other souls
as we gather, filling water
in the cups of our hands,
pouring it back into the thirsty mouths
of ghosts, stretching parched throats.
The heat presses like many hands.
I seek solace in the stone
with human shadow burned into its face.
      I want to put my mouth to it
to the shoulders of that body,
my tongue to wet its dusty heart.
      I ask the stone to speak:
          When I looked up,
          I did not see the sun
          a kind friend who has gently pulled
          my rice plants skyward.
          I worried in that moment
          that my child would not find shade
          in this unbearable heat

that melts my eyes.
No, I did not see the sun.
I saw what today
mankind has created
and I laid my body
into this cool stone,
    my merciful resting place.
Museum of ruins.
The heat wrings our bodies
with its many fingers.
Photographs remind us of a holocaust
and imagination stumbles, beaten, aghast.
    I want to put my mouth
against these ruins, the distorted teacup,
crippled iron,
melted coins,
a disfigured bowl.
    I ask the bowl to speak:
    The old man
    held his daughter
    rocking her in his lap,
    day after day after
    that terrible day,
    she weak from radiation
    could not lift this bowl.
    Her face once bright like our sunset
    now white as ash,
    could not part her lips
    as he tried to spoon okayu from this bowl
    droplet by droplet
    into the crack of her mouth
    the watered rice with umeboshi
    which he would chew to feed her.
    He did not know
    when she stopped breathing

as he put his mouth to hers
gently to pass food.
He rocked her still body
watching the red sunset
burning its fiery farewell.
Hiroshima, rising up.
I come here late
when the weather sucks at us.
      I want to put my mouth
to the air, its many fingers of heat,
lick the twisted lips
of a disfigured bowl,
the burned and dusty heart of shadow in stone,
put my mouth to the tongues
of a river,
its rhythms, its living water
weeping on the sides of lanterns
each floating flame, a flickering
voice murmuring
over and over
as I put my mouth
to echo
over and over
      never again.

We the Exiled

BRENDA PAIK SUNOO

i can understand
why
it's hard
to soften the visions of war
especially when warm tears

have fallen
upon families' bodies
soaked in red
in pools of running blood

i can understand
how relighting the memories
of promises broken
burn to ash
the million hearts
that once beat in tune

and that we, the exiled,
were forced to leave
to make families our strangers
and strangers our friends

but when will we understand
what
it was and
what
remains
that sets the stage aflame
where people kill each other
ruthlessly,
in spite of
their identical name . . .

War Story

ELAINE H. KIM

To most Americans the 1950–53 war in Korea is not familiar or interesting, not like the Second World War or the war in Vietnam. Not many Americans know that the United States has been shaping the destiny of everyone on the Korean peninsula since the turn of the century—handing Korea over to Japan by secret agreement in 1909 and helping the Soviet Union divide the country in half along political lines at the end of World War II. Even today, most Americans might be surprised to know how much American "aid" has gone into creating and propping up regimes that are supportive of American military and economic interests in Korea. Traditionally, Korea and Koreans have not been of much concern to the average American. What finally brought Korea into the consciousness of the American people was the war, in which American troops participated.

The morning the war began, my parents were still in bed when I got up. My parents never slept late; it was the only time I can remember getting up before they did. I wondered why they lay in bed and, as if to answer my unspoken question, they told me that war had broken out in Korea.

I had just finished fourth grade at a small town primary school in Maryland and was eager for a summer of bare feet and playing jacks. None of my friends had ever heard of Korea; they often accused me of making up the word "Korean" because I must have really been Chinese or Japanese after all. But Korea was important to me because my parents and all the people they knew never seemed to think or talk of anything else.

We had many relatives in Korea then, as we do now. Our family, like so many Korean families, is scattered across the world. My uncle joined the resistance movement against Japan in China, and my aunt joined the Communist movement in North Korea. My half-brother was taken to Japan by other Koreans during the Second World War. Not one of my father's blood relatives ever immigrated to America after he came in 1926, so I have first cousins in China, Japan, North and South Korea, but none in America. We were the estranged branch of the family, living among Westerners who had never even heard of Korea.

Throughout my life, it has seemed to me that being Korean meant living with *han* every day. *Han,* the anguished feeling of being far from what you wanted, a longing that never went away, but ate and slept with you every day of your life, has no exact equivalent in English. It must be a Korean feeling, born from and nurtured by what Korea and Koreans have faced over the centuries: longing for the end of the brutal Japanese rule, longing for the native place left behind when you went into exile, longing for your loved ones after being separated by war or the new boundary in your homeland, longing for the reunification of Korea as one nation of people who can trace their common roots back several millennia.

Han is by no means a hopeless feeling, however. It is something like rage. You can see it sometimes in people's eyes. South Korean poet Kim Chi Ha shows it to us in "Groundless Rumors," which is about a day worker who, jailed and executed for daring to curse his oppression, is said to roll his limbless trunk back and forth between the walls of his cell in protest. The sound strikes fear into the hearts of the powerful and lights a "strange fire" in the eyes of the oppressed everywhere.

Liberation from Japanese rule was the holy cause of Korean people my parents' age. Like many other resisters, my father left Korea for Japan as a teenager, just after Korea was annexed. He left behind his new bride who was pregnant at the time with my half-sister. Except for a brief summer visit, he did not return to his native place, not even when his wife died of consumption. Instead, he left Japan on a boat bound for America. He stayed twenty years with a student visa and had various restaurant jobs before he started to work for the U.S. and South Korean governments in Washington, D.C. He and my mother, the daughter of an immigrant Korean sugar plantation worker in Hawaii, met in Chicago and married in New York, where my older brother and I were born.

I never saw our half-sister until I visited Korea at age twenty. My Korean isn't fluent and she can't speak English, but after a year of living with her and her family, I was able to understand most of what she said and say pretty much what I wanted to to her. Because we are sisters, I am always haunted by her stories, feeling that we were like a pair of twins separated by accident. I could have been the one imprisoned for "anti-Japanese thoughts," the one married off to a man I had never met, the one drinking in the fragrance of cucumbers I could not afford to eat. I might have known nothing about American racism. In turn, she could have been the "Chink" or the "Jap" on the school playground, the one with the full stomach and the saddle shoes, diagraming English sentences for homework, ears stinging from being asked by teachers to stand in front of the room to tell her classmates "what you are."

Perhaps this mysterious feeling of being interchangeable has forged the bond welding many Americans in a nation of immigrants to the people who remained at home. This is my half-sister's story.

. . .

On 25 June 1950, when the war began, I was at church with your two little nephews when I noticed people running around outside in the streets, shouting that people from the North had crossed the 38th parallel. I didn't worry much, since I had witnessed so many shooting incidents when I lived near the 38th parallel. No one believed that our country would be divided for long, just as no one guessed that there would be such a terrible war to bring death and destruction everywhere.

The announcer on the radio said that people were being killed or captured in the streets, but I was sure there wouldn't be any fighting in Seoul. I did worry about your *hyungbu* [her husband, my brother-in-law], who had a job as a reservoir and irrigation worker near the DMZ [demilitarized zone]. Under the Japanese, we Koreans had been out of work except for the worst menial jobs because the Japanese had taken all the middle- and high-level jobs. Now that Japan had surrendered, he finally had work, and we were glad even though it meant he had to live far from home for the time being. I had returned with the children to Father-in-law's house in Seoul to escape the cross-fire in the region. But even though there were rumors that the fighting was coming closer and closer to Seoul and many people were packing up to flee across the Han River, I still didn't think anything would happen and had no thoughts of fleeing further south, since I was physically separated from my husband.

A day or two later, he arrived at our gate, so exhausted by his three-day walk to Seoul without food or sleep that he collapsed, speechless, on the floor. He wouldn't budge, even though there were gunshots all around and most our neighbors had already fled across the river. Father-in-law was jumping up and down screaming that everyone else was gone, but *hyungbu* said he couldn't move even if his life depended on it.

We finally ran out in the rain, carrying only some rice and our children on our backs, heading for his aunt's house, where we all sat around worrying about what to do. We thought that at least it would be better to be together. I had heard somewhere that bullets don't penetrate cotton comforters, so I wrapped the children up in the blankets. They were hot and I couldn't sleep, but *hyungbu,* still exhausted from his walk to Seoul, snored all night long.

When we peered outside the next morning, we saw red flags everywhere. The people from the North had arrived. On the radio, the South Korean president was telling everyone, "Don't worry, everything is all right. The North Koreans will never be able to penetrate Seoul." Later, we found out that the president had already fled, leaving behind a tape-recorded message. After he had safely crossed the Han River, the South Korean military blew up the bridge in his wake, even though many refugees on the bridge were killed.

We decided to go back home, figuring that no matter where we were the situation would be the same. The problem was that the North Korean soldiers were looking for young men to induct into their Righteous Brave Army. The North Koreans had access to all the census information and government documents, so they knew how many young men were in each household. Each night they would bang on people's gates looking for young men, who would be hiding under the floorboards or somewhere else out of sight. We would lie, saying that the young men had gone to the countryside to buy food and hadn't returned. The soldiers would ask the neighborhood children to tell them where their fathers were, and some of them would reply, "He's hiding under the floorboards." Then the men would be discovered and drafted. They didn't ask your nephew Sung-hi, though. Anyway, we had instructed him never to tell.

Since the United States was bombing everything during the day, all work had to be done under cover of night, and one person from each household was required to come out to detonate bombs and rebuild wreckage. The North Koreans were not harsh with us because our neighborhood was poor. They said I didn't have to work with a baby on my back and that Father-in-law was too old to work.

I had two bags of rice, which I hid with the linens. Rice was hard to come by then: none of the stores were open, and it was several months before the rice harvest. We bought potatoes and barley and ate that, mixed with a little rice. People were making stew from zucchini leaves and whatever vegetables they could get, boiling them with some barley in lots of water.

When *hyungbu* could no longer bear hiding under the floorboards and urinating into a bowl, he decided to try fleeing to the countryside to his relative's house. We had no idea that things were even worse there. He couldn't go alone because people were being grabbed off the streets, so he dressed up as an old farmer and took Sung-hi on his back, thinking that no one would try to take him into the army if he had a child with him. If he had gone to *Uijungbu* after all, I probably would never have seen him again, since his relatives there had become Communists, and he might have ended up in North Korea. We would have been a divided family like so many others who were separated when the borders closed and all traffic between North and South Korea stopped permanently. If he had been caught along the way, perhaps our son would have become one of those orphans crying by the side of the road.

It happened that the construction company *hyungbu* had been working in was run by men sympathetic with North Korea. Someone came to our house and told me that the people working in that company would not be drafted into the North Korean army. Instead, they would receive identification cards showing them to be draft exempt. Overjoyed, I ran all the way over the *Miari* hill to catch up with *hyungbu,* who was trudging along very slowly because he was really heartsick at leaving in the first place.

We were elated at first, but after he had worked for about one month, we began getting scared. The United Nations forces were coming closer and closer to Seoul, and we thought we'd get into trouble for cooperating with North Koreans. *Hyungbu* stopped going to work and, sure enough, when the South Korean soldiers re-entered Seoul in late September, they arrested and imprisoned all of the people who had cooperated with North Koreans, including *hyungbu*'s co-workers. Many people were murdered at that time. Now *hyungbu* was hiding from the *South*

Korean soldiers. This time, we pretended he was sick. We had him lie down next to a medicine distiller. Because he was so thin and pale, people really believed that he was ill.

By now everyone was talking about how Korea would be reunited under UN forces. We had to go on living: it was autumn, so I went ahead and made winter *kimchee* and bought firewood for the winter. But in November the UN and South Korean forces were driven back down from North Korea. The South Korean army tried to draft all the young men, many of whom were hiding or running away. *Hyungbu* was tired of hiding and decided that since he was a citizen of South Korea, it was his duty to volunteer. But how he suffered for it!

The enlisted men had to walk to Taegu [250 miles away]. They were a ragged bunch, with blankets hung over their shoulders like hoboes or beggars. What kind of an "army" was that? The road was difficult and the weather was freezing and the men had to sell their watches and possessions to buy food along the way.

In Taegu *hyungbu* failed the physical examination. Those who failed were considered of little use and unable to fight, so they were poorly fed and had to live in barns. Many men were said to have died from exposure, malnutrition, and diseases carried by vermin. Somehow, though, *hyungbu* survived. He organized people to gather wood to sell so that they could buy food. Everyone cooperated with each other, even making trips into Taegu to buy medicine for the sick among them. Finally, these men just deserted and tried to get back to their families.

Meanwhile, I was in Seoul with the babies and Father-in-law. I didn't know how we were going to flee from the battle zone. But one of *hyungbu*'s relatives had connections with a cargo train, so we got a place on top of some big drums filled with gasoline. Even though it was dangerous, everyone wanted to get a place on top of the train. We were so happy that we could get a ride, since Father-in-law was much too old to walk. Rice prices had plummeted in Seoul, so I bought two large bags of rice to carry with us. The train would go for a few hours and then stop for a few hours. Sometimes it would stop on top of some mountain and not move the whole night. We were afraid to get down to urinate, for fear the train would take off without us or that we would lose our places. It took us over a week to get to Pusan.

It was December, so it was very cold. We used our comforters for cover from the snow and freezing rain, but the wet comforters kept freezing. It was hot and sweaty under them, but if we lifted them, we would catch a chill; somehow the baby caught pneumonia. Not having any food, I tried to nurse him, but I was not producing any milk because I wasn't eating anything myself. My nipples got torn from his desperate sucking, and I was sore from his clawing little hands. He was burning up with fever by the time we finally reached Pusan, and I thought that the child was going to die.

The first thing I did in Pusan was rush to the hospital for some penicillin for the baby. We didn't have any place to sleep. Rooms were expensive, and Pusan was filled to overflowing with refugees from Seoul and other places. We were among the last to arrive—we learned that North Korean soldiers had re-entered Seoul just after we left—and we couldn't find a place to stay, so we were sleeping in the streets.

I had earlier vowed to myself that no matter how badly off I was, I would never seek out Small Uncle [Father's younger brother], because he had told us that he had no way to leave Seoul. We found out later that he had gone to Pusan in a truck sponsored by the bank where he worked. He took with him not only his entire family but even all his home furnishings. Now, with my child almost dead, there was nothing I could do but go to the bank branch in Pusan to find Uncle, who was surprised and a little embarrassed to see me. He took me to the place where he was staying with his family: it was a huge house, big enough to hold many families. The floors were heated and the people were cooking and eating almost normally, very unlike refugees. Some of the other bank employees had brought their relatives with them. It was clear that Uncle could have brought us with him. War brings out the worst in people. You never know, not even about your own relatives, until something dreadful happens . . .

Meanwhile, Father [in the United States] had put notices in the newspapers asking after us. We couldn't even wash our faces on top of those oil drums on the cargo train; how could we read the newspaper? Uncle saw one of the notices and contacted Father, who sent us a little money. Since we were living with him then, Uncle took all the money. Father asked me to write to him, and when I told him about how Uncle had left us in

Seoul, fleeing with his family and belongings to Pusan, Father was furious. I got into trouble with Uncle, but I was glad that someone knew what had happened to us.

I was surprised to see so many young men in Pusan. I had thought they would enlist in the South Korean army as they were supposed to and as *hyungbu* had. How naive we were! The young men had run away from the draft to Pusan.

Since his father was not around, your little nephew went around calling every man he saw "Daddy." I kept hearing about how many men were dying, and I didn't know whether my husband was one of them. One day, your older nephew ran into our house crying, "Mommy, Mommy, there's a beggar coming this way who looks just like Daddy!" Sure enough, it was *hyungbu,* dirty, emaciated, and dressed in rags and tatters. The new, thick pants he had been wearing when he left several months before were torn and infested with lice and fleas. We burned those clothes, and he washed and got a haircut so that he looked like a human being again. We prepared to move into our own household. Like a fool, I gave all the rice I had brought and the money I had to Uncle, so we started off on our own with nothing. People were just constructing shacks here and there with dirt floors and straw mats for walls. We too built one of these.

Hyungbu found work at the docks loading and unloading cargo, but the contractor took the workers' pay and disappeared. We were in real trouble then: the only food we could afford was bean sprouts. We couldn't even buy soy sauce, so we boiled the sprouts and ate them with a little salt. It wasn't even like eating.

When fall came, Father's friend got *hyungbu* a job. We were paid in barley, but it was better than not having any work at all. Your little nephew would see the autumn persimmons that the street vendors were selling and say, "Mommy, wouldn't it be nice to have some of those soft persimmons?" I would just tell him I'd buy him some later. He remembered my promise for a long time, and he kept reminding me about it. But people were lucky to be eating anything at all back then.

That winter, Father-in-law died. We couldn't even afford to take him to the hospital.

There should never be wars. It's the most blameless ones who are sacrificed. There was a young woman living in the shack next to us who cried all day long. It turns out that she had to leave one of her little girls behind on the road while she was fleeing. Many children were left at the side of the road or dropped into rivers if they started to cry or make noise while their parents were trying to flee under cover of night. Everyone in the group would argue that it was better for one child to die than for a whole group to be discovered and prevented from escaping. How can a mother go on living after she has thrown away her baby?

During the war, Father came to Pusan from America. Today, people can travel so easily between Korea and America, but in those days, arriving from America was like arriving from another planet. I had seen him only once before, when I was about six years old. I remember running in from playing outside to find a strange man eating on the *maru* (wooden floor veranda). People said, "That is your father." He had returned from Japan during the summer for just one visit to Cholwon. Too shy and scared to greet him, I ran out the back door. Now twenty-five years later, it was so strange to see him—he didn't seem like a father, he looked so young. I bowed to him, and he said, "Who bows to their own father?" He wanted to come to our house, and when he saw our shack, he was shocked. He didn't have much money himself, but he gave us $100, which was a huge sum then; we rented a room for six months with it. Your niece was born in the middle of the night while we were living our refugee life in Pusan. *Hyungbu* had gotten a construction job, so we had some income until the end of the war, when we returned to Seoul to try to rebuild our lives.

Now that the children are all grown up, I often think about how it was never easy. We worked so hard to send them all to school and see each one of them marry and start a family. Some people want their children to marry on auspicious days of the astrological calendar, but our children married on patriotic days, like Liberation Day or the birthdate of Korea's mythical founder.

On the small plot of land we live on in the outskirts of Seoul, we spend our time now growing vegetables of all kinds—tomatoes, cabbage, squash, onions, garlic, and corn—and taking care of our fruit trees. Now that *hyungbu* is retired, we have time to visit with three grandsons and three granddaughters. I have to work hard, since your older nephew and his family live with us. These days parents-in-law have to bend over backwards to get their children to live with them. In my time daughters-in-law had to do all the housework, but nowadays the mothers-in-law have to do everything just to keep their sons living with them. We don't have any social security or retirement income, so we have to get help from the children. In return, we try to do our best for them. I can say that we have a happy life now.

During the war, everyone was talking about how we Koreans were all going to be killed somehow, either by American bombers or by North Koreans, whom we heard were killing people everywhere. Actually, they were punishing rich people and high officials, but we didn't know what would happen to people like us. Father was trying to figure out a way to bring me to America. People would say to my sons, "Yeah! If you go to your Grandpa, you won't have to die like us." But I was afraid to go: I didn't know where my husband was then; I felt I couldn't leave my old father-in-law; I couldn't speak any English; and I had two small children. Besides, Father was a stranger to me, since I had only met him twice! So I said I didn't want to leave.

Later on I sometimes regretted missing the chance to go to America. Who knows how things would have turned out? Maybe my children would have been able to study and become successful, because in America it seems possible to get somewhere by working hard. In Korea, no matter how hard you try and how much you work, you don't necessarily get anywhere at all. Just think, if my husband or my sons had worked as hard in America as they have in Korea, they might have received a real reward for their effort. On the other hand, maybe American life would have ruined my children. It seems that people in America don't think very much about their parents or their families. And what if my own grandchildren couldn't even speak to me in our language? Or what if *hyungbu* and I had returned to Korea, leaving our children in America like so many older people do? We haven't much money and wouldn't be able to see our children and grandchildren often like we do now. And after all, we do love our country.

We are Koreans and we want to remain Koreans. My second son says that he'd rather live in the filthiest and poorest Korean place than in the most luxurious American place, just because he wants to live in his own country. Even though we aren't as comfortable, we like living in our own country. There's no place like your own country. During the past ten or fifteen years, many people have been leaving for the States and Canada. Of course ordinary people can't emigrate, since you need money to emigrate. The people who really need to emigrate so they can work to eat can't afford to go. The ones who leave are pretty well off. They sneak money out with them so they can start businesses, make money, and live out their dream of being like kings and queens in foreign countries. Sometimes these days, people in Korea criticize those who leave for America, saying they have deserted their motherland, taking all their wealth with them and leaving the problems for someone else to solve.

. . .

When my sister says this about Korean immigrants deserting their homeland, she only reinforces my own concern for the well-being of Koreans, both in America and in Korea. As a Korean American, I support movements for democratic reforms in South Korea, am critical of Japanese and U.S. exploitation of Korea, and cherish a vibrant hope for national reunification. At the same time, I live and work in the United States, and I feel I must find ways to work against racism and toward our community's strength, health, and self-sufficiency.

I often think about what it would have been like for my sister and her family to have immigrated to America, just as I wonder what my life would be like now if I had been born and raised in Korea. I always conclude that things turned out better this way. I probably would not have finished school in Korea—how could I have passed those excruciatingly difficult college entrance exams? In fact, I would probably have been married off at the "appropriate time" and pressed into a role that Korean women of my generation rarely escaped, a role that many women born and raised in the United States would find difficult and unattractive. But although my sister does not enjoy the same material possessions Americans do, she is still happy because she stayed in the country she loved, among her friends and family members, speaking her native language, instead of living as a stranger in an adopted land.

Nonetheless, there is a branch of the family she can visit in America. The last time we parted—she has visited America four times now, and I have lived at her house in Korea—I teased her about how she always weeps as if we were never going to meet again, even though we see each other every few years. She didn't shed a tear when she left Oakland this time.

The Hopeland

K. KAM

My father turned the pages slowly. His eyes shifted over several photographs in the history book, then focused on a picture taken in China during World War II. He stared at the black and white shot of several limp bodies entangled on a stairway, the corpses of families trampled in a stampede flight from a Japanese raid. Clothing had been torn from some of the dead, perhaps by desperate villagers. Children, necks bent awkwardly, were sprawled across the steps like discarded toys. On the opposite page, a clean, neat title, black on white, read: "1939–1941 Continuing Horror in China." Decades of hidden grief began to line my father's face as he closed the book. He handed it back to me, wordless, as he left the room. My father rarely talked about his boyhood in China. He kept silent about the war. The photographs spoke for him.

"Your father's youngest brother vanished during the war when he was nine," my mother confided later when I was sixteen. "Third Uncle and Fourth Uncle were inside a schoolhouse when the planes soared overhead. The children had no time to escape before the bombs exploded on them. When your grandmother heard the loud blasts and saw smoke and fire rising from the schoolhouse, she ran towards her children instead of taking cover. Later, she sifted through the rubble with the rest of the villagers, tearing her hands on jagged bricks, but she found only Third Uncle alive beneath the destruction. When you go to Hong Kong someday, ask him to show you the scars on his legs. As for Fourth Uncle, he simply disappeared in the blast. Your father's mother lost her youngest son in the war and there wasn't even a body left for her to bury. I tell you these things because you ask, but don't mention them in front of your father."

My mother has her own stories to tell, tales of fleeing to damp hillside caves for days whenever bomber planes, too small to be distinguished as ally or foe, were heard in the distance. Grabbing a handful of yams and a bottle of water kept ready for such emergencies, she bolted out the door, joining other villagers in a frenzied exodus as she wrapped the food inside an extra shirt, her only protection from the night chill. As a youngster in wartime, my barefoot mother collected leaves and boiled them, using the congealed sap to wash herself since no one had soap. Matches were a luxury, too. My grandmother would step outside and glance above the housetops before preparing a meager dinner of rice gruel. When she spotted a thin blue curl of smoke rising, she would shove my mother towards it with dry branches in hand to carry home the precious flame.

I try to imagine my mother as a young girl, small and frail with a quiet heart, shiny black hair cropped to prevent her from indulging in hours of vanity before the mirror. I laugh when she tells me some pranksters in her village filled a large vat with dung and lit a fire under it, boiling the smelly contents until they exploded.

But the funny stories are always followed by somber ones that will not let me forget the horrors my parents must have endured. I hear only bits and pieces. My mother tells of drunken soldiers banging on the doors of houses nearby, dragging out screaming girls and raping them in the night. She watched an angry crowd of villagers haul a traitor to the top of a hill, where they hanged him for selling secrets to the enemy. There were the victims forced to kneel on broken glass and the hunted ones who chose suicide. During land raids, she stared mutely as soldiers smashed windows and shot down old women barricading doorways with their bodies to protect young ones inside. During one onslaught, she hid underneath a bed as a soldier entered her house and held a bayonet to her mother's throat.

I am disturbed, yet intrigued. I listen to the stories, casting the characters and writing the script, but my mental exercise is only a game. My parents' China still eludes me.

I wonder also what their first years in America were like. I was only two when we sailed across the ocean that separates me from an ancient and remote homeland.

As a young man, my father lived in Hong Kong. He had worked hard to come to America, taking English classes at night to improve his timid, halting speech. He postponed marriage until he was thirty-one, reluctant to take a wife when he might leave for America the following year. But after a decade of pursuing his dream, he decided to marry my mother in 1959. Three years later, America opened her arms to my father, willing to embrace him after years of snubbing. My mother, less eager, stood defenseless against the powerful charms of America.

My father rarely speaks any more of his deferred dreams. But I have plowed restless fingers through his bookshelves and stumbled upon Shakespeare readers tucked between the Chinese novels with their musty trunk smells, and then a series of English grammar texts, old and yellowed with blotches of tea stains on the pages. I've raided his bookshelves section by section and have found hidden delights each time—a Sinclair Lewis novel, a Tennessee Williams play, a book of poetry. It was impossible for me to imagine my father's thickly accented syllables wrapping themselves around the elegant words.

When he first came to this country, his dreams incubated in the heat of a stuffy kitchen by day and pecked a little further out of their confining shells at night. Hard shells—language barriers, uncertainties, prejudices, fears—were chipped away bit by bit as he attended night school and struggled to become an educated man, a new success in a new land. Week after week, he sat under the glaring fluorescent lights of the classroom eking out gram-ma-ti-cal essays as English teachers with pleased smiles and small nods of approval assigned him book after book of "American reading."

But somewhere far in the past, my father stopped the weary tasks of "American reading" and writing assigned essays. He relegated his American books to the shelves and focused his energy upon the persistent questioning of his children, each of whom had gone off to college.

"What are you going to do next year when you graduate?"

"I'm not sure yet, Dad. I'm thinking of working for a couple of years, and then maybe I'll go back to school," answers his son, the one who studied economics.

"Why don't you become a dentist?" my father urges.

"It's not that easy, Dad. Besides, I don't want to become a dentist."

Once, when I worked for a group of attorneys in San Francisco, my father asked where all of them had attended law school. "Where do they go on vacations? Do they ski? Do they own houses up in the mountains?" I was reluctant to answer, not wanting to fan age-old disappointments. Before I could reply, he sighed, "You know, a very nice doctor comes into the restaurant all the time, and he always seems sad to me. I ask him what is wrong and he tells me his son is no good—uses too many drugs. Sells them, too. He asks me what my kids do and I tell him four are college graduates. He says that's beautiful, says I'm a lucky man."

His words startled me. When we had run home from grade school with near-perfect report cards, my father admonished us solemnly. "Never compare yourselves to those below you, only to those above you," he said year after year. My mother chided us, too. "You must study hard and make something of yourselves. When I was in China, I had to leave school at fourteen and start working as a seamstress in Hong Kong when I was sixteen. If I had been given the same opportunities you've received, I could have become anything I wanted—anything."

Their words seep into my blood and cause my muscles to pull taut. At times I am frustrated by the pressure to succeed, yet I am driven by guilt and sadness to redress my parents' lost dreams and regrets of an uneducated past.

Somehow, I owe another kind of debt because of their past, and so I, the American daughter, have sought jobs working with refugees in Chinatown legal clinics, resettlement agencies, and inner-city schools.

When I first started working at the high school where I am now a counselor, I would follow the Cambodian and Vietnamese refugee students with my eyes, listen for conversations about their pasts, alert myself to clues about them in their essays. I studied student transcripts that read "Birthplace: Vietnam, Year: 1969" and was astonished at the birth of tender, delicate children, all smooth flesh and soft hair, born amid bombing in the night. When I looked into the children's faces at school, their slow eyes and solemn gazes told of loss and loneliness. They opened their current distresses to me, but I remained on the periphery of their past hurts. In time, the silence of the children broke and the past poured forth.

A beautiful young girl with honeyed skin and trusting eyes sat in my office and told me of her childhood in a Khmer Rouge labor camp in Cambodia.

By day, she sat in the dirty, bleak schoolroom Pol Pot's soldiers had set up, mumbling answers, fearful that the simple-minded peasant teachers would catch a glimmer of too much intelligence in her eyes if she recited too readily or looked up too quickly. She had already seen too many bright people and their families slaughtered by the Khmer Rouge. "Never admit that your father was an engineer in Phnom Penh," her mother had warned her. "We must say he was a rice farmer."

In the fields, she cowered under the glares of the soldiers and wept, mouth shut, half starved, as she struggled to spread big pails of dung over the crops. Those around her collapsed dead from hunger, beatings, and exhaustion as they worked in the fields. When she saw them drop, she mourned for her parents, who had died within months of each other.

Not even a brother or a sister remained by her side. The soldiers had herded the biggest, strongest children, her sister among them, to another camp to build reservoirs to hoard the rainwater.

When my student watched young women in her camp forced to marry Khmer Rouge soldiers who were deformed from the war—ugly, legless men with bulging stumps—she thought of her seventeen-year-old sister now digging trenches in the strong children's camp.

"Pol Pot's soldiers shouted 'enemy' at me all the time," she told me. "I don't know why they hated me. I never hated them before."

The stories differ in time and place and intensity, but this child's voice speaks to me of the pain when a parent or brother or sister is lost forever, when a homeland is ravaged—things I wish my father could tell me but I know he cannot.

Sometimes when I walk the corridors of the high school, I see many children who look so much like me—round faces, tilted eyes, dark hair—but who are not really like me at all. A few have become sad, quiet, and crazy because of the war.

Then I notice that some of the children who have walked through fire in Southeast Asia have emerged not destroyed, but tempered with strength, hope, and resilience. For these children, obstacles simply mean finding another way.

Daily I see these young ones contend with the rigors of their new lives here. I overhear a willowy Vietnamese girl attempt to discuss a class project with her teacher, a ruddy-faced man with graying hair. Her speech stumbles along, then halts when she utters a phrase he cannot understand.

"Could you please say that last word again?"

Her eyes dart away from his face to the floor, and once more, the phrase tumbles out of her mouth in halting English. His eyebrows knit quizzically. She senses his confusion and blushes red, disgraced and flustered at not being able to make herself understood. But she tries once more. The teacher's face strains hard, trying to redeem the efforts of a nervous girl whose words hang suspended in the air between them.

I am reminded of my mother's frustrations. Once, when I was young, my mother came home weeping from the restaurant pantry where she worked. I overheard her telling my father that the loud, fat woman who sliced meats at a work station next to hers had berated her all morning until my mother felt her small voice explode within her and rise to the top of her throat like a ball of flame. She tried to yell back, but the words would not come out in English. I ran into my room and slammed the door furiously, wishing I could storm into that kitchen pantry and tongue-lash that big mean woman with all the scathing American words I knew.

When I hear tales of faceless, merciless youths who taunt refugee children, spit on them, shove them, and laugh at them as they read aloud in English classes, a bit of the same old childish rage starts to rise within me. I feel silly and impotent, like a little girl slamming doors again. Then I tell myself that my mother never really needed me to fight her daily battles for her. She waged them on her own, and now in her self-sufficiency she no longer needs her children to accompany her to stores, banks, and post offices.

As I follow these young refugees in their struggles to begin again in a land of promise, I remember my father's youthful ambitions. From the clamor and filth of refugee camps, America still shines in her splendor—sweet, clean, free. "It was a dream, but it did come true," writes one Vietnamese student about coming to this country. "It was an eager wish, yet it was fulfilled as if by magic. When stepping on this hopeland, America, I knew that I had stepped forward to a future filled with faithful promises." Only three years ago, as a child of fourteen, she had crouched stealthily in a sampan headed for sea. On the waters, she fled from Thai pirates and endured the harshness of camp life in order to reach this new country.

One student told me, "Most of my life has been spent struggling, so now that I'm in a peaceful land, my energies will go towards moving ahead." These young people pour into my office with dreams of becoming doctors, bankers, engineers, computer scientists, and accountants. Many are eager and diligent, smart and capable. Some are conscientious to an extreme, recopying applications four times over before sending them to colleges that hold within their walls the promise of a bright future.

I see all the good things America has to offer these young refugees—peace, education, opportunity, food, warmth, a future, and a hope. They are free now. I am anxious to see them accomplish what they came here hoping to achieve, but I worry that some may see their dreams unfulfilled. I am afraid that some may not be given the jobs they deserve because of their sex or the slant of their eyes or the inflections in their speech. Some of them will be called "chinks" and "gooks" and may suffer physical beatings because they have entered a society that does not automatically make room for them. Not all of them will achieve the high goals for which they aim. If they fail, will they lament the missed opportunities? Will their dreams become their children's duties, legacies of guilt and regret?

New lives in America are not easily forged. One of my brightest students, a Vietnamese war orphan, awoke one morning, and shunning the soft radio music she relied on at the start of each day to soothe what the American teachers labeled "cultural adjustment," she wandered to a nearby lake and found a wizened Chinese man playing his flute on the shore. Out of the silver instrument floated sweet, holy, tremulous notes unlike anything the girl had heard except in Vietnam.

A few days later, she appeared in my office, her eyes looking sad and aged. She told me the story of the flute and of how she lingered on, listening until the old man went away. "Now I must confess to you, my counselor, that I do not have the same heart to be in this country. I do not fit well in this society. I do not like to compete all the time. I know it cannot happen, but often, I wish I could go back to Vietnam and become a simple person again."

The homeland will never be forgotten. But I remain buoyed in my hopes for these children's futures when I recall their exuberance upon arriving in this new land. One child wrote: "I was overwhelmed by the friendly hospitality of some Americans who had given me an optimistic prediction for my next days in this country. At that moment, I had almost forgotten all the terribly dark times of my life. Wishing to fly to another promised land. . . . And now, the wish has come to reality, even though at first, I could not believe it was so. America has opened her arms and greeted us, the miserable birds struggling against the winter's coldness, with the warmest humanity."

Let it be so, I whisper. Like my parents, these children have come to the hopeland, and I celebrate them.

My Mother's Purple Dress

EVELYN LEE AND GLORIA OBERST

2 June 1985—General Hospital Emergency Unit

Huu Tien Ly, a Chinese woman from Vietnam in her early twenties, was brought in by police for psychiatric evaluation. According to the patient's aunt and younger sister, the patient behaved like a "crazy woman" after she was fired from her job two weeks ago. She wandered about the street at night and bought a round-trip ticket to Portland last weekend with no explanation given. She was easily agitated and became very verbally abusive. Yesterday, the patient threatened to kill her sister with a kitchen knife during an argument. A few hours before admission, the patient declared that all purple colored objects were dangerous and needed to be destroyed. She started to throw her aunt's purple dishes out of the apartment window and attempted to physically assault the police officer on the way to the hospital.

The patient is five feet tall, weighs ninety-two pounds, and is in good physical health. Her speech was pressured and loud. She repeatedly stated in Cantonese that she was not crazy and that her sister was the one who should be sent to the hospital. During the interview, the patient appeared to be angry, agitated, and impatient.

11 February 1975—Saigon, South Vietnam

"Wait, wait for me," her brother called down from the alley. "Don't be so quick, Little Kite. Wait for me." Huu Tien reluctantly slowed down and waited for her older brother. He seemed so tall at fifteen, one year her senior, and was very much like their father. As her brother reached her he put his hand lightly on her shoulder. "Why do you go so fast? All the time so fast. I worry for you. Too fast, too smart is not always best."

"Do I not get things done? Didn't teacher say I was best student? Quick learner. Same with father. Am I not dependable?" She teased back at him, "Are you saying I am too quick or you too slow?" Then she smiled and laughed, "I am like you, right?"

"No, yes, oh, sometimes." He shook his head and they continued down the alley. The hot Saigon sun beat down on the war-torn city. They had been born in wartime, gone to school in wartime, and now would celebrate the New Year in wartime. Everyone said the war would soon end and they would know peace at last. But for now, the two children talked, as children do, of children's problems. "Are you sure Nguyet Tien will be prepared for school tomorrow? She is not like you, she is not a quick learner." He looked down as she kicked at a rock there.

She replied very seriously, "It is hard to teach a nine-year-old sister, but I persisted and she has learned it. I plan to have her rehearse it tonight for the family. I think she will do well." As Huu Tien chased the just-kicked rock to the corner, she looked into the street. "Soldiers!" she shouted to her brother, Gia Quyen, "Soldiers!" and the game was on.

He raced past her and into the street. He was very interested in the soldiers. Soon he would have to decide whether to join the older students against the war or enlist in the army. He was disappointed that they were not American forces. He knew that the Americans had pulled out in November the year before. Still, he hoped they would come back. He was fascinated with the colorful uniforms and weapons, but mainly he watched the helicopters. He wanted to fly—like one of his kites—to soar and fly. He waited a moment and turned back to his sister. "Thank you. You are still too quick but sometimes . . . sometimes, okay." He shrugged, and they continued on home.

Before entering the house he said, "Tonight will be a good night. Mother will be happy with the dress Father had made for her. Every year she makes things for everyone else, never herself. This year will be different. Then maybe she won't be so sad that Auntie Mai is going to be leaving." Both children brushed off their clothes, and looking composed, went inside.

Black Chinese characters seemed to leap from the bright red New Year's signs. There were wishes for good health, good luck, and blessings for all who passed through the door. Huu Tien touched her favorite sign as she went to help. There was much to be done.

Soon she was in the kitchen working. She liked the sweet smell of her mother's hair as she stood next to her preparing the special New Year's vegetable dish. She watched as her mother's strong hands cut and chopped. Huu Tien's younger sister worked alongside her mother. "Nguyet! Be careful. You must tilt the knife more. I'll show you one more time." Huu Tien moved to her younger sister. "Don't be a fool. Don't embarrass me with your cutting." Taking the smaller hand in her own, she moved both of them and the knife. "Better."

Phung Tran turned to the two girls. "Huu Tien, it is good to care for your sister. But it is alright not to be so strict." Her face was lined and tired. Life had been hard since coming to Vietnam over twenty-two years ago. And while times had been hard in China, she sometimes wondered if she had made the right decision to leave her dying mother and come to this strange land—especially when one of her children had died shortly after settling here. Also, it had taken much work for her husband's grocery store to earn a profit because there had been much resentment against ethnic Chinese. And now, her sister-in-law and closest friend, was going to live in the United States. This would probably be the last New Year's they would celebrate together. "There is much to do. Huu Tien, it is important that you finish this for me and I start on the chicken."

That night there was much drinking and eating and talking. Huu Tien stood proudly as her little sister completed the rehearsal of her school lesson. Nguyet ran to her side and hugged her. "I didn't forget any words. I did good."

"You were very good. And you didn't jump around or scratch." Huu Tien then proceeded to give part of a speech she had prepared for class. She ended with, "When I finish college, I will be a teacher. And I will save money and take Mother and Father and Nguyet to visit Uncle Quak and Auntie Mai. Gia Quyen will have to watch the store. Then he can come later." With that, everyone laughed. Then Uncle Quak gave her his New Year's present.

In a quiet voice he said, "I think the war will end soon. But maybe not as you imagine." She wasn't listening. She was admiring the gold chain he had just given her. It was lovely. She thanked him and went to show it to Gia Quyen. Just then her father came forward.

They had been waiting for this moment. They knew that his gift was very special. Rarely had their mother received such a wonderful gift. Everyone watched as their father gave it to his wife. "What is this? Not for me? I don't need anything. Are you sure? Is the grocery doing this well? For me?" They had never seen her so nervous. She smiled shyly at her husband and looked down at the bundle in her lap. Slowly she opened it. It was the dress she had seen months ago. The deep, dark purple spilled down her lap as she smoothed out the material. The spiral loop buttons were so lovely that she hesitated to touch them with her rough hands. The material was so soft. Then she cried when she realized he was giving it to her because he knew of her sadness. She touched his hand and tried to compose herself. "I will save this dress for Huu Tien's wedding. Mai, you will come back for that?" Mai nodded. "Well, who is hungry?" They all laughed.

Uncle Quak hung back to talk with their father. "I do not think things will go well. I think they will go bad, very bad." He coughed. "Have you given thought as to who should go first, Hoa Troung?"

"If it comes to pass, first Nguyet Tien. She is the youngest and not capable of caring for herself. Then my wife and son, then Huu Tien and me. Huu Tien is smart and will be able to help me. But I think you are wrong."

"I hope I am wrong," said Uncle Quak.

5 June 1985—Inpatient Psychiatric Unit

The patient was uncooperative and continued to have pressured speech. She spent most of her time pacing back and forth in the ward dayroom. She was reported to be very suspicious of and hostile to Asian patients and staff, claiming that all Chinese and Vietnamese were inferior to Americans. She has difficulty with one-to-one sessions, giving little information except to warn me not to sit on the purple chair in the interviewing room because that chair is dangerous. The patient continued to deny any psychiatric history or problems and blamed her sister for causing all her troubles.

25 April 1975—Saigon, South Vietnam

Two months later, Saigon was invaded. Huu Tien and her brother ran home from school that day. There was a loud explosion three blocks away. People were screaming and yelling. A plane had fallen and hit a large building. They held tightly to each other and ran faster. There were more explosions. Shots were heard. Fires seemed to start in mid-air. Saigon was falling. Schools had been closed and the students sent home crying. For the first time, the war was at their very door. Huu Tien shrieked as a burning dog ran past them. Soon they were home. But even inside they smelled the smoke and heard the noise. Their mother was packing bags for each child while she listened to the radio. She was crying as she packed the clothes, food, and other necessities. "Where is Father?" asked Huu Tien.

"Looking for you! I told you not to go to school today. Better stay home." A yell came from the bedroom and Nguyet Tien swept into the room and flung herself into her sister's arms.

"I thought you were killed!"

She held her sister tightly. "We are fine. We will wait for Father and see what we must do. Like Father says, 'Today we pay with tears for tomorrow's joys.'" She looked at her brother. "We must fill bottles with water in case of fire. And cover windows. And find candles. The power is sure to go out." They worked quickly.

Just as they finished hiding things of value, there was a knock at the door. "Ly Phung Tran, wife of Ly Hoa Truong?" said the stranger from the hospital. Huu Tien tried not to be afraid, so she focused on his dirty, bloody uniform. The smokey smell of the man. His dry voice. Anything but his words. His awful words. "Your husband has been killed. He was standing by the hotel when it collapsed. I am sorry, but I have to go. I have other stops to make." Before he turned to go he said, "I knew him. He was a good man."

Phung Tran turned to her son and between sobs asked, "What are we going to do? What will happen to us? I don't know what to do." Turning to her daughter she asked, "Huu Tien, what shall we do?"

15 June 1985—Inpatient Psychiatric Unit

The patient continued to have disturbed sleep, but appeared to be less manic. She took her medication with less resistance and attended daily occupational therapy and group sessions. She was observed to be less hostile and started to relate to some patients. In particular, the patient seemed to be quite attached to a younger male patient, showing a great deal of interest in the way he dressed and his future plans.

In our daily individual sessions, the patient was still guarded about her past family history, but talked quite freely about the problems and frustration she encountered being a new immigrant in the United States, such as learning to speak English, looking for a job, making new friends, and waiting in lines for welfare and unemployment benefits.

5 June 1976—Saigon, South Vietnam

Huu Tien stood silently beside her mother. This was the third line they had been in today. Each time the wait had been at least three hours and even then they could never be sure they would get the items they needed. There were lines for food, clothing, and money exchange. They tried to blend into the line and not be noticed. It was especially hard for people who were ethnic Chinese. There was much prejudice against them. All the ethnic Chinese schools had been ordered closed. Businesses and jobs were taken away. There was no work for her family except to sell old clothes on the sidewalk.

She looked down at her blouse and brushed off some dirt. Soap was scarce and expensive. Finally, they reached the head of the line. Quickly they paid for the rice. "You should leave the country," said the soldier standing by the rice seller. "Soon, get out soon. We don't want you here." Moving very fast and with frozen faces, they went home. All the way not one word was said.

Then, only as the door closed behind her, Phung Tran began to let loose the torrent of words she had held back. "Always we try to work hard. Come here and work hard, try to be honest. Now this." She put up the supplies. "We would leave if we could. It takes money. We have money. But if we tell we have money, and it is too much, they will execute us. Like the others. Want to be honest—can't be honest. Want to leave. What can we do?" With this, she stopped and faced the ancestral pictures. Once again she wondered if she had been right to leave China. Maybe if she and her mother had talked more it would have been different. Silently the large pictures looked back and gave no answers. At last Phung Tran turned to her youngest daughter and asked, "Where is Gia Quyen? It is getting late."

"He went to another policy meeting and to see if he could get work or information from some of father's old friends.

"I'll go get him," said Huu Tien. When she found Gia Quyen, he was coming out of a small house. He moved to her side.

"Why are you here?" he said. "It is getting late, we must go home quickly." Together they walked down the street. "This is not like it used to be, but it's hard to remember when it was better."

She looked up to him. His eyes no longer laughed, and he never smiled. But few did these days. "Remember that you need the bad as well as the good. Like Father used to say, 'Today's tears pay for tomorrow's joys.' Later things will be better. You will see. Father was very wise." She reached up and hugged him.

He replied soberly, "It was a good thing we hid the gold and jewelry like Uncle Quak said. It costs fifteen ounces of gold each for us to leave." He pulled a letter out of his pocket. "This is the contact we must make in order to get out. It cost me mother's pin to get the name. That is why I was so late. Maybe it will be better soon." They continued on. She began to kick at the rocks on the ground.

"Maybe in the United States we will have room to fly our kites and finish school. And mother can drink tea and talk with Auntie Mai." She kicked at a large rock and watched it roll into the street. "And you can see American soldiers and the helicopters again." Laughing, she pushed him slightly and ran after the rock. In the street she saw the soldiers. Without thinking, only remembering their earlier game, she called, "Gia Quyen! Soldiers!" And he too, caught in the same memory ran into the street.

The bullet hit him in the throat and threw him into a wall, where a large purple banner said, "Giai Phone Mien Nam" (Free the People From the South). Blood was everywhere. His neck was torn almost in half. He died instantly. The soldier who had shot him ran over and saw he was only an unarmed boy.

Huu Tien couldn't stop screaming. She kept trying to use the banner to stop the bleeding. She was so distraught that later she was sent to the hospital for psychiatric treatment, and stayed there for two months.

Nguyet Tien left Saigon after her brother's death. She went to the United States with a distant relative.

20 June 1985—Inpatient Psychiatric Unit

The patient continued to do well in individual sessions. Today she talked about the tragic deaths of her father and brother, and the experiences she had on the boat with her mother.

9 July 1980—Mekong Delta Harbor, Vietnam

Nineteen-year-old Huu Tien and her mother paused on the wooden pier and looked at the boat. Their places on it had cost so much money. The name of the boat was the My Tho 175. It was a small nineteen-foot fishing boat. It was pitted and rotting, and looked as though it would sink any minute. Behind them, other refugees, carrying small bundles and worried frowns, clustered about the pier. Only the officials smiled and smirked as papers and people were processed.

Once aboard, Huu Tien found a space on the deck and helped her mother get comfortable there. Then she sat down beside her and tucked in her legs. She watched more and more people come on board until all the space was used. Children clung tightly about the legs of parents. Parents held babies. People stood pressed against one another and still more boarded. Finally, when it seemed that not one more person could get on, a few men climbed onto the boat railing and tied themselves to the ropes that secured the mast. Bags of rice from which they would eat during the journey dangled from their waists.

When the My Tho 175 left Vietnam, it carried 465 passengers and crew. In a boat that was never meant to dare the open sea, they began their journey across the Gulf of Siam to Malaysia. It would take about nine days if they were lucky.

Huu Tien closed her eyes and tried not to think of the uneasiness she felt. When this didn't work, she opened them and saw that her mother had once again taken out the pictures of her father and brother and was staring at them. More and more often, for hours at a time, this would happen. Huu Tien closed her eyes again. She felt worse. Relentlessly the memory of her mother's conversation with a friend returned. Repeatedly she could hear her mother's words, "It was the end of my family when my husband and son died." Huu Tien felt deep pain from this comment. And more pain each time her mother stared at the pictures.

But not like now, for this was worse yet. She held her stomach and called to her mother, "Mother, I am so dizzy. I feel sick." Her mother turned and held her.

"I think it is the boat. It is making many ill," said her mother as she wiped Huu Tien's face and comforted her. "It will pass. You will get used to the rocking." Later, after many times at the railing, Huu Tien slept.

On the third day, she had recovered enough to eat some rice. Cooked rice that just needed water to moisten it. As she leaned against her mother, she was aware of how they had grown far apart. Looking at the picture of her father that her mother was holding, she realized that she had been closer and more attuned to him than to her mother. She enjoyed being with him and had never missed the closeness with her mother till now. She recognized there was a barrier between them despite the fact they were so physically close—a barrier she did not want. She prayed to God to help her care for her mother. Maybe one day Huu Tien would find a way to remove this barrier. Maybe then her mother would realize that she still had some family left.

Unconsciously she reached to the neck of her blouse and fingered the small bits of hidden gold chain sewn into the collar so carefully. They would need that gold for survival in the camp. She remembered New Year's when her father had told her what to do. She smiled to herself thinking of her father's favorite saying, "Today's tears pay for tomorrow's joys." He was so wise. Then she looked at her mother and realized that she, too, was a wise person. Huu Tien felt shame for not being a better daughter.

Each day was much like the one before—children crying, people trying to find ways of resting, and more and more ocean. Huu Tien sat and watched her mother. Life had taken on a dream-like quality. Sometimes she thought of the past, then of what it would be like in the United States with her sister. How wonderful it would be for them. Slowly she awoke from her daydreams. People were shouting about something. She clutched her mother's hand in fear when she heard the cry, "Pirates!"

She stood and could see a boat approaching. The men seemed fierce and were yelling and waving knives. She was so scared there would be no escape. Then she saw the small ledge about eight inches behind her mother. They had put their belongings under it earlier to ease their backs. There wasn't much room there, but if she and her mother put more bundles in front of them, they might be able to hide beneath this ledge.

Quickly she went into action while her mother watched for the pirates. They were very near now. Huu Tien got in first, then pulled in her mother and put the extra things in front of them. Her heart beat rapidly. Through a small hole she could see only feet, but easily hear the pleading of passengers as they were being robbed.

She prayed and prayed they would not be found. Then she heard the women's high-pitched cries and the pirates' laughter as the women were raped. She had been told this might happen, and prayed harder that it would not happen to her.

She almost screamed when a girl's head hit the deck near her hiding place. Through a crack she could tell it was someone she had seen in school. Tears ran from the girl's eyes. The tearing of clothing, grunts, and flashes of a man's face were all Huu Tien could see or hear, but it was enough to fill her with dread and pain. In a few minutes, it was over, and the pirate went to look for another pretty young woman. Huu Tien hid there shaking and fearful until her mother finally pulled her out. Afterward, Huu Tien found it difficult to even look at her former classmate.

Then on the eighth day a storm struck. The sky went from blue to gray to black in minutes. The wind howled and tossed the boat up, down, back and forth. Many were ill and too afraid to move, so they vomited on themselves. The boat creaked and groaned. Each second it seemed on the verge of breaking up and sinking. Many prayed to the Dragon Queen of the Sea for protection. Huu Tien held tightly to her mother. This surely was where they would die, drowned in the sea. Then she looked at her mother and prayed that God would protect them.

The next day the boat landed in Malaysia. At first it was hard to walk to the sign that said "Paulau-Tengra Refugee Camp" without falling. But walk they did. However in the camp there was more bad news. Money was needed for everything: to get a hut, to buy plastic to make a roof, and for food. Camp officials assured the newcomers that if relatives could be reached, they would be able to get to the United States soon—in about two or three years. In the meantime, they would need money to survive. The gold that Huu Tien had hidden would not last forever. It seemed to her that tomorrow's joys would never come. There was only today's pain.

Later she had to see the official because her mother was ill. "She can't keep food down and she has sores all over her. We need a doctor to see her." He answered in a tired voice, "We have only two volunteer doctors for 3,000 people, but if necessary she can be seen within the week. The problem is if she needs medicine it could take weeks to get it."

Huu Tien was shocked and after the doctor had come to see her mother, she was even more worried. The doctor said that antibiotics were needed to fight the infection. He used what he had, but it wasn't enough. They would have to wait for more medicine to arrive.

Huu Tien prayed as she washed the sores and cared for her mother. When the old woman was sleeping, Huu Tien would go to the other women begging for herbs that could be used to help her mother. Each day she went to the camp official to see if the medicine had arrived. Each day there was no news of it.

At night when she bathed her mother, she tried not to let the running sores and awful stench bother her. She wanted to be a good daughter and heal her mother and take her to live in the United States. She touched her mother's cheek and noticed it was very hot. "Mother, the medicine will be here soon. Please hold on. Please!"

"I am trying very hard. But if I don't get to America, you must do this for me. Hear me, you must bury me in my purple dress that your father gave me. When I see your father and brother I must have it on. Do this for me. Be a good daughter." The old woman groped for the bundle under her head. "It's in here."

The thought of the dress sent a chill through her for some unknown reason. She had come to hate it. It would be very hard to fulfill her mother's last request.

The next day when she came back with news that the medicine had arrived, her mother was dead. With the help of others, she dug a grave and laid the old woman in it. Huu Tien then bartered for the use of a Polaroid camera and took a picture of her mother to take to her sister. The purple dress stood out in the color photograph.

It took another three years before Huu Tien could leave for the United States and live with her sister at her uncle and aunt's home.

25 June 1985—Inpatient Psychiatric Unit

In our weekly family session, both aunt and uncle continued to offer their support and seemed to be pleased with the patient's progress. However, the patient's relationship with her sister was still very problematic. During the session, the patient accused the sister of being too selfish and showing her no respect and gratitude. The sister expressed her anger and resentment at having a "crazy" sister who was verbally abusive and incapable of holding a steady job. In response to her sister's accusation, the patient repeatedly stated that it was a mistake for her to have come to the United States. She would rather have died in Vietnam.

20 October 1983—United States of America

Huu Tien held tightly to the tiny packet of pictures, all that she had in the world besides the clothes on her back, and knew the time of tears was over. She sat deeper into the airplane seat and took another mouthful of food from the tray in front of her. Last week she had been eating at the camp, and now she was going to the United States. Soon she would see her family. The reunion would be wonderful.

Uncle Quak had been a very successful businessman with a large company in Saigon, and should be a wealthy man in the United States. He would no doubt want her to wait before she got a job with him, but she would press him to start soon. She would not want a room alone. No, she would be happy to be with Nguyet Tien. And she would help with the housework. Her aunt would be surprised at what a good worker she was. She hoped the house had a garden. After she learned enough English, which shouldn't be too hard since she already knew some words, she would get her college degree and then teach other refugees.

She stopped daydreaming long enough to watch the stewardess

awhile. Yes, she would dress in the fine clothes of the modern woman, but of course with less makeup and not so colorful. She looked at her hands and went to the bathroom to wash them. It was wonderful to have clean water just for hand washing. As she finished she heard the call to get ready for landing. She looked down at all the buildings and saw a tiny red bridge. It was so like a toy. She felt much excitement. This was the place for happiness.

That night in bed she tried not to cry. It had been wonderful to greet her loved ones. But the meeting was not what she had expected. She was shocked to see how old and worn her aunt and uncle looked. And her sister. Her clothes were too bright and revealing. Too much makeup and she smiled at the young man on the bus. Plus she didn't take well the advice she was given. Younger sisters should listen to older sisters. And she was disappointed when she found that the house was not a house, but a small apartment. But very clean. Better than the camp, but still not like she imagined. And Uncle Quak was no factory owner, but worked as a dishwasher. Auntie Mai, who had never worked at all, now worked in a garment factory. Only Nguyet Tien had a job that seemed to have a future—in a bank, and just because she spoke good English.

Huu Tien was already beginning to hate English. The few words she thought she knew had made her sister laugh. It would be very hard to fit in here. No, the time of joy was not yet. Nonetheless she was no longer in a city at war, or on a sickening boat with pirates around, nor in a camp. She was with her family at last, and she could be happy. She would be happy. But as her silent tears fell in the dark, she knew she was not happy, and she felt even more ashamed.

18 July 1985—Inpatient Psychiatric Unit

The patient continued to do well. She was elected as patient representative to chair the ward community meeting today, and appeared to be very proud of her leadership. In our individual sessions, the patient seemed to be more responsive and trustful. She talked quite freely about the hardships she has encountered the past few years. Her relationship with her sister has also improved. Both were able to share more positive feelings toward each other in the family sessions. No manage-

ment problem was reported by the nursing staff, except that the patient occasionally complained of having nightmares.

20 July 1985—Inpatient Psychiatric Unit

Dr. Wong met with Huu Tien. "The night nurse said you seemed very frightened and wanted to see me as soon as I came in this morning. Can you tell me what is wrong?" The doctor leaned forward. She noted Huu Tien sat very still in the chair, her hands folded in her lap.

"I am very sad. I think I am going to die. I am very afraid." Her voice was so soft that it was almost inaudible. Tears were in her eyes. She looked at the doctor and then down to the floor. "I had a bad dream last night. It scared me. I called for the nurse to stay with me." It seemed hard for her to talk. Her breathing got quicker and and she swallowed several times.

"It was New Year's in Saigon. Like the last time. It was our old house. I was home. At first it seemed nice. I saw all the red signs, but I couldn't read them." The doctor only nodded. "It made me worry. Something was wrong. Then I saw my mother." She began to cry softly. Tears dropped on her hands. The doctor reached over and gave her some tissues. "I loved my mother. But she scared me."

"How did she scare you?" asked Dr. Wong. "Can you tell me?"

"She was wearing the purple dress my father gave her. I was surprised and scared when I saw her in it. Then I looked and there was my brother and father, they both had on purple suits. I stepped back, but I could go no farther. They kept saying over and over, 'Come join us. Come join us.' I woke up so afraid." Her tears continued to flow. The doctor gave her some water.

"What frightened you most? Can you tell me?"

She sipped some water and replied, "All that purple. It scares me. I'm scared I must die too." Her voice got shakier and louder. "I have failed her, and Gia and Father. They all died because I failed them. I am a bad daughter. Now I must die. I don't want to. But what can I do?"

Dr. Wong wondered if this dream held the key to her problems. If they could learn more about her failure, they could examine it and ease her guilt. Dr. Wong saw she was in pain, but still asked, "How did you fail your mother?"

In a stronger voice, she replied, "I did not do as she asked. I failed her." Her voice became even more forceful. "I was supposed to put her purple dress on her and I *did not. I just put it in on* top *of her. Just on top."* Huu Tien shouted, *"I failed her!"* The patient wept, and then in a soft, very gentle voice, she said, *"I loved my mother, but I failed her. I am sorry."*

"Did you fail Gia Quyen also?"

Hurt showed in her face. *"Yes, I failed him, too. And even Father. If he had not been looking for me, he would be alive. It is all my fault."*

"Huu Tien, can you remember your father for a minute?" She nodded. *"You know he loved you, right?"* Dr. Wong continued, *"A parent who is worried for a child would look for that child. It was the war that caused his death. Not you."*

In a tender tone the therapist explained to her, *"You were children, it was a game. Do you really believe that you wanted to kill your brother? Didn't you love him?"*

"I would never have hurt Gia Quyen. Never. But . . . I still feel so bad." She cried into her hands. *"I miss him so."*

"Sometimes it is easier to blame ourselves than to just miss someone we love."

She looked up in despair. *"But what about my mother? There I really failed. She asked me to do something and I did not. I couldn't do it."*

Gently Dr. Wong asked, *"What were you feeling then? Not just what a 'good daughter' should feel, but what you truly felt. Even 'bad daughter' feelings."*

Ashamed, she turned to the wall. It was very difficult for her to talk. *"I was—I was angry with her. I was mad she would leave me. She left me all alone. I was mad at her. I loved her and I was mad at her for leaving me. I tried to put the dress on her, but I couldn't. I was too scared I would die if I touched the dress too long. I didn't want her to die. I didn't want her to leave me. I loved her and I didn't get a chance to prove it."* Now the sobs were wracking, breathless gasps. It took many minutes for the crying to lessen. *"I really miss my mother. I am sorry she died."*

"Sometimes it is very hard to be the one left." Huu Tien agreed. *"And it is very hard not to get angry or even hate the person we love for leaving us."* She was listening closely now. *"Facing that fact can free us and we can then forgive ourselves for doing things that are very human."*

"I should forgive myself for not putting the dress on her? For being angry with my mother? For failing? That will not be easy."

"No, it will not be easy. But I think you have done the hard part here. Looking at the unwanted feelings is very hard to do. It will still take more work

on your part—thinking and remembering. But it will also get easier for you to keep living and not feel so guilty about failure."

Huu Tien was much more composed and not crying when she rose to leave. "I have to think some more about this. Can we talk later?"

"Yes, of course," said the doctor as she left. And they did talk again, many times.

30 July 1985—Inpatient Psychiatric Unit

The patient was discharged today. She will go back with her sister to live at their aunt and uncle's home. She agreed to continue her medication and see an outpatient therapist once a week. She has also enrolled at City College to improve her English. There are still problems to be worked on, but given time and ongoing therapy, she should do well. As a refugee woman, she has demonstrated a great deal of courage to endure the scars of war and the pain of mental illness. It is hoped that now will begin the time of joy for her.

Nisei Women and Resettlement during World War II

VALERIE MATSUMOTO

The uprooting of Japanese Americans from the West Coast to crude relocation camps during World War II profoundly affected the lives of three generations. Examining the wartime experience of Japanese American women reveals the complexity of its impact. This essay focuses on one facet of the experiences of nisei women (the American-born second generation), a large number of whom left the camps to relocate in the Midwest and East during the war years.[1] These women, who pursued work and education in unfamiliar regions of the country, were sustained by fortitude, family ties, discipline, and humor. My understanding of their history derives from several collections of evacuees' letters, assembly center and relocation camp newspapers, census records, and taped oral history interviews that I conducted with eighty-four nisei and eleven issei (immigrant first generation). Two-thirds of these interviews were with women.[2]

Evacuation: Hostile Whirlwind

The bombing of Pearl Harbor on 7 December 1941 unleashed war between the United States and Japan and triggered a wave of hostility against Japanese Americans. Despite some official doubts regarding the necessity of their removal from the West Coast, the voices of anti-Japanese American sentiment prevailed. On 19 February 1942, President Franklin Delano Roosevelt signed Executive Order 9066, arbitrarily suspending the civil rights of American citizens by authorizing the "evacuation" of 120,000 Japanese and their American-born children from the western half of the Pacific Coastal states and southern third of Arizona.[3] This number included 50,000 women, of whom approximately 60 percent were nisei.[4]

The numbing whirlwind of forced evacuation began in the spring of 1942 when the Japanese Americans were sent to fourteen temporary assembly centers. By November of the same year, the War Relocation Authority had moved them to ten permanent relocation camps established in desolate areas: Topaz, Utah; Poston and Gila River, Arizona; Amache, Colorado; Manzanar and Tule Lake, California; Heart Mountain, Wyoming; Minidoke, Idaho; Denson and Rohwer, Arkansas.[5]

The conditions of camp life profoundly altered family relations and affected women of all ages and backgrounds. Family unity deteriorated in the crude communal facilities and cramped housing. Overcrowding and lack of privacy drove many away from the one-room barrack "apartments," and family members gradually began to eat separately in the large mess halls: mothers with small children, fathers with other men, and older children with their friends. All family members spent more time than ever before in the company of their peers.

Women's work experiences changed in complex ways during the years in the relocation camps. Each camp offered a wide range of jobs, which resulted from the organization of the camps as model cities managed through a system of departments headed by Caucasian administrators. Even before the war many family members had worked, but within the camps men and women, children and parents, all received the same low wages.[6] The new equity in pay and the variety of jobs—ranging from clerical work, medical care, and art to mess hall busing and technical services—gave some women unprecedented opportunities for experimentation.

Camp life also increased the leisure time of many. A good number of issei women, accustomed to long days of work inside and outside the home, found that the communally prepared meals and limited living quarters provided them with spare time. Many attended adult classes involving handcrafts and traditional Japanese arts such as flower arrangement, sewing, and knitting. To the issei women these courses were not merely hobbies but represented access to new skills and a means to contribute to the material comfort of the family. In addition to classes, the internees filled their time with religious meetings, cultural programs, athletic events, and visits with friends.

Like their non-Japanese American contemporaries, most young nisei women envisioned a future of marriage and children. They—and their parents—anticipated that they would marry other Japanese Americans,[7] but these young women also expected to choose their own husbands and to marry "for love." This mainstream American ideal of marriage differed greatly from the issei's view of love as a bond that might evolve over the course of an arranged marriage that was firmly rooted in less romantic notions of compatibility and responsibility. The discrepancy between issei and nisei conceptions of love and marriage had sturdy prewar roots; relocation camp life fostered further divergence from the old customs of arranged marriage.

Resettlement: A Difficult Decision

Many nisei, among them a large number of women, were anxious to leave the limbo of camp and return "to normal life again."[8] With all its work, social events, and cultural activities, camp was still an artificial, limited environment. It was stifling "to see nothing but the same barracks, mess halls, and other houses, row after row, day in and day out; it gives us the feeling that we're missing all the freedom and liberty."[9]

Resettlement began slowly in 1942. Concerned educators provided a way out for some nisei college students when they organized the National Japanese American Student Relocation Council that year. The nongovernmental organization persuaded institutions outside the restricted western defense zone to accept nisei students and facilitated their admissions and leave clearances. In the years 1942 to 1946, it provided invaluable placement aid to 4,084 nisei.[10] A study of the first four hundred students to leave camps showed that a third of them were women.[11]

The decision to relocate was a difficult one. An aspiring teacher wrote: "Mother and father do not want me to go out. However, I want to go so very much that sometimes I feel I'd go even if they disowned me. What shall I do? I realize the hard living conditions outside but I think I can take it."[12] Women's developing sense of independence in the camp environment and their growing awareness of their abilities as workers contributed to their self-confidence and hence their desire to leave. Significantly, issei parents, despite initial reluctance, were gradually beginning to sanction their daughters' departures for education and employment in the Midwest and East—opportunities increasingly available after 1943. One nisei noted:

> [Father] became more broadminded in the relocation center. He was more mellow in his ways. . . . At first he didn't want me to relocate, but he gave in. . . . I said I wanted to go [to Chicago] with my friend, so he helped me pack, so I thought, "Well, he didn't say no."[13]

For some women, the issue of resettlement posed additional problems because they felt obligated to stay and care for elderly or infirm parents, like the Heart Mountain nisei who observed wistfully, "It's getting so more and more of the girls and boys are leaving camp, and I sure wish I could, but mother's getting on and I just can't leave her."[14]

Many internees worried about their acceptance in the outside world. The nisei considered themselves American citizens, and they had an allegiance to the land of their birth: "The teaching and love of one's own birth place, one's own country was . . . strongly impressed upon my mind as a child. So even though California may deny our rights of birth, I shall ever love her soil."[15] But forced evacuation had taught the Japanese Americans that in the eyes of many of their fellow Americans, theirs was the face of the enemy. Many nisei were torn by mixed feelings of shame, frustration, and bitterness at the denial of their civil rights. These factors created an atmosphere of anxiety that surrounded those who contemplated resettlement: "A feeling of uncertainty hung over the camp; we were worried about the future. Plans were made and remade, as we tried to decide what to do. Some were ready to risk anything to get away. Others feared to leave the protection of the camp." [16]

Thus, those first college students were the scouts whose letters back to camp marked pathways for others to follow. May Yoshino sent a favorable report to her family in Topaz from the nearby University of Utah, indicating that there were "plenty of schoolgirl jobs for those who want to study at the University." [17]

Correspondence from other nisei students shows that although they succeeded in making the dual transition from high school to college and from camp to the outside world, they were not without anxieties as to whether they could handle the study load and the reactions of the Caucasians around them. One student at Drake University in Iowa wrote to her interned sister about a professor's reaction to her autobiographical essay, "Evacuation":

Today Mr.———, the English teacher that scares me, told me that the theme that I wrote the other day was very interesting. . . . You could just imagine how wonderful and happy I was to know that he liked it a little bit. . . . I've been awfully busy trying to catch up on work and the work is *so* different from high school. I think that little by little I'm beginning to adjust myself to college life. [18]

Several incidents of hostility did occur, but the reception of the nisei students at colleges and universities was generally warm. Topaz readers of *Trek* magazine could draw encouragement from Lillian Ota's "Campus Report" from Massachusetts. Ota, a Wellesley student, reassured them: "During the first few days you'll be invited by the college to teas and receptions. Before long you'll lose the awkwardness you might feel at such doings after the months of abnormal life at evacuation centers." [19] Although Ota had not noticed "that my being a 'Jap' has made much difference on the campus itself," she offered cautionary and pragmatic advice to the nisei, suggesting the burden of responsibility these relocated students felt, as well as the problem of communicating their experiences and emotions to Caucasians.

> It is scarcely necessary to point out that those who have probably never seen a Nisei before will get their impression of the Nisei as a whole from the relocated students. It won't do you or your family and friends much good to dwell on what you consider injustices when you are questioned about evacuation. Rather, stress the contribution of [our] people to the nation's war effort.[20]

Given the tenor of the times and the situation of their families, the pioneers in resettlement had little choice but to repress their anger and minimize the amount of racist hostility they encountered.

In her article "a la mode," Marii Kyogoku also offered survival tips to the departing nisei, ever conscious that they were on trial not only as individuals but as representatives of their families and their generation. She suggested criteria for choosing clothes and provided hints on adjustment to food rationing. Kyogoku especially urged the evacuees to improve their table manners, which had been adversely affected by the "unnatural food and atmosphere" of mess hall dining:

> You should start rehearsing for the great outside by bringing your own utensils to the dining hall. It's an aid to normality to be able to eat your jello with a spoon and well worth the dishwashing which it involves. All of us eat much too fast. Eat more slowly. All this practicing should be done so that proper manners will seem natural to you. If you do this, you won't get stagefright and spill your water glass, or make bread pills and hardly dare to eat when you have your first meal away from the centers and in the midst of scrutinizing Caucasian eyes.[21]

Armed with advice and drawn by encouraging reports, increasing numbers of women students left camp. A postwar study of a group of one thousand relocated students showed that 40 percent were women.[22] The field of nursing was particularly attractive to nisei women; after the first few students disproved the hospital administration's fears of their patients' hostility, acceptance of nisei into nursing schools grew. By July 1944, there were more than three hundred nisei women in over one hundred nursing programs in twenty-four states.[23] One such student wrote from the Ashbury Hospital in Minneapolis: "Work here isn't too hard and I enjoy it very much. The patients are very nice people and I haven't had any trouble as yet. They do give us a funny stare at the beginning but after a day or so we receive the best compliments." [24]

The trickle of migration from the camps grew into a steady stream by 1943, as the War Relocation Authority developed its resettlement program to aid evacuees in finding housing and employment in the East and Midwest. [25] A resettlement bulletin published by the Advisory Committee for Evacuees described "who is relocating":

> Mostly younger men and women, in their 20s or 30s; mostly single persons or couples with one or two children, or men with larger families who come out alone first to scout opportunities and to secure a foothold, planning to call wife and children later. Most relocated evacuees [have] parents or relatives whom they hope and plan to bring out "when we get re-established." [26]

In early 1945, the War Department ended the exclusion of the Japanese Americans from the West Coast, and the War Relocation Authority announced that the camps would be closed within the year. By this time, 37 percent of the evacuees of sixteen years or older had already relocated, including 63 percent of the nisei women in that age group. [27]

Adjustment: A Different Life

For nisei women, like their non-Japanese sisters, the wartime labor shortage opened the door into industrial, clerical, and managerial occupations. Prior to the war, racism had excluded the Japanese Americans from most white-collar clerical and sales positions, and, according to sociologist Evelyn Nakano Glenn, "the most common form of non-agricultural employment for the immigrant women (*issei*) and their American-born daughters (*nisei*) was domestic service." [28] The highest percentage of job offers for both men and women continued to be requests for domestic workers. In July 1943, the Kansas City branch of the War Relocation Authority noted that 45 percent of requests for workers were for domestics, and the Milwaukee office cited 61 percent. [29] However, nisei women also found jobs as secretaries, typists, file clerks, beauticians, and factory workers. By 1950, 47 percent of employed Japanese American women were clerical and sales workers and operatives; only 10 percent were in domestic service.[30] The World War II decade, then, marked a turning point for Japanese American women in the labor force.

Whether they were students or workers, and regardless of where they went or how prepared they were to meet the outside world, nisei women found that leaving camp meant enormous change in their lives. Even someone as confident as Marii Kyogoku, the author of much relocation advice, found that reentry into the Caucasian-dominated world beyond the barbed wire fence was not a simple matter of stepping back into old shoes. Leaving the camps—like entering them—meant major changes in psychological perspective and self-image.

> I had thought that because before evacuation I had adjusted myself rather well in Caucasian society, I would go right back into my former frame of mind. I have found, however, that though the center became unreal and was as if it had never existed as soon as I got on the train at Delta, I was never so self-conscious in all my life.[31]

Kyogoku went on to describe how she was amazed to see so many men and women in uniform and that, despite her "proper dining" preparation, she felt strange sitting at a table set with clean linen and a full set of silverware.

> I felt a diffidence at facing all these people and things, which was most unusual. Slowly things have come to seem natural, though I am still excited by the sounds of the busy city and thrilled every time I see a street lined with trees, I no longer feel that I am the cynosure of all eyes.

Like Kyogoku, many nisei women discovered that relocation meant adjustment to "a life different from our former as well as present way of living," [32] and, as such, posed a challenge. Their experiences in meeting this challenge were as diverse as their jobs and living situations.

"I live at the Eleanor Club No. 5 which is located on the west side," wrote Mary Sonoda, working with the American Friends Service Committee in Chicago:

I pay $1 per day for room and two meals a day. I also have maid service. I do not think that one can manage all this for $1 unless one lives in a place like this which houses thousands of working girls in the city. . . . I am the only Japanese here at present. . . . The residents and the staff are wonderful to me. . . . I am constantly being entertained by one person or another. The people in Chicago are extremely friendly. Even with the Tribune screaming awful headlines concerning the recent execution of American soldiers in Japan, people kept their heads. On street cars, at stores, everywhere, one finds innumerable evidence of good will.[33]

Chicago, the location of the first War Relocation Authority field office for supervision of resettlement in the Midwest, attracted the largest number of Japanese Americans seeking to resettle. Not all found their working environment as congenial as Mary Sonoda did. Smoot Katow, a nisei man in Chicago, painted "another side of the picture":

I met one of the Edgewater Beach girls. . . . From what she said it was my impression that the girls are not very happy. The hotel work is too hard, according to this girl. In fact, they are losing weight and one girl became sick with overwork. They have to clean about fifteen suites a day, scrubbing the floors on their hands and knees. . . . It seems the management is out to use labor as labor only. . . . The outside world is just as tough as it ever was.[34]

These variations in living and work conditions and wages encouraged—and sometimes necessitated—a certain amount of job experimentation among the nisei.

Many relocating Japanese Americans received moral and material assistance from a number of service organizations and religious groups, particularly the Presbyterians, the Methodists, the Society of Friends, and the Young Women's Christian Association. One such nisei, Dorcas Asano, enthusiastically described to a Quaker sponsor her activities in the big city:

Since receiving your application for hostel accommodation, I have decided to come to New York and I am really glad for the opportunity to be able to resume the normal civilized life after a year's confinement in camp. New York is really a city of dreams and we are enjoying every minute working in offices, rushing back and forth to work in the ever-speeding sub-way trains, counting our ration points, buying war bonds, going to church, seeing the latest shows, plays, operas, making many new friends and living like our neighbors in the war time. I only wish more of my friends who are behind the fence will take advantage of the many helpful hands offered to them.[35]

The nisei also derived support and strength from networks—formed before and during internment—of friends and relatives. The homes of those who relocated first became way stations for others as they made the transition into new communities and jobs. In 1944, soon after she obtained a place to stay in New York City, Mine Okubo found that "many of the other evacuees relocating in New York came ringing my doorbell. They were sleeping all over the floor!"[36] Single women often accompanied or joined sisters, brothers, and friends as many interconnecting grapevines carried news of likely jobs, housing, and friendly communities. Ayako Kanemura, for instance, found a job painting Hummel figurines in Chicago; a letter of recommendation from a friend enabled her "to get my foot into the door and then all my friends followed and joined me."[37] Although they were farther from their families than ever before, nisei women maintained warm ties of affection and concern, and those who had the means to do so continued to play a role in the family economy, remitting a portion of their earnings to their families in or out of camp, and to siblings in school.

Elizabeth Ogata's family exemplifies several patterns of resettlement and the maintenance of family ties within them. In October 1944, her parents were living with her brother Harry who had begun to farm in Springville, Utah; another brother and sister were attending Union College in Lincoln, Nebraska. Elizabeth herself had moved to Minneapolis to join a brother in the army, and she was working as an operative making pajamas. "Minn. is a beautiful place," she wrote, "and the people are so nice. . . . I thought I'd never find anywhere I would feel at home as I did in Mt. View [California], but I have changed my mind."[38] Like Elizabeth, a good number of the thirty-five thousand relocated Japanese Americans were favorably impressed by their new homes and decided to stay.

Conclusion: Complicated Alterations

The war years had complex and profound effects upon Japanese Americans, uprooting their communities and causing severe psychological and emotional damage. The vast majority returned to the West Coast at the end of the war in 1945—a move that, like the initial evacuation, was a grueling test of flexibility and fortitude. Even with the assistance of old friends and service organizations, the transition was taxing and painful; the end of the war meant not only long-awaited freedom but also more battles to be fought in social, academic, and economic arenas. The Japanese Americans faced hostility, crude living conditions, and a struggle for jobs. Few evacuees received any compensation for their financial losses, estimated conservatively at $400 million, because Congress decided to appropriate only $38 million for the settlement of claims.[39] It is even harder to place a figure on the toll taken in emotional shock, self-blame, broken dreams, and insecurity. One Japanese American woman still sees in her nightmares the watchtower searchlights that troubled her sleep forty years ago.

The war altered Japanese American women's lives in complicated ways. In general, evacuation and relocation accelerated earlier trends that differentiated the nisei from their parents. Although most young women, like their mothers and non-Japanese peers, anticipated a future centered around a husband and children, they had already felt the influence of mainstream middle-class values of love and marriage and in the camps quickly moved away from the pattern of arranged marriage. There, increased peer group activities and the relaxation of parental authority gave them more independence. The nisei women's expectations of marriage became more akin to the companionate ideals of their peers than to those of the issei.

As before the war, many nisei women also worked while they were in camp, but the new parity in wages altered family dynamics. And though they were expected to contribute to the family economy, a large number did so in settings far from the family, availing themselves of opportunities provided by the student and worker relocation programs.

In meeting the challenges facing them, nisei women drew not only upon the disciplined strength inculcated by their issei parents but also upon firmly rooted support networks and the greater measure of self-reliance and independence that they developed during the crucible of the war years.

PART THREE

Moving Currents: Work

Introduction

Long before the advent of the popular media images of the "working mother" and the "working woman," Asian American women were very active participants in the labor force. While the quest for a better livelihood may have served as a reason to immigrate, arrival in this country did not bring any guarantees of an improved life. This is evidenced by the fate of the young women in Kathy Wong's "And All the Girls Cried," which is based on the cries used by Chinese prostitutes in the 1860s and 1870s. Kitty Tsui's "Chinatown Talking Story" focuses on an actress who must still do menial chores to make ends meet.

As pointed out in "Issei Working Women in Hawaii," by Gail Nomura, working days were long regardless of whether the women worked in the growing towns and cities or out on rural sugar plantations. Like many Asian American women, they worked at more than one job: in addition to working for wages, they toiled in the home, taking care of husbands, children, and other relatives.

To help their families meet the financial demands of survival in a new country, immigrant women and men worked long hours for only marginal economic or psychological returns. According to Diane Yen-Mei Wong and Dennis Hayashi's "Behind Unmarked Doors: Developments in the Garment Industry," the conditions under which early Asian immigrants worked persists to this day. And they have also spread to other industries that draw many of their low-paid employees from the increasing ranks of Asian immigrants who have limited language and job skills but who need to work. In "Women in the Silicon Valley" by Rebecca Villones and "Ladies on the Line" by Marcelle Williams, we see similar working conditions among Filipina electronics assemblers and South Asian fruit and vegetable cannery workers.

In the past few decades, more and more Asian women in America have entered professional fields and other financially rewarding and prestigious occupations, as illustrated in Felicia Lowe's "Asian American Women in Broadcasting." But even those women must still deal with discrimination in their fields.

In "The Gap between Striving and Achieving: The Case of Asian American Women," Deborah Woo uses California census data as the basis for her argument that the rewards of education and work experience are higher for white men and women and men of color than for Asian American women. Her analysis disputes the much-touted myth of Asian Americans as a "model minority."

The powerful currents that once pushed and pulled pioneer working women—economic need, emotional satisfaction, racism, sexism, and the precarious balancing act between being a wage-earner and wife—continue to affect Asian American women today. Their inequitable impact on the lives of contemporary working women—whether immigrant or American-born, in professional or more traditional occupations—persists, but now with growing resistance from the women themselves.

And All the Girls Cried

KATHY WONG

Madam screamed
"Get off your butt!"

So slave girls had to cry:
"China girl here! You come inside, please?
Your father, he just go out!"

From Jackson St. to Washington St.
down echoing alleyways
cribs were filled with
seductive cries

moanings that accompanied
half-clad girls
in black silk blouses.

Syphilitic Chinamen
groped through the dark
searching for their favorite trick.

And white boys came
to the dens
to stare
and compare the exotic
to the norm—
disappointed but jacked-up
just the same
by the sight of
gyrating flesh.

And all the girls cried:
"Two bittee lookee, flo bittee feelee, six bittee doee!"

Day and night
lesions bled and blisters oozed.

Men mounted
pounding into ruptured depths
leaving satisfied.

The next man waited to receive.

And all the girls cried:
"Two bittee lookee, flo bittee feelee, six bittee doee!"

Auctioned for a price
enslaved for life.

Disease reeked
through shriveled bodies
and those diseased were:

Left on shelves to rot
Left with moldy rice to eat
Left with rusted drinking tins
Left with bare candle light—

Old hags died at age twenty.

And all the girls cried:
"Two bittee lookee, flo bittee feelee, six bittee doee!"

Chinatown Talking Story

KITTY TSUI

the gold mountain men said
there were two pairs of eyes
so beautiful
they had the power
to strike you dead,
the eyes of
kwan ying lin
and mao dan so.

kwan ying lin, my grandmother,
and mao dan so
were stars of the cantonese opera
and women
rare
in a bachelor society.

when my grandmother first came
to gold mountain in 1922
she was interned on angel island
for weeks, a young chinese girl,
prisoner in a strange land.

when mao dan so
first arrived
she came on an entertainer's visa
and made $10,000 a year.

it cost $1.25 to see a show,
a quarter after nine.
pork chop rice was $.15.

when theater work was slow
or closed down
other work was found:
washing dishes,
waiting tables,
ironing shirts.

in china
families with sons
saved and borrowed
the $3,000
to buy a bright boy
promise in a new land.

in china
girls born into poverty
were killed or sold.
girls born into
prosperity
had their feet bound,
their marriages arranged.

on angel island
paper sons and blood sons
waited
to enter *gum san*
eating peanut butter on crackers
for lunch and
bean sprouts at night.

the chinamen who passed the interrogations
were finally set free.
the ones who failed
were denied entry and deported
or died by their own hands.

in 1940, the year
angel island detention center
was closed,
a job at macy's
paid $27 a week.
only chinese girls
without accents please apply.

my grandfather had four wives
and pursued many women
during his life.
the chinese press loved to write of his affairs.

my grandmother,
a woman with three daughters,
left her husband
to survive on her own.
she lived with another actress,
a companion and a friend.

the gold mountain men said
mao dan so was as graceful
as a peach blossom in wind.

she has worked since
she was eight.
she is seventy-two.
she sits in her apartment
in new york chinatown
playing solitaire.
her hair is thin and white.

her eyes, sunken in hollows,
are fire bright when she speaks.

the gold mountain men said
when kwan ying lin
went on stage
even the electric fans stopped.

today
at the grave
of my grandmother
with fresh spring flowers,
iris, daffodil,
i felt her spirit in the wind.
i heard her voice saying:

born into the
skin of yellow women
we are born
into the armor of warriors.

Issei Working Women in Hawaii

GAIL M. NOMURA

Japanese women first came to Hawaii to work as laborers on the sugar plantations. Although a few women arrived in 1868 with the first formal importation of Japanese labor to Hawaii,[1] the main immigration of Japanese women started in 1885, with the beginning of government contract labor importation from Japan. These issei, first-generation, women were married and accompanied their husbands who had contracted to work on the Hawaiian sugar plantations. Within five years of their arrival issei women comprised the majority of wage-earning women in Hawaii; and in succeeding decades Japanese women continued to compose the majority of wage-earning women in Hawaii. Most at first worked as field hands on the sugar plantations.

While the sugar industry remained the most important employer for Japanese women until 1920, issei women gradually moved into other occupations. They played a major, if not dominant, labor role in such fields as the newly-developing pineapple industry, domestic and personal service, and clothing trade. They often were creative in developing income-producing jobs in their homes using their skills of cooking, washing, and sewing—all of which were highly valued by the bachelor-dominated society of Hawaii in the late-nineteenth and early-twentieth century. While the work these issei women performed was critical to the development of Hawaii's key industries, it also provided needed services for Hawaii's society and was vital to the economic survival of the Japanese American family in Hawaii.

Immigrating as Wives and Workers

The Hawaii sugar planters were eager to sponsor the immigration of Japanese laborers. Labor needs had greatly increased with the boom in the sugar industry due to the securing of duty-free entrance into the United States for Hawaii's sugar under the 1876 Reciprocity Treaty. The Hawaiian government was actively searching the world for labor for its key industry and for people to repopulate the islands, whose native population had been decimated by disease brought in by foreigners to which the natives had no immunity. The dwindling Hawaiian population could not supply the needed labor for the growing sugar industry, and other labor was either too expensive to import or posed special problems; Chinese immigration, for example, had been limited by legislation. The importation of Japanese women laborers was advocated as part of the Hawaiian government's efforts not only to secure laborers for the sugar plantations but also to prevent too great an imbalance of males over females in the immigrant population and to encourage the growth of a native-born population.

Robert W. Irwin was Hawaii's representative in Japan handling the first immigration of Japanese government contract laborers. He first reported in 1884 that the Japanese preferred that the proportion of immigrants sent be four-fifths men and one-fifth women, with children numbering one-tenth of the total of men and women.[2] He held out the hope for more women and stated that "if the Japanese like the country those who go without their wives will send for them subsequently, just as the early Emigrants to America from Europe did in the beginning of this century."[3]

On 8 February 1885 the first shipload of Japanese laborers arrived aboard the *City of Tokio* with the required proportion, which remained the usual ratio of men to women for the next twenty-five shiploads of contract laborers.[4] Throughout the government contract period (1885–1894) and the later emigration company period (1894–1900), a proportion of 20 to 25 percent of the total immigrants continued to be women accompanying their husbands. This meant that some 40 to 50 percent of the immigrants came as family units. Moreover, within a year of the arrival of the first group of immigrants, the men who had not come with their wives were already sending for their wives just as Irwin had predicted.[5]

The Hawaiian Board of Immigration and the sugar planters supported the immigration of Japanese wives for they determined that "if their wives come, the men will probably remain permanently; otherwise they will probably return to Japan at the expiration of their contracts."[6] Irwin, too, believed that the continued importation of wives was essential, since "the women can do certain things that men cannot and will not do, namely nurse the sick, cook nice dishes, clean the quarters, sew and keep clothes in order and numberless small matters necessary to the comfort, health and happiness of the men."[7]

Another aim of bringing Japanese women to Hawaii was to have them work on the plantations. Initially, in negotiations with Japanese Foreign Minister Inoue in the summer of 1885, Irwin had agreed to the stipulation that thirty wives for each one hundred men be sent and that the women were not to work in the fields. Ten of the thirty wives were to be paid ten dollars a month to cultivate vegetables for the entire group.[8] But Hawaii's Minister of Foreign Affairs, Walter Murray Gibson, wrote Irwin that the prohibition of women working in the fields "is unnecessarily and as I think improperly to interfere with the liberty of the women themselves."[9]

In the summer of 1887, the Hawaiian government sought to modify the labor convention with Japan to pay for the passage of "women who desire to come to this country to work" rather than the blanket payment of passage for wives who might or might not work.[10] By that fall Irwin could write that he was devoting himself "assiduously to the work of sending good strong young men and women" and sending "very few children."[11] In December of that year Irwin wrote the president of the Board of Immigration that of the immigrants he would send, "all would be young men and women (wives of emigrants), used to agriculture, strong, able-bodied first class laborers."[12] From 1889 Irwin always described the emigrants he was sending with the set phrases, "strong, able bodied men and women, fit for any work on any Plantation in the Hawaiian Islands."[13]

By 1890 two-thirds of the wage-earning women in Hawaii were Japanese, numbering 1,418 out of 2,143. Nearly all employed issei women were laborers (1,404 of 1,418).[14] The 1890 census states that 61.6 percent of all Japanese females in Hawaii (1,404 of a total 2,281) were laborers and that this figure represented "after deducting the children, the sick, the infirm and the otherwise incapacitated, pretty much all the adult females of that nationality who are capable of engaging in downright and continuous physical toil." The census report commented that "the Japanese are peculiar in this respect, being, with the exception of Polynesians, the only people among us whose women are engaged as common laborers to any extent."[15]

In 1890 issei women worked as laborers mainly on the sugar plantations where they comprised 5.9 percent of the total sugar laborers (1,114 of 18,959) and 76 percent of the female sugar work force. Japanese women received the lowest pay of all sugar workers because of ethnic and sex differentials in pay although they performed the same field work that men did.[16]

The women worked from 6:00 A.M. to 4:30 P.M., ten hours in the fields with half an hour for lunch, six days a week.[17] The women were usually assigned to *hoe hana,* cultivating and weeding the fields with hoes. For *kalai* (weeding) work the women would line up in parallel rows piling the weeds in mounds as they weeded. The women did *hanawai* (irrigation) by irrigating two rows at a time while weeding the field. They had to properly gauge the speed of the flowing water in order to shut off the water supply before it overflowed the bottom row, or they would be penalized.[18] They also did *hole hole* (stripping leaves off cane stalks) and *pula pula* (cutting seed cane). *Pula pula* required the women to cut tops of selected healthy cane stalks into pieces about the length of a cane knife, yielding three or four pieces per stalk. This seed cane was bundled into bags weighing about sixty pounds and loaded onto trucks or trains.[19]

The women did most kinds of field work, especially if they were doing contract or *konpan* (sharecropping) work with their husbands. They did difficult and heavy work such as *kachi ken* (cutting cane) and *hapai ko* (carrying and loading cane). As one issei woman declares, "I did anything that the men did. . . . I did any and all kinds of work."[20]

In fact it was reported that "although a woman's rate of pay is usually 75 per cent that of a man's, there are certain operations in which she can equal a man day's work. Irrigating, weeding, fertilizing, picking up cane, piling cane, cutting seed, setting seed, covering and planting are all operations in which she may excel. . . ."[21] Payment for these types of work was usually determined by the amount of work actually done. Therefore, if the women did the same amount of work as that done by men, they could earn as much as men. Some plantations were reported to reserve certain fields to be cultivated by day laborers with a view to employing women.[22]

Women often worked side by side with the men and performed heavy work. But it was not easy. One issei woman remembers that "at the beginning I could work only three or four days at a time. My neck would be so stiff I could not move. My husband used to get disgusted with me, but gradually I got accustomed to the work, and I continued that work for seventeen years."[23] Another issei woman recalls being reprimanded constantly until she had acquired the necessary skills. In one unforgettable incident, "I was scolded many times, but I didn't understand what the *luna* (foreman) was saying. Finally in exasperation, he grabbed the knife away from me and yelled something. Although I didn't understand his words, I knew he was very angry and was using abusive language . . . I sat down and cried and wondered why I had come to Hawaii."[24]

Though the work was grueling and the conditions difficult, the women did not quit. A labor report said they are "not strong physically, but perform hard and exhausting work, keeping up through sheer force of spirit."[25]

Most issei women were still working outside the home in 1900, with the majority of them continuing to labor in the sugar plantations. The commissioner of labor report noted in 1901 that while most other wives "engaged solely in home duties," a Japanese wife "almost without exception engaged in work outside of her home." The income brought in by the Japanese wife was critical for the family finances because, due to ethnic differentials in pay, the average income of the Japanese husband was the lowest of all ethnic groups. The average yearly income of the Japanese wife was estimated at $91.42. Since the average income of her husband was only $258.66, her income added a significant 35 percent to their family income.[26]

The number of Japanese women in Hawaii increased greatly after the Gentlemen's Agreement (1907–1908) restricted Japanese immigration primarily to only the wives and children of Japanese men already working in the United States. More and more men began to send for their families. Some unmarried men who could not go back to Japan to marry had their families or "go-betweens" arrange marriages for them with picture brides in Japan. Pictures and information were exchanged between the prospective bride and groom, and they were married by proxy. About one-fourth of all wives who immigrated during the period from 1908 to 1924 were picture brides.

The issei women who came during the picture bride era provided labor for the plantations. Although this period showed a marked decline in the overall numbers of Japanese working on the sugar plantations, the number of Japanese women workers held steady due to the influx of these new wives. This retention of issei women workers resulted in an increase in the proportion of Japanese women to Japanese men employed on the sugar plantations. While Japanese women did not supply a large percentage of the entire work force in the sugar industry, they constituted a steady and important labor source, especially in a time of labor shortage.[27]

After 1900 Japanese women who had arrived earlier had begun moving to urban jobs in domestic and personal service, clothing trades, and pineapple canneries. A 1905 labor report noted, for instance, that the clothing industry was being monopolized by Japanese and Chinese, and that most domestic servants were "Asiatics."[28] In 1910 Japanese women were 65 percent of all women gainfully employed (7,337 of 11,271) with 44 percent of all Japanese women working (7,337 of 16,643), 48.5 percent of Japanese women were still in agriculture and 36 percent were now in domestic and personal service.[29]

However, by 1920 the new picture brides had increased the numbers of Japanese women working in agriculture and particularly on the sugar plantations. The majority of Japanese women were now once again in agriculture. Sixty percent of Japanese issei women were in agriculture and only 26.9 percent were in domestic and personal service. Japanese women represented 65 percent of all women in gainful employment (9,233 of 14,263).[30]

The arrival of wives and brides during the so-called picture bride era led not only to an increase in the number of issei women in agriculture, but also led to an increase in the number of children born to the Japanese.

Work or Children?

In the beginning the vast majority of issei women were able to work outside the home because in part, unlike other ethnic women, Japanese women had few children. At the time this was due to governmental and planter policy, for the issue of children had become very important to the planters. Because of their experiences with importing Portuguese laborers who brought large families with them, the planters were now anxious to restrict the numbers of unproductive immigrants, that is, children and other relatives who did not work.[31]

In the first shipload of Japanese contract workers in 1885, there were 108 children, but in the subsequent three loads there were fewer children (14, 4, and 7), and from the fifth load to the twenty-sixth there were none.[32] According to the 1890 census, many issei women left children back in Japan. Most of the Japanese women who emigrated with their husbands did not have children; only 25.7 percent of Japanese women of legal age of marriage and physiological age of motherhood had born any children.[33] Furthermore, these few Japanese mothers had an average of only 1.56 children, the lowest average among all ethnic groups.[34]

In the first years of immigration the women may have wanted to restrict the birth of children in order to work and save money. But even as late as 1901 it was reported that "the large proportion of Japanese families without children is noticeable." The report went on to state that only 50.8 percent of Japanese families had children and that Japanese families with children continued to have the lowest number of children of all ethnic groups.[35]

We begin to see a different tone in the 1902 report which stated that with regard to the new Japanese wives coming to Hawaii, "their children are numerous."[36] In the subsequent years of permanent settlement, when more men sent for wives and picture brides, there was a great increase in the birthrate. A 1912 survey of industrial conditions in Honolulu found that "whereas a generation ago few Japanese children were born in Hawaii, abortionists abounded among them, the past five years has brought a change and families of at least moderate size are now the rule and are found in every part of the community. . . ."[37]

The children represented a commitment to settle in Hawaii, and for the working issei mother, they posed a special problem as well as joy. Childcare was uppermost in their minds. As the women began to have children, the percentage of Japanese women working in the fields dropped. But with the increase in family members, there was an increase in family expenditures, so many issei mothers found it necessary to continue to work somehow.

The women who arrived in Hawaii early on worked with children strapped to their backs or placed nearby.[38] One issei said that she worked in the fields while tending to her baby. "I placed my baby in a wagon in the field. It was difficult to work and baby-sit at the same time because the baby would cry off and on. I carried the baby on my back, too." [39]

Some issei mothers were lucky to be employed by plantations that set up day nurseries and kindergartens to free the women for work in the fields. On the island of Oahu, Waialua Plantation set up a kindergarten in 1900,[40] Kahuku Plantation had a day nursery for infants and children in 1905, and Ewa Plantations had a free kindergarten at about the same time.[41] One issei woman explained her childcare arrangements: "There was a large baby home. The plantation hired three ladies, and all the working women left their children there. It was a free service provided by the plantation for working mothers. Until the children became of school age, that is where they all stayed." [42]

Other women had to pay for nursery care. One woman reported that she paid five dollars a month for childcare.[43] Some reported that other issei mothers took in children in a private childcare arrangement. This provided needed income for the mother who babysat and a needed service for the mothers who worked elsewhere. However, if a mother had more than one or two children, the cost of childcare equaled or exceeded their wages for working in the fields.[44]

Many of the issei women worked in the fields until nearly the end of their pregnancy and rested only a few months after giving birth before going back to work. One issei woman said, "When the second child came, I stayed home three months. I was expecting the second child in February; yet I worked in January. . . ." She recalls being ridiculed for working so hard. "I would hear fellow workers saying, "Look at Kumasaka-san. Work comes before her children, and she calls herself a mother!" Yet to her mind she was working so hard because she wanted to be a good mother, for "I grew up poor and had a poor education. I did not want our children to be like me, so I made up my mind to work." [45]

Decades later, however, the common guilt complex of a working mother still plagued her. In a 1984 interview she stated, "Our children were left at the baby home where many children of all ages were cared for by a few sitters. The children did not have individual attention. I think I really did an injustice to my children." Vivid memories of painful daily separations from her very young children still haunted her. "The younger child was too young to know, but the older one used to cry every day when I left them at the baby home. Even now I can hear her wailing." She concludes that "in retrospect, I was terribly mistaken . . . about my thinking that I should work to save money. Rather, I should have taken care of the children." [46]

While some women continued to work in the fields even after having children, others found it difficult to work while having to care for preschool children and increasingly so after the birth of additional children. But with each child born, the family expenditures increased, and the wife's income was sorely missed if she quit working.

But the women were resourceful and found means other than field work to contribute to the family income, including providing domestic services such as cooking, laundering, and sewing for the bachelor laborers. One issei is reported to have originally worked in the sugar mill and sugar fields but after the birth of her youngest child started to cook for ten to seventeen bachelors in the camp. By charging five dollars per boarder she netted an income that was a little higher than the average of a woman field worker. Another woman reported that when things got difficult financially, she took in sewing. After quitting field work, another did laundry for bachelors. [47]

One issei woman explained that she quit field work for a time and did laundry and heated bath water for Filipino bachelor workers "because I had children . . . little children." She was paid five dollars per month by each man for doing his laundry and thirty cents a month each for drawing the bath water and heating it with firewood. The pay was good but the "profit was slim." Doing the laundry for ten men was a full-time job: two days of washing by hand using a washing board and then another two or three days pressing with a charcoal-heated iron. She says that field work was "more leisurely" because there was no predetermined amount of work to do, but with laundry "no matter how much there is to do, you have to finish it no matter what." [48]

This same issei woman also later cooked for the field workers of her husband who was a *luna* (foreman). She got up at three in the morning to make them breakfast and worked until eight at night making lunch and dinner and cleaning up in addition to her own household tasks and childcare. But this job was a lucrative one for "even with inflation, cooks' pay was relatively good." Besides, "I couldn't go out to the field because the children were all small." [49]

Even when these women did field work, they often supplemented their wages. One woman said that "besides working in the field during the day, I took in washing on the weekends and ironed at night." [50] Another related the same: "On Sunday, I washed, and then, at night, I ironed. Sunday night and workday nights I ironed until I finished all the ironing—every night." [51]

By 1910 the commissioner of labor stated that the Japanese were demanding higher wages and seeking more independent positions than that of field laborers since expenses were higher with families to support. [52] As a matter of fact, Japanese female urban workers were characterized in a 1912 report as "fighters among the women wage earners of the city. . . ." [53] The writer noted that the "kicks" (i.e., demands) by Japanese women were said to be the reason for the pay raise in all the pineapple canneries in 1912. Also even though Japanese were not hired by commercial laundry operators "because of the fear of cut prices if processes are learned," the Japanese women managed to overcome the exclusion by operating their own nonlicensed laundries with the Japanese women operators collecting laundry from individuals and hiring other Japanese women to do the work. [54]

Japanese women were fighters in the fields, too. The Japanese led strikes to increase wages and improve working conditions, and Japanese women participated actively. The 1901 commissioner of labor report figures indicate that on many plantations all Japanese women employees took part in strikes although not all the Japanese men did. In one particular incident the report notes that on a large sugar plantation Japanese and Portuguese women demanded an increase in wages from eight to ten dollars per month. The employers tried an unsuccessful ten-day lockout of the women, but later the women were able to return to work at the higher wage. [55]

The first major Japanese sugar strike was the 1909 strike. One of the reasons cited for the strike was the demand for higher wages to support the men's growing families.[56] In stating reasons for demanding a wage increase, the Japanese of the Higher Wage Association wrote that "the wives of the family with three or four children cannot help their husbands increase the income of the family. Their time is entirely for the care of the house and the children."[57] A major demand of the 1920 Oahu Sugar Strike was for paid maternity leave for female workers of two weeks before delivery and six weeks after delivery.[58]

The Move from Rural to Urban Work

After the 1920 strike, the number of Japanese working on the sugar plantations declined drastically. This trend continued until 1929; only 18.5 percent of the male sugar labor force was Japanese. But Japanese women still represented by far the major source of female labor for the sugar plantations at 84.6 percent of the 1,636 female workers.[59] As the Japanese began to leave the plantations in great numbers, they were replaced with laborers imported from the Philippines. By 1929 Filipino sugar workers accounted for 69.5 percent of the adult male labor force on the sugar plantations (34,681 of 49,890).[60] No replacement was found for the Japanese women workers.

Most Japanese women were no longer on the sugar plantations. As had happened before the arrival of picture brides, there was a definite shift in the employment pattern of Japanese women by 1930 from agriculture to urban occupations. In 1930 only 16.7 percent of Japanese working women were in agriculture, while 50.2 percent were in domestic and personal services, and 13.7 percent were in manufacturing and mechanical industries.[61]

The developing pineapple industry provided alternative and better-paying agricultural and urban jobs for those leaving the sugar plantations. Japanese women formed an important segment of pineapple field and cannery workers. In 1915 although few women worked in the fields, 68 percent of them were Japanese. They received an average daily wage of sixty-four cents. The Japanese women field workers in the sugar industry, who worked a similar average sixty-hour week, earned a daily average of only fifty-five cents.[62] In 1920, 89.4 percent of female pineapple laborers were Japanese (473 of 529). By 1930 women workers in the pineapple fields were still predominantly Japanese and worked there with their husbands. [63]

Japanese women also provided the major source of pineapple cannery workers, though the ethnic composition was somewhat more evenly distributed among other groups. Japanese women represented some 37 percent of female cannery workers in 1915 (557 out of 1,501). [64] In a 1930 report 32.1 percent of women working in five pineapple canneries were Japanese, and half of the reported Japanese women working were nisei, second-generation, women. [65]

The short canning season—which peaked in July and August—required a large number of workers, thus the major canneries were located in the more urban labor market of Honolulu. The short season of full operation accounted for the relatively higher rate of pay in the canneries as compared to that paid on the sugar plantations. For example, in 1915 the average daily wage for Japanese women working in canneries as trimmers and packers was sixty-nine cents as compared to fifty-five cents for Japanese women working as field workers on the sugar plantations. [66] Cannery work drew a great deal of its female labor from Japanese domestic servants who found the shorter hours and higher pay to their liking and Japanese housewives who wanted to add to the family income by working temporarily out of the home during the summer.

The pineapple canneries were important sources of jobs for issei women, but by 1930 domestic and personal services provided more jobs in Hawaii for women than any other single industry. In 1930 half of Japanese working women held domestic and personal service jobs. Thirty percent of Japanese working women were employed as servants and two-thirds of all the women servants in Hawaii were Japanese (2,472 of 3,540). [67] Japanese women were almost unanimously preferred by employers of household help according to studies done in 1936 and 1940 because, as the 1936 report stated, "they are usually quiet, scrupulously neat and clean in appearance, not given to gossip (at least not beyond their own racial group) and do not find detail and routine as monotonous as do the more temperamental members of other races." [68]

Laundry work and barbering were other domestic and personal service trades that Japanese women dominated. Although in the large commercial laundries Japanese women were not employed in great numbers,

Japanese women had developed laundry work as a home industry. Three-fourths (658 of 885) of laundresses not working in commercial laundries were Japanese women in 1930.[69] In 1930 88.5 percent (354 of 400) of barbers and hairdressers in Hawaii were Japanese women. And in a 1939 study of Honolulu barber shops, 84 percent (32 of 38) were run by Japanese women of which 46.9 percent (15 of 32) were issei women. Barbering actually came to be thought of as a "woman's trade" dominated by Japanese women.[70]

Japanese women were also prominent in the dressmaking trade. In 1930 three-fourths of dressmakers not employed in factories were Japanese (456 of 606). By 1940 there was a Japanese dressmakers' association "whose purpose [was] to interest its members in cooperating to raise standards and increase profits of their trade."[71]

By 1940 most issei women were no longer working as sugar workers; they had left for jobs in other industries. A 1940 labor report on women-employing industries in Hawaii declared that "women are employed to a limited extent on the plantations, but they are not considered an important part of the general economy. . . ."[72] However, Japanese women had once played an important role in the development of the sugar industry and were continuing to play an important role in other occupations.

One issei woman said of her life that "I worked constantly all my life."[73] That simple statement seems to sum up the life of all issei working women: Their constant work contributed to the growth and development of the key industries of Hawaii as well as to the economic survival of their families.

Ladies on the Line: Punjabi Cannery Workers in Central California

MARCELLE WILLIAMS

"Well, those ladies on the lines, they have it pretty easy," Mr. Singh replied when I asked Mrs. Singh about her job as a cannery worker. Mrs.

Singh's husband continued to answer for her: "And now that she has seniority, you know, she can sit around and drink tea or something like that." While I tried to talk to Mrs. Singh about her life and work at a nearby food-processing plant, she moved industriously around the kitchen, preparing snacks for her two little granddaughters and me. As a guest in their home, an old farmhouse that they had recently refurbished, I was ushered into the formal living room where I sat drinking tea with Mr. Singh, a married daughter who was visiting, and an unmarried, teen-age daughter. Although the entire family was very gracious and hospitable, whenever I asked Mrs. Singh questions about herself, the other members present frequently answered instead.

This situation did not occur only with this family. In fact, it happened over and over again during my interviews with Punjabi Sikh women who work in the California canning industry. Even though I requested to speak directly with the women, they were often busy in the kitchen while their family members spoke for them.[1]

At first glance my interviews seem to support previous research which stereotypes Asian Indian women as restricted to the domestic sphere of home and hearth, passive and unable to speak for themselves. In a review of the few studies of South Asian immigrant women, Pratibha Parmar states that they usually are depicted as "limited to the kitchen, the children and the religious rituals, and . . . emotionally and economically dependent upon their husbands."

However, my interviews with Punjabi cannery workers contradict the commonly held view that Indian immigrant women are economically dependent on men and do not work outside of the home. At the very least, my study documents that these women work hard *outside* as well as *inside* the house, in both the public and the private realms. Very rarely, whether at work or home, did they "sit around and drink tea." Moreover, a closer examination of my interviews shows that these women are extremely active and that their actions may speak more loudly than their apparent lack of words.

I intend to illustrate in this essay that the Punjabi women with whom I talked are anything but passive, and that they actively influence and interlink the public sphere of work and the private sphere of family. Indeed, they are often able to gain the upper hand by manipulating the stereotypic images of their supposed domesticity, passivity, and inarticulateness.[2]

The Singhs Arrive in California

In order to convey the idea that Punjabi women are active in both the workplace and the home and to show the extent to which the two realms overlap, this essay will focus on one particular woman, Mrs. Singh, her work, and her family. I met Mrs. Singh and her family during the spring of 1985, when I began interviewing Indian immigrant women who worked in the fruit and vegetable canneries of Stanislaus County in central California. Mrs. Singh knew of approximately one hundred Punjabi Sikhs who worked as seasonal laborers at a specific plant in Modesto run by Tri/Valley Growers, Inc. While I spoke with some of the women who worked at this cannery, and to women from other food processing plants, I will concentrate on Mrs. Singh since her experiences are representative, for the most part, of the larger group of Punjabi women. When her life history appears atypical, however, I will note this and provide illustrative material from other sources.

Mrs. Singh and her husband, like 30 to 40 percent of the 59,674 Asian Indians currently in California, belong to the Sikh religion, which predominates in the state of Punjab in India. Mr. Singh left the Jullundur district in the Punjab in 1971 and settled with his sister's family north of Sacramento, in the Marysville-Yuba City area, which has had a sizable Punjabi Sikh population since the early 1900s. Mrs. Singh, also born and raised in the Jullundur district where she married her husband in 1958 at the age of seventeen, followed him to America a year later with their four children.

Many scholars have traced the historical development of the Punjabi community in rural California and have commented on its inception as a bachelor group of agricultural laborers. Mr. Singh was able to immigrate because of his relationship to this earlier group through his sister. She could sponsor her brother because she had married a man whose father had entered California as a farm worker. In turn, after immigrating as Mr. Singh's wife, Mrs. Singh became a United States citizen as soon as possible so that she could sponsor the entry of her own brothers and sisters.

So, contrary to the studies of Asian Indian immigrant women that stress their dependent status and imply that they migrate only because of men, Mrs. Singh, like her sister-in-law and many other women before her, served as a vital link in the immigration cycle—men bringing over women relatives who then bring their own relatives. Unlike the usual portrayal of Asian Indian women, Mrs. Singh took an active role in migration strategies.[3]

In their search for land and new opportunities, the Singhs, like many of the Sikhs in northern California, moved southward into Stanislaus County. In 1973, Mr. and Mrs. Singh left his sister's ranch, where they had worked picking peaches and tending the orchard, and moved to Stanislaus County, which is located about sixty miles south of Sacramento near the middle of the Central Valley. They settled on the outskirts of Modesto, the largest city in the county, in the hopes of acquiring some orchard land of their own.

Although there is no official estimate of the size of the Punjabi community, the 1980 census calculates a total Asian Indian population of only 1,150 out of 293,400 people in the county. This figure may be a gross underestimation, however. Based on the Sikh temples in the area and the estimated number of families they each serve, there appear to be almost a thousand Punjabi Sikhs alone. Asian Indians other than Punjabi Sikhs reside in the county—they are primarily from the northern states, but probably every state in India is represented, as well as there being some Indians from Fiji, England, and Africa. And among them there is a fairly well-defined residential and class division. The Punjabi Sikhs tend to live in the smaller towns and more rural areas, in Turlock, Ceres, Patterson, Hughson, Denair, and Delhi; and they tend to be working-class, waged workers who also own or lease a little land. In contrast, the other Asian Indians seem to reside more often within the city of Modesto and to work in business or are professionals.[4]

Soon after they settled in Stanislaus County, the Singhs sought gainful employment. As one of the state's top ten producing agricultural

counties, the county has well over three hundred food processing, packing, and distributing companies. Mr. Singh, who had been a taxi driver
in India, found a year-round job as a forklift driver for a large food
processing plant. Mrs. Singh worked in the fields picking various crops,
sometimes along with the children of the family.

Just months after the Singhs moved into the area, Mrs. Singh found a
seasonal job as an assembly line worker for Tri/Valley Growers, Inc.
Fortunately Mrs. Singh was at the right place at the right time: she
began working at Tri/Valley Plant 7, the world's largest "supercannery,"
soon after the company opened it and began expanding its holdings in
Stanislaus County.

Since then, Tri/Valley Growers, a cooperative association of several
hundred farming operations, has grown until it is now the largest fruit
and vegetable processor in the state. This development is unfortunate for
cannery workers at other plants, though, because Tri/Valley's growth
has been related to an industry "shakedown" and merger mania that have
resulted in numerous plant closures and shutdowns.[5]

Working at the Cannery

When asked how she got her job at Tri/Valley, Mrs. Singh said that she
"just went down to the [plant] office, filled out an application, and that
was it." Unlike most of the other cannery workers with whom I spoke,
she did not hear about, or get her job, through word-of-mouth since she
was among the first Punjabis hired. Another Punjabi woman who was
hired at Tri/Valley explained:

> Okay, you just talk to your friends and family about where they work,
> and you usually hear who is hiring. You know from talking to them if
> they [the companies] are any good to work for. You know, Tri/Valley
> is usually good to work for, and Del Monte is not so good. It used to
> be that if you knew the floorlady or the foreman, you could tell them
> that so-and-so, your brother, needs a job and he's a good worker, and
> he'd get on. I don't think it's like that anymore.

Through word-of-mouth communication, it is not uncommon for
relatively large numbers of Indian immigrants, often related by kinship

and friendship, to work together at the same plant. Of course, this kind of networking also occurs with groups other than Asian Indians and, as a result, many canneries have clusters of particular ethnic groups. One nut processing plant in Modesto, for example, has a majority of Assyrian immigrant employees; another plant has mostly Chicanos; a third has mostly "Okies." Most plants, though, like Tri/Valley's Plant 7, have a combination of several ethnic groups.

There are many Punjabi Sikhs employed by Tri/Valley Growers, but it is difficult to know the exact percentage because the company does not keep any kind of tally of their Indian immigrant employees. Based on my discussion with the workers there, I estimate that Punjabis make up about 2 percent of the work force. According to company records for 1984, over half of this labor force is Hispanic (51.26 percent), while the rest is comprised of almost 3 percent black, 5 percent "Asian" (many of whom are Southeast Asian refugees), and the remainder unspecified (presumably white).[6]

Although being 2 percent of the Tri/Valley work force may not seem numerically significant, it is socially significant in the daily lives of the Punjabi Sikhs who work there. They interact in a very close-knit social world composed of kith and kin with whom they work, at the height of the canning season, for up to ten hours a day, and with whom they may then visit afterwards. An Anglo cannery worker with whom I talked complained about the Punjabi worker's social habits:

> Yeah, they're really very clannish. You know, they sit together during breaks, and they usually manage to work together on the lines or wherever. The women are really the worst about sticking to themselves and sitting in gangs. It really bugs me when you walk past them, and they start giggling and talking about you in their language, you know, Indian or whatever it is. I don't know, it sort of sounds like Spanish.

As this comment inadvertently recognizes, the social world of the Punjabi Sikh women—who make up a little more than half of all the Sikh cannery workers—may be even more closely knit because they often do not speak English fluently. Quite often the Punjabi women state explicitly that they do cannery work because English language skills are not crucial in most of the work. Mrs. Singh points out that when Tri/Valley hired her in the early 1970s, when their business was booming, the hiring personnel were not interested in whether or not she spoke English.

> I just filled out the application, and they asked me some questions. I just said "yes" to everything that they asked me; I didn't even know what they were asking. A couple of times when I said "yes," they looked at me kind of funny, so I guess I should've said "no" then. They didn't care that I didn't know the language.[7]

The Punjabi Sikh women who work at the canneries share more than a small social world and the inability to speak English fluently; they share other cultural characteristics as well. Like Mrs. Singh, most of them immigrated to California during the 1970s from either the Jullundur or Ludhiana districts of the Punjab, and since their arrival most of them have been involved in agribusiness as pickers, packers, cannery workers, and small-scale farmers. Most were hired by Tri/Valley or by other canneries during the 1970s, and consequently have ten or more years of seniority.

The vast majority of the Punjabi Sikh women who work in the cannery are middle-aged. This fact is due to immigration cycles and hiring patterns in the canning industry resulting from "boom and bust" trends since World War II. As Mrs. Singh's daughter emphasized, most of the cannery workers, including her mother, are in their forties and fifties because "only the first ladies that came over here, the very first like them, you know, they're the only ones that work there [at the cannery]. But like the children, they don't work there."

In addition to sharing similar backgrounds and characteristics, most of the Punjabi Sikh women share similar work at the canneries. Most of them work in the lower paying jobs on the assembly lines or conveyor belts in preparation and canning, two of the three departments—preparation, canning, and warehouse—at the cannery.

The preparation department is made up almost exclusively of women and consists of numerous conveyor belts that move the produce from the trucks, through a lye solution that peels it, and ultimately into machines that fill the cans. In the canning department the cans move through seamer and cook machines, which are tended by both women and men. After the cans have been filled, seamed, and cooked, they proceed to the warehouse area where almost only men work to pack, store, and later distribute the canned goods. In most of the departments, but especially in the preparation and canning departments, the work is subdivided into minute single tasks. Women on the lines, for example, grade the produce by standing alongside the belt and tossing away the unsuitable fruit, hour after hour, day after day.

Not only is work in the cannery monotonous, it is also usually uncomfortable and sometimes dangerous. The noise level is so high that it is practically impossible to carry on a conversation in many of the work areas, so workers have developed a sign language instead. The stench of the processed food is at times overpowering and causes the nausea that most line workers experience at one time or another. One woman working at a cannery summed it up: "I don't like the monotony of the belt. I hate standing all day. It's noisy; it gives me a headache. The line makes me dizzy, and sometimes I get sick." Also workers sometimes become ill because of the disorientation from working the "swing" (usually 2:00 to 10:00 P.M.) or the "graveyard" (usually 10:00 P.M. to 6:00 A.M.) shift.

Overall these conditions can be very harsh, especially during the peak part of the season—July to mid-September—when workers may put in as many as ten hours a day, with only two twelve-minute breaks and a half-hour lunch, six or seven days a week. In addition, conditions at the cannery can be dangerous. Mrs. Singh, along with most other cannery workers, recounted stories of various cannery accidents, such as the story of a woman's finger being severed by the machinery and then "canned" with the peaches.[8]

Despite the implementation of affirmative action policies, cannery work is still difficult for women because of the de facto sex segregation of the work that keeps women in the lower-paying, lower-bracket jobs in the preparation and canning departments, which are more seasonal, more monotonous, and more strictly supervised. Although there are not official distinctions made between "male" and "female" jobs or their pay scales, the job brackets—eight levels that are hierarchically ranked according to the job description and wages—are divided by sex. On the whole, men occupy the upper brackets, women the lower. As of 1984, after a decade of reform measures, women at Tri/Valley still made up 71.38 percent of the less-skilled, lower-paying, lower job brackets.

For the Punjabi women, this situation of sex discrimination is aggravated by racial or ethnic discrimination. Affirmative action measures have not changed the fact that cannery work is also ethnically segregated, with people of color occupying the lower job brackets. After working at the cannery for thirteen years, Mrs. Singh, like all of the other Punjabi women, is still a seasonal worker. She is a Bracket Five worker and, as of last year, was finally moved off the lines to a higher level job running a seamer machine. Out of all the Punjabi women working at Tri/Valley, there are only two who have been able to reach even lower-ranking supervisory positions.

Although Mrs. Singh did not complain about discrimination at the cannery, many other workers have. In another study, a Chicana testified: "Discrimination is blatant. If you're white, or know the bosses, you last maybe a week on the lines. If you're brown or a woman, you work for years and never get promoted."[9]

Given the harsh conditions at work and the discrimination that exacerbates them, why do Punjabi Sikh women continue to work in the canneries? Aside from the more obvious reasons, their previous experience in agribusiness, their language limitations, and a competitive labor market, the Punjabi women I spoke with insisted that they actively sought out cannery work because it suited their purposes: to provide more income for their families while fulfilling their domestic roles as wives and mothers.

With seasonal cannery work lasting four or five months and then unemployment benefits the remainder of the year, Punjabi women earn up to a third of the family's income and yet can also be around the house as much as possible. In a sense, they use to their own advantage the cannery management's notion that they are expendable, secondary workers, a reserve army of labor.

Work and the Family

The key to understanding why Punjabi women work is to know that they do not view work and the family as incompatible, dichotomized spheres. According to most Punjabi women, they gain prestige from participating in both spheres, and as it happens, these very spheres overlap anyway. As Mrs. Singh laughingly said, "My work is sort of my family, you know, with all my relatives and friends there; and, of course, my family is my work."

Nearly all the Punjabi women emphasize that they are wage workers for their families' economic benefit. I heard over and over again, "It is good for Indian ladies from good families to work here. You see, everybody works because the pay is good, and it's good for the families." Punjabi families encourage every able-bodied adult to help finance the family goal of purchasing a small plot of orchard land. The women in the families are able to aid in this endeavor by working at the canneries, and they often can secure cannery jobs for other family members too. For example, Mrs. Singh was able to refer both her brother and her husband to Tri/Valley where both took on seasonal work to supplement their year-round jobs.

It is interesting to note that the women claimed they worked at the cannery in order to contribute to the welfare of their families, thereby fulfilling their domestic obligations. Essentially, they are legitimizing their departure from traditional domesticity, by saying their entry into the workplace is for domestic reasons. While these women are undoubtedly working outside of their homes for economic reasons, they are also hoping, according to what I learned in my interviews, to change their traditional roles within the family. They use their stereotypic image of devoted domesticity to justify becoming wage earners, but at the same time actually gain more control and decision-making power within the household. Many Punjabi women told anecdotes about their increased power in the family. One woman said with great satisfaction, "Now my husband, he listens to me when I say something; when I want to buy something, I do; and when I want to go in the car, I go." Although the family as a whole usually makes the decisions about where a family member will work, Mrs. Singh showed that she could break precedent and decide herself when to quit a job:

I worked at another plant once, and they gave me a "man's" job. It was cutting this turkey into three pieces; it [the belt] was too fast and [the

work was] too hard. I was the only woman working there. I worked
hard all day to show that I could do it, that I could do a "man's" job.
But I quit the next day 'cause it was too hard. It was too much work,
and I didn't like it.

Other Punjabi women told of using their stereotypic image as passive
and inarticulate workers to avoid doing certain jobs at the cannery. For
instance, since the Punjabi women cannery workers form a close-knit
social group at work, they sometimes do not want to leave the lines
where that group interacts the most. One woman explained: "I work
very hard, but I don't want to move away from the lines, from the belt,
you know, 'cause that's where my friends are. So, I don't act all gung ho
when the floorlady comes by and says there's a spot for someone on the
filler machines or something." Another woman who usually worked the
seamer machines resisted the authority of the supervisors in this small
but effective way: "When a floorlady I don't like brings over someone
and tells me to train them, you know, on my machine, I act like I don't
understand her. I speak Punjabi back to her and act like I don't understand English. That way I don't have to fool with them." Someone else
related that sometimes when she doesn't want to do a particular job,
clean-up for instance, she says, "Okay, okay," and then just stands
around and chats with her friends. When the supervisor chides her, she
acts as though she doesn't understand what the supervisor wants her to
do and says, "No English."

These women indicated to me that they were satisfied with working
at the cannery, which, after all, was better than doing farm work. They
were happy at being able to contribute to their families' income and
fulfill domestic duties, while simultaneously being able to change their
families' expectations of them. In order to do this, the women often used
the traditional stereotype of their being domestic to their advantage. In
the workplace, they also sometimes manipulated the stereotypes about
passivity and inarticulateness to do what they wanted versus what their
supervisors told them to do. In talking about their work and family
experiences, it was evident that they sometimes said little or, even more
often, said what fit their stereotypic image as domestic, passive, and
inarticulate women. However, these statements sometimes obscured

what was really happening in their lives. The actions of the women, these Punjabi Sikh "ladies on the lines," may well speak more loudly than their words.

Behind Unmarked Doors: Developments in the Garment Industry

DIANE YEN-MEI WONG WITH DENNIS HAYASHI

Machines emit a low hum accented by occasional bursts of power. Conversations ebb and flow, punctuating the mechanical sounds with phrases in Taishanese (Toisanese), Vietnamese, or Korean, and occasionally with a universally understood laugh or sympathetic clucking of the tongue. Multicolored fabric forms haphazard stacks of reds, blues, plaids, and prints. Light is limited to a few naked bulbs, each suspended from the ceiling by a single cord, and a few focused crook-necked desk lamps.

Black- and gray-haired grandmothers, mothers, sisters, and daughters bent over their machines, cast quick glances at the hanging sample garment, at the slow-paced clock on the wall, and at each other. Rows of material, machines, and women are hidden in small rooms behind unmarked doors and bedsheet-covered windows. Only the infrequent opening of the door releases the sounds and sights of these small nonunion sewing factories, the lowest rungs of the international garment industry, the sweatshops.

In the larger nonunion shops, women, who comprise the vast majority of the industry's workers, may fare a bit better: heat in the winter, ventilation in summer, and better lighting. Sometimes in the unionized shops they have the employee benefits that characterize other American jobs: regular hours, overtime pay, holidays, health and pension benefits, sick leave, and paid vacations; sometimes they work under the same conditions as their nonunion colleagues, and pay union dues as well.

The industrialized nature of the garment business has always kept women from positions of leadership and gaining control over their work.

160

Yet, with the rising cost of living, more and more women enter the job market in the hopes of making ends meet. How did this industry develop, how much has changed, and what lies in its future?

Role of the Subcontractors

In the Bay Area alone, the garment industry grosses about $3.5 billion a year in business, and provides work for about twenty-five thousand workers, most of whom are Asian and Latino. About 80 percent of the garments produced in San Francisco come from small Chinatown shops.[1] Most of these shops, regardless of size, rely on work meted out to them by large clothing manufacturers: Byers, Esprit, Fritzi, Foxy Lady, Gunne Sax, North Face, and Twin Peaks for the nonunion shops; Koret of California for the union shops. The manufacturers provide the shops with precut fabric and a sample of how the finished work should look and hang. The women take the pieces and assemble them into reasonable facsimiles of the sample.

Manufacturers also control the prices at each level of production and sale. Though most of the smaller subcontractors have little say over the final retail price of the garments, they do have a limited ability to bargain with manufacturers about the contract price paid to them for putting the garments together.

In contrast, the women who actually sew the garments have no power in regard to their price. Both retailers and manufacturers are looking for ways to increase their respective profit margins, and subcontractors are fiercely competing with each other for their small portion. Thus, the fee paid to the women often decreases, unaffected by any minimum wage rate set by state or federal governments.

With an investment from as little as ten thousand to fifty thousand dollars, an entrepreneur can set up a sewing factory employing five to ten workers who assemble clothes cut at one site, designed at another, and sold at yet another.[2] The money is just enough to rent a store front or upper floor space, rent or buy a few secondhand sewing machines, and pay for electricity. Success of the enterprise depends heavily on the availability of cheap labor, not on having fancy machines or the latest technology. Fast-changing clothing styles prevent it being cost-effective to purchase machines that automate the steps involved in creating a garment from nondescript piles of fabric. As far as the industry is concerned, the only way to keep up with style changes is to train human beings individually to incorporate the new lines.

The Women Who Sew

Though most of the Asian garment workers trace their roots to China, many come from other countries in Asia. For instance, at one nonunion factory in Seattle where about 70 percent of the total work force was comprised of Asian American women, 34 percent were Chinese, 20 percent Filipino, 14 percent Korean, and 5 percent Vietnamese.[3] Despite the working conditions, in many cases there are more women wanting to sew than there are jobs available, especially with increased layoffs because of a depressed economy and the continuing immigration of Asian women to the United States.

In describing the lot of many Korean women who work in the sewing factories, University of California senior Kathleen Pai stated:

> The life of the typical Korean immigrant worker in the garment industry is one of continual hard work in order to provide a better life for her family. It [is] out of economic necessity that she takes to the clothing industry. In a society geared toward high education and high-skilled professions, sewing is one of the few marketable skills she has.[4]

Researchers Chalsa Loo and Paul Ong found that this description aptly applies to Chinese American seamstresses as well. About 80 percent of the families they surveyed were multiple wage earning and said that they could "barely get by" if there was only one person bringing in an income.[5]

For some of the women, sewing is the only type of work they know how to do. For others the job is attractive because of the convenient location, flexible hours, and proximity to friends or relatives who also work in the factory. Bernice Tom, a fifty-six-year-old woman who came to San Francisco Chinatown almost thirty-six years ago, has worked in a garment factory since she arrived. She readily admits the same reasons when asked how she got into the industry:

I knew how to sew in Hong Kong and had a cousin here in the factory. I like working here because I can go home anytime. This was important when my children were small. I like being in Chinatown and I like the flexible hours, the independence. I can visit my friends and go shopping.[6]

Tom works in a factory right in Chinatown, but unlike most of her colleagues, she works in a union shop. While she approaches her work with a relatively positive attitude, for the majority of women in the industry, sewing clothes is a matter of "expediency and not of choice."[7]

Given even a small choice, many of the women opt for a different, better work situation, opined Reverend Norman Fong, who with his wife, Sui Ying, established the Chinatown Workers' Center in San Francisco.[8] Those who learn to speak more English, he noted, are willing to leave the comparatively safe boundaries of Chinatown to go to the factories downtown where they can earn more and increase the likelihood of working in a unionized shop. "They need more English [skills] to talk to the supervisor, to go through the interviewing and for filling out the applications," said Fong, or to find a job outside of the industry. Mrs. Lee, a worker from Naline Lee Sewing, Inc. in San Francisco Chinatown, stated, "If I could speak English, I wouldn't be a seamstress for long. But since I can't, it is either this or washing dishes. I don't know anything else."[9]

Young Hai Shin, director of a community-based immigrant women's group in California, concurred about the women's desire to find other work if possible. However, she and her co-workers have found that many women remain in the garment industry much longer than they had initially anticipated.

For a large percentage of Korean women in the industry, . . . regardless of the educational background, they go through sewing factories because it is easy to get a job there. . . . Once they get the job, they tell other newcomers about it. . . . They may not have the original idea to stay, but they establish a life pattern and then they do not leave.

Even when they do think about changing jobs, the choices they see before them are limited. Garment workers want to become hotel maids because the work is unionized and pays more; maids want to work in restaurants because the work seems less backbreaking; restaurant workers want to go into the garment industry because there might be more flexibility. "They can't seem to get out of the dead-end jobs," lamented Shin.[10]

Efforts to Improve Conditions

Getting out of a "dead-end" job in the garment industry or improving work conditions there have not been easy to achieve. Even so, contrary to their stereotypic image as passive and docile workers, Asian women have participated in union fights against employers when they thought such action might be effective. For instance, Chinese women comprised the main picketing force in the thirteen-week strike in 1938 against the National Dollar Stores, a clothing manufacturer in San Francisco. Though the employer had fought against the entry of International Ladies' Garment Workers' Union (ILGWU), National Dollar finally acceded to the union's demands for a closed shop; a wage increase; and time-and-a-half for overtime, weekend, and holiday work. Unfortunately, the union's inability to obtain an agreement that National Dollar buy exclusively from that factory eventually led to the plant's closure the next year.[11]

In 1974 workers at the Esprit de Corp. subsidiary, Great Chinese American Sewing Company (also known as Jung Sai), voted to have the ILGWU represent them in collective bargaining. Shortly thereafter the mostly Chinese and Filipino workers found themselves locked out of the factory in what the National Labor Relations Board and the U.S. Ninth Circuit Court of Appeals later found to be an unlawful closure. After ten years of litigation, the company finally was ordered to pay 126 illegally discharged employees back pay and interest totaling about $1.2 million.[12]

The largest organized response by Asian American garment workers took place in New York City in the summer of 1982, when over fifteen thousand Chinese and Korean seamstresses rallied in support of ILGWU, Local 23–25's contract negotiations. Chinatown employers appealed to the workers for racial solidarity against the contract, which had been proposed by the larger white-owned manufacturers and the union, which historically had never involved the immigrant women in its negotiations. Because the key contract issues of job security and medical and pension benefits had a direct impact on their families' welfare, the women supported the union. A mass march through Chinatown prompted the employers to eventually sign the contract.[13]

These women were unusual, though, because most garment workers are reluctant to bring any action against their employers. They fear possible deportation, loss of jobs, blacklisting from further employment in the field, and generally do not trust the government and its agencies. Others despair at the length of time it takes to achieve resolution in legal disputes. In addition, because the women and their bosses are often of the same ethnic group or are even related, there is pressure from the family and community not to sue. Consequently workers often ignore problems or just move to another shop.[14]

In larger shops where ties between the boss/owner and the workers are not so close, dissatisfied seamstresses may find it easier to assert their rights. In December 1983 eleven seamstresses sued their former employer T & W Fashions Inc., an unusually large subcontractor owned by Tammy Ho and employing three hundred workers. The women alleged failure to comply with labor regulations pertaining to overtime and holiday pay, minimum wage, and several other state and federal laws. They had long endured the violations because "jobs were so difficult to come by and . . . because they are unable to read English, they hardly knew anything about the benefits to which they were entitled under the labor law." The workers, however, had finally reached their breaking point.[15]

Two other aspects of the case make it fairly unique. First, the women's attorneys also sued the manufacturer, Fritzi of California, asserting that it too should be held liable for the violations of its subcontractors. "The garment industry operates on a cheap work force, and an action like this sends a message out to all garment contractors and manufacturers that they should get in line with the law," said Dennis Hayashi, an attorney with the Asian Law Caucus and one of the lawyers representing the women. Second, the U.S. Department of Labor later filed its own lawsuit against T & W on behalf of the workers, citing labor violations amounting to $800,000.[16]

In 1986 Fritzi asked the court for dismissal as a defendant in the case, stating that it could not be held responsible for its contractors' illegal acts. In an unprecedented move the court ruled that Fritzi could possibly be liable and refused to dismiss the charges. This led the manufacturer to settle the case brought by the thirteen plaintiffs for $172,500, which included full back pay and damages.[17]

Runaway Shops

The fear underlying many of the actions and inactions of the seamstresses and their supporters is the potential loss of jobs. Shop owners who become unhappy with lawsuits or public and political scrutiny, can and do close up shop and move to more hospitable locales. "Hospitable" in this case means a place where there is a concentration of Asian immigrants who have no support network to help them assert their rights as workers, according to Eugene Moriguchi, an attorney with Legal Services of Northern California in Sacramento.[18]

While not unique to the garment industry, the phenomenon of runaway shops is very common among sewing factory owners. Because the location of the factories depends primarily on the availability of cheap and passive labor, and because the capital investment required is relatively small, many owners would rather relocate to what they perceive is a less hostile site than acquiesce to demands for better working conditions, more pay, and other worker's benefits.

Manufacturers' representatives state that the mere presence of "large ethnic communities [which have] people willing to work at sewing machines, something American women will not do," is what determines a plant's locale. However, seeing the trend of many San Francisco Bay

Area shops moving north to Sacramento indicates there are other factors involved. Even though the Asian immigrant population of Sacramento has grown, so has that of the Bay Area. The union influence in the Bay Area is small (about 20 percent of the factories), but it is even less in Sacramento. One Sacramento human rights worker feels this is what has made his hometown more attractive to factory owners and manu-facturers.[19]

Many manufacturers have sought a greater profit margin through cheaper labor outside this country's borders. In the late 1950s only one out of twenty-five garments bought in the United States was made abroad. Now about 60 to 65 percent of the sewing work is sent to Asian countries. Moving to another site is often one of the most attractive alternatives for manufacturers who feel pressured to improve working conditions and wages for employees, said union representative Teng.

> Esprit is 100 percent imported and the United States only does the warehousing. Liz Claiborne, Calvin Klein—they are all overseas. . . . How can we stop runaway shops? You can't. This is one of the most difficult things about the industry. . . . As a union, we can go after them wherever they are *if* they're in the country. . . . Maybe through legislation we could impose a tax to make it less profitable for corpora-tions [to manufacture abroad]. Even with shipping costs, they are still making a 400 percent profit![20]

The overseas seamstresses are a bargain. According to Walter Man-koff, associate research director for the union, the average garment worker earns 25¢ an hour in the Philippines, 16¢ in China, $1.18 in Hong Kong and 63¢ in South Korea—hard prices to beat.[21]

Prosecuting the Victims

While wages in this country may not be quite as low as those in Asia, they often do not even reach the minimum wage rate established by the government. This practice can lead to unexpected problems. For in-stance, in 1982 after a lengthy investigation which included surveillance of the factory, workers at the Naline Lee Sewing, Inc. factory in San Francisco Chinatown found themselves facing charges of unemployment insurance fraud. The district attorney's office said that the women had claimed unemployment payments for a period during which they worked full time. The women countered that they had been paid less than minimum wage for the hours they worked and that the shop owner had filed partial unemployment claims for them. [22]

The issue split the community. Some groups, even those that normally advocated fair employment, had problems supporting the women who had technically "broken the law" by applying for unemployment while working full-time hours. What the women should have done was to try to force the state to enforce the minimum wage law, they said. Others, however, argued that the women were being punished unfairly because it was the shop owner who had broken the law by paying less than minimum wage and by forcing the women to apply for unemployment compensation in order to support their families. If anyone should be penalized, it should be the owner not the workers, asserted this group.

Instead of making the women go through the criminal justice system, the judge gave the women an alternative. Though some still had to pay fines, all were directed to participate in English classes, where they could learn the language as well as their legal rights and responsibilities as workers with the hope of avoiding similar trouble in the future. The community responded by starting the Chinatown Workers' Center.

In 1985 investigators filed criminal charges of unemployment insurance fraud against a Sacramento contractor and several employees. After a year-long surveillance, the state agency alleged that the women had claimed unemployment compensation for days which they had been seen working at the factory. The contractor was charged with knowledge of the actions and with noncompliance with other labor regulations. Though negotiations resulted in the criminal charges being dropped against the women, the state decided to pursue its civil case against the contractor.

Clement Kong, an attorney who represented the shop owner and eleven of the employees, stated, "The contractors I have talked with feel terrible [about what is happening]. Though it's not an excuse, they say that 'everyone is doing it,' that they can't make a living if they [pay] minimum wages because the employees want the flexibility to go home when they please, to see their children, and to bring their work home. They're not supposed to do that according to labor laws." [23]

Alternatives Explored

Changes in the industry are needed, but where to begin? When women workers have a chance to operate their own shop, many hesitate. They fear that they will not be able to attract enough work to support the business and to make even a small profit, especially if they must pay the legal minimum wage. One possibility recently opened up when, because of a building renovation, the owner of a small factory in San Francisco Chinatown announced the sale of his entire business for only $5,000. A bargain, thought Norman Fong of the Workers' Center, especially since the new landlord, a community-based redevelopment agency, offered the space for $800 a month, with a promise to keep the rent low for an indefinite period of time thereafter.

However after visiting the site and discussing the issue in an all-day retreat, the center's coordinating committee, comprised largely of workers, unanimously voted *against* the purchase of the factory. "Given the industry, they thought they would not get that much out of it," remarked Fong. He noted that they were concerned about their ability to compete with other factories. "'Where would we get contracts from?' they asked. Even if we could make the cooperative work, they figured there would not be that much profit. If the Workers' Center ran it, we would have to pay at least minimum wage." Other concerns were raised including disparities in the amount of time each worked versus the distribution of profits and the possible loss of independence and flexible hours. [24]

On the other hand, some enterprising women did take up the challenge to run their own shop. In October 1984 Sierra Designs, a large manufacturer based in California, announced plans to close its local operations and contract that work with foreign shops. [25] After a long campaign—including a boycott of Sierra Designs products—the company finally retreated from its initial, resistant posture and began to cooperate with the women to work out a way to save their jobs.

What the women wanted was to convert Sierra Designs to a cooperatively owned and operated factory. What they got was a compromise: They could use the company's equipment and were promised at least $450,000 of subcontracts from Sierra Designs annually. So on 1 April 1985 thirty-three former employees of Sierra Designs opened a factory they would run and manage themselves.

When they opened for business, not only did they have the Sierra Designs contract, but also some others. Those were with what Plant Closures Project coordinator Jan Gilbrecht described as mostly "local designers with limited designs . . . without resources to go elsewhere." The women—of whom 50 percent were Chinese and the remainder divided among Filipino, black, Hispanic, and white—hoped they could succeed knowing earlier similar efforts had failed. Their plans were hinged on many years of experience in the specific field of outdoor wear and their emphasis on quality work with domestically-produced synthetics.

Hopes ran high, but one year later in 1986 the factory was shut. "A financial crisis was caused when the co-op went after a new market and expanded its work force but couldn't get high enough prices to support the payroll," said Gilbrecht.[26] Reports from two groups which had made loans to the cooperative cited other factors: poor general and financial management; low productivity; a weak and ineffective board; disagreements between owner/workers and employees, between business and social goals, and between manager and president.[27]

Because significant improvements in working conditions are hard to effect—even with financial and societal support—many of the women and their advocates have looked to less ambitious solutions than the workers at Sierra Designs. When the Chinatown Workers' Center was in operation, co-founder Norman Fong acknowledged that, while he personally hoped the women would fight for changes beyond their immediate workplace, the emphasis at the center was on educating individuals. "To change the whole industry is unrealistic; it's too big."[28]

Asian Immigrant Women's Advocates also tries to be pragmatic about its organizing work, says the group's director, Young Shin. Many of its activities are more social in nature—field trips, fruitpicking, and potluck dinners—but they lay the groundwork for a future network among the women. This is especially true when the women discover they share the same problems at work.

> For many of them this is the first time they have had a chance to sit down with each ethnic group [Korean, Chinese, Southeast Asian] and communicate with each other. This [organizing process] takes a long time, and the more time I work with them, the more I realize how long that is.[29]

Another solution may come from Sacramento. According to legal services attorney Moriguchi, at least one contractor wants to run a "wide open shop" that could provide basic decent working conditions.

> [However], if [just] one contractor attempted to run a wide open shop, he would not be competitive; the manufacturers would just go around him. . . . The contractors have to form a united front against the manufacturers so that the manufacturers cannot go around them. Without undercutting, we could have an established and legitimized industry.[30]

In New York City, where the garment workers' union is stronger, prospects for better employment conditions are increasing. While less than 1 percent of the Bay Area's Asian American garment workers belong to the ILGWU, about 95 percent of the New York Chinatown garment workers are union members. With a membership of over fifteen thousand representing about five hundred different shops, the union itself has been able to establish and financially support services for the seamstresses—including a childcare center, English classes, and shop steward training. In addition, because almost every Chinatown household has a member in the garment workers' union, the well-being of the community and the seamstresses are inextricably linked. Thus, the union has become involved in issues beyond those strictly within the industry, issues such as adequate low-income housing and redevelopment priorities for Chinatown. Though some non-Asian union members initially resented this move, the changing membership base from "mostly Jewish, black, and Spanish members" to "mainly Chinese, Korean, and Filipino" has supported the actions.[31] Not all locals are as responsive to their membership's needs. Translators, non-English versions of bargaining agreements, and other services are not viewed as essential or sometimes even desired, by most locals.

Conclusion

No one believes the road to improved working conditions for garment workers is an easy one. No one really thinks that change will come quickly; some even lament that change may not come within "our lifetime." Still, hope remains and it motivates the women and their supporters in the community to keep trying. The recognition of the situation as a community-wide problem has at times prompted the rare alliance of seamstresses and contractors against manufacturers. In a recent San Francisco Chinatown redevelopment case, a subcontractor wanted to open her shop in the renovated building at a reasonable rent in order to keep her factory in Chinatown and employees working. She sought help from the Asian Law Caucus, the same group that had earlier filed lawsuits against other subcontractors for failure to comply with wage regulations!

Cooperation among lawmakers, governmental agencies charged with enforcing wage and labor regulations, and garment workers and their supporters also aids the effort toward improved working conditions. This has already occurred when, for example, spurred by a lawsuit filed by a few former workers at one company, the federal government stepped in on behalf of all women. And on another occasion testimony provided by workers and their advocates, as well as media coverage, prompted the California state legislature to pass some of the most stringent laws in the country requiring registration by contractors and imposing fines for noncompliance. Discussions have also begun about laws which would hold manufacturers strictly liable for labor law violations committed by contractors.

These developments have not happened suddenly. Instead they reflect the fruit of many long years of labor. So the hope remains. "I know it's a long process and [problems] cannot be overcome in one day," said Shin. "I have to be patient and remind myself that if I see one person change . . . then being involved is worth it." [32]

Women in the Silicon Valley

REBECCA VILLONES

For the last twenty-five years, the so-called Silicon Valley, which includes all of Santa Clara County and parts of San Mateo and Alameda Counties in Northern California, has been a magnet for people seeking employment. The American Electronics Association reported that in 1984 sixteen hundred electronics and information technology firms were located in the area. Until 1982, when a recession hit the industry, the valley had been one of the few areas in the United States where employment opportunities remained high. As the demand grew for semi-conductors, computers, and other electronic equipment, the populations of South Bay cities mushroomed. San Jose's population in 1980 was 671,800, making it a new major American city.

The electronics industry is the major source of jobs in Santa Clara County, employing 25 percent of the labor force.[1] Thirteen percent of the Silicon Valley work force commutes into the area from the two adjacent counties, Alameda and San Mateo.

Of the 200,500 people employed in the Silicon Valley electronics industry, 50 percent are involved in production-related jobs. They form the lines of workers who assemble the integrated circuits for computers, radios, televisions, watches, stereos, microwave ovens, calculators, missiles, and other electronic equipment. Eighty percent of the production workers are women, and a majority of them are members of minority groups. As many as thirty thousand of the workers are recent immigrants to the United States, the largest ethnic group being the Filipinos, followed by the Vietnamese (most of whom came to this country as refugees), Mexicans, Koreans, and Portuguese.

Because of their large numbers in the electronics industry—approximately twenty thousand—Filipino workers are the focus of this essay. They are mostly recent immigrants and tend to be unskilled. A small percentage of them do have professional backgrounds in electronics, but are unable to find jobs commensurate with their training and experience. This contrasts greatly with the earlier wave of Filipino immigrants who came in 1965 and were primarily professionals.

Minority and especially immigrant workers are concentrated in the most dangerous and low-paying jobs.[2] Because of their immigrant status, their lack of knowledge about comparable wages, and their tendency to compare their salaries with the even lower wages they received in their homelands, immigrant workers accept less pay. But the consequence of such low wages is that many Filipino workers hold two jobs in an effort to support their families. Starting pay at most plants is four dollars an hour, with seven dollars per hour the top wage for production workers. (In a unionized company, such as General Electric, starting pay is nine dollars per hour, with a top pay for skilled production workers of fifteen dollars.)[3]

By hiring disproportionately large numbers of immigrant workers, the electronic corporations reap at least two benefits: they save on money paid out in wages and benefits, and they exercise control regarding working conditions, especially in the area of union organizing.

The electronics industry in the Silicon Valley is largely nonunion. Though there have been many attempts over the years to unionize, the electronics corporations maintain their aggressive policy against the unions. During the most recent union drives (conducted in the early- to mid-1980s) by the United Electrical Radio and Machinists Union and the Glaziers Union, the companies unleashed harsh anti-union practices. Workers visibly involved with union drives lost jobs; other workers faced threats of job loss if they attended union organizing meetings or distributed union literature. Immigrant workers felt especially intimidated and vulnerable because they were threatened with the loss of immigrant status if they joined the unions.[4]

The unfair labor practices the unions hoped to rectify continue to persist. "The employment practices of the corporations keep workers segregated. Companies specialize in workers of different races," asserts Pat Sacco, member of the United Electrical Workers Organizing Committee. "One company will only hire Filipino workers for swing shifts and only Vietnamese workers for another shift. Or they will keep a whole department Vietnamese or Korean. Because of their [the workers'] inability to speak English and the efforts of the companies to keep them segregated, immigrant workers cannot communicate with other workers," she continued.[5]

David Bacon, another member of the United Electrical Workers Organizing Committee, believes that these practices encourage racism between workers. "The companies use the 'divide and conquer' technique to fuel the racism of white workers. They tell white workers that they are better than immigrant workers and that they better watch out for their jobs because the immigrants want them. They [the companies] encourage them in thinking that the white workers should get the training and promotions and not the immigrant or minority workers."[6]

The corporations' employment practices have not only built up the differences between white and nonwhite, but also between men and women. Men and white employees are paid higher wages and have the chance to advance to higher positions, while women and minority workers are paid less and are relegated to only production jobs. In many companies women are actually discouraged from entering training programs that could lead to higher positions and more pay.[7]

The general structure of the electronics industry bears out the union's observations. The 5 percent of the industry's employees in management are largely white and some European. However, as already mentioned, most of the production workers, who make up about 50 percent of the industry's work force, are women and minorities. Men make up the 13 percent of the work force that is in technical and maintenance areas, nonimmigrants comprise the 12 percent that are clerical workers, and the remaining 20 percent of the industry's work force are male engineers, with immigrant engineers earning less money than white engineers.[8]

Production workers not only earn less money, they are also in jobs that can be hazardous to their health. The National Institute of Occupational Safety and Health has placed the electronics industry on its select list of health-risk industries, that is, those that use the greatest numbers of toxic substances. For example in the process of producing integrated circuits for electronic devices, workers must dip the silicon chips into chemical baths, while inevitably inhaling fumes from the chemicals.

Chemical exposure also occurs in other ways. In 1972 the International Labor Office in Geneva, Switzerland, reported that the chemical xylene irritated both blood-producing organs and the central nervous system. Yet it is still widely used in the electronics industry. Another substance, trichlorethylene (TCE), is a suspected carcinogenic in humans, but it too remains in usage because it is a powerful cleaning solvent.[9] Other health problems are caused by hydrofluoric and arsine gas leaks, chemical spills, and even such obvious dangers as open containers of toxic chemicals and solvents in work areas. There are but few warnings given to the workers about these potential hazards.

The workers talk of constant headaches, sinus problems, repeated miscarriages, skin allergies, and other difficulties.[10] However, few actually file complaints or take sick leave for fear they will lose their jobs if absent from work too long.[11] Other workers consult doctors who are untrained in diagnosing ailments caused by constant exposure to dangerous chemicals and who declare the health problems are allergic reactions not related to their working conditions.[12]

As employees fight for better working conditions, they now face an additional threat that affects their individual economic survival and that of their communities, which depend so heavily on the electronics industry. In the last few years several major electronic corporations have developed a long-term strategy for product development that would move all of the production jobs out of the Santa Clara Valley area. The only work remaining in Silicon Valley would be research related. The companies would move production jobs to areas such as Oregon, Utah, Texas, and Arizona, where they could take advantage of a labor force paid even lower wages than in California.

According to union representative David Bacon, another reason for their decision to leave the area has been the work of the unions. "We must stop the electronic corporations from running away. One reason they are running away is that corporations don't want to deal with the demands of unionized workers."[13] With unions, plants have to provide safer working conditions, including the use of chemicals which are not a threat to the health and safety of the labor force. Wages have to be in line with what unionized plants pay. And there is more insurance against plants running away and leaving behind thousands of displaced workers.[14]

Most of the major corporations, including National Semiconductors,

Signetics, Hewlett-Packard, and Intel, have ascribed to the new strategy and moved jobs to other plants in and outside the United States. The Plant Closures Project Research Group at the University of California at Berkeley recorded 15,510 jobs were lost in high technology industries between 1981 and 1984 in the Santa Clara Valley alone. Of those, 31.6 percent were lost permanently as a result of plant closures.

Minority communities with tens of thousands of workers will be adversely affected by these moves. The impact on the Filipino community alone, which has twenty thousand workers in the industry, will be particularly devastating.

For many years, the electronics industry has been touted as clean and safe, but in light of the many studies conducted by unions and health and safety groups it is now clear that electronics workers face a myriad of hazards. Continued unequal treatment of immigrant and Asian employees also refutes any idea that the industry might be a better alternative to the other problem-riddled, semiskilled jobs—such as those in the garment and restaurant industries—which are available to immigrants. Until working conditions are improved, the Asian American communities must continue to be aware of these problems and support clean-up efforts.

Asian American Women in Broadcasting

FELICIA LOWE

For those of us Asian American women in broadcast journalism, the story of our careers began around 1970, on the heels of the civil rights movement, Vietnam, student self-determination, the drug culture, women's liberation, the sexual revolution, rejection of traditional American values—anything that smacked of change. *Change* was the key word in those days, and in some convoluted amalgamation of what was happening then, the Federal Communications Commission ordered television stations across the country to begin hiring women and minorities.

Wherever there was a sizable Asian American population, many individuals and community groups added to the federal pressure by advocating affirmative action hiring of Asian American reporters and writers. Most opportunities turned out to be in the Northwest (Seattle and Portland); California (San Francisco, Sacramento, and Los Angeles); Hawaii; and some pockets on the East Coast.

A handful of independent souls also created their own training situations. On the East Coast, Connie Chung started out as a copyperson at WTTG-TV in Washington, D.C. Linda Shen, fresh out of Radcliffe, got her first production assistant job at WNEW-TV in New York, and at KOMO-TV in Seattle, Washington, Barbara Tanabe became the first Asian American female reporter. The year was 1971.

The Early Years

A steady stream of would-be reporters and anchors—trained by station-run programs, stipended by foundation and network grants, and motivated by sheer determination—followed in the early years. Aspirants sometimes received inspiration from the few trailblazers on the air. Seattle native Wendy Tokuda, now a San Francisco news anchor, remembers, "When Barbara [Tanabe] was on, the whole family rushed to the television set. . . . Seeing her on air made me realize what was possible." After meeting personally with the reporter, Tokuda was even more encouraged by Tanabe's willingness to help in any way possible.

Most of us worked at entry-level positions or volunteered time at community newspapers and radio and television stations just for the exposure and the chance to absorb the many skills needed for broadcasting. As summarized by Connie Chung, "I was a schlep like everyone else."

By 1974 Asian faces on television were no longer a novelty. By then each of the San Francisco stations had their "first Asian American reporter"—usually a female. KRON-TV had Suzanne Joe; KPIX hired Linda Shen; at KGO I joined reporter David Louie as a vacation relief reporter.

Some names cropped up in other stations and locales; old names were replaced by new ones. In San Francisco KQED-TV hired Pamela Young away from KPIX's Public Affairs Department. In Los Angeles Tritia Toyota reported for KNBC, and Joanne Ishimine took over Linda Yu's trainee job when Yu moved to Portland, Oregon, for her first reporting and anchoring position. Tanabe, the first Asian American to anchor news, moved from Seattle to Honolulu, and at her old Seattle station, KING-TV, Tokuda landed her first media job as a production secretary in public affairs.

It was an intense period for us reporters and the Asian American communities we were hired to represent. Community people, especially the older generation, were happy and proud that the racial barrier had finally been broken in this highly visible and powerful medium. But learning how to trust and work with one another took time. We were often made to feel "suspect." Linda Shen recalls, "It was devastating to find the [San Francisco] community did not automatically support us. Since I was from Connecticut, it made it all the more difficult, even though I truly aspired to help."

I, too, remember a meeting in 1974, with community members who attacked me for "being an outsider who couldn't possibly understand the problems of the community." It was awkward and frustrating. I thought: here I am, born and raised in the Bay Area, moved to New York on my own to get training, and I return to find an unwelcome community. I responded by saying it was unfair to prejudge me and that a reporter's accountability to the community should be questioned only after he or she failed to generate more stories than had previously been reported.

Being Aggressive

Satisfying the community was just one requirement. Beyond that hurdle was another: learning the basics. We had to know where and how to get background information quickly, interview people efficiently, write clearly and concisely, use our voices effectively, and deliver information believably before the camera. Having to report two to four stories daily—always under deadline—helped hone those skills.

Almost all of us agree, however, that one of the most difficult aspects of reporting is overcoming a cultural tendency *not* to be aggressive. As Asian Americans, we are taught to be polite and to stay out of other people's business—tenets contrary to the requirements of the job. How to develop assertiveness on and off camera and how to be direct became our greatest challenges. Assertiveness went beyond obtaining the information needed for a story; it went to the very basis of survival in the business. As reporters we had to communicate what we wanted to the mostly male camera crew. Cooperation was not necessarily forthcoming. The older, more experienced technicians generally resented taking orders from young, inexperienced, minority women. Film editors, assignment editors, and writers often shared that attitude. We had to learn how to develop effective communication skills with our co-workers as well as the audience.

Chicago anchor, Linda Yu says the work changed her. "People won't believe today that this person that I am used to barely speak above a whisper, always went to the back of the line, and glued herself to the wall. For a shy, retiring little girl, this is the one profession which got me out, forced me to stay outgoing, and develop confidence."

We learned that self-confidence and a strong sense of ourselves are needed to sustain us in the field. Emerald Yeh, news anchor with a San Francisco station, and formerly a reporter for Cable News Network in Atlanta, Georgia, and a Portland, Oregon, station, says "One has to become strong within—emotionally and psychologically. Being an anchor puts you on the line. You are an easy scapegoat if things aren't going well. But you can't let other people feel good or bad about you. You have to make your own judgment and do the best you can, based on *your* range of experience. Know yourself and be secure in that."

Conflicts on the Job

Television reporting is not for everyone, as some of us trailblazers soon discovered. After working as a reporter for CBS News in New York, Atlanta, and Chicago for nearly two years, Genny Lim eventually found the job unsuitable to her temperament. She recalls the excitement of covering the story of Wounded Knee, stealthily entering the Indian compound that had been restricted to news personnel, and obtaining an exclusive interview with American Indian Movement leader Dennis Banks.

"CBS wouldn't run it. . . . They said the pieces were too sympathetic to Indians, too slanted. I had no intention of doing that. I was reporting what I saw." But, the incident crystallized for Lim what she believed to be the racist, sexist, and paternalistic attitudes of the network. "I felt we [Asian American women] were ten years ahead of the times." She resigned. She took on some freelance assignments with East Coast educational stations and hosted a San Francisco public affairs show, but left television for good in 1977. Since that time Lim has concentrated on creative writing.

Roberta Wong, formerly with KRON-TV in San Francisco, has also left television. Though she has been able to apply her reporting, writing, and broadcasting skills to her work in public relations, she prefers the economic freedom and less demanding schedule of her new job.

Linda Shen, now a small business entrepreneur, has harsh memories of her journalism work, which took her from New York to San Francisco and then Washington, D.C. "I was the '60s idealist. I wanted to work for social change but found few opportunities to do so. There were minor triumphs, but most of the stories I found despicable. . . . One time, I was sent out to interview a black welfare mother who had lost everything in a fire. On my return, the desk asked, 'Did you get her to cry on camera?' Personally, I was heartbroken because I had caused this woman public anguish. Even though I was handsomely rewarded, it wasn't worth it. I was miserable, and it wasn't made any better by office politics." In the end, Shen says, "Nobody's to blame. It was just a conflict of values."

But Shen also recalls some fonder moments. "There were aspects of the job I liked. With my liberal arts background, reporting was perfect for the overeducated dilettante. You could dabble in this and that, then leave. You were exposed to different segments of society. I especially liked the visual experience and the teamwork involved in putting together stories."

Sherry Hu, a reporter for KPIX in San Francisco since 1980, also loves these aspects of the job. "I love learning new things, meeting

different people, and the pace. I've found a niche for myself. I feel fulfilled at the end of the day, and I love the people I work with."

Though the job is exciting, San Francisco reporter Linda Yee quickly
points out that "it's not a glamorous job. You work long, hard hours,
and because of the visibility of the job, you lack some privacy outside of
work." Public recognition, awards, speaking engagements, breaking
news stories, and big money certainly sound glamorous, but these
things alone could never sustain anybody in this high-pressure, competitive field where job security is nonexistent. The more enduring
traits, such as a love of the business and determination, are essential to
survival in broadcast journalism.

One who intends to stay is Wendy Tokuda. "I am committed to the
work and love what I do. There are aspects of the job that bother me. I
find the tendency toward entertainment a matter of concern and am
troubled that the medium being visual sometimes affects the kinds
of stories that are reported, but I try to know the entire newscast, edit
and write as much copy as possible, and maintain high journalistic
standards."

Personal Life

Kaity Tong, WABC-TV News anchor in New York, formerly with Sacramento's KCRA and San Francisco's KPIX, has learned to live with
critics, but she has had a harder time adjusting to job relocations. A
Bryn Mawr graduate and native of the East Coast, Tong says being back
in New York suits her, though professional moves have sometimes been
hard on her personal life. She is married to Bob Long, a television
producer whose work used to keep him in Los Angeles a great deal. The
couple maintained two residences for many years, commuting back and
forth from Sacramento. Her job in New York increased the commute by
three thousand miles for nearly a year and a half. Her husband now lives
in New York, but personal sacrifices had to be made in the name of
professional ambition.

Linda Yu thinks that any woman who chooses a time-consuming and
competitive career, such as journalism, must make some sacrifices when
it comes to time for herself and her relationships. "I worked a lot of

seven-day weeks, twelve- to fifteen-hour days for years until I met my husband and decided it was time to slow down to a more reasonable five- or six-day week, and occasionally eight-hour days."

For Wendy Tokuda, who anchored news at 6 P.M. and 11 P.M. for seven years, maintaining private time has become "like a career." She guards it judiciously so she has time to spend with her family. "Before I had the children, I concentrated on developing my career; there was some control in my life, but I had to relinquish those controls the minute Mikka was born." Though the birth of her second child initially caused Tokuda to doubt whether she could successfully "juggle another ring," Maggie's arrival helped Tokuda understand how much she wanted both family and career.

But Tokuda has had to make some major adjustments to balance the demands of children and work. "I try to do everything, but I realize I can't," she admits. For example, she has cut back some of her participation in time-consuming community benefits, and in 1987 she asked her station to relieve her of her late-night anchor slot. Though this cuts her exposure substantially, the new schedule yields two much-desired results: she now can do reporting again and also spend more time with her two girls and husband, all of whom she happily acknowledges as the "best things that have happened to me." A live-in nanny provided help in the early days, but Tokuda largely credits her husband, independent producer Richard Hall, for his support and contribution in raising the family. "Richard and the girls . . . keep my life in balance," she says.

The schedule of street reporters generally is more time-consuming and erratic than that of news anchors. Of the street reporters at KPIX in San Francisco who have had children in recent years, Sherry Hu points out that several have elected to work only part time. Shortly before the birth of her child, Linda Yu said, "I realize now that professional ambition isn't everything. Perhaps, I will feel again that I've made it [if] after my child is born, I learn to balance one more important element in life."

Future Trends

With the presence of Asian American women in the major television stations across the country and our involvement in organizations such as the Asian American Journalists Association, which formed in the early 1980s to encourage professional development and to offer scholarships to aspiring journalists, the future looks promising to many. But some major problems remain.

Senior member of the broadcasting community, Barbara Tanabe, is bothered that so few Asian American men are given a chance in the business. While less than a handful have co-anchored news in the smaller markets, including Seattle, Washington, where Ken Woo once anchored, and Honolulu, Hawaii, where Dalton Tanaoka recently began as a news anchor, no male has anchored in the larger markets. Veteran reporters, David Louie of KGO-TV in San Francisco and ABC correspondent Ken Kashiwahara both aspire to anchor, but neither has been approached. "It's been the women who have been nurtured for anchoring," says Louie.

The pressure applied in the early years was not about hiring Asian men or women; it was applied to hiring Asians. Yet Asian females had an automatic edge. We were both minority and women, "two-pointers," making us particularly attractive to television management. As a result, more job opportunities were open to Asian women and remain so today. Vic Lee, reporter for San Francisco's KRON-TV and former member of the management team at the station, has seen the issue from both sides. "Years ago when there were quotas, Asian females had the advantage of being minority and women. Then the consultants were brought in, and they conducted surveys which showed viewers found [white] male/minority female anchor teams acceptable but not the other way around. This makes it difficult for Asian males to find jobs, and with so few role models around, young men are discouraged."

In 1985 Asian American women anchored news in four out of the five largest markets in the country: Kaity Tong and Connie Chung in New York; Tritia Toyota and Joanne Ishimine in Los Angeles; Linda Yu in Chicago; and Wendy Tokuda and Emerald Yeh in San Francisco. It is the absence of Asian American male anchors in these major markets that is noteworthy.

This stark imbalance of females and males on television screens across the country raises questions about the greater and continued acceptability of Asian women by television management and viewers. The

stereotypes attributed to Asian Americans have had a large part in establishing and perpetuating the pattern. The Asian male stereotype is less
positive than the female's, says San Francisco reporter David Louie.
"Asian men are seen as houseboys, cowering servants, not intellectual.
We just don't fit in." Tokuda feels that the presence of Asian reporters
and anchors has exposed viewers to another view of Asian women—as
professionals—but admits there is ongoing testing as well. The stereotyping of Asian females as "exotic," "mysterious," "China dolls," "sex
kittens" is not dead. But as one reporter points out, "You can play up
that role as much as you want. Still you have to be good, if not better, at
the job to keep it."

The call for social change in the 1970s inaugurated the presence of
Asian women in the broadcast industry. But we still are constantly proving ourselves as competent veteran writers, reporters, and anchors in
order to remain in the profession, and to open doors for other Asian
Americans. At the same time, and like many other working women, we
learn to survive in the business while balancing our family and personal
lives. The challenges now before Asian American women journalists,
and the chance for professional and personal fulfillment in today's electronic age, can and often do offset the conflicts we have all faced in the
past fifteen years of broadcasting history. However, as long as there is the
sex imbalance—the lack of Asian men in broadcasting—we have not
reached equity. This situation is a bittersweet success for us as Asian
American women.

EDITOR'S NOTE: Author Felicia Lowe left television reporting in the
late 1970s. She turned her skills to independent documentary filmmak-
ing so that she could work on longer pieces that also had a longer life
than a broadcast news story. Her credits include *China: Land of My
Father* and *Carved in Silence*. Both documentaries have won awards and
are being shown in schools and libraries across the country.

The Gap between Striving and Achieving: The Case of Asian American Women

DEBORAH WOO

Much academic research on Asian Americans tends to underscore their success, a success which is attributed almost always to a cultural emphasis on education, hard work, and thrift. Less familiar is the story of potential not fully realized. For example, despite the appearance of being successful and highly educated, Asian American women do not necessarily gain the kind of recognition or rewards they deserve.

The story of unfulfilled dreams remains unwritten for many Asian Americans. It is specifically this story about the gap between striving and achieving that I am concerned with here. Conventional wisdom obscures the discrepancy by looking primarily at whether society is adequately rewarding individuals. By comparing how minorities as disadvantaged groups are doing relative to each other, the tendency is to view Asian Americans as a "model minority." This practice programs us to ignore structural barriers and inequities and to insist that any problems are simply due to different cultural values or failure of individual effort.

Myths about the Asian American community derive from many sources. All ethnic groups develop their own cultural myths. Sometimes, however, they create myths out of historical necessity, as a matter of subterfuge and survival. Chinese Americans, for example, were motivated to create new myths because institutional opportunities were closed off to them. Succeeding in America meant they had to invent fake aspects of an "Oriental culture," which became the beginning of the Chinatown tourist industry.

What has been referred to as the "model minority myth," however, essentially originated from without. The idea that Asian Americans have been a successful group has been a popular news media theme for the last twenty years. It has become a basis for cutbacks in governmental support for all ethnic minorities—for Asian Americans because they apparently are already successful as a group; for other ethnic minorities because they are presumably not working as hard as Asian Americans or they would not need assistance. Critics of this view argue that the portrayal of Asian Americans as socially and economically successful ignores fundamental inequities. That is, the question "Why have Asians been successful vis-à-vis other minorities?" has been asked at the expense of another equally important question: "What has kept Asians from *fully* reaping the fruits of their education and hard work?"

The achievements of Asian Americans are part reality, part myth. Part of the reality is that a highly visible group of Asian Americans are college-educated, occupationally well-situated, and earning relatively high incomes. The myth, however, is that hard work reaps commensurate rewards. This essay documents the gap between the level of education and subsequent occupational or income gains.

The Roots and Contours of the "Model Minority" Concept

Since World War II, social researchers and news media personnel have been quick to assert that Asian Americans excel over other ethnic groups in terms of earnings, education, and occupation. Asian Americans are said to save more, study more, work more, and so achieve more. The reason given: a cultural emphasis on education and hard work. Implicit in this view is a social judgment and moral injunction: if Asian Americans can make it on their own, why can't other minorities?

While the story of Asian American women workers is only beginning to be pieced together, the success theme is already being sung. The image prevails that despite cultural and racial oppression, they are somehow rapidly assimilating into the mainstream. As workers, they participate in the labor force at rates higher than all others, including Anglo women. Those Asian American women who pursue higher education surpass other women, and even men, in this respect. Moreover, they have acquired a reputation for not only being conscientious and industrious but docile, compliant, and uncomplaining as well.

In the last few decades American women in general have been demanding "equal pay for equal work," the legitimation of housework as work that needs to be recompensed, and greater representation in the professional fields. These demands, however, have not usually come from Asian American women. From the perspective of those in power, this reluctance to complain is another feature of the "model minority." But for those who seek to uncover employment abuses, the unwillingness to talk about problems on the job is itself a problem. The garment industry, for example, is a major area of exploitation, yet it is also one that is difficult to investigate and control. In a 1983 report on the Concentrated Employment Program of the California Department of Industrial Relations, it was noted:

> The major problem for investigators in San Francisco is that the Chinese community is very close-knit, and employers and employees cooperate in refusing to speak to investigators. In two years of enforcing the Garment Registration Act, the CEP has never received a complaint from an Asian employee. The few complaints received have been from Anglo or Latin workers.[1]

While many have argued vociferously either for or against the model minority concept, Asian Americans in general have been ambivalent in this regard. Asian Americans experience pride in achievement born of hard work and self-sacrifice, but at the same time, they resist the implication that all is well. Data provided here indicate that Asian Americans have not been successful in terms of benefitting fully, (i.e., monetarily), from their education. It is a myth that Asian Americans have proven the American Dream. How does this myth develop?

The working consumer: income and cost of living. One striking feature about Asian Americans is that they are geographically concentrated in areas where both income and cost of living are very high. In 1970, 80 percent of the total Asian American population resided in five states—California, Hawaii, Illinois, New York, and Washington. Furthermore, 59 percent of Chinese, Filipino, and Japanese Americans were concentrated in only 5 of the 243 Standard Metropolitan Statistical Areas (SMSA) in the United States—Chicago, Honolulu, Los Angeles/Long Beach, New York, and San Francisco/Oakland.[2] The 1980 census shows that immigration during the intervening decade has not only produced dramatic increases, especially in the Filipino and Chinese populations, but has also continued the overwhelming tendency for these groups to concentrate in the same geographical areas, especially those in California.[3] Interestingly enough, the very existence of large Asian communities in the West has stimulated among more recent refugee populations what is now officially referred to as "secondary migration," that is, the movement of refugees away from their sponsoring communities (usually places where there was no sizeable Asian population prior to their own arrival) to those areas where there are well-established Asian communities.[4]

This residential pattern means that while Asian Americans may earn more by living in high-income areas, they also pay more as consumers. The additional earning power gained from living in San Francisco or Los Angeles, say, is absorbed by the high cost of living in such cities. National income averages which compare the income of Asian American women with that of the more broadly dispersed Anglo women systematically distort the picture. Indeed, if we compare women within the same area, Asian American women are frequently less well-off than Anglo American females, and the difference between women pales when compared with Anglo males, whose mean income is much higher than that of any group of women.[5]

When we consider the large immigrant Asian population and the language barriers that restrict women to menial or entry-level jobs, we are talking about a group that not only earns minimum wage or less, but one whose purchasing power is substantially undermined by living in metropolitan areas of states where the cost of living is unusually high.

Another striking pattern about Asian American female employment is the high rate of labor force participation. Asian American women are more likely than Anglo American women to work full time and year round. The model minority interpretation tends to assume that mere high labor force participation is a sign of successful employment. One important factor motivating minority women to enter the work force, however, is the need to supplement family resources. For Anglo American women some of the necessity for working is partly offset by the fact that they often share in the higher incomes of Anglo males, who tend not only to earn more than all other groups but, as noted earlier, also tend to receive higher returns on their education. Moreover, once regional variation is adjusted for, Filipino and Chinese Americans had a median annual income equivalent to black males in four mainland SMSAs—Chicago, Los Angeles/Long Beach, New York, San Francisco/Oakland.[6] Census statistics point to the relatively lower earning capacity of Asian males compared to Anglo males, suggesting that Asian American women enter the work force to help compensate for this inequality. Thus, the mere fact of high employment must be read cautiously and analyzed within a larger context.

The different faces of immigration. Over the last decade immigration has expanded the Chinese population by 85.3 percent, making it the largest Asian group in the country at 806,027, and has swelled the Filipino population by 125.8 percent, making it the second largest at 774,640. Hence at present the majority of Chinese American and Filipino American women are foreign-born. In addition the Asian American "success story" is misleading in part because of a select group of these immigrants: foreign-educated professionals.

Since 1965 U.S. immigration laws have given priority to seven categories of individuals. Two of the seven allow admittance of people with special occupational skills or services needed in the United States. Four categories facilitate family reunification, and the last applies only to refugees. While occupation is estimated to account for no more than 20 percent of all visas, professionals are not precluded from entering under other preference categories. Yet this select group is frequently offered as evidence of the upward mobility possible in America when Asian Americans who are born and raised in the United States are far less likely to reach the doctoral level in their education. Over two-thirds of Asians with doctorates in the United States are trained and educated abroad.[7]

Also overlooked in some analyses is a great deal of downward mobility among the foreign-born. For example, while foreign-educated health professionals are given preferential status for entry into this country, restrictive licensing requirements deny them the opportunity to practice or utilize their special skills. They are told that their educational credentials, experience, and certifications are inadequate. Consequently, for many the only alternatives are menial labor or unemployment.[8] Other highly educated immigrants become owner/managers of Asian businesses, which also suggests downward mobility and an inability to find jobs in their field of expertise.

"Professional" obscures more than it reveals. Another major reason for the perception of "model minority" is that the census categories implying success, "professional-managerial" or "executive, administrative, managerial," frequently camouflage important inconsistencies with this image of success. As managers, Asian Americans, usually male, are concentrated in certain occupations. They tend to be self-employed in small-scale wholesale and retail trade and manufacturing. They are rarely buyers, sales managers, administrators, or salaried managers in large-scale retail trade, communications, or public utilities. Among foreign-born Asian women, executive-managerial status is limited primarily to auditors and accountants.[9]

In general, Asian American women with a college education are concentrated in narrow and select, usually less prestigious, rungs of the "professional-managerial" class. In 1970, 27 percent of native-born Japanese women were either elementary or secondary school teachers. Registered nurses made up the next largest group. Foreign-born Filipino women found this to be their single most important area of employment, with 19 percent being nurses. They were least represented in the more prestigious professions—physicians, judges, dentists, law professors, and lawyers.[10] In 1980 foreign-born Asian women with four or more years of college were most likely to find jobs in administrative support or clerical occupations.

Self-help through "taking care of one's own." Much of what is considered ideal or model behavior in American society is based on Anglo-Saxon, Protestant values. Chief among them is an ethic of individual self-help, of doing without outside assistance or governmental support. On the other hand, Asian Americans have historically relied to a large extent on family or community resources. Their tightly-knit communities tend to be fairly closed to the outside world, even when under economic hardship. Many below the poverty level do not receive any form of public assistance.[11] Even if we include social security benefits as a form of supplementary income, the proportion of Asian Americans who use them is again very low, much lower than that for Anglo Americans. [12] Asian American families, in fact, are more likely than Anglo American families to bear economic hardships on their own.

While Asian Americans appear to have been self-sufficient as communities, we need to ask, at what personal cost? Moreover, have they as a group reaped rewards commensurate with their efforts? The following section presents data which document that while Asian American women may be motivated to achieve through education, monetary returns for them are less than for other groups.

The Nature of Inequality

The decision to use white males as the predominant reference group within the United States is a politically charged issue. When women raise and push the issue of "comparable worth," of "equal pay for equal work," they argue that women frequently do work equivalent to men's, but are paid far less for it.

The same argument can be made for Asian American women, and the evidence of inequality is staggering. For example, after adjustments are made for occupational prestige, age, education, weeks worked, hours worked each week, and state of residence in 1975, Chinese American women could be expected to earn only 70 percent of the majority male income. Even among the college-educated, Chinese American women fared least well, making only 42 percent of what majority males earned. As we noted earlier, the mean income of all women, Anglo and Asian, was far below that of Anglo males in 1970 and 1980. This was true for both native-born and foreign-born Asians. In 1970 Anglo women earned only 54 percent of what their male counterparts did. Native-born Asian American women, depending on the particular ethnic group, earned anywhere from 49 to 57 percent of what Anglo males earned. In 1980, this inequity persisted.

Another way of thinking about comparable worth is not to focus only on what individuals do on the job, but on what they bring to the job as well. Because formal education is one measure of merit in American society and because it is most frequently perceived as the means to upward mobility, we would expect greater education to have greater payoffs.

Asian American women tend to be extraordinarily successful in terms of attaining higher education. Filipino American women have the highest college completion rate of all women and graduate at a rate 50 percent greater than that of majority males. Chinese American and Japanese American women follow closely behind, exceeding both the majority male and female rate of college completion. [13] Higher levels of education, however, bring lower returns for Asian American women than they do for other groups.

While education enhances earnings capability, the return on education for Asian American women is not as great as that for other women, and is well below parity with white males. Data on Asian American women in the five SMSAs where they are concentrated bear this out. [14] In 1980 all these women fell far behind Anglo males in what they earned in relation to their college education. Between 8 and 16 percent of native-born women earned $21,200 compared to 50 percent of Anglo males. Similar patterns were found among college-educated foreign-born women.

The fact that Asian American women do not reap the income benefits one might expect given their high levels of educational achievement raises questions about the reasons for such inequality. To what extent is this discrepancy based on outright discrimination? On self-imposed limitations related to cultural modesty? The absence of certain social or interpersonal skills required for upper managerial positions? Or institutional factors beyond their control? It is beyond the scope of this paper to address such concerns. However, the fact of inequality is itself noteworthy and poorly appreciated.

In general, Asian American women usually are overrepresented in clerical or administrative support jobs. While there is a somewhat greater tendency for foreign-born college-educated Asian women to find clerical-related jobs, both native- and foreign-born women have learned that clerical work is the area where they are most easily employed. In fact, in 1970 a third of native-born Chinese women were doing clerical work. A decade later Filipino women were concentrated there. In addition Asian American women tend to be overrepresented as cashiers, file clerks, office machine operators, and typists. They are less likely to get jobs as secretaries or receptionists. The former occupations not only carry less prestige but generally have "little or no decision-making authority, low mobility and low public contact." [15]

In short, education may improve one's chances for success, but it cannot promise the American Dream. For Asian American women education seems to serve less as an opportunity for upward mobility than as protection against jobs as service or assembly workers, or as machine operatives—all areas where foreign-born Asian women are far more likely to find themselves.

Conclusion

In this essay I have attempted to direct our attention on the gap between achievement and reward, specifically the failure to reward monetarily those who have demonstrated competence. Asian American women, like Asian American men, have been touted as "model minorities," praised for their outstanding achievements. The concept of model minority, however, obscures the fact that one's accomplishments are not adequately recognized in terms of commensurate income or choice of occupation. By focusing on the achievements of one minority in relation to another, our attention is diverted from larger institutional and historical factors which influence a group's success. Each ethnic group has a different history, and a simplistic method of modeling which assumes the experience of all immigrants is the same ignores the sociostructural context in which a certain kind of achievement occurred. For example, World War II enabled many Asian Americans who were technically trained and highly educated to move into lucrative war-related industries. [16] More recently, Korean immigrants during the 1960s were able to capitalize on the fast-growing demand for wigs in the United States. It was not simply cultural ingenuity or individual hard work which made them successful in this enterprise, but the fact that Korean immigrants were in the unique position of being able to import cheap hair products from their mother country. [17]

Just as there are structural opportunities, so there are structural barriers. However, the persistent emphasis in American society on individual effort deflects attention away from such barriers and creates self-doubt among those who have not "made it." The myth that Asian Americans have succeeded as a group, when in actuality there are serious discrepancies between effort and achievement, and between achievement and reward, adds still further to this self-doubt.

While others have also pointed out the myth of the model minority, I want to add that myths do have social functions. It would be a mistake to dismiss the model minority concept as merely a myth. Asian Americans are—however inappropriately—thrust into the role of being models for other minorities.

A closer look at the images associated with Asians as a model minority group suggests competing or contradictory themes. One image is that Asian Americans exemplify a competitive spirit enabling them to overcome structural barriers through perseverance and ingenuity. On the other hand, they are also seen as complacent, content with their social lot, and expecting little in the way of outside help. A third image is that Asian Americans are experts at assimilation, demonstrating that this society still functions as a melting pot. Their values are sometimes equated with white, middle-class, Protestant values of hard work, determination, and thrift. Opposing this image, however, is still another, namely that Asian Americans have succeeded because they possess cultural values unique to them as a group—their family-centeredness and long tradition of reverence for scholarly achievement, for example.

Perhaps, then, this is why so many readily accept the myth, whose tenacity is due to its being vague and broad enough to appeal to a variety of different groups. Yet to the extent that the myth is based on misconceptions, we are called upon to reexamine it more closely in an effort to narrow the gap between striving and achieving.[18]

PART FOUR

Where Rivers Merge: Generations

Introduction

Learning about ourselves and our history is an ongoing process. The lessons come from sources all around us—historical events, mass media, conversations, introspection, and especially our families. What we learn may not always be what we wish to pass on to our children. So we are spurred to assess and reassess what we feel is important. Sometimes the lessons involve cultural and generational conflicts that cannot be reconciled easily, but leave an indelible imprint on our minds and hearts nonetheless.

One case of generational and cultural conflict developed as American-born children adopted more Western behaviors and attitudes. In Beheroze Shroff's "Mother," the speaker reflects angrily on restriction of women to motherhood in South Asian cultures. A strong-willed Kartar Dhillon in "Parrot's Beak" recounts conflicts with her immigrant mother and her traditional husband, which convince her to raise her own children differently. Generational tensions are quietly presented and lovingly resolved among the members of a Japanese American family in "The Loom" by R. A. Sasaki. The sansei, or third-generation, daughters learn to recognize and respond to their mother's culturally different ways of communicating, grieving, and maturing.

The father-daughter tie is the subject of Cecilia Brainard's "Waiting for Papa's Return," in which a Filipina eagerly awaits the return of her adored father who can no longer comfort her.

There are other elders in the community besides parents from whom we learn about our cultural heritage and life in general. Most early Asian immigrants to America were male. Some were married but could not bring their wives with them. Others came as bachelors and remained unmarried during the decades they lived in this country. These men formed the original ethnic communities which came to be known as

Chinatown and Manilatown. The woman in Virginia Cerenio's "Dreams of Manong Frankie" shares friendly moments with one of these elderly bachelors.

Like the inevitable merging of river into sea, sea into ocean, our lives are connected with those of our ancestors. Through these bonds, we discover what contributes to the way we are today, what ties we have to the past, and how to strengthen ourselves for the future.

Mother

BEHEROZE F. SHROFF

Sucked into currents
of married life at nineteen,
your youth and energy were harnessed
to serve a mother-in-law's sickbed.

Husband, pushed into background,
the family machine took over;
Speculating the promise
of the bride's fruitful womb,
they turned uneager
after the yield of three years:
"Only daughters?"

They required your reproductive organs
to function again,
and as aids offered prayers,
holy water from Babas
and charms from Gurus.

Like a bucket of water
scraped out of a low-lying well,
a son was obtained from you,

claimed from birth by each aunt and uncle
to be the product of *their* holy effort.

The Father, made hero
was congratulated, praised, feted.

The Mother was given
tips on child-rearing.

The Loom

R. A. SASAKI

And out of a pattern of lies, art weaves the truth.
—*D. H. Lawrence*

It was when Cathy died that the other Terasaki sisters began to think that something was wrong with their mother. Sharon and Jo were home for the weekend, and when the phone call came they had gone up to her room with the shocking news, barely able to speak through their tears. Sharon had to raise her voice so her mother could hear the awful words, choked out like bits of shattered glass, while Jo watched what seemed like anger pull her mother's face into a solemn frown.

"You see?" their mother said. Her voice, harsh and trembling with a shocking vehemence, startled the two sisters even in their grief. "Daddy told her not to go mountain climbing. He said it was too dangerous. She didn't listen."

Recalling her words later, Jo felt chilled.

They had always known about their mother's "ways"—the way she would snip off their straight black hair when they were children as soon as it grew past their ears, saying that hair too long would give people the wrong idea. Then later, when they were grown and defiant and wore their hair down to their waists, she would continue to campaign by lifting the long strands and snipping at them with her fingers. There was also the way she would tear through the house in a frenzy of cleaning just before they left on a family vacation, "in case there's a fire or someone breaks in and *yoso no hito* have to come in." They never understood if it was the firemen, the police, or the burglar before whose eyes she would be mortally shamed if her house were not spotless. It was even in the way she cooked. She was governed not by inspiration or taste, but by what "they" did. The clothes she chose for them were what "they" were wearing these days. Who is this "they," her daughters always wanted to ask her. Her idiosyncrasies were a source of mild frustration to which the girls were more or less resigned. "Oh, Mom," they would groan, or, to each other: "That's just Mom."

But this.

"It was as though she didn't feel anything at all," Jo recounted to her eldest sister, Linda, who had come home from Germany for the funeral. "It was as though all she could think about was that Cathy had broken the rules."

It wasn't until their father had come home that their mother cried, swept along in the wake of his massive grief. He had been away on a weekend fishing trip, and they had tried to get in touch with him, but failed. Jo had telephoned the highway patrol and park rangers at all his favorite fishing spots, saying, "No, don't tell him that his daughter has died. Would you just tell him to come home as soon as possible?" And it was Jo who was standing at the window watching when his truck turned the corner for home. The three women went down to the basement together. He and his fishing buddy had just emerged from the dusty, fish-odorous truck, and he was rolling up the garage door when they reached him. He was caught between the bright spring sunlight and the dark coolness of the basement. His hand still on the garage door, he heard the news of his daughter's death. Their mother told him, with a hint of fear in her voice. He cried, as children cry who have awakened in the night to a nameless terror, a nameless grief; and for a suspended moment, as he stood alone sobbing his dead daughter's name, the three women deferred to the sanctity of his suffering. Then Sharon moved to encircle him in her arms, clinging flimsily to him against the tremendous isolation of grief.

It was only then that their mother had cried, but it seemed almost vicarious, as if she had needed their father to process the raw stuff of life into personal emotion. Not once since the death had she talked about her own feelings. Not ever, her daughters now realized.

"It would probably do Mom good to get away for a while," Linda said. "I was thinking of taking her to Germany with me when I go back, just for a few weeks. She's never been anywhere. A change of scene might be just what she needs. Don't you think?"

"I suppose it's worth a try," said Jo.

So it was decided that when Linda flew back to join her husband, who was stationed in Heidelberg, their mother would go with her and stay a month. Except for a visit to Japan with her own mother when she was sixteen, it was their mother's first trip abroad. At first she was hesitant, but their father encouraged her; he would have gone too if he didn't have to stay and run the business.

It was hard to imagine their mother outside the context of their house. She had always been there when the children came back from school; in fact, the sisters had never had babysitters. Now, as they watched her at the airport, so small and sweet with her large purse clutched tightly in both hands and her new suitcase neatly packed and properly tagged beside her, they wondered just who this little person was, this person who was their mother.

She had grown up in San Francisco, wearing the two faces of a second generation child born of immigrant parents. The two faces never met; there was no common thread running through both worlds. The duality was unplanned, untaught. Perhaps it had begun the first day of school when she couldn't understand the teacher and Eleanor Leland had called her a "Jap" and she cried. Before then there had never been a need to sort out her identity; she had met life headlong and with the confidence of a child.

Her world had been the old Victorian flat in which her mother took in boarders—the long, narrow corridor, the spiral stairway, the quilts covered with bright Japanese cloth, and the smell of fish cooking in the kitchen. She had accepted without question the people who padded in and out of her world on stockinged feet; they all seemed to be friends of the family. She never wondered why most of them were men, and it never occurred to her child's mind to ask why they didn't have their own families. The men often couldn't pay, but they were always grateful. They lounged in doorways and had teasing affectionate words for her and her sister. Then they would disappear, for a month, for six months, a year. Time, to a child, was boundless and unmeasurable. Later crates of fruit would arrive and be stacked in the corridor.

"From Sato-san," her mother would say, or "*Kudoh-san kara.*" The young men sometimes came back to visit with new hats set jauntily on their heads, if luck was good. But often luck was not good, and they came back to stay, again and again, each stay longer than the last; and each time they would tease less and drink more with her father in the back room. The slap of cards rose over the low mumble of their longing and despair. All this she accepted as her world.

The Victorian house which contained her world was on Pine Street, and so it was known as "Pine" to the young adventurers from her parents' native Wakayama prefecture in Japan who made their way from the docks of Osaka to the lettuce fields and fruit orchards of California. "Stay at Pine," the word passed along the grapevine, "Moriwaki-san will take care of you."

It was a short walk down the Buchanan Street hill from Pine to the flats where the Japanese community had taken root and was thriving like a tree whose seed had blown in from the Pacific and had held fast in this nook, this fold in the city's many gradations. When she was a little older her world expanded beyond the Victorian called Pine. It expanded toward the heart of this community, toward the little shops from which her mother returned each day, string bag bulging with newspaper-wrapped parcels and a long white radish or two. She played hide-and-seek among the barrels of pickles and sacks of rice piled high in the garage which claimed to be the American Fish Market, while her mother exchanged news of the comings and goings of the community over the fish counter. "Ship coming in Friday? Do you think Yamashita-san's picture bride will come? She's in for a surprise!"

At the age of five she roller skated to the corner of her block, then on sudden impulse turned the corner and started down the Buchanan Street hill. Her elder sister, Keiko, who had expected her to turn around and come right back, threw down her jumprope and ran after her, screaming for her to stop. But she didn't stop. She made it all the way to the bottom, cheeks flushed red and black hair flying, before shooting off the curb and crumpling in the street. Her hands and knees were scraped raw, but she was laughing.

Before that first day of school there had been no need to look above Pine Street, where the city reached upwards to the Pacific Heights area and the splendid mansions of the rich, white people. The only Japanese who went to Pacific Heights were the ones employed to do housecleaning as day laborers. She had always known what was on the other side of Pine Street, and accepted easily that it was not part of her world.

When it came time for her to go to school, she was not sent to the same school as the other Japanese American children because Pine was on the edge of Japantown and in a different school district. She was the only Japanese in her class. And from the instant Eleanor Leland pulled up the corners of her eyes at her, sneering "Jap!," a kind of radar system went to work in her. Afterward she always acted with caution in new surroundings, blending in like a chameleon for survival. There were two things she would never do again: One was to forget the girl's name who had called her a Jap; the other was to cry.

She did her best to blend in. Though separated from the others by her features and her native tongue, she tried to be as inconspicuous as possible. If she didn't understand what the teacher said, she watched the other children and copied them. She listened carefully to the teacher and didn't do anything that might provoke criticism. If she couldn't be outstanding she at least wanted to be invisible.

She succeeded. She muted her colors and blended in. She was a quiet student and the other children got used to her; some were even nice to her. But she was still not really a part of their world because she was not really herself.

At the end of each school day she went home to the dark, narrow corridors of the old Victorian and the soothing, unconscious jumble of two tongues which was the two generations' compromise for the sake of communication. Theirs was a comfortable language, like a comfortable old sweater that had been well-washed and rendered shapeless by wear. She would never wear it outside of the house. It was a personal thing, like a hole in one's sock, which was perfectly alright at home but would be a horrible embarrassment if seen by *yoso no hito*.

In the outside world—the *hakujin* world—there was a watchdog at work which rigorously edited out Japanese words and mannerisms when she spoke. Her words became formal, carefully chosen and somewhat artificial. She never felt they conveyed what she really felt, what she really was, because what she really was was unacceptable. In the realm of behavior, the watchdog was a tyrant. Respectability, as defined by popular novels and Hollywood heroines, must be upheld at all costs. How could she explain about the young men lounging in the doorways of her home and drinking in the back room with her father? How could she admit to the stories of the immigrant women who came to her mother desperate for protection from the beatings by their frenzied husbands? It was all so far from the drawing rooms of Jane Austen and the virtue and gallantry of Hollywood. The Japanese who passed through her house could drink, gamble, and philander, but she would never acknowledge it. She could admit to no weakness, no peculiarity. She would be irreproachable. She would be American.

Poverty was irreproachably American in the Depression years. Her father's Oriental art goods business on Union Square had survived the 1906 earthquake only to be done in by the dishonesty of a *hakujin* partner who absconded with the gross receipts and the company car. The family survived on piecework and potatoes. Her mother organized a group of immigrant ladies to crochet window shade rings. They got a penny apiece from the stores on Grant Avenue. Her father strung plastic birds onto multicolored rings. As they sat working in the back room day after day, they must have dreamed of better times. They had all gambled the known for the unknown when they left Japan to come to America. Apparently it took more than hard work. They could work themselves to death for pennies. Entrepreneurial ventures were risky. They wanted to spare their sons and daughters this insecurity and hardship. Education was the key that would open the magical doors to a better future. Not that they hadn't been educated in Japan; indeed, some of them were better educated than the people whose houses they cleaned on California Street. But they felt the key was an American education, a college education. Immigrant sons and immigrant daughters would fulfill their dreams.

She and her peers acquiesced in this dream. After all, wasn't it the same as their own? To succeed, to be irreproachable, to be American? She would be a smart career girl in a tailored suit, beautiful, and bold—an American girl.

After the Depression her father opened a novelty store on Grant Avenue, and she was able to go to college. She set forth into the unknown with a generation of immigrant sons and daughters, all fortified by their mutual vision of the American dream.

They did everything right. They lived at home to save expenses. Each morning they woke up at dawn to catch the bus to the ferry building. They studied on the ferry as it made the bay crossing, and studied on the train from the Berkeley marina to Shattuck, a few blocks from the majestic buildings of the University of California. They studied for hours in the isolation of the library on campus. They brought bag lunches from the dark kitchens of old Japantown flats and ate on the manicured grass or at the Japanese Students' Club off campus. They went to football games and rooted for the home team. They wore bobby socks and Cal sweaters. The women had pompadours and the men parted their hair in the middle. They did everything correctly. But there was one thing they did not do: they did not break out of the solace of their own society to establish contact with the outside world.

In a picture dated 1939, of the graduating members of the Nisei Students' Club, there are about sixty people in caps and gowns standing before California Hall. She is there, among the others, glowing triumphantly. No whisper of Pearl Harbor to cast a shadow on those bright faces. Yet all these young graduates would soon be clerking in Chinatown shops or pruning American gardens. Their degrees would get them nowhere, not because they hadn't done right, but because it was 1939 and they had Japanese faces. There was nowhere for them to go.

When the war came, her application for a teaching job had already been on file for two years. Since graduation she had been helping at her father's Grant Avenue store. Now she had to hand-letter signs for the store saying "Bargain Sale: Everything Must Go." Her father's back slumped in defeat as he watched the business he had struggled to build melt away overnight. America was creating a masterpiece and did not want their color.

They packed away everything they could not carry. Tom the Greek, from whom they rented Pine, promised to keep their possessions in the basement, just in case they would be able to come back someday. The quilts of bright Japanese cloth, Imari dishes hand-carried by her mother from Japan, letters, photos, window-shade rings made in hard times, a copy of her junior college newspaper in which she had written a column, her Cal yearbook, faded pictures of bright Hollywood starlets—she put all her dreams in boxes for indefinite keeping. As instructed, they took along only what was functional, only what would serve in the uncertain times to come—blankets, sweaters, pots, and pans. Then, tagged like baggage, they were escorted by the U.S. Army to their various pick-up points in the city. And when the buses took them away, it was as though they had never been.

They were taken to Tanforan Racetrack, south of the city, which was to be their new home. The stables were used as barracks, and horse stalls became "apartments" for families. As she viewed the dirt and manure left by the former occupants, she realized, "So this is what they think of me." Realization was followed by shame. She recalled how truly she had believed she was accepted, her foolish confidence, and her unfounded dreams. She and her nisei friends had been spinning a fantasy world that was unacknowledged by the larger fabric of society. She had been so carried away by the aura of Berkeley that she had forgotten the legacy left her by Eleanor Leland. Now, the damp, dusty floor and stark cots reminded her sharply of her place. She was twenty-four. They lived in Tanforan for one year.

After a year they were moved to the Topaz Relocation Center in the wastelands of Utah. Topaz, Jewel of the Desert they called it sardonically. Outside the barbed wire fence, the sagebrush traced aimless patterns on the shifting gray sands. Her sister Keiko could not endure it; she applied for an office job in Chicago and left the camp. Her brother enrolled at a Midwestern university. She stayed and looked after her parents.

After a time she began to have trouble with her hearing. At first, it was only certain frequencies she could not hear, like some desert insects. Then it was even human voices, particularly when there was background noise. She couldn't be sure, but sometimes she wondered if it was a matter of choice, that if she only concentrated, she would be able to hear what someone was saying. But the blowing dust seemed to muffle everything anyway.

She left camp only once, and briefly, to marry the young man who had courted her wordlessly in the prewar days. He was a *kibei*—born in America and taken back to Japan at the age of eight. He had then returned to San Francisco to seek his fortune at the age of eighteen. He got off the boat with seven dollars in his pocket. He was one of those restless, lonely young men who would hang out at the Japantown poolhall, work at odd jobs by day, and go to school at night. He lived with a single-minded simplicity that seemed almost brash to someone who had grown up with so many unspoken rules. He wanted this sophisticated, college-educated American girl to be his wife, and she was completely won over. So she got leave from camp, and he from his unit, which was stationed at Fort Bragg, and they met in Chicago to cast a humble line into the uncertain future, a line they hoped would pull them out of this war into another, better life. Then they each returned to their respective barracks.

As defeat loomed inevitable for Japan, more and more people were allowed to leave the camps. Some of them made straight for the Midwest or East Coast where feelings did not run so high against their presence, but her family could only think of going back home. The longing for San Francisco had become so strong that there was no question as to where they would go when they were released. They went straight back to Pine, and their hearts fell when they saw the filth and damage caused by three years of shifting tenancy. But they set about restoring it nevertheless because it was the only thing left of their lives.

The three years that had passed seemed like wasted years. The experience had no connection to the rest of her life; it was like a pocket in time, or a loose string. It was as though she had fallen asleep and dreamed the experience. But there was certainly no time to think about that now; they were busy rebuilding their lives.

She was pregnant with her first child. Her husband pleated skirts at a factory that hired Japanese. Later he ventured into the wholesale flower business where the future might be brighter. His hours were irregular; he rose in the middle of the night to deliver fresh flowers to market. Her sister had an office job with the government. Her parents were too old to start over, though her father hired out to do day work. But it shamed him so much that he did not want anyone else to know, and he died shortly afterward.

She was busy with the babies who came quickly, one after another, all girls. She was absorbed in their nursing and bodily functions, in the sucking, smacking world of babies. How could she take time to pick up the pieces of her past selves, weave them together into a pattern, when there were diapers to be changed and washed, bowel movements to be recorded, and bottles sterilized. Her world was made up of Linda's solicitude for her younger sister Cathy, Cathy's curiosity, and the placidity of the third baby Sharon. Then there was Jo, who demanded so much attention because of her frail health. The house was filled with babies. Her husband was restless, fiercely independent—he wanted to raise his family in a place of his own.

So they moved out to the Avenues, leaving the dark corridors and background music of mixed tongues for a sturdy little house in a predominantly *hakujin* neighborhood, where everyone had a yard enclosed by a fence.

When their mother died, Keiko also moved out of Pine and closed it up for good. The old Victorian was too big for one person to live in alone. But before all the old things stored away and forgotten in the basement were thrown out or given away, was there anything she wanted to keep? Just her college yearbook from Cal. That was all she could think of. She couldn't even remember what had been so important, to have been packed away in those boxes so carefully when the war had disrupted their lives. She couldn't take the time with four babies to sift through it all now. It would take days. No, just her yearbook. That was all.

Sealed off in her little house in the fog-shrouded Avenues, the past seemed like a dream. Her parents, the old Victorian, the shuffling of slippered guests, and the low mumble of Japanese, all gone from her life. Her college friends were scattered all over the country, or married and sealed off in their own private worlds. But she felt no sense of loss. Their lives, after all, were getting better. There was no time to look back on those days before the war. The girls were growing. They needed new clothes for school. She must learn to sew. Somer & Kaufman was having a sale on school shoes. Could she make this hamburger stretch for two nights?

Linda was a bright and obedient child. She was very much the big sister. Jo, the youngest, was volatile, alternating between loving and affectionate, and strong and stubborn. Sharon was a quiet child, buffered from the world on both sides by sisters. She followed her sister, Cathy, demanding no special attention. Cathy was friendly and fearless, an unredeemable tomboy. When she slid down banisters and bicycled down the big hill next to their house in the Avenues, her mother's eyes would narrow as if in recognition, watching her.

As a mother, she was without fault. Her girls were always neatly dressed and on time. They had decent table manners, remembered to excuse themselves and say thank you. They learned to read quickly and loved books because she always read to them. She chose the books carefully and refused to read them any slang or bad grammar. Her children would be irreproachable.

She conscientiously attended PTA meetings, although this was a trial for her. She wasn't able to tell people about her hearing problem; somehow she was unable to admit to such a deficiency. So she did her best, sometimes pretending to hear when she didn't, nodding her head and smiling. She wanted things to go smoothly; she wanted to appear normal.

Linda, Cathy, and Jo excelled in school and were very popular. Linda held class offices and was invariably the teacher's pet. "A nice girl," her teachers said. Cathy was outgoing and athletic, and showed great talent in art and design—"a beautiful girl," in her teachers' estimation. Jo was rebellious, read voraciously, and wrote caustic essays and satires. Teachers sometimes disliked her, but they all thought she was "intelligent." Sharon was termed "shy." Although she liked the arts, Cathy was the artist of the family. And though Sharon read quite a bit, Jo was the one who liked to read. Sharon was not popular like Linda, and of all the Terasaki girls, she had to struggle the hardest, often unsuccessfully, to make the Honor Roll. But all in all, the girls vindicated their mother, and it was a happy time, the happiest time of her life.

Then they were grown up and gone. They left one by one. The house emptied room by room until it seemed there was nothing but silence. She had to answer the phone herself now, if she heard it ring. She dreaded doing so because she could never be sure if she was hearing correctly. Sometimes she let the telephone ring, pretending not to be home. The one exception was when her sister called every night. Then she would exchange news on the phone for an hour.

When her daughters came home to visit she came alive. Linda was doing the right things. She had a nice Japanese American boyfriend; she was graduating from college; and she was going to get married.

Cathy was a bit of a free soul, and harder to understand. She wore her hair long and straight, and seldom came home from Berkeley. When she did she seemed to find fault: Why didn't her mother get a hearing aid? Did she enjoy being left out of the hearing world? But Cathy had friends, interesting friends, *hakujin* friends, whom she sometimes brought home with her. She moved easily in all worlds, and her mother's heart swelled with pride to see it.

Sharon sometimes came home, sometimes stayed away. When she did come home she did not have much to say. She was not happy in school. She liked throwing pots and weaving.

Then there was Jo, who would always bring a book home, or notebook, and whose "evil pen" would pause absently in midstroke when her mother hovered near, telling her little bits of information that were new since the last visit. Jo, whose thoughts roamed far away, would gradually focus on the little figure of her mother. She had led such a sheltered life.

And then Cathy had died, and her mother didn't even cry.

Linda sent pictures from Germany of their mother in front of Heidelberg Castle, and cruising down the Rhine. "She's just like a young girl," her letters proclaimed triumphantly. "She's excited about everything." But when their mother came home she talked about her trip for about a week. Then the old patterns prevailed, as if the house were a mold and her soul molded to it. In a month, Germany seemed like another loose thread in the fabric of her life. When Jo visited two months later, her mother was once again effaced, a part of the house almost, in her faded blouse and shapeless skirt, joylessly adding too much seasoned salt to the dinner salad.

"If only," Jo wrote Linda facetiously, "we could ship her out to some exotic place every other month."

In the fall Jo went to New York to study. "I have to get away," she wrote Linda. "The last time I went home I found myself discussing the machine washability of acrylics with Mom. There has got to be more to life than that." In the spring she had her mother come for a visit. No trip to the top of the Empire State Building, no Staten Island ferry, with Jo. She whisked her mother straight from Kennedy Airport to her cramped flat in the Village, and no sooner had they finished dinner than Jo's boyfriend, Michael, arrived.

Her mother was gracious. "Where do you live, Michael?" she asked politely.

He and Jo exchanged looks. "Here," he said.

Despite her mother's anxiety about the safety of New York streets, the two of them walked furiously in the dusk and circled Washington Square several times, mother shocked and disappointed, daughter reassuring. At the end of an hour they returned to the flat for tea, and by the end of the evening the three of them had achieved an uneasy truce.

"I knew you wouldn't be happy about it," Jo said to her, "but I wanted you to know me. To know the truth. I hate pretending."

"Things were different when we were your age," her mother said. "What's Daddy going to say?"

She stayed for two weeks. Every morning Michael cooked breakfast, and the three of them ate together. Her attitude towards the situation softened from one of guarded assessment to tentative acceptance. Michael was very articulate, Jo as level-headed as ever. Their apartment was clean and homey. She began to relax over morning coffee at the little round table by the window.

She remembered the trip she made to Chicago during the war to get married. She had traveled from Topaz to Chicago by train. It was her first trip alone. Her parents and camp friends had seen her off at Topaz, and her sister and future husband had met her at the station in Chicago. But as the train followed its track northeastward across the country, she had been alone in the world. Her senses had been heightened. She remembered vividly the quality of light coming through the train window, and how it had bathed the passing countryside in a golden wash. Other passengers had slept, but she sat riveted at the window. Perhaps the scenery seemed so beautiful because of the bleakness and sensual deprivation of Topaz. She didn't know why she remembered it now.

Jo took her to the Metropolitan and to the Statue of Liberty. In a theater on Broadway they sat in the front row to see Deborah Kerr, her all-time favorite, and afterwards she declared she had heard every word.

When she left she shook Michael's hand and hugged Jo, saying, "I'll talk to Daddy."

But by the time Jo came home to visit a year later, the house, or whatever it was, had done its work. Her mother was again lost to her, a sweet little creature unable to hear very well, relaying little bits of information.

"I give up," said Jo. "We seem to lose ground every time. We dig her out, then she crawls back in, only deeper."

Linda loyally and staunchly defended the fortress in which her mother seemed to have taken refuge.

Jo defiantly wanted to break through. "Like shock treatment," she said. "It's the only way to bring her out."

Sharon, the middle daughter, gave her mother a loom.

And so, late in life, she took up weaving. She attended a class and took detailed notes, then followed them step by step, bending to the loom with painstaking attention, threading the warp tirelessly, endlessly winding, threading, tying. She made sampler after sampler, using the subdued, muted colors she liked: Five inches of one weave, two inches of another, just as the teacher instructed.

For a year she wove samplers, geometric and repetitious, all in browns and neutral shades, the colors she preferred. She was fascinated by some of the more advanced techniques she began to learn. One could pick up threads from the warp selectively, so there could be a color on the warp that never appeared in the fabric if it were not picked up and woven into the fabric. This phenomenon meant she could show a flash of color, repeated flashes of the color, or never show it at all. The color would still be there, startling the eye when the piece was turned over. The backside would reveal long lengths of a color that simply hadn't been picked up from the warp and didn't appear at all in the right side of the fabric.

She took to her loom with new excitement, threading the warp with all the shades of her life: Gray, for the cold, foggy mornings when she had, piece by piece, warmed little clothes by the heater vent as Jo, four, stood shivering in her underwear; brown, the color of the five lunch bags she packed each morning with a sandwich, cut in half and wrapped in waxed paper, napkin, fruit, and potato chips; Dark brown, like the brownies they had baked "to make Daddy come home" from business trips—Sharon and Jo had believed he really could smell them, because he always came home.

Now when the daughters came home they always found something new she had woven. Linda dropped by almost every week to leave her own daughter, Terry, at "Bachan's house" before dashing off to work. When Linda's husband came to pick her up, Terry never wanted to leave "Bachi" and would cling to her, crying at the door.

She continued to weave: White, the color of five sets of sheets, which she had washed, hung out, and ironed each week—also the color of the bathroom sink and the lather of shampoo against four small black heads; blue, Cathy's favorite color.

Sharon came by from time to time, usually to do a favor or bring a treat. She would cook Mexican food or borrow a tool or help trim trees in the garden. She was frustrated with the public school system where she had been substitute teaching and was now working part time in a gallery.

Sometimes Sharon brought yarn for her mother to weave: Golden brown, the color of the Central Valley in summer. The family had driven through the valley on their way to the mountains almost every summer. They would arrive hot and sweating and hurry into the cool, emerald green waters of the Merced River. The children's floats flashed yellow on the dark green water. Yellow, too, were the beaten eggs fried flat, rolled, and eaten cold, with dark brown pickled vegetables and white rice balls. She always sat in the shade.

Jo was working abroad and usually came home to visit once a year. She and Michael had broken up. During the visits the house would fill with Jo and her friends. They would sit in the back room to talk. Jo visited her mother's weaving class and met her weaving friends.

"So this is the daughter," one of them said. "Your mother's been looking forward to your visit. She never misses class except when her daughters are home."

Soon it was time for Jo to leave again. "Mom's colors," she remarked to Sharon as she fingered the brown muffler her mother had woven for her.

"Put it on," said Sharon.

Jo did, and as she moved toward the light, hidden colors leaped from the brown fabric. It came alive in the sunlight.

"You know, there's actually red in here," she marveled, "and even bits of green. You'd never know it unless you looked real close."

"Most people don't," Sharon said.

The two sisters fell silent, sharing a rare moment together before their lives diverged again. The muffler was warm about Jo's neck.

At the airport, Jo's mother stood next to Jo's father, leaning slightly toward him as an object of lighter mass naturally tends toward a more substantial one. She was crying.

When Jo was gone she returned to the house, and her loom. And amidst the comings and goings of the lives around her, she sat, a woman bent over a loom, weaving the diverse threads of life into one miraculous, mystical fabric with timeless care.

The Parrot's Beak

KARTAR DHILLON

My mother was sure she would die after surgery. A doctor told her she would have to go to the county hospital in Fresno to have a tumor removed. Her first sight of the doctor in the hospital confirmed her fears.

"That man does not like Indians," she told us. "He is the one who let Labh Singh die."

She had never before been a patient in a hospital. Her eight children had been born at home with the help of midwives. The day before entering the hospital she lay in her bed and brooded about the fate of her children. She was forty-one years old, widowed for five years. Her youngest child, born after the death of our father, was five years old, and her first-born, delivered a few weeks after her arrival in the United States in 1910, was twenty-one. Her husband had promised his brother in India that his first-born son would be his son because he had no children of his own. So they taught their first-born to call them "uncle" and "aunt," which he did, and the other children, all seven of us, hearing these terms, called our father and mother uncle and aunt also. "Chacha" and "Chachi" were our names for them, uncle and aunt on the father's side.

My parents had five sons and three daughters, and it was the daughters who worried our mother the most. Whatever we did that was different from the proper behavior of young girls in her village in India signified danger. And because most things here were different, I was in constant trouble.

At a very early age, I became convinced that my mother hated me. It seemed to me that whatever I did, or didn't do, was wrong. She cursed and beat me so much that I automatically ducked if she lifted her hand. When entering a room, I kept to the edges to stay out of her arm's reach.

"Get up, you black-faced witch," was a usual eye-opener for me in the morning. And throughout the day, it was, "You parrot's beak," to remind me of my long, ugly nose.

Sometimes when I was no more than six or seven years old, I would wonder why she hated me so much. Watching her nurse the newest baby, I would wonder what she felt about having carried me in her body.

She frequently talked to us about God. "He made parents to be as God over their children," she explained once. "If children do not obey their parents, they will surely go to hell after they die." Hell was a place, she said, where the disobedient would have to pass through walls set so close together it would be almost impossible to squeeze through them, and she would indicate a tiny space with her thumb and forefinger. I wasn't able to envision my soul, so I suffered endlessly imagining my body trying to squeeze through that tiny space.

Sometimes when she was particularly exasperated with me, she would say, "God must have given you to me to punish me for something I did in my previous life."

I went about feeling guilty most of the time, but I was never sure what I had done wrong. In time, I decided my crime was being a girl.

One day before she entered the hospital, she summoned me to her bedside, like a sovereign might summon a serf. I entered her room braced for a scolding. I knew she wouldn't hit me, because as I had grown older—I was sixteen then—she had given up on physical punishment, saying, "You are too old for whippings now. I can only appeal to your reason." The truth was, I had grown a head taller than my mother; I was too big.

I had learned long before not to speak when she scolded me for something. If I ever dared to protest an unjust accusation, she shouted, "Do not speak back to your elders."

At first I did not speak back because of her order; later I found not speaking to be a useful form of resistance. I would stand mute before her at times, even when being questioned, which added to her rage and frustration.

I went into her bedroom that day, tall and gangly, head hanging, waiting for an outpouring of abuse. But it did not come. Instead she said, "You probably know that I don't expect to come out of the hospital alive. You will be alone now, with neither father nor mother to guide you."

She had never spoken to me in a confiding manner before. I felt a rush of sorrow for her, this frail woman lying before me out of whose body I had come, and I felt guiltier than ever. Two days earlier she had paid a doctor in Merced with chickens, eggs, and vegetables, to learn that her tumor, grown to the size of a melon, had to be surgically removed.

"Your father wanted to arrange marriages for you and your sisters before he died," she continued, "but I absolutely refused. I told him, 'We came to this country to give our children an education. What good will it do them if they have to marry men they do not know and perhaps might not like?' You were only eleven years old when he died, you know."

"Oh yes, Chachi," I wanted to cry out to her, "I know. How well I know. But I thought it was only he who cared about me; it was only he who was kind to me. He would stop you from beating me, and when you pointed out my faults, he would say, she will learn better when she gets older, and you would reply, I doubt it. And yet it was you who saved me from a commitment I would have hated." I wanted to pour out words of gratitude, I wanted to comfort her, but I was too confused to say anything, and I remained silent.

"You will marry whom you please," she went on, "but it is my duty to teach you how to conduct yourself in marriage.

"You must remember that a woman is subservient to a man. When she is a child, she obeys her father; if he should die, then she must obey her oldest brother.

"When a woman marries, her husband is her master."

"If she becomes a widow, then she must defer to her sons."

The year was 1932. My mother did die in the hospital, a few days after the surgery. Her youngest child, my brother, was not old enough for grade school yet, so we took him to high school with us for the remainder of my senior term.

I had dreams of becoming an artist; I planned to work actively for India's freedom from British rule. I looked upon marriage as a prison. But even though I abhorred the idea of marriage, that same year, right out of high school, I got married.

My oldest brother already had planned to send me to India to marry the "right person." But the man I married, a political activist, born and raised in India, warned me, "You will have no rights in India. Your brother can force you to marry anyone he chooses. Marry me, then he will have no power over you."

I idolized this man. I had been impressed from the start by his fiery speeches at meetings of the Gadar Party, an organization formed to fight British rule in India. He already had a degree in political science from the University of California in Berkeley.

"But I want to go to the university," I said.

"You can do both," he insisted. "I will help you."

We got married secretly so that I could go on caring for my younger brothers and sister. But I did not keep my secret for long, because soon I had morning sickness and was frequently running out of the house to throw up behind the trees and bushes. "No children," I had said to my husband. "Political activism and babies don't go together." Though he had agreed with me, I found myself pregnant nonetheless.

My oldest brother was so furious when he found out that he kicked me out of the house. "Go live off your husband," he said, though he had bragged to people earlier about how much I did for the family. "Give her two empty bowls," he would say, "and she can produce a delicious dinner for the whole family."

I wanted to take the two youngest children with me, but my next oldest brother said, "You will have problems enough being married." A month later, all four of the younger children were brought to live with me and my husband—one of them had accidentally burned down the house.

Caring for the family was nothing new to me. When we were no more than seven and eight years old, my mother used to assign a baby apiece to me and my sister to watch for the day. At twelve, I was doing the entire family's wash on a washboard by hand, and taking turns with my sister to cook meals. By high school, the job of milking thirty cows every morning and night was tacked onto my other duties.

When I was in my eighth month of pregnancy, I had had no medical care. The clinics in the area where my husband leased land on a share-crop basis had refused me because I had not been in that county a full year. So in an effort to obtain care, all the children and I had moved back to the farm that my brothers sharecropped. We slept on large raisin boxes under the open sky, and I cooked meals on a grill placed over a hole in the ground for the wood fire.

A family friend was shocked to learn I was not getting medical treatment and took me to the director of the same county hospital where my mother had died. But she also refused me admission, saying, "If these people can afford to farm, they can afford medical care." My friend pointed out that we did not have any money, that we could not even buy enough milk for all the children. "They buy one quart of milk a day, and take turns drinking one cup every other day." She told her that my teeth were breaking off in pieces for lack of calcium, but the director remained adamant.

"She can't have her baby on the street," my friend said.

The hospital official fixed her eyes on my friend and asked, "Then why do these people have babies?"

As we walked out the door, a nurse who had been in the room whispered to us, "The hospital can't turn you away in an emergency. Come in when you are in labor."

And that's what I did. My joy was great at learning my baby was a girl. Because I was slipping in and out of the anesthesia, I asked three times to be assured I had heard right. I had indeed. I was so happy it was a girl because I wanted to prove to the world that she could be the equal of any boy ever born. Above that, I wanted a girl to give her the love and understanding that had been withheld from me.

In the hospital the nurses wouldn't believe that I was married because I wore no wedding ring and I gave my own last name instead of my husband's. I told them my mother had not worn a wedding ring, that it was a cultural thing. Also, I saw no reason for changing my name to someone else's.

One day the superintendent of nurses came into my ward, sat down on the edge of my bed, and took my hand in hers. "You can tell me, dear," she said gently. "You're really not married, are you?"

"But I am," I said.

"Then why don't you use your husband's name?"

"Why doesn't he use mine?"

She let go of my hand. "Is your husband English?"

"No, we're both Indian."

"But his name is Sharman. He must have borrowed it from the English."

"The English probably borrowed it from us," I replied. "After all the Indian civilization has been here much longer."

I eventually lost the battle to keep my identity when I went to work in a war plant and was asked once too often why, if I was really married, didn't I use my husband's name and wear a wedding ring. I went to the dime store and bought a "gold" ring which I wore until the day I decided not to be married anymore.

My husband couldn't understand.

"What have I done wrong?" he begged to know.

I didn't have the courage to confront him, to tell him how he cheated me out of an education. You see, the day I was to sign up for classes at the university, he accused me of wanting to be around other men.

I didn't confront him about how he put an end to my political work either. The day I was to cover a strike for the workers' paper, he asked me, "And who will take care of the children if you are arrested?"

When he asked me what had he done wrong, I only told him, "Last week when I asked you to buy me some white sewing thread, you said you had bought some another time, and what had I done with it."

He looked at me as if I was crazy. "We've been married eleven years, and when I ask you what is wrong, you tell me I wouldn't buy you five cents' worth of thread."

"That's it exactly," I said. "It cost only five cents, but I didn't have even *that* much money of my own. I had to ask you for it."

I had been in the habit of keeping silent about my real feelings for too many years and was unable to articulate all my grievances. I decided at that moment that I was not going to be a servant any longer—and an unpaid one at that.

Freedom from marriage at the age of twenty-seven with no job skills and three children to support is not quite the stuff of dreams, but I had finally taken my destiny into my own hands. I could wait on tables, and my typing ability could get me work in offices. Most important, I could live in a city to avail myself of evening classes and guarantee a good education for my children.

My cardinal rules for raising children were: no physical punishment, no discrimination between boys and girls, and no unfairness. When I was a child, my mother sometimes punished me for someone else's misdeed because she thought I looked guilty. I decided to believe my children.

In the house where I lived with my son and two daughters in San

Francisco, there was no girls' work and no boys' work. The three of them helped me according to their ability. My son became the best cook because he started learning how the earliest.

Education topped the list of priorities for us. We took classes in everything that was available. I studied shorthand and bookkeeping to increase my earning power, and art and literature to fulfill my real aspirations. The children took classes in dance, art, and biology. They attended lectures by prominent world figures, went to the symphony with donated tickets, and took music lessons on the second-hand piano and violin I had purchased. With the leanest of budgets, we could be seated in only the top rows of the theaters and opera house, but we enjoyed the performances of many talented artists nevertheless.

In high school I had always been on the outside looking in. When my classmates stayed after school to rehearse plays, take part in sports, or play musical instruments, I went home to do housework and milk cows. I was determined to help my children expand their horizons by taking advantage of all the things the city offered. On weekends we rented bicycles and rode through Golden Gate Park; we picnicked on the ocean beaches; we visited the zoo; we saw the exhibits at the museums. At home, when our studies were done, we played chess. When I was a child, if I was not studying, I had to be working, or if I was not working, I had to be studying. So now I played with my children—chess, tennis, swimming. I believed that life was meant to be enjoyed, not suffered.

We may have lived in the slums at times, but our apartments were sunny with life. Our rooms were filled with books and music, social activity, and intellectual endeavor. No matter how shabby a place we moved into, I could make it beautiful with paint and paintings. I sometimes think back to the many homes I lived in as a child. I cannot recall a single house that had running water or a rug on the floor. But I can recall vignettes of my mother and father seated at the rough kitchen table. On one occasion my mother was drawing a scroll of birds and flowers entwined with leafy vines around the borders of a letter to her family written in Punjabi script. On another occasion my father sat at the table in the light of a kerosene lamp writing poetry on a schoolchild's lined tablet.

Was that where my interest in art and literature was born? Was it their artistic creativity which sustained them in the harsh reality of their barren existence? Sometimes, when I look beyond my own hurts, I try to envision my mother's life before I arrived. I marvel at her survival as the family trekked around California and Oregon, living as they could wherever my father found work. He had the company of other men, friends and workers on the job. My mother had no one, no other Indian women to keep her company, no sisters or relatives to give her a hand with the housework. She had to do it all—all, that is, until her daughters grew old enough to help.

Both my father and mother were pioneers in those days of the early West. My father arrived at the port of San Francisco in 1899 as a matter of choice, an economic choice. He left his village in India of his own volition. Yet when my mother came to California, it was not her choice, but her husband's. My father had returned to India, and brought back to the United States the wife selected for him by his father. At the age of seventeen, she had been picked up virtually like a piece of baggage and taken off to a foreign land by a man whom she never saw before her marriage.

It was her good fortune that he was a kind and generous man who taught her to write in Punjabi so that she could communicate with the family she left behind, the family she would never see again. Neither of my parents went to school, but my father had learned to read and write both Punjabi and English in the course of his years of service in the British army. His was the vision that motivated me to educate my children.

With what wisdom I have gained, I now realize that some of the bitterness my mother projected onto me, came from her status as a woman in a world controlled by men. I think my mother would agree, if she could, I consider my greatest accomplishment summed up in a compliment paid to one of my children: "She is not afraid to think."

Waiting for Papa's Return

CECILIA MANGUERRA BRAINARD

When Reverend Mother Superior tells Remedios her father died, all she can think is how ugly the nun looks. Remedios stares at the mustache fringing the nun's upper lip; Reverend Mother Superior stares back with pale watery eyes.

"This morning, child. Heart attack," the nun says.

In the distance the three o'clock bell rings as if repeating the nun's words. It is an October Thursday, warm and humid. The sound stays with Remedios as the nun takes her to the chapel. "Let us pray so your father will go straight to heaven," she whispers. They kneel in the front pew and Remedios closes her eyes. The ringing that echoes in her head fades and she hears her father's voice loud and clear: I'll be back in two weeks.

She clings to those words, mulling over them. I'll-be-back-in-two-weeks. That means next week because Mama and Papa have already been gone for a week. She pictures her father with his oval face, his gold-rimmed glasses, and his balding head. He was leaning on his cane when he asked, "What do you want me to bring?"

"Mama says she'll buy me shoes, clothes, candies, and chocolates."

"But what do you want?" his gentle voice prodded.

"A walking doll and a tea set like Mildred's. Not the plastic tea set, I want the kind that breaks."

"All right," he replied, tousling her dark hair. "I'll scour all of Hong Kong and I'll bring you your doll and tea set."

Her father said those words and he never lies. Remedios is confused. Reverend Mother Superior is the most important person in school and she doesn't lie either. She must have made a mistake. Papa and Mama will be back next week from their vacation.

Remedios thinks things over, trying to find a reason for this mis-understanding. Was it because she and Mildred giggled in church at the fat woman singing with a warbling voice? Mildred elbowed her in the ribs and they had been bad, no doubt about it, snickering in the back row instead of paying attention to Father Ruis's novena.

The chapel smells of melted wax and when Remedios opens her eyes, she studies the bleeding Jesus nailed to the cross. "I'm sorry for having been bad," she prays over and over, until Reverend Mother Superior stands up and says, "Your aunt is picking you up, child."

They find Tiya Meding waiting in the office. She is wearing a brown dress; her face is pale, her eyes, pink-rimmed. "Poor, poor child," she mumbles. In the car she looks at Remedios in a way that makes Remedios think her aunt is trying to discover something in her—and Remedios does not know what.

Feeling awkward, Remedios rolls down her window and watches the hawkers selling lottery tickets, boiled bananas, and soft drinks. Her aunt delicately blows her nose and sniffles.

"Look, there's the woman in black dancing in front of the church," Remedios points out.

"Crazy woman," Tiya Meding answers.

"Papa says she's pathetic."

"Pathetic my foot. She's as loony as they come."

Remedios keeps quiet; pathetic is how her father describes the woman in black.

Her aunt's chauffeur—that is what Tiya Meding calls her driver— takes them to Vering the dressmaker. Remedios is surprised she will have a dress sewn, and she nods approvingly at the design: puffed sleeves, boat neck, and shirred skirt.

"And pockets, two square pockets," Remedios suggests.

Vering sketches in the pockets.

"And I don't want this black cloth. Yellow organdy would be nicer."

The two women eye each other.

"But the dress has to be black," Tiya Meding insists.

"I don't like black. Papa says I look prettiest in yellow."

"The dress will be black, Remedios." Her aunt sets her jaw and Remedios knows there is no use arguing.

Before leaving the dressmaker's shop, Tiya Meding asks for pieces of black cloth the size of postage stamps. She pins one on Remedios's blouse, right above her heart—a little bit of black cloth that flutters when the warm breeze blows.

At school she is the center of attention, like the actress Gloria Romero or the one-eyed freak with the Chinese Acrobatic Troupe, stared at by everybody. When she picks up her schoolbag, the children glance curiously at her. The visitors, streaming into Tiya Meding's house look at her, and when she and her aunt go to the funeral parlor and church "to make arrangements," people study her. Remedios feels as if her nose were growing from her forehead. Pairs of glassy eyes follow her around and she does not know what they want, how to escape them.

At her aunt's house, she tries to amuse herself by inspecting the numerous porcelain figures in the living room—pretty dainty women with ducks beside them, little angels kneeling down in prayer, but her aunt snaps: "Don't touch those. They're breakable." She goes to the piano and plays "Chopsticks," but her aunt lifts a reprimanding finger. "The noise," she complains. Tiya Meding is on the phone and Remedios listens to her.

"Thank you," her aunt says. "Heart attack. Isn't that too bad? I warned my sister. An older man like that." Tiya Meding's diamond earrings dangle from her elongated ears and a huge diamond solitaire sparkles on her finger.

"Baubles," her father often says about Tiya Meding's jewelry. "She is a silly woman who likes baubles."

Remedios leaves the main house thinking to herself: Silly, silly woman. She goes to the kitchen and has a second lunch with the servants. Using her fingers, she makes a ball of rice and eats it with stewed fish. Later she helps the cook peel cassava and grate coconuts.

"Your father was a good man," the cook says. "He made my son foreman of the road construction."

"Yes," Remedios replies, "I can't wait until he comes home."

After speaking, she wonders why she said those words. She understands what Reverend Mother Superior said, what all the commotion is about, yet deep within herself she knows her papa will return.

The kitchen is sooty and smells of grease and bay leaves. The cook, who stands next to the huge wood-burning stove, looks at her. Remedios continues grating. She watches the curly slivers of white coconut meat fall into the basin. The kitchen smoke seems to engulf her and she feels warm. The pungent smell makes her temples throb. She begins to feel weak, just as she felt when her cousin told her she was adopted. He had lost in a game of checkers, and angrily, he told Remedios that her parents picked her up from a pile of trash, that she had been covered with fat flies. She did not cry; she crawled into bed to sleep off her tiredness. Her mother called the boy an idiotic pervert. Her father later placed her on his knee.

"See this bump on my nose?" he asked.

"Yes."

"Don't you have a bump on your nose like mine?" His warm forefinger traveled down her nose over the slight protrusion.

She nodded.

"That means that you are my very own little girl. We didn't adopt you."

The darkness lifted and the next time she saw her cousin she stuck her tongue out at him. But now the tiredness stays and she drags around until bedtime. It seems she has just tucked the mosquito net under the mattress when she falls asleep and begins dreaming.

It is Sunday, and she, Mama, and Papa are driving over bumpy, dusty roads to Talisay Beach. Remedios is happy because she enjoys clamming in the small inlet. But when they arrive, the sea is blood red and smells foul. Remedios cries and her papa asks why.

"Something terrible has happened," she says.

"It's all right," he answers. "I'm right beside you."

She dries her eyes, noticing that the water has turned blue and the air is clean once more. She laughs and hugs her papa.

"Don't cry. It makes me sad," her father says in the dream.

She wakes to Tiya Meding's voice telling her the plane is arriving in less than an hour. Trying to get excited, she bathes with her aunt's Maja soap and dabs Joy perfume behind her ears. Like a sleepwalker, she puts on her new black dress, white socks, and black patent leather shoes. Remedios ties yellow ribbons at the ends of her braids but Tiya Meding removes them. "Not for a year," she says.

Heavy-faced people wearing somber clothes crowd the airport. They stare at Remedios and she tries hard to figure out what they want from her. She laughs. "I can hardly wait to see them," she exclaims in a high thin voice. Pairs of eyes follow her, letting go only when the noisy plane arrives with a loud screech. The special cargo plane stops near the terminal, and some men open the side doors and struggle to bring down a casket. When Remedios spots her mother walking down the ramp, she runs shouting, "Ma!" The mourners around her pause. "Ma, where's my walking doll and tea set?" Her aunt tells her to be quiet. "She's just a child," someone else says. "Just a child."

Her mother appears dreary in her black dress—Remedios really hates that color—and she weeps constantly. She will not talk, nor will she tell Remedios that everything will be fine.

A hollow feeling grows inside Remedios. Sometimes she feels like the conch shell sitting on the writing desk. Other times it seems she is hanging on a thin thread, like the gray spider swinging back and forth from the ceiling. She feels odd, as if waiting for something to happen so all the staring will end, so the strangeness that has invaded her life will disappear.

The next day there is a mass. Then the men carry the coffin to the funeral car, so black and slick. When it starts raining, people scramble for umbrellas or newspapers and they mutter, "Ah, a good sign, heaven is weeping." She, Mama, and Tiya Meding walk behind the funeral car to the old cemetery with gray crumbling crypts. Some women hold umbrellas over them to keep their heads dry. Remedios trudges along, splashing in puddles, watching the slum children playing in the rain.

At the cemetery, the men pick up the coffin, carry it to the family crypt and open it. The priest sprinkles holy water inside. Her mama, who emits wailing sounds and whose shoulders are shaking, bends over to kiss the man inside. Remedios has not looked but she knows that a man is in there. She heard people talking: "Looks like he's sleeping, doesn't he? They sure did a good job."

Her mama turns to her and Remedios walks toward the casket. She tiptoes and peers in. The man's face is a waxy mask. He doesn't wear glasses and his tight little smile is a grimace. There is a smell like mothballs. Remedios feels faint. She wants to giggle, but stopping herself, she bends over and plants a kiss on the wax-man's cool cheek.

The men close the coffin and slide it into the crypt making a grating sound. There is a dull thud when the marble slab covers the niche, and briefly Remedios feels a lurching inside her stomach. She closes her eyes and hears that voice loud and clear: I'll be back in two weeks. I'll bring you your doll and tea set.

When she opens her eyes and sees the mourners crying, for just a moment she understands that they want her to weep, that they are waiting for her to cry. But soon she is thinking of dainty tea cups, the smooth feel of delicate china, the clinking sound as the cup hits the saucer. She is seeing her father smiling broadly as she hands him his cup and they make a toast pretending to sip tea under the cool shade of the lush star apple trees.

Dreams of Manong Frankie

VIRGINIA CERENIO

manilatown memories
too many
　　to fill
　　　　one photo album
pages cannot hold the music
of clapping hands and dancing feet
"such foolish things
　　remind me
　　　　of you. . . ."

summer/chinatown

the cable cars danced up california street, a slow samba line of tourists hugging cameras. bell sounds flew in the air like quick bird wings. a sunlit afternoon poured like a gold rush into the cool brick alleys of chinatown. i walked out onto the sidewalk, watching the people in perpetual motion from shadow to sunlight. fish swimming upstream, scales glistening in noon light.

then i saw him, lumbering slowly up the river of sunlight like a lazy carabao in the warm day, fish scattering in his wake.

"Ay, Virgie! . . . my beautiful pinay . . . by golly girl . . . whatcha doing here . . . I been looking for you so long my eyes hurting me already." his hands big and leathered swallowed my slender ones in their darkness. manong frankie, fast frankie, one hundred miles per hour on his feet dancin' frankie, hizzoner commissioner frankie, five-wives frankie, my dear heart frankie, how are you?

"Well . . . I'm doing all right for an old man. Where you been? I thought you're hiding from me . . . ahhh . . . you work too much . . . where you going now? . . . are you busy? . . . would you like to take a walk in the park with an old man? . . . it's a beautiful day."

we held hands like teenagers, the carabao and the rice-bird playing in the sun and shadow of chinatown. anyone would have thought we were a loving grandfather and granddaughter. little did they know that the grandfatherly old man was in love with the thought of being in love again and the young woman was regretting being reincarnated too late in life. so, frankie, what have you been doing?

". . . going crazy without you . . . just finished dancing at Manila-town . . . then I'll go for the pinochle game at St. Paul's . . . then dinner, then to bed early, cause I got to be dancing all weekend!" he squeezed my arm with the enthusiasm of someone who never tired of doing what they did best. smiling, i maneuvered my precious cargo across narrow streets, between parked and moving cars, through the flowing streams of tourists and chinatown residents.

all during our walk, manong frankie behaved like a lovesick teenager—squeezing my hand until it felt like one of those bruised bananas, left loose and single on sale, murmuring "oh, Virgie, who've you been seeing . . ." and yet like a gentleman walking me down the street with all the dignity 79 years could carry.

swimming downstream to clay and kearny streets we ended up at portsmouth square park for the proposed walk. of course, this wasn't just any casual stroll, but a chance for frankie to walk me around in full view of all his kababayans, amigos, pungyao, friends. showing off his girl. "Ay, talagang Frankie! Magandang babae!" frankie waving, walking slowly and proudly like a datu surveying his barangay. the sunlight of surprise and curiosity appearing in faces lined with past winters, old men sprouting like dusty mushrooms on park benches, clustering around the card games. all of them like village elders whose responsibility of age has made them idle and called them wise, carrying on the recreation of men with nothing to do—smoking, gambling, drinking, storytelling, ogling. and manong frankie was giving them a chance to practice the latter by parading me through portsmouth square. "Hey, Frank! You sonuvagun! You always fooling around with those women! Don't you know? Old men aren't supposed to do those kinda stuff!" frankie would smile quietly, the silence of his proud walk giving enough response to the remarks of the park bench crowd.

"Frankie, really!" I protested. "You're embarassing me!"

"Don't worry," he said, patting my hand. "I'll just tell them you're my granddaughter."

autumn/portsmouth square playground

the breeze like cool careless fingers brushed through chinatown, leaves and litter danced waltzes in the sidewalk squares. the old women and bums wore layers of clothing like cocoons, eyes peering out beneath hats, between folds. only the occasional hooker dared to show her long pale legs, pedestaled on four-inch heels and shivering slightly into her short woolworth's trenchcoat. the breeze carried the stale smell of the city, a faint hint of oceans a hill away, a dream of rains and the winter to come.

"Egypt," frankie said.

"What?"

"Alexandria, Egypt. That's where I learn palm reading."

"Frankie, you know how to read palms?" i was incredulous, especially after i had been told by my friends not to believe any of frankie's stories, because even he believed in the myths he had created about himself.

"Oh, yesss. I was in the merchant marines, you know, we went all over the world. And I met this old lady there in Egypt, who knows the secrets of palm reading and she taught it to me. I can tell your past and your future."

"Really?!"

"I'm not kidding. Here, I'll read your palm." we walked over to a park bench and sat down causing a mass exodus of pigeons. frankie held my hand, palm up, peering with the concentration he usually reserved for a keno ticket at reno, smoothing my palm with his thumbs as though it were a map of wrinkles. silence. another cool breeze shimmied through the park. "Your boyfriend is coming from far away. Maybe from the Philippines." frankie looked at me with a twinkle in his eye, awaiting my reaction. . . . *oh frankie, that happened a long time ago . . . broken hearts never mend, they just stay cracked* . . . "Maybe this boyfriend is already here. Your palm says it's someone maybe you know, a friend, someone who lives close by, maybe in your own neighborhood." frankie seemed very pleased by this pronouncement. he looked at me. "Hmmm . . . you better be careful . . . there's a married man in your future. Maybe someone you know is trying to fool you." he looked at me with concern.

i laughed. "Frankie, you're too serious. Tell me, how many children will I have?"

he turned my hand into a fist, reading the wrinkles cornered below my little finger. "Four children . . . but only three will live." the solemn tone of his words got carried away by yet another chill breeze, winging over the pyramid. his hand held mine in comfort, already mourning a dead child, not yet conceived.

frankie had sad stories in every pocket today. "C'mon Manong. It's almost time for lunch. It's too cold to be sitting out here." the chilly breezes chased us back to the warmth of manilatown. the pigeons reclaimed the park bench giving no respect to the art of palm-reading.

winter/manilatown senior center

". . . hernando's hideaway, ole! . . ." the melody drifted up from the basement onto clay street, being washed away by the chilly winter rains into the sounds of a wet city. the sharp slick sounds of city traffic were exchanged abruptly for the latin rhythms and crying clarinets of the manilatown senior center band. the band played as loudly and raucously as possible to compete with the sounds of the lunch crowd—shouted conversations into deaf ears, plates and tablespoons clattering in rhythm.

frankie, always the picture of sartorial splendor, was dressed in green polyester slacks, matching double-breasted jacket, tie. his tie had the remains of lunch—chicken adobo, squash, rice, sabao, fruit cocktail for dessert. not bad for a sixty-cent lunch.

frankie, as usual, was dancing. he loved to dance, would dance with anybody, for he was as he put it "a dancing fool."

"Virgie, you just in time to dance!" frankie greeted me with glee. there was no escape now. "I been waiting for you!" he took my hand and led me to the small space between the band and the dining area. scattered applause and shouts of admiration for frankie's boldness. frankie led me gracefully into a foxtrot, while I tried not to step on his feet or bump his belly.

dancing with frankie called for maximum concentration. he would stare into my eyes with all seriousness and romantic drama, barely smiling, while his large hand pressing into the small of my back brought me ever closer into his embrace. for all his grace, his dance steps often did not match the music. there was always one point during the dance when he would show off his fancy footwork—his feet would move at about ninety miles per hour in a figure-eight shuffle making his rotund body move like a gaily dancing balloon. it did not seem to matter that his dancing partner could not keep up with him. but that was frankie—always dancing to the music inside his head.

> the oldest pinoy around manilatown
> 79 and still dancing
> since 1917 found him
> waltzing his way
> into the heart of america
> chicago's marathon manong
> he latined his way into the navy
> not seeing the world

but only as a blur thru finely coiffed hair
a perfumed shoulder
an upturned face
lip smiling promises
dance with me always dancing
never a misstep
but one-two one-two cha cha cha
thirteen grandchildren later
"one of them had to come out looking filipino
dark brown, flat nose . . . like me"
a wallet full of memories
i hear his voice whispering
now he's asking *me* to dance . . .

autumn/home

the phone rang one sunday afternoon.
   "Hello?"
   "Hello? Virgie?"
   "Yes—who's this? . . . Frankie, is that you?"
   "Yeah, it's me."
   "Frankie, is everything all right? Where are you?"
   "Chinese Hospital. But I'm okay, don't worry."
   "What are you doing in the hospital?"
   "You know old men need a tune-up once in a while just like cars. So I got tuned up and I'm leaving tomorrow."
   "Are you sure everything's all right? What did the doctors say? Do you want me to come see you?"
   "Of course, always. But that's not why I called."
   "Okay." I said patiently. "Why did you call me, Frankie?"
   "I just wanted to tell you . . . you're not going to forget me are you?"
oh, god, frankie—don't talk like that. being in a hospital doesn't mean you have to die. "I know I'm just a crazy old man, but don't forget—I love you."
   "Frankie, don't be silly, of course I won't forget."
   "Do you still love me, Virgie?"

"Of course, manong. Listen, don't worry. I'll come dance with you next weekend at Manilatown."

He laughed. "That damn doctor told me not to dance, but he's so young, what does he know? Dancing is good for the heart. It's good for an old man." he was silent for a moment. "Okay . . . don't forget me now."

no, manong. i won't. i can't. because i have dreams about you. and i never forget my dreams . . .

dream

he reached into one of those mysterious pockets men always have and brought out his wallet. he took out his photos, neatly ordered and fanned them like playing cards in his hand. the photos ranged from sepia-tone to color. in each one was frankie, a girl friend—blonde or redhead—or a relative. he invited me to look at them and i bent closer to see

> one photo, black and white
> a nightclub dark
> cigarette smoke
> frankie smiling
> with his arms holding
> his dancing partner
> not a blondie, but me
> with soft curls and
> cadillac-red lipstick
> holding on to my carabao
> in the storm of music
> darkness and light
> we moved in a precious bubble
> dancing in that merry-go-round
> of people, knowing that if we
> stopped dancing, the dream
> would end and we would be
> only a photo in frankie's wallet.

i held the small photo in my fingers, wanting to see the couples dance to the silent music. frankie put his wallet away, and looked at me sadly, shaking his head, then held my hands like china cups in his big dark hands.

suddenly he put his hand to his head as though he were in pain and started doing a clumsy but graceful box step across the sidewalk, bumping into people as he went. he danced to the throbbing of pain inside his head, his hands trying to contain the loudness which seemed to be deafening him. the crowd of tourists waiting at the corner became his last obstacle as they parted like a gate to let him race onto the street like a horse with a broken leg. a cable car, coasting down california street, stopped too late and as the crowd cried in horror, the silent music frankie had been hearing inside his head came to an abrupt halt.

and in the photo, everything had gone dark, as though the band had stopped playing and the drunk swaying couples had gone home to sleep and could dance no more.

PART FIVE

Clearing the Mist: Identity

Introduction

Identity is a simple word yet it raises many complex issues and causes much introspection. We grapple not only with our individual understanding of ourselves, men, and other women, but also with broader influences of history, society, cultural heritage, and traditional structures. Who am I as an Asian American? Who am I as an Asian American woman? "Growing Up Asian in America," by Kesaye Noda, tries to address some of these difficult questions.

Our identity as Asian American women is influenced by how others see us; of more importance is how we see ourselves. Both Nellie Wong's "Broad Shoulders" and Angela Lobo-Cobb's "Behind the Shadow" present strong women who are not content living within the stereotype of the Asian American female as passive and submissive. The chance encounter between a nisei woman and a long lost love in "Makapuu Bay," by Wakako Yamauchi, gives the woman a chance to redefine her relationship with the man and with her daughter.

We are diverse not only in terms of ethnicity and generation but also many other factors. Barbara Posadas's article "Mestiza Girlhood," and Jonny Price's "Double Doors" look at one of those factors: interracial marriage. Amerasian children face unique identity issues because they embody disparate cultures and histories.

Sexual preference and physical disabilities are other factors that shape the identities of some Asian American women. Pam H. in "Asian American Lesbians: An Emerging Voice in the Asian American Community" describes attempts by Asian American lesbians to survive in a community that either condemns or ignores them. The tendency to look the other way when confronted by someone who is different extends to Asian American women who are physically handicapped. "You're Short, Besides!" by Sucheng Chan, is about her struggles to overcome disabilities caused by polio, as well as the prejudices of her family, community, and professional colleagues.

As Asian American women, we are taking risks to describe and define ourselves. As we reveal more of ourselves, we become more vulnerable. But at the same time we affirm each other and help clear away the cloud of misinformation and negative stereotypes perpetuated by our society, and by our own doubts and insecurities.

Behind the Shadow

ANGELA LOBO-COBB

Why should I be
    the remnants of Ajanta's fresco,
Lotus-eyed mists
    of your perception,
A black shock of hair?

Why should I awaken
    from ancient ruins,
A rib caged
    female Torso,
Embalmed
    into the joints of bones
Contoured into the passage
    of floating pelvis's
Flute tone
    in silent stone?

My song is one of breaking
    not the rhythms
Of some ancient rite.
Art for me
    cannot be arranged with

Strung flowers
     but breathes in the struggle
     of water reeds.

I cannot be the instrument
     you strum,
     The loose silk you drape
          your designs upon.

I shall wash the henna
     off my hands,
Clear the film
     from my eyes,
To perceive the substance
     behind the shadow.

Double Doors

JONNY SULLIVAN PRICE

To my Great-great Aunt Leila, an eighth-generation Jordan

Winter light sifts
through the curtains
of your small room,
          blessing
your white head bent
over the writing table.
               And your hair
brightens like milkweed.
Your pen moves with steady
emphasis, underlining
words with a fervor

"Papa's mother was a Washburn. John
Washburn came to Duxbury, Mass. about
1631. His son John married Elizabeth
Mitchell, granddaughter of *Francis
Cook, the Pilgrim*."

Glass squeaks as
         branches
skew against the
window panes,
       exotic with ice.
Fathers and strange brides.

"*What* was there for me *to forgive* about
your father's marriage? I had no *feeling
against* the *Japanese*. It was *strange* to me
to have a marriage with someone of
another race, but your grandmother told
me your mother was a Christian, which was
of more importance."

My first birthday, I was dressed in a red silk kimono.
I ate
rice wrapped in seaweed,
small fish.
Sitting on Ojiichan's knee. I reached
for the single candle.
        Who can explain
this world to you?

Twenty-two years since
we met in Tucson the autumn
I was four. I thought
you'd always been old.
You sang to me songs,
taught me how to stretch
my fingers as I chanted:
       Here's the church, Here's the steeple

"They were all ones I was taught when I
was in first grade. You did the motions
with me, as I sang, and I enjoyed it.
When your sister Kei got home, she tried
so hard. The rhyme was: Open the door,
And here are the people. (Mama taught
me that.)"

O Leila. I want to
sing for you again.
        My two hands
parting like doors.
        My fingers
unlocking
something your hands taught them.

Growing Up Asian in America

KESAYA E. NODA

Sometimes when I was growing up, my identity seemed to hurtle toward me and paste itself right to my face. I felt that way, encountering
the stereotypes of my race perpetuated by non-Japanese people (primarily white) who may or may not have had contact with other Japanese
in America. "You don't like cheese, do you?" someone would ask. "I
know your people don't like cheese." Sometimes questions came making
allusions to history. That was another aspect of the identity. Events that
had happened quite apart from the me who stood silent in that moment
connected my face with an incomprehensible past. "Your parents were in
California? Were they in those camps during the war?" And sometimes
there were phrases or nicknames: "Lotus Blossom." I was sometimes
addressed or referred to as racially Japanese, sometimes as Japanese
American, and sometimes as an Asian woman. Confusions and distor-
tions abounded.

How is one to know and define oneself? From the inside—within a context that is self defined, from a grounding in community and a connection with culture and history that are comfortably accepted? Or from the outside—in terms of messages received from the media and people who are often ignorant? Even as an adult I can still see two sides of my face and past. I can see from the inside out, in freedom. And I can see from the outside in, driven by the old voices of childhood and lost in anger and fear.

I am racially Japanese

A voice from my childhood says: "You are other. You are less than. You are unalterably alien." This voice has its own history. We have indeed been seen as other and alien since the early years of our arrival in the United States. The very first immigrants were welcomed and sought as laborers to replace the dwindling numbers of Chinese, whose influx had been cut off by the Chinese Exclusion Act of 1882. The Japanese fell natural heir to the same anti-Asian prejudice that had arisen against the Chinese. As soon as they began striking for better wages, they were no longer welcomed.

I can see myself today as a person historically defined by law and custom as being forever alien. Being neither "free white," nor "African," our people in California were deemed "aliens, ineligible for citizenship," no matter how long they intended to stay here. Aliens ineligible for citizenship were prohibited from owning, buying, or leasing land. They did not and could not belong here. The voice in me remembers that I am always a *Japanese* American in the eyes of many. A third-generation German American is an American. A third-generation Japanese American is a Japanese American. Being Japanese means being a danger to the country during the war and knowing how to use chopsticks. I wear this history on my face.

I move to the other side. I see a different light and claim a different context. My race is a line that stretches across ocean and time to link me to the shrine where my grandmother was raised. Two high, white banners lift in the wind at the top of the stone steps leading to the shrine. It is time for the summer festival. Black characters are written against the sky as boldly as the clouds, as lightly as kites, as sharply as the big black crows I used to see above the fields in New Hampshire. At festival time there is liquor and food, ritual, discipline, and abandonment. There is music and drunkenness and invocation. There is hope. Another season has come. Another season has gone.

I am racially Japanese. I have a certain claim to this crazy place where the prayers intoned by a neighboring Shinto priest (standing in for my grandmother's nephew who is sick) are drowned out by the rehearsals for the pop singing contest in which most of the villagers will compete later that night. The village elders, the priest, and I stand respectfully upon the immaculate, shining wooden floor of the outer shrine, bowing our heads before the hidden powers. During the patchy intervals when I can hear him, I notice the priest has a stutter. His voice flutters up to my ears only occasionally because two men and a woman are singing gustily into a microphone in the compound, testing the sound system. A pre-recorded tape of guitars, samisens, and drums accompanies them. Rock music and Shinto prayers. That night, to loud applause and cheers, a young man is given the award for the most *netsuretsu*—passionate, burning—rendition of a song. We roar our approval of the reward. Never mind that his voice had wandered and slid, now slightly above, now slightly below the given line of the melody. Netsuretsu. Netsuretsu.

In the morning, my grandmother's sister kneels at the foot of the stone stairs to offer her morning prayers. She is too crippled to climb the stairs, so each morning she kneels here upon the path. She shuts her eyes for a few seconds, her motions as matter of fact as when she washes rice. I linger longer than she does, so reluctant to leave, savoring the connection I feel with my grandmother in America, the past, and the power that lives and shines in the morning sun.

Our family has served this shrine for generations. The family's need to protect this claim to identity and place outweighs any individual claim to any individual hope. I am Japanese.

I am a Japanese American

"Weak." I hear the voice from my childhood years. "Passive," I hear. Our parents and grandparents were the ones who were put into those

246

camps. They went without resistance; they offered cooperation as proof of loyalty to America. "Victim," I hear. And, "Silent."

Our parents are painted as hard workers who were socially uncomfortable and had difficulty expressing even the smallest opinion. Clean, quiet, motivated, and determined to match the American way; that is us, and that is the story of our time here.

"Why did you go into those camps," I raged at my parents, frightened by my own inner silence and timidity. "Why didn't you do anything to resist? Why didn't you name it the injustice it was?" Couldn't our parents even think? Couldn't they? Why were we so passive?

I shift my vision and my stance. I am in California. My uncle is in the midst of the sweet potato harvest. He is pressed, trying to get the harvesting crews onto the field as quickly as possible, worried about the flow of equipment and people. His big pickup is pulled off to the side, motor running, door ajar. I see two tractors in the yard in front of an old shed; the flat bed harvesting platform on which the workers will stand has already been brought over from the other field. It's early morning. The workers stand loosely grouped and at ease, but my uncle looks as harried and tense as a police officer trying to unsnarl a New York City traffic jam. Driving toward the shed, I pull my car off the road to make way for an approaching tractor. The front wheels of the car sink luxuriously into the soft, white sand by the roadside and the car slides to a dreamy halt, tail still on the road. I try to move forward. I try to move back. The front bites contentedly into the sand, the back lifts itself at a jaunty angle. My uncle sees me and storms down the road, running. He is shouting before he is even near me.

"What's the matter with you," he screams. "What the hell are you doing?" In his frenzy, he grabs his hat off his head and slashes it through the air across his knee. He is beside himself. "Don't you know how to drive in sand? What's the matter with you? You've blocked the whole roadway. How am I supposed to get my tractors out of here? Can't you use your head? You've cut off the whole roadway, and we've got to get out of here."

I stand on the road before him helplessly thinking, "No, I don't know how to drive in sand. I've never driven in sand."

"I'm sorry, uncle," I say, burying a smile beneath a look of sincere apology. I notice my deep amusement and my affection for him with great curiosity. I am usually devastated by anger. Not this time.

During the several years that follow I learn about the people and the place, and much more about what has happened in this California village where my parents grew up. The issei, our grandparents, made this settlement in the desert. Their first crops were eaten by rabbits and ravaged by insects. The land was so barren that men walking from house to house sometimes got lost. Women came here too. They bore children in 114 degree heat, then carried the babies with them into the fields to nurse when they reached the end of each row of grapes or other truck farm crops.

I had had no idea what it meant to buy this kind of land and make it grow green. Or how, when the war came, there was no space at all for the subtlety of being who we were—Japanese Americans. Either/or was the way. I hadn't understood that people were literally afraid for their lives then, that their money had been frozen in banks; that there was a five-mile travel limit; that when the early evening curfew came and they were inside their houses, some of them watched helplessly as people they knew went into their barns to steal their belongings. The police were patrolling the road, interested only in violators of curfew. There was no help for them in the face of thievery. I had not been able to imagine before what it must have felt like to be an American—to know absolutely that one is an American—and yet to have almost everyone else deny it. Not only deny it, but challenge that identity with machine guns and troops of white American soldiers. In those circumstances it was difficult to say, "I'm a Japanese American." "American" had to do.

But now I can say that I am a Japanese American. It means I have a place here in this country, too. I have a place here on the East Coast, where our neighbor is so much a part of our family that my mother never passes her house at night without glancing at the lights to see if she is home and safe; where my parents have hauled hundreds of pounds of rocks from fields and arduously planted Christmas trees and blueberries, lilacs, asparagus, and crab apples; where my father still dreams of angling a stream to a new bed so that he can dig a pond in the field and fill it with water and fish. "The neighbors already came for their Christmas tree?" he asks in December. "Did they like it? Did they like it?"

I have a place on the West Coast where my relatives still farm, where I heard the stories of feuds and backbiting, and where I saw that people survived and flourished because fundamentally they trusted and relied upon one another. A death in the family is not just a death in a family; it is a death in the community. I saw people help each other with money, materials, labor, attention, and time. I saw men gather once a year, without fail, to clean the grounds of a ninety-year-old woman who had helped the community before, during, and after the war. I saw her remembering them with birthday cards sent to each of their children.

I come from a people with a long memory and a distinctive grace. We live our thanks. And we are Americans. Japanese Americans.

I am a Japanese American woman

Woman. The last piece of my identity. It has been easier by far for me to know myself in Japan and to see my place in America than it has been to accept my line of connection with my own mother. She was my dark self, a figure in whom I thought I saw all that I feared most in myself. Growing into womanhood and looking for some model of strength, I turned away from her. Of course, I could not find what I sought. I was looking for a black feminist or a white feminist. My mother is neither white nor black.

My mother is a woman who speaks with her life as much as with her tongue. I think of her with her own mother. Grandmother had Parkinson's disease and it had frozen her gait and set her fingers, tongue, and feet jerking and trembling in a terrible dance. My aunts and uncles wanted her to be able to live in her own home. They fed her, bathed her, dressed her, awoke at midnight to take her for one last trip to the bathroom. My aunts (her daughters-in-law) did most of the care, but my mother went from New Hampshire to California each summer to spend a month living with grandmother, because she wanted to and because she wanted to give my aunts at least a small rest. During those hot summer days, mother lay on the couch watching the television or reading, cooking foods that grandmother liked, and speaking little. Grandmother thrived under her care.

The time finally came when it was too dangerous for grandmother to live alone. My relatives kept finding her on the floor beside her bed when they went to wake her in the mornings. My mother flew to California to help clean the house and make arrangements for grandmother to enter a local nursing home. On her last day at home, while grandmother was sitting in her big, overstuffed armchair, hair combed and wearing a green summer dress, my mother went to her and knelt at her feet. "Here, Mamma," she said. "I've polished your shoes." She lifted grandmother's legs and helped her into the shiny black shoes. My grandmother looked down and smiled slightly. She left her house walking, supported by her children, carrying her pocket book, and wearing her polished black shoes. "Look, Mamma," my mom had said, kneeling. "I've polished your shoes."

Just the other day, my mother came to Boston to visit. She had recently lost a lot of weight and was pleased with her new shape and her feeling of good health. "Look at me, Kes," she exclaimed, turning toward me, front and back, as naked as the day she was born. I saw her small breasts and the wide, brown scar, belly button to pubic hair, that marked her because my brother and I were both born by Caesarean section. Her hips were small. I was not a large baby, but there was so little room for me in her that when she was carrying me she could not even begin to bend over toward the floor. She hated it, she said.

"Don't I look good? Don't you think I look good?"

I looked at my mother, smiling and as happy as she, thinking of all the times I have seen her naked. I have seen both my parents naked throughout my life, as they have seen me. From childhood through adulthood we've had our naked moments, sharing baths, idle conversations picked up as we moved between showers and closets, hurried moments at the beginning of days, quiet moments at the end of days.

I know this to be Japanese, this ease with the physical, and it makes me think of an old, Japanese folk song. A young nursemaid, a fifteen-year-old girl, is singing a lullaby to a baby who is strapped to her back. The nursemaid has been sent as a servant to a place far from her own home. "We're the beggars," she says, "and they are the nice people. Nice people wear fine sashes. Nice clothes."

> If I should drop dead,
> bury me by the roadside!
> I'll give a flower
> to everyone who passes.
>
> What kind of flower?
> The cam-cam-camellia {tsun-tsun-tsubaki}
> watered by Heaven:
> alms water.[1]

The nursemaid is the intersection of heaven and earth, the intersection of the human, the natural world, the body, and the soul. In this song, with clear eyes, she looks steadily at life, which is sometimes so very terrible and sad. I think of her while looking at my mother, who is standing on the red and purple carpet before me, laughing, without any clothes.

I am my mother's daughter. And I am myself.

I am a Japanese American woman.

Epilogue

I recently heard a man from West Africa share some memories of his childhood. He was raised Muslim, but when he was a young man, he found himself deeply drawn to Christianity. He struggled against this inner impulse for years, trying to avoid the church yet feeling pushed to return to it again and again. "I would have done *anything* to avoid the change," he said. At last, he became Christian. Afterwards he was afraid to go home, fearing that he would not be accepted. The fear was groundless, he discovered, when at last he returned—he had separated himself, but his family and friends (all Muslim) had not separated themselves from him.

The man, who is now a professor of religion, said that in the Africa he knew as a child and a young man, pluralism was embraced rather than feared. There was "a kind of tolerance that did not deny your particularity," he said. He alluded to zestful, spontaneous debates that would sometimes loudly erupt between Muslims and Christians in the village's public spaces. His memories of an atheist who harangued the villagers when he came to visit them once a week moved me deeply. Perhaps the man was an agricultural advisor or inspector. He harrassed the women. He would say:

> "Don't go to the fields! Don't even bother to go to the fields. Let God take care of you. He'll send you the food. If you believe in God, why do you need to work? You don't need to work! Let God put the seeds in the ground. Stay home."

The professor said, "The women laughed, you know? They just laughed. Their attitude was, 'Here is a child of God. When will he come home?'"

The storyteller, the professor of religion, smiled a most fantastic, tender smile as he told this story. "In my country, there is a deep affirmation of the oneness of God," he said. "The atheist and the women were having quite different experiences in their encounter, though the atheist did not know this. He saw himself as quite separate from the women. But the women did not see themselves as being separate from him. 'Here is a child of God,' they said. 'When will he come home?'"

Makapuu Bay

WAKAKO YAMAUCHI

That was the time I went to Hawaii, the first real vacation I'd ever had, one I'd earned myself. I had a small windfall, a story I wrote was accepted for television, and also I was asked to do a presentation in Hawaii for an Ethnic American Writers Conference, and so my airfare, a per diem, and a small fee were offered. At that time, I invited Kay who had been my loyal supporter, cook, confidante, and nurse since the time of my divorce from her father. In spite of the uneven marriage, I had assumed I would always be married to Joe; divorce among Japanese Americans is uncommon and I was not prepared for it.

That was the worst period of my life. I became a walking zombie with no interest at all in day-to-day reality—the eating, sleeping, the laughing, and loving of life. I finally pulled through without a psychiatrist; I made Kay the receptacle for all my poisonous feelings and she held them for me (I didn't know this then) until I could put them in their proper places, which I have since done, and I wanted to thank her for her support. And for a change she agreed to go with me.

I look at these vacation snaps and relive that time; I take a magnifying glass (my eyes are getting so bad) and minutely examine the pictures in case there's an expression I'd missed, a mood I'd lost—in case I'd forgotten the time of day for each picture. I look for the source of light: shadows are long on this one, changing the green on the ground; a yellow glow catches the palm fronds; skies are heavy for the night's rain.

And the pictures at Makapuu—that hot day at the bay—those tiny figures in the background of a family on a picnic, so long gone (the children must be grown now), strangers caught in my camera, strangers sitting in my album. I had nearly forgotten how white the sand was in the afternoon light, or the magnificent blues of the sea. And the hot sun, yes.

Today I sit with my album and peruse the pictures as though my life depended on remembering the sand, the afternoon light, the sea at Makapuu Bay. I did not mean to think about it.

It was a wonderful conference with writers, poets, chanters, dancers, and actors. Kay and I had agreed, since we were both adults, not to stay too close to each other. She was often in the company of one young man, whom she did not introduce to me, and when I veered near, I heard the kind of laughter a mother doesn't often hear from her daughter. And I was happy.

Kay was fifteen when Joe and I split up. Though I didn't relate it to the divorce then, I noticed she began to stick very close to home, and the few attachments she formed were one-to-one, as though she reasoned that more people meant more chances for abandonment. It wasn't until much later, in fact just before we left for Hawaii, that she confessed the best time of her life was the fifteen years before the divorce. Though intellectually she realized her father was happier now with his new wife and family, and I was happier with my many love affairs (actually there were only two), we had left her at that place in the past. For years she prayed we would return for her so she could resume life.

I cried then and said I was returning for her now. I told her the old concept I'd been taught and also imposed on her, of a nuclear family— one man, one family—was no longer viable for us and we must push on, not necessarily together, but forward to explore and discover more work- able philosophies for ourselves. I told her I would never withdraw my love and support. No matter where she stood, she would not be alone. She should not be afraid to love; that joy was worth the risk of pain. After all, one does not die from pain unless one chooses to. I am witness to that.

With all that said, we went to Hawaii to have a good time, and I was happy to hear Kay's tinkling laughter. Hawaii would not have been my first choice of places to visit. I'd heard how commercialized the islands had become, high-rise hotels dominating the landscape, waters sullied by tourist droppings. I was not prepared for the incredible beauty of the islands, the magnificent colors, the trade winds, the tropical rains.

I asked Kay as I have always done, "Are you having fun?"

She answered as she has always done, "Yes."

I asked, "Don't you just love it here?"

She said, "Yes, I do."

My presentation was scheduled for the last day of the conference. I was asked to speak on the literature of the camp experience in World War II. During the war with Japan, all Japanese and Japanese Americans were incarcerated in internment centers in the more remote areas of the American Midwest. These places were commonly called camps. The year before, I'd written a similar paper on camp poetry, so I added some new material and read the piece and quickly went on to the discussion. The first question was too involved, I simply shrugged and said, "I don't know." The rest was easy; questions dealt with my own writing, where my characters come from, where the plot originates, do I outline first, etc., like the questions people ask painters, I paint too: "What size brush do you use? Do you make small sketches first?" I said, no, my stories start with a character and a situation, then they write themselves, although . . . yes, there is an underlying vein, like an earthquake fault that yields to a certain destiny.

After the talk my throat felt dry, so I went out to find a coffee machine. Several people followed me, some to congratulate me while I edged my way to the coffee. I was fumbling for coins in my purse when someone slipped the money in for me and asked, "Black, wasn't it, Pinky?"

Pinky! I hadn't heard that name for twenty-five years. After I married Joe, he decided it was too cute, too frivolous a name for his wife and banned it, stamped it out wherever he heard it.

I got the name in camp—Poston, Arizona, where my father and I were sent (my mother had died two years before the war). The dust there was so malevolent I was often afflicted with a condition called pink eye. They called me "Pinky," and the name stuck even after my environment changed—until Joe decided to obliterate the name along with my past.

My heart leaped as I thought about Mitch Ochiai.

I'd met him at the camp swimming hole. The "hole" was a deep excavation filled with stagnant Colorado River water set in the center of a fire break. On one end was a crude diving board and in the deepest middle was a floating barge. I passed by the swimming hole one evening while Mitch was doing one of his perfect swan dives, and for several evenings thereafter I watched for this perfect dive and then moved on. He was always alone—a young man of twenty who swam alone, who sat on the barge and watched the sun go down, who could soar like a bird and suspend himself in the Arizona sky.

I couldn't swim, but I decided to get in the same water with this young man. For a while I endured the murky green water, the slimy mud and algae, to stand neck deep in it until I worked up the courage to ask him, as he moved close to the shallow edge, if he would teach me to swim.

Mitch was an enthusiastic teacher. He manually worked my head and arms to get the technique just right, and in other ways tried hard to teach me the rudiments—even going underwater to watch my kick. But I was inept and could not even float without his hand under my belly. Besides, I had other things in mind.

Between gurgles ("Pinky, you'll get sick drinking all that bad water") I learned that Mitch was attending the university in Berkeley at the outbreak of the war and was originally sent to a camp in Utah. He had enlisted in a special military service and was scheduled to train in the fall in Minneapolis. He had come to Poston to spend his remaining time as a civilian with his father. I learned also that Mitch was gentle and, unlike other boys I knew, he was not forever trying to impress me with his cleverness, what we now call "macho." He said, "I have no herd instinct." I was a loner too, and it seemed I had at last found one of my own. Mitch did not speak of a mother. We were both motherless.

One evening while we were laughing and splashing at the pool's edge, I noticed an old man watching us carefully. Mitch introduced him as his father and they invited me to their barrack. While Mr. Ochiai brewed tea, he sent Mitch to the canteen for cookies. And as he went slowly through the ritual of tea—the boiling of the water, the mixing of the herbs, and the steeping—he talked about Mitch: that he was a brilliant scholar and had many stories published in the university magazine, and that finally in his junior year he'd been made the editor.

"I'm proud of Michio. He's the first Japanese American in the university's history to become editor of this scholarly journal—the *only* Japanese," he said. He brought out the paperback and pointed to Mitch's name.

"How old are you, Pinky-san?" he asked.

"Eighteen," I said.

"Ah!" He was delighted. "You are so young. You have much to look forward to: so many boyfriends . . . a pretty girl like you will have many boyfriends."

Then summer was over. Those were the war years and men and boys were constantly leaving us. Our lives, already complicated by the incarceration and hostilities with the country of our heritage, were always threatened with separations that conceivably were final. Mitch went away to Minneapolis.

He wrote wonderful letters. He was often very funny. Sometimes he remembered our summer idyll; he was lonely too.

Within a short time I cleared the camp security board and my father and the government released me to go to Chicago. I got a job in a candy factory and shared an apartment with a religious old woman from

Croatia, and I waited for Mitch's letters and his weekend passes. Mrs. Creta did not like me to keep company with Mitch in the apartment, so we went to movies and coffee shops and walked up and down the deserted avenues at night. When the weather warmed, we walked barefoot along the shores of Lake Michigan.

That's the way it was. We sang songs, we laughed, talked, and often walked hand in hand in silence. In spite of the harried times, the imminence of separation, I felt a quiet joy with him. We did not speak of marriage or of love. I lived for these weekends, those letters. I smile now at the things that gave me such intense pleasure: a pressure on the arm, a certain look, a space between words. It was a different time.

The last time I saw Mitch, he kissed me ("I think you are as innocent as I am in these matters"). And shortly after that I was called back to Poston by Joe Noda, the block manager. My father was dying.

The train from Chicago took three days; I did not get back to Poston in time. I arrived on the night of the wake. Joe and the mortician arranged the funeral for the next day; they explained the weather was too warm to delay the ceremony. I was now an orphan.

I was in Poston two weeks putting my father's affairs in order when I got a letter forwarded from Chicago in Mrs. Creta's wavering and inaccurate hand. Mitch said he had gone to see me and a strange young woman had answered the door . . . no, she knew no Pinky; no, Mrs. Creta was out of town. He walked down the stairs and for the first time noticed how worn the steps were. He said he smelled cabbage cooking in the hall (was it supper time then?). He said he was shipping out to parts unknown in the morning and had come to say goodbye to me.

By this time the dispersal of camp was ordered and I had to decide where to relocate. I didn't have the heart to return to Chicago. Joe suggested I go with his family to Los Angeles. I thought in Los Angeles I might still make contact with Mitch. Maybe he would be detained there.

I traveled with them and then stayed in a hostel until I could find an apartment and a job. I ended up hand-painting shower curtains in a factory and spent one bleak year waiting to hear from Mitch. When Joe Noda pressed me for attention, I explained about Mitch and he waited a while and then pressed me again. Finally I put an end to that lonely year. And at that point Joe began to call me by my given name: Sachiko.

Much later I read in the Japanese newspapers that Mr. Ochiai died in San Francisco (did he wait for Mitch to return to the university?); and I supposed that Mitch, listed as his surviving son, had come back to claim his father. By that time I had little Kay and I'd begun to write and paint and my life with Joe was secure in its ups and downs. I did not care to see Mitch.

Still, once in a while he would appear in my dreams and the sweet-sad feeling of unfinished business, of being close to something very important awakened me and I would wonder if I didn't try hard enough to contact him, or he me, those many years ago. With the reality of morning—Joe's warm body against me, Kay's need for attention—this feeling slipped back into its own dimension like songs sung from another room or stories of someone else's pain. I supposed Mitch, like me, had gone on to marry someone and probably had a family and certainly would have written several novels. If there was a memory of me at all, it was probably as distant as mine of him.

My marriage almost lasted forever, but not quite long enough or short enough, and in my middle age I was facing life alone again. No, I wasn't alone. Kay was with me this time—a child leading me, following the bread crumbs, picking our way back to sanity. Then through a fluke, some of the stories I'd written while still married found their way to publication and one was bought for television and *voilà!* I was doing a minor lecture circuit.

And so in Hawaii, with the word "Pinky," feelings of youth and love and girlish laughter returned to me and my heart jumped there in front of the coffee machine. I didn't raise my head until it cleared.

He hadn't changed much—a little gray, almost as slim, a tired look around his eyes, but still the boyish smile. With our two coffees in our hands, our embrace was only a body contact, a kiss like wind against my cheek. (The scent of wine on his lips; was it so difficult to come?) He'd read in the papers about the conference and the presentation on camp literature, and wondered if Sachiko Noda could be the Pinky he once knew. And he'd come to see. He lived in Honolulu.

We drove to Waikiki and the shallows of Hanauma and we stopped at Makapuu Bay. Mitch pointed out Rabbit Island and the cove where he spent much of his free time ("Waves come fast and clean here—the best for body surfing"). We briefly remembered the Poston swimming hole ("Why wouldn't you learn to swim, Pinky?"); we did not speak of the days in Chicago, what took me away, the death of his father or mine. We passed over the years between:

"You never married?" I asked.

"No, I'm free still."

"You like it this way?"

"Well, it's better for me. I'm free."

"Of course, your writing. . . ."

"I've freed myself from that too. I have no novel for you, Pinky."

"But why?"

"Because," he laughed dryly. "Here you are, still literally seething with innocence, even after all these years, and I must be the one to tell you things are not what they seem; that sometimes the illusion and the enlightenment are found at the same place, are one and the same. So does it matter whether one takes the long trip around to arrive at the same place?"

"Is this the truth or is it your theory?"

"Each finds one's own truth."

"And you've wandered over the face of the earth?"

"In a manner of speaking, yes."

"To the Himalayas—the gurus of India?" I tried to make light.

"The Diamond Head of Oahu."

"The monasteries of Japan, at least."

"At least."

"And you've chosen this green and blue and gold island with the swaying palms."

"Well, I'm stationed here, Pinky."

"You're still with the military?"

"Yes." A smile died in his eyes.

We returned to Makapuu the next day. Mitch swam while I waited on the rocks, tasting the salt wind, snapping pictures, writing in my journal, trying to find the exact words for the color of the sea, trying to nail down an elusive feeling of living a recurring dream. But this was Makapuu—another time, another era, not a fragment of the past dislodged from its time frame. This was now, and Mitch was one of those little dots in the changing blue, moving with the surf, almost coming ashore, drawing out to sea again. I wrote in my journal: "This moment *is*. No more, no less." I stood on the black rocks and snapped a family of picnickers under the palms, freezing an instant of their laughter.

We went one more time to Makapuu ("I'll wave my arm and you'll know which dot is me") and later stopped at a terrace cafe facing the sea. We were alone, the sun was setting, and a strange sense of endlessness prevailed. I was thinking that we were the intruders here, that the sun would continue to set like this on this island forever while we died in agony or joy or ennui and cafe terraces crumbled and cities decayed. So why shouldn't a small persistent dream also perish here in Makapuu with the last of the day's sun? Mitch touched my hand.

"You look so sad," he said.

"I'm releasing a dream."

"The past is not retrievable," he said.

Kay and I finished the vacation with a tour of the islands. We tramped through miles of volcanic ash, cane and pineapple fields and factories, lush valleys, stuffy museums, and scores of souvenir shops. In Lahaina I found a paperweight—a fragile heart-shaped shell, a heart cockle, encased in a bubble of plastic. A man I know said he'd been twenty years in medicine but had never seen the cockles of a body's heart, and I meant to carry it two thousand miles across the emerald sea to him ("You've been looking in the wrong places, sir"). I bought strings of coral, T-shirts, black sand in tiny bottles, and I bought ti leaf liquor and macadamia nut chocolates.

That was a long time ago—seven, eight years? When I look at these photos of Hawaii I can almost smell the salt spray. The sun is forever suspended at late afternoon, a moment standing still. Sometimes, along with a certain sadness, a kind of joy returns. Then I remember Mitch again, the conference, and I remember Kay's laughter.

Kay was never the same after Hawaii. She dropped out of college, enrolled in an airline training program, and became a flight attendant. She now sleeps in many of the major cities of the world. She stops by now and then with expensive gifts which I've put in the room which used to be hers: a samovar, Persian stone rubbings, Indian baskets, ivory and jade carvings, a piece of a Roman relic. I keep the relic in a dish with the broken coral we collected in Maui.

The heart cockle paperweight is in the room too. I didn't give it to my friend; I couldn't part with it. It has all the beautiful colors of the shores of Hawaii, and depending on how I hold it, it is greener or bluer. Sometimes the light catches the shell and it shines all gold and white and blue and green. Yet if I hold it directly at eye level, it is clearly only a plastic bubble and one can see that the colors are just at the base of the paperweight. I suspect there is a way to look at things so that truth clearly separates itself from illusion.

Broad Shoulders

NELLIE WONG

How she loved broad shoulders. Hadn't she always admired Joan Crawford for her shoulders, not her shoulder pads, not her pageboy haircut, nor her full, painted mouth? She loved the broad shoulders of leaders, women leaders. She wanted to be a leader, but she didn't know how.

The woman picked at her heart with dry fingers. Her fingers smelled of ointment that she lathered to quell the itching, the swelling from within that lemon juice attacked, or oranges, or white wine. Broad shoulders. The image rose in her mind. Shoulders were ladders to climb on, to stand on, to rise above the world. Shoulders with muscles that flexed, arms of a warrior, with hands that typed, filed, scrubbed, peeled, embroidered, jommed. She peeled off a corn with the bravery of a woman who once was shoulderless, backless, eyeless, empty. Her left foot felt better with the corn peeled off. Her poor little piggy toes. How they squealed. Her legs were the curse of her and yet she loved them the way she loved her own broad shoulders. Sometimes her fingers traveled over the roadmaps on her legs. Sometimes she got lost over the roadmaps and thought that the flakes of dry skin became arrows pointing to freedom.

Love was all she ever asked for: to be loved by a man, a husband, of course, and the woman's shoulders grew and grew. Her shoulders were tofu that absorbed the heat of the Fourth of July, when her skin rose hot and wild as she wore a wool sweater to cover up her neck as firecrackers exploded in Chinatown. Undercover. Coverup. Hide beneath the surface, the skin, the rough, dry skin that erupted tiny red mountains, that itched and itched, that made her scratch, so that on the hottest day of the summer she had to wear a long-sleeved sweater to cover up her eruptions while the boys and girls of Chinatown ran around in tee-shirts and shorts, short-sleeved cotton dresses, or blouses and pleated skirts. She didn't know the meaning of the word leader. But it tantalized her and touched her broad shoulders. It danced as if in a trance. It pirouetted and leaped high into the air, high above the woman's shoulders, then disappeared.

She knew the meaning of the word heart. Her heart grew so big she thought the moon fell from the heavens and resided inside. The moonbeams became her longings, her wishes, as they shot at her from within her body, her red, red heart. And so she dreamed of becoming heroic, not like Wonder Woman who fought America's enemies with her steel bracelets and short, short skirt, but more like Marilyn Monroe, perhaps, with a mouth that invited touch. Touching lived as far away as a distant cousin in China from this woman's heart. Her fingers were too dry, she insisted. Her knuckles were too big, too ugly, and so she taught herself that her fingers and body weren't hers. They belonged outside to the world, detached from her person, her dry skin, her eyes that danced on top of her hand, as she saw herself lying on a beach in St. Tropez with the sun blazing on a body that she would never have. She was a woman who had learned to live under cover and under cover pointed the toes of a dancer thudding against her wild heart.

But her shoulders, her broad shoulders, she secretly admired. They didn't slope. She wasn't skinny. She always felt full, like her heart that blossomed red-hot peonies, flowers she thought she had never seen, but which she loved the sound of. And she smelled the tea that she drank with her mother and father in dim sum tea houses. Peony tea. *Po-nay cha* in Chinese. But fullness never hung around like a good friend, a pal. When the moonbeams inside her heart went to sleep, the woman's heart drained tears into the sea. The sea was a safe place, a refuge for feeling, a habitat that fed her emptiness though she always felt full because she loved rice crusts burnt to a golden brown. She would burn the pan and then she had to scrub it until her fingers ached. Ah, the shoulders of youth. Ma's eyes that bored through her heart and landed on her shoulders. Bah Bah's eyes that smiled even when he growled unspoken messages. Her shoulders grew so broad, the world entered her mind and her soul. The world whirled inside her stomach and the fullness grew. The fullness roared inside her, beneath her skin and snuck outside like thieves stealing strands form her black, black hair.

Love and romance: what shoulders she lived on, sought. The mountains of China weren't within her reach, nor the Himalayas, nor the buttes of Montana, nor Dorothy's Wizard of Oz. Only her shoulders on which the world sat, rolled around, teasing her, entrancing her, building bridges of steel that gleamed in the sunsets of Acapulco Bay. Wanderlust captured her broad shoulders, brushed her like a falling star, tantalized her like her father's midnight meals of golden porkchops. She would travel far on her shoulders even if she never left home, even if she typed for the rest of her life, even if she was afraid of taking risks. To speak out was taking a risk. To give an opinion, to let others know that she had thoughts, ideas, tables spread with roast duck, asparagus spears, and mandarin oranges.

The woman's shoulders consumed her daily walks to work, past the skyscrapers, the city lake, past the parking lots and construction sites where men welded and drilled and gulped paper cups of hot coffee. And still she delighted at the spring iris, the Japanese magnolias that bloomed in front of her dark eyes. She admired the shoulders of women now. Shoulders that didn't slope. Shoulders that held themselves up like stars suspended in a midnight sky. Shoulder pads no longer needed to be worn, but they were making a comeback on designer sweatshirt dresses, on batwing-sleeved jackets, even in jogging-suit tops. The woman examined the shoulder pads one day in a department store. They were attached with Velcro. Removable for the wash. Fullness. The woman wanted fullness, not shoulder pads she could remove. She hungered for fullness and yet she knew her body would never yield a child now.

Fullness, she told herself, was not necessarily becoming a mother. Fullness surrounded her: every time she read about children, women, and men being murdered in the name of democracy, for the sake of an economic system that placed profits over people, that took food stamps away from the poor. It was too much for her eyes to see. She once felt eyeless, but she knew she lied. She didn't like what she saw: the men of her youth who shot themselves with opium to dream away the misery of working fourteen-hour days, missing their loved ones in China; the arguments of her parents in their closed bedroom over money, the lack of it; the trips to her father's cousin's grocery store to borrow food on credit; men lying in doorways sleeping away in drunkenness, women who fought over lettuce and bokchoy scraps in the garbage bins of Chinatown.

Shut your eyes, she told herself. Put your fingers in your ears. Don't see, don't hear, and so she obeyed her red, red heart, but her shoulders were stubborn and cradled the images for her, toward the fullness she sought, toward the expression that found its way into the moonbeams that shot through her detached body. If she had never learned to type, where would her fullness be? If her mother and father had had the money to send her to college at seventeen, where would she be now? Not here, in this room, typing after midnight, not here, alone, without husband, without children, without a fire crackling to warm her tender bones.

She still had a full head of hair though she often pretended she had no gray. Sometimes in a fit of vanity she'd yank out a white hair or two, telling herself she would never get old. No, no, not she, who had always lived under cover, not she who talked about how she didn't mind getting old. However, the act of pulling a white hair or two only lived like a moonbeam that escaped from her red, red heart.

She would look at her skin and know she was aging. She would touch the crow's feet beneath her eyes, and the fullness returned, a child coming home wanting her mother's touch. She wanted to travel from one end of the world to the other, but she circled around her shoulders. She often stood on them to see how far, how high, how wide the world could be. If the world could expand inside her stomach, surely it could enhance her vision. Now she heard rifle shots in El Salvador, and she saw peasants lying in heaps in a hamlet. Now she felt the hunger of a child suffering from malnutrition in Somalia. Now she saw a five-year-old girl begging in Mexico City in front of a luxury hotel. Now she saw a poet in Korea in jail for writing about repression, and in her own home in California, she saw the elderly living on the streets, chancing their meals from workers' lunch scraps in the financial districts.

Now her dreams plunged through the silver screen of her youth, and Joan Crawford, that dear woman with broad shoulders, that "dancing lady," fought to dance instead of wearing an organdy apron, a mink coat, even when Franchot Tone was ready to devour her and yet love her, even when Clark Gable was waiting in the wings.

Her shoulders, her shoulders. Would they never stop growing? Would they never stop being tofu? Would the world on her shoulders never fall off? The woman rubbed her eyes. She was tiring now and yet she felt full. The perfume of rice crusts steeping in boiled water rose through her nostrils. Ma sat across from her at the blue formica kitchen table. Ma was smiling, in a dream: her gold tooth gleamed in a field of white daisies. "Ma!" the woman cried out, "thank you for my broad shoulders! I've never had a chance to tell you that I love you." The woman's voice snapped off. Ma's gold tooth was gone. Ma was gone and the white daisies vanished into the silence of the cold night air.

The woman rubbed her shoulders. They were indeed broad. And so what if the shoulders were tofu, the firm, Chinese-style kind? Moon-beams still resided in her heart and now when shots of silver streaked through her body, she came home to rest, and her shoulders rose and rose until she thought she would float. Her shoulders would guide her toward fullness, on the roadmaps on her legs, inside her red, red heart, outside her knuckly fingers. Her sisters would always be around her: the blood sisters, but especially her revolutionary sisters, the ones who spoke out defending her and themselves, the ones who wrote letters to the editor protesting racist stereotypes in a play, the ones who unflinchingly and eloquently spoke about the strength and leadership of women workers, lesbians, women of all colors, women of all ages, women of all nations. These revolutionary sisters, her comrades, with the broadest, most beautiful shoulders of all. She learned from them because her eyes were wide open now. Somehow her eyes had decided to come out from hiding and nudged her tofu shoulders, firm and yet tender, and as she looked out into the night, she saw the women, walking shoulder to shoulder, she saw the dark violets blooming around them as they rose and lifted the world from her red, red heart.

You're Short, Besides!

SUCHENG CHAN

When asked to write about being a physically handicapped Asian American woman, I considered it an insult. After all, my accomplishments are many, yet I was not asked to write about any of them. Is being handicapped the most salient feature about me? The fact that it might be in the eyes of others made me decide to write the essay as requested. I realized that the way I think about myself may differ considerably from the way others perceive me. And maybe that's what being physically handicapped is all about.

I was stricken simultaneously with pneumonia and polio at the age of four. Uncertain whether I had polio of the lungs, seven of the eight doctors who attended me—all practitioners of Western medicine—told my parents they should not feel optimistic about my survival. A Chinese fortune teller my mother consulted also gave a grim prognosis, but for an entirely different reason: I had been stricken because my name was offensive to the gods. My grandmother had named me "grandchild of wisdom," a name that the fortune teller said was too presumptuous for a girl. So he advised my parents to change my name to "chaste virgin." All these pessimistic predictions notwithstanding, I hung onto life, if only by a thread. For three years, my body was periodically pierced with electric shocks as the muscles of my legs atrophied. Before my illness, I had been an active, rambunctious, precocious, and very curious child. Being confined to bed was thus a mental agony as great as my physical pain. Living in war-torn China, I received little medical attention; physical therapy was unheard of. But I was determined to walk. So one day, when I was six or seven, I instructed my mother to set up two rows of chairs to face each other so that I could use them as I would parallel bars. I attempted to walk by holding my body up and moving it forward with my arms while dragging my legs along behind. Each time I fell, my mother gasped, but I badgered her until she let me try again. After four nonambulatory years, I finally walked once more by pressing my hands against my thighs so my knees wouldn't buckle.

My father had been away from home during most of those years because of the war. When he returned, I had to confront the guilt he felt about my condition. In many East Asian cultures, there is a strong folk belief that a person's physical state in this life is a reflection of how morally or sinfully he or she lived in previous lives. Furthermore, because of the tendency to view the family as a single unit, it is believed that the fate of one member can be caused by the behavior of another. Some of my father's relatives told him that my illness had doubtless been caused by the wild carousing he did in his youth. A well-meaning but somewhat simple man, my father believed them.

Throughout my childhood, he sometimes apologized to me for having to suffer retribution for his former bad behavior. This upset me; it was bad enough that I had to deal with the anguish of not being able to walk, but to have to assuage his guilt as well was a real burden! In other ways, my father was very good to me. He took me out often, carrying me on his shoulders or back, to give me fresh air and sunshine. He did this until I was too large and heavy for him to carry. And ever since I can remember, he has told me that I am pretty.

After getting over her anxieties about my constant falls, my mother decided to send me to school. I had already learned to read some words of Chinese at the age of three by asking my parents to teach me the sounds and meaning of various characters in the daily newspaper. But between the ages of four and eight, I received no education since just staying alive was a full-time job. Much to her chagrin, my mother found no school in Shanghai, where we lived at the time, which would accept me as a student. Finally, as a last resort, she approached the American School which agreed to enroll me only if my family kept an *amah* (a servant who takes care of children) by my side at all times. The tuition at the school was twenty U.S. dollars per month—a huge sum of money during those years of runaway inflation in China—and payable only in U.S. dollars. My family afforded the high cost of tuition and the expense of employing a full-time *amah* for less than a year.

We left China as the Communist forces swept across the country in victory. We found an apartment in Hong Kong across the street from a school run by Seventh-Day Adventists. By that time I could walk a little, so the principal was persuaded to accept me. An *amah* now had to take care of me only during recess when my classmates might easily knock me over as they ran about the playground.

After a year and a half in Hong Kong, we moved to Malaysia, where my father's family had lived for four generations. There I learned to swim in the lovely warm waters of the tropics and fell in love with the sea. On land I was a cripple; in the ocean I could move with the grace of a fish. I liked the freedom of being in the water so much that many years later, when I was a graduate student in Hawaii, I became greatly enamored with a man just because he called me a "Polynesian water nymph."

As my overall health improved, my mother became less anxious about all aspects of my life. She did everything possible to enable me to lead as normal a life as possible. I remember how once some of her colleagues in the high school where she taught criticized her for letting me wear short skirts. They felt my legs should not be exposed to public view. My mother's response was, "All girls her age wear short skirts, so why shouldn't she?"

The years in Malaysia were the happiest of my childhood, even though I was constantly fending off children who ran after me calling, "*Baikah! Baikah!*" ("Cripple! Cripple!" in the Hokkien dialect commonly spoken in Malaysia). The taunts of children mattered little because I was a star pupil. I won one award after another for general scholarship as well as for art and public speaking. Whenever the school had important visitors my teacher always called on me to recite in front of the class.

A significant event that marked me indelibly occurred when I was twelve. That year my school held a music recital and I was one of the students chosen to play the piano. I managed to get up the steps to the stage without any problem, but as I walked across the stage, I fell. Out of the audience, a voice said loudly and clearly, "Ayah! A *baikah* shouldn't be allowed to perform in public." I got up before anyone could get on stage to help me and, with tears streaming uncontrollably down my face, I rushed to the piano and began to play. Beethoven's "Für Elise" had never been played so fiendishly fast before or since, but I managed to finish the whole piece. That I managed to do so made me feel really strong. I never again feared ridicule.

In later years I was reminded of this experience from time to time. During my fourth year as an assistant professor at the University of California at Berkeley, I won a distinguished teaching award. Some weeks later I ran into a former professor who congratulated me enthusiastically. But I said to him, "You know what? I became a distinguished teacher by *limping* across the stage of Dwinelle 155!" (Dwinelle 155 is a large, cold, classroom that most colleagues of mine hate to teach in.) I was rude not because I lacked graciousness but because this man, who had told me that my dissertation was the finest piece of work he had read in fifteen years, had nevertheless advised me to eschew a teaching career.

"Why?" I asked.

"Your leg . . ." he responded.

"What about my leg?" I said, puzzled.

"Well, how would you feel standing in front of a large lecture class?"

"If it makes any difference, I want you to know I've won a number of speech contests in my life, and I am not the least bit self-conscious about speaking in front of large audiences. . . . Look, why don't you write me a letter of recommendation to tell people how brilliant I am, and let *me* worry about my leg!"

This incident is worth recounting only because it illustrates a dilemma that handicapped persons face frequently: those who care about us sometimes get so protective that they unwittingly limit our growth. This former professor of mine had been one of my greatest supporters for two decades. Time after time, he had written glowing letters of recommendation on my behalf. He had spoken as he did because he thought he had my best interests at heart; he thought that if I got a desk job rather than one that required me to be a visible, public person, I would be spared the misery of being stared at.

Americans, for the most part, do not believe as Asians do that physically handicapped persons are morally flawed. But they are equally inept at interacting with those of us who are not able-bodied. Cultural differences in the perception and treatment of handicapped people are most clearly expressed by adults. Children, regardless of where they are, tend to be openly curious about people who do not look "normal." Adults in Asia have no hesitation in asking visibly handicapped people what is wrong with them, often expressing their sympathy with looks of pity, whereas adults in the United States try desperately to be polite by pretending not to notice.

One interesting response I often elicited from people in Asia but have never encountered in America is the attempt to link my physical condition to the state of my soul. Many a time while living and traveling in Asia people would ask me what religion I belonged to. I would tell them that my mother is a devout Buddhist, that my father was baptized a Catholic but has never practiced Catholicism, and that I am an agnostic. Upon hearing this, people would try strenuously to convert me to their religion so that whichever God they believed in could bless me. If I would only attend this church or that temple regularly, they urged, I would surely get cured. Catholics and Buddhists alike have pressed religious medallions into my palm, telling me if I would wear these, the relevant deity or saint would make me well. Once while visiting the tomb of Muhammad Ali Jinnah in Karachi, Pakistan, an old Muslim, after finishing his evening prayers, spotted me, gestured toward my legs, raised his arms heavenward, and began a new round of prayers, apparently on my behalf.

In the United States adults who try to act "civilized" towards handicapped people by pretending they don't notice anything unusual sometimes end up ignoring handicapped people completely. In the first few months I lived in this country, I was struck by the fact that whenever children asked me what was the matter with my leg, their adult companions would hurriedly shush them up, furtively look at me, mumble apologies, and rush their children away. After a few months of such encounters, I decided it was my responsibility to educate these people. So I would say to the flustered adults, "It's okay, let the kid ask." Turning to the child, I would say, "When I was a little girl, no bigger than you are, I became sick with something called polio. The muscles of my leg shrank up and I couldn't walk very well. You're much luckier than I am because now you can get a vaccine to make sure you never get my disease. So don't cry when your mommy takes you to get a polio vaccine, okay?" Some adults and their little companions I talked to this way were glad to be rescued from embarrassment; others thought I was strange.

Americans have another way of covering up their uneasiness: they become jovially patronizing. Sometimes when people spot my crutch, they ask if I've had a skiing accident. When I answer that unfortunately it is something less glamorous than that, they say, "I bet you *could* ski if you put your mind to it!" Alternately, at parties where people dance, men who ask me to dance with them get almost belligerent when I decline their invitation. They say, "Of course you can dance if you *want* to!" Some have given me pep talks about how if I would only develop the right mental attitude, I would have more fun in life.

Different cultural attitudes toward handicapped persons came out clearly during my wedding. My father-in-law, as solid a representative of middle America as could be found, had no qualms about objecting to the marriage on racial grounds, but he could bring himself to comment on my handicap only indirectly. He wondered why his son, who had dated numerous high school and college beauty queens, couldn't marry one of them instead of me. My mother-in-law, a devout Christian, did not share her husband's prejudices, but she worried aloud about whether I could have children. Some Chinese friends of my parents, on the other hand, said that I was lucky to have found such a noble man, one who would marry me despite my handicap. I, for my part, appeared in church in a white lace wedding dress I had designed and made myself—a miniskirt!

How Asian Americans treat me with respect to my handicap tells me a great deal about their degree of acculturation. Recent immigrants behave just like Asians in Asia; those who have been here longer or who grew up in the United States behave more like their white counterparts. I have not encountered any distinctly Asian American pattern of response. What makes the experience of Asian American handicapped people unique is the duality of responses we elicit.

Regardless of racial or cultural background, most handicapped people have to learn to find a balance between the desire to attain physical independence and the need to take care of ourselves by not overtaxing our bodies. In my case, I've had to learn to accept the fact that leading an active life has its price. Between the ages of eight and eighteen, I walked without using crutches or braces but the effort caused my right leg to become badly misaligned. Soon after I came to the United States, I had a series of operations to straighten out the bones of my right leg; afterwards though my leg looked straighter and presumably better, I could no longer walk on my own. Initially my doctors fitted me with a brace, but I found wearing one cumbersome and soon gave it up. I could move around much more easily—and more important, faster—by using one crutch. One orthopedist after another warned me that using a single crutch was a bad practice. They were right. Over the years my spine developed a double-S curve and for the last twenty years I have suffered from severe, chronic back pains, which neither conventional physical therapy nor a lighter work load can eliminate.

The only thing that helps my backaches is a good massage, but the soothing effect lasts no more than a day or two. Massages are expensive, especially when one needs them three times a week. So I found a job that pays better, but at which I have to work longer hours, consequently increasing the physical strain on my body—a sort of vicious circle. When I was in my thirties, my doctors told me that if I kept leading the strenuous life I did, I would be in a wheelchair by the time I was forty. They were right on target: I bought myself a wheelchair when I was forty-one. But being the incorrigible character that I am, I use it only when I am *not* in a hurry!

It is a good thing, however, that I am too busy to think much about my handicap or my backaches because pain can physically debilitate as well as cause depression. And there are days when my spirits get rather low. What has helped me is realizing that being handicapped is akin to growing old at an accelerated rate. The contradiction I experience is that often my mind races along as though I'm only twenty while my body feels about sixty. But fifteen or twenty years hence, unlike my peers who will have to cope with aging for the first time, I shall be full of cheer because I will have already fought, and I hope won, that battle long ago.

Beyond learning how to be physically independent and, for some of us, living with chronic pain or other kinds of discomfort, the most difficult thing a handicapped person has to deal with, especially during puberty and early adulthood, is relating to potential sexual partners. Because American culture places so much emphasis on physical attractiveness, a person with a shriveled limb, or a tilt to the head, or the inability to speak clearly, experiences great uncertainty—indeed trauma—when interacting with someone to whom he or she is attracted. My problem was that I was not only physically handicapped, small, and short, but worse, I also wore glasses and was smarter than all the boys I knew! Alas, an insurmountable combination. Yet somehow I have managed to have intimate relationships, all of them with extraordinary men. Not surprisingly, there have also been countless men who broke my heart—men who enjoyed my company "as a friend," but who never found the courage to date or make love with me, although I am sure my experience in this regard is no different from that of many able-bodied persons.

The day came when my backaches got in the way of having an active sex life. Surprisingly that development was liberating because I stopped worrying about being attractive to men. No matter how headstrong I had been, I, like most women of my generation, had had the desire to be alluring to men ingrained into me. And that longing had always worked like a brake on my behavior. When what men think of me ceased to be compelling, I gained greater freedom to be myself.

I've often wondered if I would have been a different person had I not been physically handicapped. I really don't know, though there is no question that being handicapped has marked me. But at the same time I usually do not *feel* handicapped—and consequently, I do not *act* handicapped. People are therefore less likely to treat me as a handicapped person. There is no doubt, however, that the lives of my parents, sister, husband, other family members, and some close friends have been affected by my physical condition. They have had to learn not to hide me away at home, not to feel embarrassed by how I look or react to people who say silly things to me, and not to resent me for the extra demands my condition makes on them. Perhaps the hardest thing for those who live with handicapped people is to know when and how to offer help. There are no guidelines applicable to all situations. My advice is, when in doubt, ask, but ask, in a way that does not smack of pity or embarrassment. Most important, please don't talk to us as though we are children.

So, has being physically handicapped been a handicap? It all depends on one's attitude. Some years ago, I told a friend that I had once said to an affirmative action compliance officer (somewhat sardonically since I do not believe in the head count approach to affirmative action) that the institution which employs me is triply lucky because it can count me as nonwhite, female and handicapped. He responded, "Why don't you tell them to count you four times? . . . Remember, you're short, besides!"

Mestiza Girlhood: Interracial Families in Chicago's Filipino American Community since 1925

BARBARA M. POSADAS

This essay about the Filipino community in the years since 1925, explores one element of Filipino American group diversity and culture by focusing on the daughters born to interracial couples of Chicago's old-timer generation.[1] My examination of mestiza girlhood is divided into three areas: the women's absorption and perpetuation of the ethnic heritage of their parents; the level of their interracial consciousness within and outside the nuclear family; and their subsequent integration into both Chicago's Filipino American community and the wider world as measured by such indices as education, occupation, and social interaction. I have chosen to separate the offspring by sex so as to determine the extent of sex-stereotyped patterns of female childrearing with regard to schooling and dating. Further, the dynamics of mother-daughter and father-daughter bonds across the color line provide a unique opportunity to analyze minority divergence from dominant norms and problems.

The Community

Filipino American ethnicity in Chicago today constitutes an amalgam born of time and circumstance. While records show that the first arrival of a Filipino in Chicago occurred in 1906,[2] the substantial immigration, which would later be termed the "old timers' generation," was confined to the period between 1925 and 1934. By the latter date Chicago's Filipino population had undoubtedly surpassed the 1,796 noted in the 1930 federal census. The overwhelming majority of the migrants were young, unmarried men whose search for feminine company and whose establishment of an ethnic community were complicated by the absence of eligible Filipinas, by racism, and by the passage of the Tydings-McDuffie Act in 1934. This legislation set the Philippines on a course toward independence from the United States, but at the same time limited the previously unrestricted immigration of Philippine nationals to fifty per year. The effects of this law, together with problems stemming from the Depression, caused a reduction of approximately fifty in Chicago's official Filipino population for 1940.[3]

Detail provided in the 1940 census permits the construction of a group portrait of Chicago Filipinos. In that year, the sex ratio of Filipinos in the city reflected past patterns and continued isolation; among the 1,259 Filipinos over twenty-five years of age, the proportion of men to women stood at twenty-five to one. Yet approximately 44 percent of these men were married. The presence of only forty-two married Filipinas in the city indicates that most marriages were interracial. For Filipino men in Chicago, choice of a white bride of Eastern or Southern European background was the typical course; 92 percent of those who married had done so outside their ethnic group.[4]

Given the categories of the 1940 census, it is impossible to determine as precisely the figures for interracial childbearing. Of the 1,740 Filipinos in Chicago, 422 were under the age of fifteen, most likely living with their parents. Since the number of endogamous marriages in Chicago was so small, most of these children were presumably born to interracial couples. While males still outnumbered females, the sex ratio among this age group was much more evenly balanced: 1.5 to 1.0.[5]

Subsequent censuses have failed to replicate the categories of the 1940 survey and to provide data on individual cities. In 1950, Filipinos were lumped with Koreans and Asian Indians in an "All Other" classification. The 1960 census reveals only that the Filipino population in Illinois had grown to 3,587, an 85.9 percent increase during the preceding twenty years. Happily, however, the 1970 census gives more detail and permits a tentative contrast between old-timers' and newcomers' marriage patterns. Of those men over forty-five years of age, 59 percent were married to women of another race, while among those under forty-four, intermarriage was restricted to 16 percent. Given the decade's 252.8 percent growth rate of the Filipino population in Illinois, and the persistence of this rate throughout the 1970s—an increase of over forty thousand in twenty years—the contrast within the community between the old generation and the new is not surprising.[6] Further complicating the pattern, an unknown number of men of the old-timer generation, once married to white women, found Filipino wives in their later years.

The Context

Little has been written about Filipino American mestizo children. During the 1930s, as academicians and policy makers investigated what they called the Filipino "problem," University of Southern California graduate students Benicio T. Catapusan and Severino F. Corpus focused on interracial family life. Catapusan stressed cultural conflict within the home:

In the husband's traditional home the father was the head of the family. . . . But in the current American situation . . . authority . . . is now exercised by the mother . . . under the presupposition that she is better adapted; she can think and act more quickly in American ways than does her Filipino husband.[7]

Four years later, in further treatment of the subject, Catapusan posited this consequence: "increasingly, in language, manners, ideals, and loyalties the mestizos . . . conform approximately to . . . American standards." Could they, however, assimilate? Corpus theorized that second-generation Filipinos would experience (or constitute) a "social problem" if their small numbers forced them to seek spouses of "other races," as had their Filipino fathers.[8]

More recent analysis has been contradictory. Writing in 1971, Alfredo N. Munoz argued:

> While looking more American than Filipino, the mestizos and mestizas feel more [like] Filipinos than Americans. They are rice-eaters instead of flour-consumers, Catholics instead of Protestants. They are at home with Filipinos more than they are with Americans.[9]

By contrast, anthropologist Edwin B. Almirol found that in Salinas, California, at Filipino kin and community gatherings

> . . . the English-speakers are a minority; . . . Filipinos of different generations, from grandparents to grandchildren, eat, sing, drink, and dance together to the music of recorded Filipino folk songs played loudly on a turn-table. The American-born and the mestizo often express their feelings of being left out during these occasions.[10]

Perhaps this study of ten Filipino American daughters in the Chicago area—ranging in age from mid-twenties to mid-fifties, in education from high school graduate to Ph.D., and in occupation from homemaker to university professor—can help reconcile these divergent views and, in addition, indicate how the mestizas' cultural orientation was established.

The Families

The Chicago Filipino old-timers migrated to the Middle West in search of education and middle-class employment.[11] Many had finished high school in the Islands and then completed at least a year at a Midwestern college or university or attended an urban commercial or technical institute. Though most had intended to return to the Islands with an American degree in hand, for various reasons those who made up the Chicago old-timer community failed to do so. As they struggled to support themselves and their new families, they found work as chauffeurs, bus-boys, and barbers—all service occupations shunned by white workers. More permanent employment was available in the late 1920s when the Pullman Company systematically recruited Filipinos to serve as atten-dants on railroad club cars, a job classification segregated by race from black sleeping car porters. At one time as many as three hundred Chi-cago Filipinos worked for the Pullman Company. [12]

While the old-timer Filipinos had more education than most males of their age in Chicago, the same was not true of their spouses. In most instances, the Filipinos married young women who either were the daughters of Eastern European immigrants or who were themselves mi-grants from rural America. Many of these women had dropped out of school after the eighth grade to begin factory work and contribute to their families' income. They met their future Filipino husbands at dance halls and often suffered at least temporary ostracism from their families after their marriages. The interracial couples tended to cluster together with their husbands' province-mates or fellow Pullman employees on the near North or West Sides of Chicago in apartment buildings whose owners were willing to rent to racially mixed couples. It is within this setting that two-thirds of the mestiza daughters grew to maturity be-tween the early 1930s and the mid-1960s.

Throughout their lives in their parents' households, the women of this study were encouraged by Filipino fathers and white mothers alike to assimilate to the dominant society and to reject, in a sense, their ethnicity and race. Chicago made this task difficult: the city's milieu emphasized ethnic and racial identity, frequently defining neighbor-hoods by it. Ethnic inhabitants, particularly in the city's older sections, used language, food, and homeland traditions to reinforce group ties and to provide a heritage even for the mobile ethnics of their group who had left the neighborhoods of their youth. Blacks lived in segregation on the city's South and West Sides, creating a virtual "city within a city" that was their own. [13]

In this setting, interracial couples and their children were an anomaly. Most women were from close-knit European ethnic backgrounds, but found that their unapproved marriages had shattered many old ties. Filipino men, defined by race, were confined with their families to marginal areas. Yet these interracial families were too few in number to establish a fully viable community. For them, then, disappearance into larger society promised escape from here-and-now difficulties. [14]

Parental backgrounds were not totally abandoned. Both crocheted handiwork from Polish grandmothers and straw handbags sent from the Philippines might be admired and used. Ethnic foods from each nationality might be served daily in some homes and on holidays in others. Filipino dialects and European languages might be heard when relatives and friends visited. Nonetheless parents generally sought to free their daughters from any practices or habits which might label them as different. Learning a language other than English at home was not considered, for a foreign tongue seemed to conflict with desired American behavior patterns. One daughter recalled her mother's veto of brightly colored clothing: "You look like you just got off the boat." Similarly, mestizas rejected pierced ears until teenage girls in general sought gold posts and dangling hoops. And as adolescents they spent their summers avoiding the darkening effects of the sun.

The contrasting ethnic appearance between mothers and daughters could be traumatic for both. In the early 1950s a young mother walking with her two small daughters was stopped by a stranger who complimented her generosity in adopting war orphans. "They're mine," said the mother, an exchange which her then four-year-old child remembers to this day. In contrast, another pair recalled happy smiles when a casual acquaintance saw likeness enough to link the two as parent and offspring in a crowd.

Most daughters, though, resembled their fathers more than their mothers, a fact which seems to have strengthened the normally close bond between fathers and their small daughters; no one could mistake Daddy's little girl. Even in one rare instance when the child bore her mother's blond hair and blue eyes, their almond shape and her slightly broad, flat nose testified to her Filipino father's influence. Thus, throughout the years, as their daughters grew to maturity, Filipino fathers enjoyed a rare freedom from curiosity when in public with their children, a freedom regularly denied when husbands and wives, or mothers and children, ventured from home.

The strength of the father-daughter bond could be noticed in other ways as well. Daughters generally recall that day-to-day responsibility for their rearing rested with their mothers. Many Filipino fathers, who worked as railroad attendants for the Pullman Company, were away from home for as long as a week at a time. Given these regular absences and the fact that few married women worked outside the home before World War II, discipline fell to them while their children were small.[15]

Fathers of preadolescent daughters reserved roles for themselves as companions and advisors. Work trips for Pullman employees were followed by layovers, periods of several days during which railroad workers recovered from the exertions of their most recent travel. Daughters uniformly recall anxiously waiting for their fathers' return. Treats could be expected—ice cream, magazines, and occasionally a scarf or other trinket left by a forgetful passenger. During their long hours at home, fathers played board games and cards with their daughters; mothers continued their household chores. Similarly, because most mothers could not drive the family car, plans for special trips to doctors and dentists, and to museums and the distant zoo, were put off until those days when fathers would be in town.

Because most Filipino men had more formal education than their wives, decisions concerning their children's schooling commonly became the fathers' responsibility. Many Filipino men had originally migrated from the Islands in the hope of obtaining an American high school or college education.[16] When these dreams were dashed in their own lives, Filipino fathers hoped to fulfill them through the lives of their children. Because they came from a society that values the education of females as well as males,[17] Filipino fathers encouraged their daughters to get as much education as they could, for schooling still seemed to them the most likely route to mobility in America.

The mestizas' level of educational achievement appears to have been affected by the generation during which they matured. Children born in the late 1920s and early 1930s rarely attended college. Given the absence of large scholarship and loan programs, families just emerging from the Depression found college tuition to be an insurmountable burden. So, after completing high school, the mestizas secured office work, white-collar employment which represented a step up from the light factory jobs their mothers had held before marriage and from the service occupations of their Filipino fathers. In the years immediately after World War II, Filipino American women responded, as did their peers, to the social pressure to marry and bear children. Even if they intended to resume work when their children reached school age, these mestizas thought of jobs and income levels rather than careers.[18]

In contrast more of the daughters who finished high school during the 1960s attended college. The society as a whole moved toward a four-year degree as the norm,[19] and Filipino American families, like many others, endured sacrifices, juggled the monthly budget, and completed the confidential financial assistance forms that might result in funding. Fathers in particular worried over the courses in which their daughters enrolled. For some the urgency of parental concern, as well as modest resources, dictated that daughters live at home while pursuing higher education. One young woman who graduated from college in 1965 remembered her lack of freedom vividly: her father chose each class through her sophomore year, ultimately selecting mathematics as her major. She welcomed her graduation from a community college, which enabled her to flee to a public university in another state.

While her example was atypically severe, other daughters were reminded that technical fields offered greater financial rewards and more prestige than traditional occupations such as teaching and nursing. Irrespective of the fields they ultimately chose, however, the daughters of this era were more likely than older daughters to regard their work as a lifelong career and to view their fathers' influence as central to their educational achievement. As one professional woman in her mid-thirties remarked:

When I was growing up and we socialized with my mother's ethnic relatives, it was clear that I was different from my cousins, not only because I was part Filipino, but also because I intended to go to college. All the other girls viewed an office job and marriage as their ultimate goal. If my father hadn't pushed so hard, I'm sure I would have been caught in their world.

If strong bonds were forged with their fathers in these areas, daughters turned more frequently to their mothers for understanding and intervention as they began dating, because conflicts with their fathers often arose. Mothers and fathers alike upheld traditional standards of morality—"sex before marriage was a no-no." Yet parents still disagreed over behavior. Filipino fathers, recalling both the customs of the Islands, when chaperones had been ever-present, and their own conduct as single men cut loose in America, argued for strict hours and close supervision. Mothers favored a middle ground. "She didn't want me to run wild, but she was prepared to be reasonable," said one daughter. Another daughter recalled:

> My mother was more liberal in the situation, let's say, of people living together. She knew my sister had been living with her boyfriend [in the late 1960s] and never would tell my father. . . . It would have killed him.

So long as they remained in their parents' homes, so long as they continued to be single, daughters found these tensions to be constant.

Ironically, given the strictness of their fathers, the ethnic identity of the boys they dated and the men they married was rarely at issue. So long as their beaus were moral, respectful, sociable, and potentially good providers, ethnicity mattered little. None of the mestiza daughters married men wholly or even part Filipino—but neither did they choose spouses of their mothers' ethnic backgrounds. These marriages, the births of their own children, their ties to their husbands' families, and their own diverse friendships drew the mestiza daughters into a world that was more heterogeneous and more American.

Race has handicapped the Chicago mestizas in rare, isolated instances. Each woman recalls an instance in which she was singled out as different—denied a party invitation as a child, subjected to a racial slur as an adult—but once on their own or married, they escaped their parents' difficulties in finding housing or employment. If anything, affirmative action in recent years may have added a competitive edge: the

Spanish surnames of their fathers have been known to catch the attention of job recruiters.

Mestiza Identity

As should be clear by now, the perpetuation of Filipino culture was not a major emphasis in the upbringing of these mestiza daughters. To love one's father, to be proud of one's father, was not synonymous with knowledge of and pride in a Filipino heritage. The Islands themselves were a distant mystery to most. Those who visited the Philippines were shocked by the abject poverty and by the wide gulf between social classes. But even in this assessment, fathers lent support. Decades had passed and the land to which these men returned was rarely the land of their memories.

The daughters of the old timers' generation were educated before "black power" and "white pride" spurred many other Americans to consider their own roots. Yet even if they had explored their ancestry, group identity would have remained elusive. The Filipino immigrant population grew in Chicago after immigration law changes in 1965, but many offspring of the old-timers' generation found little of themselves in the imported culture of the newcomers. Daughters might gather at Chicago's Rizal Center when the child of a family friend was married, but none belonged to the more than forty Filipino organizations in Chicago. The mestizas, like many others of multiple heritage, acknowledge their parental background, but function more as the products of an American mass culture than of an ethnic enclave.

Asian American Lesbians: An Emerging Voice in the Asian American Community

PAMELA H.

Among the voices in the Asian American women's community, one has yet to be heard and recognized—that of the Asian American lesbian. In literature on Asian American women, a discussion of lesbianism is usually absent, and similarly in lesbian literature, Asian Americans continue to be an elusive subject. The need for information about Asian American lesbians increases as the Asian American lesbian movement grows and demands to be heard. By refusing or failing to recognize lesbians, the Asian American women's community will divide itself and consequently lose out on a potential resource.

Around 1980 Asian American lesbians began forming organizations with Asian American gay men and recognizing their potential as a force in the Asian American community. While most of these organizations initially attracted more male members than female, in recent years the organizations have witnessed either a growth in the number of women members or the establishment of separate and autonomous sister organizations by women. But whatever the organizational configuration, Asian American lesbians are becoming more visible and promise to become more vocal.

The path to visibility is not without obstacles though. As a minority within a minority, Asian American lesbians face many problems. These problems spring from their unique status as Asian American lesbians and also from their identity as Asian American women in general. This essay will explore these obstacles within three contexts: personal identity, the larger lesbian and gay community, and the Asian American community.

Personal Acceptance: Self-Image

On the most basic level, Asian American lesbians must first accept their homosexuality. This first step is the most arduous and is a process that continues throughout their lives.

Many Asian American women are not encouraged to develop their self-image at all. Instead they must completely submerge their identities within the family structure. In traditional Asian cultures, females are devalued in comparison with males; males enjoy a higher social status and are encouraged to forge their own identities in the public sphere. Even in the 1980s female infanticide in China is practiced because of the government policy limiting families to one child. Couples having a female baby are disappointed because the family name will not be continued. And in Japan, which is often referred to as a "man's country," women are prevented from occupying positions in business or in the nation's political structure.

If Asian American women are discouraged from developing even a basic sense of self-worth or self-identity, then developing a sexual identity remains an especially difficult task. Women have been indoctrinated to believe that anything dealing with sex is shameful and must be avoided. Even interpersonal activity on a casual friendship level does not include as much touching or physical contact as in mainstream American society. For instance, instead of a handshake upon meeting a person, the traditional Japanese greeting is a deep bow. Conversely, men are allowed to deal with sexual feelings as youths and are even encouraged by peers to be sexually active.

When Asian American parents or schools try to educate students about sexuality, the emphasis is on heterosexual behavior and heterosexual interaction. Sex education classes are designed to inform students about their sexuality, but beyond basic biological functioning, these courses meticulously avoid discussion of sexual orientation. If a teacher is adventurous enough to discuss sexual attraction and activity, the focus is on male-female interactions; discovering and exploring sexual feelings for another woman is usually a solitary activity for a lesbian just beginning to examine her sexuality.

A lesbian exploring her sexuality usually does not receive much support from her family, who may, in fact, discourage her "coming out." Most Asian families are oblivious to the lesbian and gay movement, especially the former, and may not even consider homosexuality an option.

Homosexuality is seen as a Western concept, a product of losing touch with one's Asian heritage, of becoming too assimilated. One Asian American woman, when she revealed to her parents that she was a lesbian, was met with shocked stares. Her parents said, "But how can that be? Being gay is a white disease. We're Korean; Korean people aren't gay." The perception that homosexuality does not "afflict" Asians is pervasive. Asian parents are incredulous when they learn *their* daughter is a lesbian; indeed, most Asian languages do not even have a word meaning "lesbian." In essence, Asian lesbians do not exist for many Asian cultures. Saying "I'm a lesbian" to parents who do not understand the word "lesbian" is like speaking a foreign language—comprehension is minimal.

Furthermore, media projections about homosexuality usually depict white lesbians and gays, perhaps including an occasional black homosexual. Major studio movies like *Making Love* featured upwardly mobile white males; Tony Award–winning stage productions like *La Cage Aux Folles* and television dramas have also focused primarily on whites. White males have appeared on the cover of national magazines and in weekly situation comedies on television. White lesbian singers such as Holly Near and Cris Williamson have begun to be recognized by the general public, and white women dominated movies such as *Entre Nous, Lianna,* and *Desert Hearts.* Insofar as the media influences our perceptions of others and ourselves, the popular (and Asian parents') perceptions of homosexuals would be unsurprisingly exclusively white.

Thus, an Asian American lesbian must first strive to develop a basic sense of self-identity before taking the next step of developing a sexual identity. Then she will be better able to hurdle the more difficult obstacle—developing an identity as a lesbian.

Community Acceptance: The Larger Lesbian and Gay Community

Finding little support from school, friends, or family, many Asian lesbians turn to the larger lesbian and gay community to find peers and a sense of belonging. Each major city has its lesbian and gay community center, a starting point for the lesbian just coming out. Usually, people learn about the center through a telephone listing or media coverage. These centers, however, are staffed predominantly by white gay males and are inadequately staffed to deal with lesbians of color. Each city also has its share of lesbian organizations, but these are populated mainly by white women, and several lesbian or women's bars, but bars are primarily for socializing. Thus, an Asian American lesbian's initial entrance into the larger lesbian and gay community brings her in contact with few or no Asian lesbians.

In such a limited community, some women have nevertheless developed lesbian identities, but this was done by forsaking ethnic background. Many Asian lesbians encounter racist attitudes in the lesbian community and are discouraged from exploring their ethnicity. Asian lesbians experience the same racism encountered by other Asian women. They are sometimes seen as passive, quiet, and servile in comparison to white women and this view affects how some white women interact with Asians. Clearly the alleged sisterhood of lesbians is not devoid of its share of stereotypes about Asian American women.

Some lesbian bars discriminate against women of color and seek to exclude them. This discrimination can take many forms. For instance, women of color may be asked for three pieces of identification to prove age while white women must provide only one. Or, women of color may have a harder time than white women getting the bartender's attention. Because frequenting bars has been the predominant social activity among lesbians, forced exclusion means isolation from the larger lesbian community. Simply because a woman is a lesbian does not mean that all lesbians are her sisters; many racist attitudes carry over despite sexual preferences.

There exist some progressive groups within the larger lesbian community that do incorporate the needs of Asian American lesbians, but Asian American concerns constitute only a part of these organizations. As a result many Asian American lesbians feel a void in their lives because their ethnic background is ignored or given second-class status to the developing lesbian culture—one based on mainstream white lesbian issues.

Community Acceptance: The Asian American Community

Until 1980 the larger lesbian community was the only community which provided a supportive atmosphere for Asian lesbians. As mentioned earlier, Asian American parents are usually oblivious to the idea of lesbianism and think it incomprehensible that their daughter could be inflicted with this "Western disease." And those parents who do recognize that lesbianism exists regard it as shameful or as a temporary disorder.

In Asian culture where marriage and family are stressed for every woman, the Asian American lesbian often succumbs to the familial pressure. Parents' expectations are that she fill the "dutiful daughter" role and become a loyal, obedient wife, an asset to her husband's career. Being a lesbian would smear the perfect Asian image and reflect negatively on the woman's family. One Japanese American lesbian was told by her irate parents that she was the first in their family ever to be homosexual and that it would irreparably harm her chances of marriage.

Concern that family honor will be tarnished motivates many women to hide their lesbianism. This family shame factor reflects the tightness of many Asian communities and how one's community itself may inhibit a woman from coming out. For instance one woman whose father was prominent in the Chinese American community avoided associating with any lesbian or gay Asian American groups after she encountered one of her father's business acquaintances at a meeting. She feared that her parents would discover her homosexuality from someone else before she was prepared to tell them herself. Therefore, it is not uncommon for Asian American lesbians to move outside the Asian community so as not to be found out. In fact the general Asian American community may be too close-knit for the closeted lesbian.

When several Asian lesbian and gay groups began forming around the country in 1980, their collective general purpose was to provide a sense of community for Asian lesbians and gays and to make their presence known in the larger Asian and homosexual communities. They sought to alleviate many of the problems facing lesbian and gay Asians. Boston, Chicago, Honolulu, Los Angeles, New York, Philadelphia, and San Francisco have Asian lesbian and gay men groups; each city's group takes on its own unique characteristics from its members' needs. Some organizations tend to be predominantly male or female, and some are involved in more political activities than others.

For instance in Los Angeles the organization proper, Asian/Pacific Lesbians and Gays (A/PLG), is now composed primarily of Asian and white men. At its inception in August 1980, both men and women sought to build an organization for both Asian gays and lesbians. But as the organization grew, men greatly outnumbered women. Expecting to find more than just a small handful of women, some lesbians drifted away after one general meeting at which they were outnumbered by men twenty-five to one. These disappointed women wanted a ready-made community and left when they did not find it. Expectations such as these created a nonproductive cycle: lesbians wanting to meet other Asian women left rather than trying to increase the numbers. Some women felt uncomfortable around men, preferring to live in an exclusively women's world. Still others felt that the gay Asian American men were not supportive of women's interests and were sexist. And finally some Asian lesbians did not want to join a formal organization or associate with a radical group because of professional or immigration reasons.

Consequently in Los Angeles some Asian lesbians began organizing their own social activities along more loosely structured lines. (San Francisco's Association of Lesbian and Gay Asians and the Boston Area Gay Men and Lesbians have experienced a similar phenomenon.) The women's group has since been renamed Asian/Pacific Lesbians and Friends (A/PLF). Since the women broke away from the original organization, their numbers have increased from about six in 1980, to a mailing list of over seventy in 1985. The women's group concentrates primarily on social, cultural, and educational activities and attracts women of several ethnic backgrounds, including Chinese, Filipina, Japanese, and Korean. The group has also tried to establish contact with the San Francisco women's group via softball challenges and with the New York–based Asian Lesbians of the East Coast by exchanging newsletters.

In contrast to the Los Angeles group, the New York group began in 1983 as a strictly Asian lesbian organization and has a distinctly political nature. Many of the members were active in other community groups, but this organization gave them an opportunity to reclaim their Asian heritage.

June Chan, one of the main organizers of the East Coast group, has produced a slide presentation on Asian lesbians and has attended many conferences to discuss Asian lesbianism. She has also tried to make inroads into the New York Chinatown community, but says, "it's hard to get in . . . they were scared of us." However June continues to become more vocal and visible and wants to gain the "political leverage" to work with other established groups—both Asian American and women's groups. For the present, target areas for the Asian Lesbians of the East Coast are racism, homophobia in the Asian women's community, and sexism. In the future, Chan hopes to research the history of lesbianism in Asian cultures and create more of a bond among the women.

The importance of networking among Asian lesbians in their own cities and with other cities' groups is tremendous. Women are able to combat, or at least discuss, the problems they face as Asian American lesbians with women from similar backgrounds and with similar experiences. Making such contact gives many Asian lesbians a new family, one that is finally sensitive to their needs.

Some of the A/PLF women are also involved in political activities concerning the lesbian and gay movement. Working in conjunction with A/PLG, others speak on panels about the organization and some have been interviewed by the Radio Lil' Tokyo's "Radio Active" program in Los Angeles and by UCLA's gay and lesbian special interest newspaper *Ten Percent*. In addition, members have marched in the Christopher Street West Gay Pride parade in West Hollywood; provided the Chinese translation for the newsletter of Parents and Friends of Gays; taken part in the Los Angeles–based civic group Pacific/Asian American Round Table; and participated in a panel discussion before the San Fernando chapter of the Japanese American Citizen's League. Reactions from the larger Asian American community have either been positive or mild surprise, but generally not negative. However homosexuality necessarily brings up the subject of sexuality, a subject that has been rarely broached in public in the Asian American community. So part of the unease with these recent organizing efforts may be in response to the basic topic of sexuality.

Beyond the issue of sexual preference, many Asian American lesbians hope to convert lesbianism into a political force, one that can effect progressive change. The burgeoning Asian American lesbian movement is just beginning to gain notice from more well-established movements, and much of this is through organizing efforts and writing. Barbara Noda, Kitty Tsui, and Merle Woo are presently among the best known writers and voices for the Asian American lesbian community. But there are hundreds of other Asian lesbians beginning to collect their voices, and they want to be heard.

PART SIX

Thunderstorms:
Injustice

Introduction

Asian American women face discrimination on the basis of many factors. Among them are their status as women, their membership in a visibly different ethnic community, and often their economic status, sexual preference, or physical disabilities.

The women in "Factory Girls" by Chea Villanueva labor under an economically oppressive situation in the free trade zone. With few job alternatives, the women must sell their bodies—figuratively and literally—in order to survive, and they dare not complain. The stereotypes of the passive and submissive woman begin in Asia, but they do not stop there.

Stereotypes reinforced by the American film and television media are discussed by Renee Tajima in "Lotus Blossoms Don't Bleed: Images of Asian Women." Generalizations of women in Asia are carried over to Asian American women as well. The message from the screen is that all Asian American women are passive, submissive, and either exotically sexy or totally asexual.

The primary danger of stereotypes is that they limit how people view these women and how the women may view themselves. In "Two Deserts" by Valerie Matsumoto, a nisei woman living in a Central California farming community learns that the racist and sexist views about Asian women held by her new neighbor require a nonstereotypical response.

"Matchmaking in the Classifieds," by Rashmi Luthra, focuses on the difficulties facing South Asian women in America in establishing their own, contemporary identities, when their parents and immigrant community follow practices which reinforce the traditional second-class status of women. In this case, the practice involves the use of newspaper advertisements to find spouses, a practice that all too often fails to take into account the desires of the women.

Popular images have prompted many American men to send for and marry Asian women, as Venny Villapando points out in "The Business of Selling Mail-Order Brides." These women who seek a way to flee the poverty of their homelands, see marriage to a pen pal from across the ocean as a viable means to economic stability for themselves and their families. The men who bring them to the United States are often searching for women who can live out their dream of a subservient wife. Though the results can be disastrous for both parties, the lucrative business of bringing bride and groom together will continue as long as the Asian American female stereotypes feed the demand.

The disparity between stereotype and reality can create stress between women and men and within women themselves. In turn that tension can sometimes erupt into violence within the family. Nilda Rimonte in "Domestic Violence among Pacific Asians" discusses the incidence of spousal and child abuse in the Asian American community, the cultural factors that contribute to their occurrence, and the response of the women involved.

Violence, as a function of exerting power over the powerless, is the topic of Meena Alexander's "Mosquitoes in the Main Room," which retells the story of a woman raped by a group of police officers in India. The woman becomes a pawn in the brutal sex game. Often Asian women are assaulted because they fit the fantasy of a rapist who wants to subjugate people he perceives as passive and submissive. Though this particular incident motivated protests among Indian women across India and in America, many rapes pass unrecorded and unprotested.

Women of Asian descent have lived in the United States for many decades. And though they can be found in cities throughout the country, many people still perceive them through eyes clouded by the false images portrayed in the media. These stereotypes merely describe what some people *think* Asian American women should be rather than who they truly are.

Factory Girls

CHEA VILLANUEVA

in the Philippines
women sell their bodies
to buy rice
they live in
factory dormitories
along the "free trade zone."
free
trade
zone. . . .
freedom for business
less freedom for women
incarcerated inside the
barbed wire labor camps.
at Mattel toy "motel"
women are told
to lay down or
lay off
free trade
free women's bodies.
at Subic naval base
Filipina flesh is worth
$7 U.S. money
in america they're worth
at least fifty.
on the news today another
woman is kidnapped
via male-order bride
domestic help
secretarial employment.
U.S. fronts for

sexual slavery
free
trade
zone. . . .
in the Philippines
the earth is red
death lurks
in revolution
sisters Alma, Puri, Mia and Lorrie
murdered
by the U.S.-Marcos dictatorship.
the sisters died
with their guns
in hand
murdered
by the
free
trade
zone. . . .

Mosquitoes in the Main Room

MEENA ALEXANDER

This prose piece is based on a true episode that took place in Hyderabad in 1978. A woman who was visiting the town was dragged into a police station and gang raped by policemen.

Rameeza is almost my age, just a year and a half younger. Her mouth is filled with dust. She is numb, she doesn't even scratch herself. For an instant, she squints at the old woman who peers in through the bars. She tries to shake her head no, she doesn't want any water. She stares at the old woman's scrawny feet, and the stained waterpot.

There is nothing Rameeza can say. Does she know there is blood, crushed bone in her pelvis? Nothing hurts her. It would be true to say she feels nothing. A single mosquito whirrs above her lips. In a blur, she watches its wings.

Hours later, a whole day later, she feels a single sore on the inside of her thigh, where the stray cur had licked. Had she felt it then? Hard prods of the lathi in her ribs, the racking pain in her belly, the hairs on her exposed vulva, burning shamefully.

Did the policemen take fright at what they had done, under cover of darkness? It might be more correct to say that as true sons of the Indian bureaucracy, they were overcome by the urge to clean up. Two of them dragged Rameeza by the armpits. As her hips hit the stone steps, they burst in pain, each bone in cadence as the marble struck.

Tin cans clattering on his bicycle, the milk man approached. It was dawn already, opening the swamp, shutting the eyes of the night owls. A decent fellow, the milkman fell off his vehicle in shock. The milk cans spilled over the red pebbles, the dried bloodstains, the eyelids of the mongrel, and even over the boots of the satiated policemen a slim line of milk flowed. The sparrows stirred in the tall grasses beside the swamp.

Her sari stretched under her, a mere rag, dark with blood. She does not have Draupadi's [1] luck. Would the blessed Draupadi have survived a rape, outside a police station? Would the mystic fabric have guarded her virtue, shimmering as it bound her flesh and burnt the hands of miscreants?

The cell door is rusty, it clangs like an old bell left by the British. Now the blood has dried in her eyes, in her mouth. Another twelve hours pass before the old woman returns with her waterpot, before the dog filled with a woman's blood vomits into the swamp. The swamp is behind the cell window. Sparrows rustle in the tall grasses. The milk- man trembles as he gathers his cans together and races away from the policeman in charge. He pushes his bent bicycle ahead of him, away from the stone steps with the two slender men at the top.

Make no mistake, the police station is a modest building as befitting a place of justice. Like all the public service buildings in Hyderabad it is whitewashed. In the main room there is a low wooden platform with three chairs on it, all in a row. In front of the three chairs is a large wooden table, a leather bound book propped open on it, a steel pen attached to the spine with a bit of string. Behind the chairs are two small cells. If you peer beyond the policeman who sits in the middle chair, his face overshadowed by a stiff cap, you can see into the cells—only partially, however, for when Rameeza curls up into a tight ball, on the mud floor of her cell, it's impossible to see her from the main room of the police station.

In the main room, the floor under the platform is depressed and deepens in the cells. At monsoon time stagnant water pools in the hole breeding mosquitoes. In the dry season the depression is damp, cool to the flesh, welcoming the parched prisoners. Rameeza makes it a habit to curl up in the darkness. The mud soothes her a little; she barely feels the mosquitoes.

Mosquitoes surround the two portraits hanging above the platform in the main room of the police station. To the right, in faded brown ink, is a man with parted lips, tiny round spectacles, and a bent nose. He looks puzzled, but he is smiling a little. He is bald and he holds a telephone in his hand. Where did the phone come from? Is the line good? It's Gandhi. The mosquitoes crowd into his eyes. One even seems to have bored through his spectacles and into the lime dust behind.

On the left is Nehru, erect, handsome, his cap pointed, polished on his head. His teeth are visible, clearly brushed each morning. An aristocrat, lacking a phone line with the future. Both these visitors from our history watched as the mosquitoes shimmered over her wrist. Then, as she was tossed into the cell and her knees folded under her, they saw the mosquitoes flock, beating their wings, hovering over her mouth seeking entry. Do they know that her story is not finished?

Two Deserts

VALERIE MATSUMOTO

Emiko Oyama thought the Imperial Valley of California was the lone-
liest place she had ever seen. It was just like the Topaz Relocation Camp,
she told her husband, Kiyo, but without the barbed wire fence and
crowded barracks. Miles of bleached desert, punctuated sparsely by creo-
sote bush and debris, faced her from almost every window in their small
house. Only the living room had a view of the dirt road which ended in
front of their home, and across it, a row of squat, faded houses where
other farmers' families lived. They waved to her and Kiyo in passing,
and Jenny played with the Garcia children, but Emiko's Spanish and
their English were too limited for more than casual greetings.

Emiko felt a tug of anticipation on the day the moving van pulled up to
the Ishikawa's place across the road—the house which in her mind had
become inextricably linked with friendship. She had felt its emptiness as
her own when Sats, Yuki, and their three children gave up farming and
departed for a life which later came to her in delicious fragments in Yuki's
hastily scrawled letters. Yuki made the best sushi rice in the world and had
given her the recipe. She could draw shy Kiyo into happy banter. And her
loud warm laugh made the desert seem less drab, less engulfing.

The morning of moving day Emiko had been thinking about Yuki as
she weeded the yard and vegetable plot in preparation for planting. Sats
and Yuki had advised her to plant marigolds around the vegetables to
keep away nematodes, and she liked the idea of a bold orange border.
Emiko liked bright colors, especially the flaming scarlet of the bougainvillea which rose above the front door, where Kiki their cat lay sunning
himself. There was a proud look in those amber eyes, for Kiki the hunter
had slain three scorpions and laid them in a row on the porch, their backs
crushed and deadly stingers limp, winning extravagant praise from
Jenny and Emiko. The scorpions still lay there, at Jenny's insistence,
awaiting Kiyo's return that evening. Emiko shuddered every time
she entered the house, glancing at the curved stingers and thinking of
Jenny's sandaled feet.

Emiko had finished weeding the front border and was about to go inside to escape the heat, when she saw the new neighbor woman plodding across the sand toward her. A cotton shift could not conceal her thinness, nor a straw hat her tousled gray curls. Her eyes were fragile lilac glass above a wide smile.

"Hello, I'm Mattie Barnes. I just thought I'd come over and introduce myself while Roy is finishing up with the movers. Your bougainvillea caught my eye first thing, and I thought, 'Those are some folks who know what will grow in the desert.' I hope you'll give me some advice about what to plant in my yard once we get settled in."

They talked about adjusting to desert life and Emiko learned that Mattie's husband Roy had recently retired. "We decided to move here because the doctor said it would be better for my lungs," Mattie explained, wiping her brow.

"Would you like a glass of lemonade?" Emiko offered. "Or maybe later, after you've finished moving."

"Oh, I'd love something cold," Mattie said, adding vaguely, "Roy will take care of everything—he's more particular about those things than I am."

Emiko led Mattie into the house, hoping that Jenny was not lying on the cool linoleum, stripped to her underwear. As she crossed the threshold, Mattie gave a shriek and stopped abruptly, eyeing the scorpions lined up neatly on the porch.

"What on earth are these things doing here?"

"Our cat killed them," Emiko said, feeling too foolish to admit her pride in Kiki's prowess. "Jenny wants me to leave them to show her father when he comes home from the field."

"Awful creatures," Mattie shuddered. "Roy can't stand them, but then he can't abide insects. He said to me this morning, 'Of all the places we could have moved to, we had to choose the buggiest.'"

There was no buggier place than the Imperial Valley, Emiko agreed, especially in the summer when the evening air was thick with mosquitoes, gnats, and moths, and cicadas buzzed in deafening chorus from every tree. They danced in frenzied legions around the porch light and did kamikaze dives into the bath water, and all of them came in dusty gray hordes, as though the desert had sapped their color, but not their energy. And late at night, long after Kiyo had fallen into exhausted sleep, Emiko would lie awake, perspiring, listening to the tinny scrabble of insects trapped between the window glass and screen.

". . . but I like the desert," Mattie was saying, dreamily clinking the ice cubes in her glass. "It's so open and peaceful. As long as I can have a garden, I'll be happy."

Within a few weeks after their arrival, the Barneses had settled into a routine: Roy made daily trips to the local store and the Roadside Cafe; Mattie tended her garden and walked to church once a week with Emiko and Jenny. By the end of June, Mattie had been enlisted with Emiko to make crepe paper flowers for the church bazaar.

"My, your flowers turned out beautifully," Mattie exclaimed one morning, looking wistfully at the cardboard box filled with pink, yellow, scarlet, and lavender blossoms set on wire stems. "They'll make lovely corsages." She sighed. "I seem to be all thumbs—my flowers hardly look like flowers. I don't know how you do it. You Japanese are just very artistic people."

Emiko smiled and shook her head making a polite disclaimer. But the bright blur of flowers suddenly dissolved into another mass of paper blooms, carrying her more than a decade into the past. She was a teenager in a flannel shirt and denim pants with rolled cuffs, seated on a cot in a cramped barrack room, helping her mother fashion flowers from paper. Her own hands had been clumsy at first, though she strived to imitate her mother's precise fingers which gave each fragile petal lifelike curves, the look of artless grace. The only flowers for elderly Mr. Wasaka, shot by a guard in Topaz, were those which bloomed from the fingertips of issei and nisei women, working late into the night to complete the exquisite wreaths for his funeral. Each flower was a silent voice crying with color, each flower a tear.

"I did a little flower making as a teenager," Emiko said.

"Will you come over and show me how?" Mattie asked. "I'm too embarrassed to take these awful things, and I've still got lots of crepe paper spread all over the kitchen."

"Sure," Emiko nodded. "I'll help you get started and you'll be a whiz in no time. It isn't too hard; it just takes patience."

Mattie smiled, a slight wheeze in her voice when she said, "I've got plenty of that, too."

They were seated at the Barnes's small table, surrounded by bright masses of petals like fallen butterflies, their fingers sticky from the florist tape, when Roy returned from shopping. When he saw Emiko, he straightened and pulled his belt up over his paunch.

"A sight for sore eyes!" he boomed, giving her a broad wink. "What mischief are you ladies up to?"

"Emi's teaching me how to make flowers," Mattie explained, holding up a wobbly rose.

"Always flowers! I tell you," he leaned over Emiko's chair and said in a mock conspiratorial voice, "all my wife thinks about is flowers. I keep telling her there are other things in life. Gardening is for old folks."

"And what's wrong with that?" Mattie protested, waving her flower at him. "We *are* old folks."

"Speak for yourself," he winked at Emiko again. "What's so great about gardens, anyway?"

"I hold with the poem that says you're closest to God's heart in a garden," said Mattie.

"Well, I'm not ready to get that close to God's heart, yet." There was defiance in Roy's voice. "What do you think about that, Emi?"

"I like working in the yard before it gets too hot," she said carefully. Her words felt tight and deliberate, like the unfurled petals on the yellow rose in her hands. "I don't have Mattie's talent with real flowers, though—aside from the bougainvillea and Jenny's petunias, nothing ever seems to bloom. The soil is too dry and saline for the things I used to grow. Now I've got my hopes pinned on the vegetable garden."

"Vegetables—hmph!" Roy snorted, stomping off to read the paper.

"Oh, that Roy is just like a boy sometimes," Mattie said. "I tell you, don't ever let your husband retire or you'll find him underfoot all day long."

"Doesn't Roy have any hobbies?" Emiko thought of her father and his books, his Japanese brush painting, his meetings.

"He used to play golf," Mattie said, "but there's no golf course here. He says this town is one giant sand trap."

"There have been times when I felt that way, too," Emiko admitted lightly.

"Well, don't let Roy hear you say that or you'll never get him off the topic," Mattie chuckled. "The fact is, Roy doesn't much know how to be by himself. I've had forty years to learn, and I've gotten to like it. And I suppose maybe he will, too."

Her voice trailed off, and Emiko suddenly realized that Mattie didn't much care whether he did or not.

One day while Emiko was engrossed in pinning a dress pattern for Jenny, she suddenly heard a tapping on the screen, like the scrabbling of a large beetle. She half turned and felt a jolt of alarm at the sight of a grinning gargoyle hunched before the window. It was Roy, his nose pushed up against the glass, hands splayed open on either side of his face, the caricature of a boy peering covetously into a toystore.

"Hey there! I caught you daydreaming!" he chortled. "Looks to me like you need some company to wake you up."

"I'm not daydreaming; I'm trying to figure out how to make a two-and-a-half yard dress out of two yards," she said. "Jenny is growing so fast, I can hardly keep up with her."

Roy walked into the house unbidden, confident of a welcome, and drew a chair up to the table. He fingered the bright cotton print spread over the table and gazed at Emiko, his head cocked to one side.

"You must get pretty lonesome here by yourself all day. No wonder you're sitting here dreaming."

"No," she said, her fingers moving the pattern pieces. "There's so much to do, I don't have time to be lonesome. Besides, Jenny is here, and Kiyo comes home for lunch."

"But still—cooped up with a kiddie all day." Roy shook his head. He chose to disregard Kiyo, who had no place in his imagined scenarios, and was hard at work miles away.

Emiko delicately edged the cotton fabric away from Roy's damp, restless fingers. "I'll be darned if I offer him something to drink," she thought, as he mopped his brow and cast an impatient glance at the kitchen. "I haven't seen Mattie outside this week. How is she feeling?"

"Oh, 'bout the same, 'bout the same," he said, his irritation subsiding into brave resignation. "She has her good days and her bad days. The doctor told her to stay in bed for awhile and take it easy."

"It must be hard on Mattie, having to stay indoors," Emiko said, thinking of her peering out through the pale curtains at the wilting zinnias and the new weeds in the back yard.

"I suppose so—usually you can't tear Mattie away from her garden." Roy shook his head. "Mattie and me are real different. Now, I like people—I've always been the sociable type—but Mattie! All she cares about are plants."

"Well, Kiyo and I have different interests," Emiko said, "but it works out well that way. Maybe you could learn a few things from Mattie about plants."

Even as the suggestion passed her lips, she regretted saying it. Roy viewed the garden as the site of onerous labor. To Mattie, it was the true world of the heart, with no room for ungentle or impatient hands. It was a place of deeply sown hopes, lovingly nurtured, and its colors were the colors of unspoken dreams.

"Plants!" Roy threw up his hands. "Give me people any time. I always liked people and had a knack for working with them—that's how I moved up in the business."

"Why don't you look into some of the clubs here?" Emiko tried again. "The Elks always need people with experience and time."

"Sweetheart, I'm going to spend my time the way I want. I'm finished with work—it's time to enjoy life! Besides, how much fun can I have with a bunch of old geezers? That's not for me, Emily, my dear." She stiffened as he repeated the name, savoring the syllables. "Emily . . . Emily . . . Yes, I like the sound of that—Emily."

"My name is Emiko," she said quietly, her eyes as hard as agate. "I was named after my grandmother." That unfaltering voice had spoken the same words in first, second, third, fourth, fifth, and sixth grades. All the grammer school teachers had sought to change her name, to make her into an Emily: "Emily is so much easier to pronounce, dear, and it's a nice American name." She was such a well-mannered child, the teachers were always amazed at her stubbornness on this one point. Sometimes she was tempted to relent, to give in, but something inside her resisted. "My name is Emiko," she would insist politely. I am an American named Emiko. I was named for my grandmother who was beautiful and loved to swim. When she emerged from the sea, her long black hair would glitter white with salt. I never met her, but she was beautiful and she would laugh when she rose from the waves. "My name is Emiko; Emi for short."

"But Emily is such a pretty name," Roy protested. "It fits you."

"It's not my name," she said, swallowing a hard knot of anger. "I don't like to be called Emily!"

"Temper, temper!" He shook his finger at her, gleeful at having provoked her.

"Well, I guess I'll be in a better temper when I can get some work done," she said, folding up the cloth with tense, deliberate hands. She raised her voice. "Jenny! Let's go out and water the vegetable garden now."

If Jenny thought this a strange task in the heat of the afternoon, it did not show in her face when she skipped out of her room, swinging her straw hat. It still sported a flimsy, rainbow-hued scarf which had been the subject of much pleading in an El Centro dime store. At that moment, Emiko found it an oddly reassuring sight. She smiled and felt her composure return.

"Tell Mattie to let me know if there's anything I can do to help," she told Roy, as he unwillingly followed them out of the house and trudged away across the sand. After they went back inside, Emiko, for the first time, locked the door behind them. When Kiyo returned home, his face taut with fatigue, she told him it was because of the hoboes who came around.

Emiko went to see Mattie less and less frequently, preferring instead to call her on the phone, even though they lived so close. Roy, however, continued to drop by, despite Emiko's aloofness. His unseemly yearning tugged at her with undignified hands, but what he craved most was beyond her power to give. She took to darning and mending in the bedroom with the curtains drawn, ignoring his insistent knock; she tried to do her gardening in the evening after dinner when her husband was home, but it was hard to weed in the dusk. She was beginning to feel caged, pent up, restless. Jenny and Kiyo trod quietly, puzzled by her edginess, but their solicitude only made her feel worse.

Finally one morning Emiko decided to weed the vegetables, sprouting new and tender. Surely the midmorning heat would discourage any interference. Although perspiration soon trickled down her face, she began to enjoy the satisfying rhythm of the work. She was so engrossed she did not notice when Roy Barnes unlatched the gate and stepped into the yard, a determined twinkle in his faded eye.

"Howdy, Emi! I saw you working away out here by your lonesome and thought maybe you could use some help."

"Thanks, but I'm doing all right," she said, wrenching a clump of puncture vine from the soil and laying it in the weed box careful to avoid scattering the sharp stickers. Jenny was close by, digging at her petunias and marigolds, ignoring Mr. Barnes, who had no place in the colorful jungle she was imagining.

"If I had a pretty little wife, I sure wouldn't let her burn up out here, no sir." His voice nudged at her as she squatted on the border of the vegetable plot. If Mattie looked out of the window, she would see only a pleasant tableau: Roy nodding in neighborly fashion as Emiko pointed out young rows of zucchini and yellow squash, watermelon, cantaloupe, eggplant, and tomatoes. Mattie would not see the strain on Emiko's face, which she turned away when Roy leaned over and mumbled, "Say, you know what I like best in this garden?"

Emiko grabbed the handle of the shovel and stood up before he could tell her, moving away from him to pluck a weed. "I know Mattie likes cantaloupe," she said. "So do I. Kiyo prefers Crenshaws, but I couldn't find any seeds this year. What do you and Mattie have in your garden?"

"Just grass," he said, undeterred. "Mattie's always fussing over her flowers—you know what she's like," he chuckled indulgently. "But I'd rather spend my time doing other things than slaving in the yard."

Emiko hacked away at the stubborn clumps of grass roots and the persistent runners with myriad finer roots, thread-thin, but tough as wire. She worked with desperate energy, flustered, her gloved hands sweating on the shovel handle, forehead damp. She was groping for the language to make him understand, to make him leave her in peace, but he was bent on not understanding, not seeing, not leaving until he got what he wanted.

"You know what, Emi?" He moistened his dry lips, beginning to grin reminiscently. "You remind me of somebody I met in Tokyo. Have you ever been to Tokyo?"

"No," she said, digging hard. "Never."

"You'd like it; it's a wonderful place, so clean and neat, and the people so friendly. When I was in Tokyo, I met up with the cutest geisha girl you ever saw—just like a little doll. She'd never seen anybody with blue eyes before, and couldn't get over it." He chuckled. "I couldn't think who you reminded me of at first, and then it just hit me that you are the spitting image of her."

"Did Mattie like Tokyo, too?" Emiko said, continuing to spade vigorously, as his eyes slid over her, imagining a doll in exotic robes.

"She didn't go—it was a business trip," he said impatiently. Then his voice relaxed into a drawl, heavy with insinuation. "After all, I like to do some things on my own." He was moving closer again.

Then she saw it. Emiko had just turned over a rock, and as she raised the shovel, it darted from its refuge, pincers up, the deadly tail curved menacingly over the carapaced back. It moved a little to the left and then the right, beginning the poison dance. Emiko glanced to see where Jenny was and saw Roy jump back hastily; the scorpion, startled by his movement, scuttled sideways toward Jenny, who lay on her stomach, still dreaming of her jungle.

The blood pounded in Emiko's head. She brought down the shovel hard with one quick breath, all her rage shooting down the thick handle into the heavy crushing iron. She wielded the shovel like a samurai in battle, swinging it down with all her force, battering her enemy to dust. Once had been enough, but she struck again and again, until her anger was spent, and she leaned on the rough handle, breathing hard.

"Mommy! What did you do?" Jenny had scrambled to Emiko's side. There was fear in her eyes as she gazed at the unrecognizable fragments in the dirt.

"I killed a scorpion," Emiko said. She scornfully tossed the remains into the weed box, and wiped her brow on her arm, like a farmer, or a warrior. "I don't like to kill anything," she said aloud, "but sometimes you have to."

Roy Barnes recoiled from the pitiless knowledge in her eyes. He saw her clearly now, but it was too late. His mouth opened and closed, but the gush of words had gone dry. He seemed to age before her eyes, like Urashima-taro who opened the precious box of youth and was instantly wrinkled and broken by the unleashed tide of years.

"You'll have to leave now, Mr. Barnes. I'm going in to fix lunch." Emiko's smile was quiet as unsheathed steel. "Tell Mattie I hope she's feeling better."

She watched him pick his way across the dirt, avoiding the puncture vine and rusted tin cans, and looking as gray as the rags that bleached beneath the fierce sun. Jenny stared past him and the small houses of their neighborhood, to the desert sand beyond, glittering like an ocean with shards of mica.

"Do you think we might ever find gold?" she asked.

They gazed together over the desert, full of unknown perils and ancient secrets, the dust of dreams and battles.

"Maybe." Emiko stood tall, shading her eyes from the deceptive shimmer. "Maybe."

Lotus Blossoms Don't Bleed: Images of Asian Women

RENEE E. TAJIMA

In recent years the media have undergone spectacular technical innovations. But whereas form has leaped toward the year 2000, it seems that content still straddles the turn of the last century. A reigning example of the industry's stagnation is its portrayal of Asian women. And the only real signs of life are stirring far away from Hollywood in the cutting rooms owned and operated by Asian America's independent producers.

The commercial media are, in general, populated by stereotyped characterizations that range in complexity, accuracy, and persistence over time. There is the hooker with a heart of gold and the steely tough yet honorable mobster. Most of these characters are white, and may be as one-dimensional as Conan the Barbarian or as complex as R. P. McMurphy in *One Flew Over the Cuckoo's Nest*.

Images of Asian women, however, have remained consistently simplistic and inaccurate during the sixty years of largely forgettable screen appearances. There are two basic types: the Lotus Blossom Baby (a.k.a. China Doll, Geisha Girl, shy Polynesian beauty), and the Dragon Lady (Fu Manchu's various female relations, prostitutes, devious madames). There is little in between, although experts may differ as to whether Suzie Wong belongs to the race-blind "hooker with a heart of gold" category, or deserves one all of her own.

Asian women in American cinema are interchangeable in appearance and name, and are joined together by the common language of non-language—that is, uninterpretable chattering, pidgin English, giggling, or silence. They may be specifically identified by nationality—particularly in war films—but that's where screen accuracy ends. The dozens of populations of Asian and Pacific Island groups are lumped into one homogeneous mass of Mama Sans.

Passive Love Interests

Asian women in film are, for the most part, passive figures who exist to serve men, especially as love interests for white men (Lotus Blossoms) or as partners in crime with men of their own kind (Dragon Ladies). One of the first Dragon Lady types was played by Anna May Wong. In the 1924 spectacular *Thief of Bagdad* she uses treachery to help an evil Mongol prince attempt to win the Princess of Bagdad from Douglas Fairbanks.

The Lotus Blossom Baby, a sexual-romantic object, has been the prominent type throughout the years. These "Oriental flowers" are utterly feminine, delicate, and welcome respites from their often loud, independent American counterparts. Many of them are the spoils of the last three wars fought in Asia. One recent television example is Sergeant Klinger's Korean wife in the short-lived series "AfterMash."

In the real world, this view of Asian women has spawned an entire marriage industry. Today the Filipino wife is particularly in vogue for American men who order Asian brides from picture catalogues, just as you might buy an imported cheese slicer from Spiegel's. (I moderated a community program on Asian American women recently. A rather bewildered young saleswoman showed up with a stack of brochures to promote the Cherry Blossom companion service, or some such enterprise.) Behind the brisk sales of Asian mail-order brides is a growing number of American men who are seeking old-fashioned, compliant wives, women they feel are no longer available in the United States.

Feudal Asian customs do not change for the made-for-movie women. Picture brides, geisha girls, concubines, and hara-kiri are all mixed together and reintroduced into any number of settings. Take for example these two versions of Asian and American cultural exchange:

1. It's Toko Riki on Japan's Okinawa Island during the late 1940s in the film *Teahouse of the August Moon*. American occupation forces nice guy Captain Fisby (Glenn Ford) gets a visit from Japanese yenta Sakini (Marlon Brando).

Enter Brando: "Hey Boss, I Sonoda has a present for you."

Enter the gift: Japanese actress Machiko Kyo as a geisha, giggling.

Ford: "Who's she?"

Brando: "Souvenir . . . introducing Lotus Blossom geisha girl first class."

Ford protests the gift. Kyo giggles.

Brando sneaks away with a smile: "Good night, Boss." Kyo, chattering away in Japanese, tries to pamper a bewildered Ford who holds up an instructive finger to her and repeats slowly, "Me . . . me . . . no." Kyo looks confused.

2. It's San Francisco, circa 1981, in the television series "The Incredible Hulk." Nice guy David Banner (Bill Bixby a.k.a. The Hulk) gets a present from Chinese yenta Hyung (Beulah Quo).

Enter Quo: "David, I have something for you."

Enter Irene Sun as Tam, a Chinese refugee, bowing her head shyly.

Quo: "The Floating Lotus Company hopes you will be very happy. This is Tam, your mail-order bride."

Bixby protests the gift. Sun, speaking only Chinese, tries to pamper a bewildered Bixby who repeats slowly in an instructive tone, "you . . . must . . . go!" Sun looks confused.

Illicit Interracial Love

On film Asian women are often assigned the role of expendability in situations of illicit Asian-white love. In these cases the most expedient way of resolving the problems of miscegenation has been to get rid of the Asian partner. Thus, some numbers of hyphenated (made-for-television, war-time, wives-away-from-home) Asian women have expired for the convenience of their home-bound soldier lovers. More progressive-minded GI's of the Vietnam era have returned to Vietnam years later to search for the offspring of these love matches.

In 1985 the General Foods Gold Showcase proudly presented a post-Vietnam version of the wilting Lotus Blossom on network television. "A forgotten passion, a child he never knew. . . . All his tomorrows forever changed by *The Lady From Yesterday.*" He is Vietnam vet Craig Weston (Wayne Rogers), official father of two, and husband to Janet (Bonnie Bedelia). She is Lien Van Huyen (Tina Chen), whom Weston hasn't seen since the fall of Saigon. She brings the child, the unexpected consequence of that wartime love-match, to the United States. But Janet doesn't lose her husband, she gains a son. As *New York Times* critic John J. O'Connor points out, Lien has "the good manners to be suffering from a fatal disease that will conveniently remove her from the scene."

The geographic parallel to the objectification of Asian women is the rendering of Asia as only a big set for the white leading actors. What would "Shogun" be without Richard Chamberlin? The most notable exception is the 1937 movie version of Pearl Buck's novel *The Good Earth.* The story is about Chinese in China and depicted with some complexity and emotion. Nevertheless the lead parts played by Louise Rainer and Paul Muni follow the pattern of choosing white stars for Asian roles, a problem which continues to plague Asian actors.

Other white actresses who have played Asian roles include Katharine Hepburn, sporting adhesive tape over her eyes, in the 1944 film *The Dragon Seed,* Jennifer Jones as a Eurasian in *Love is a Many Splendored Thing,* Ona Munson as Gin Sling, the "Chinese Dietrich" in Josef von Sternberg's *Shanghai Gesture,* and Angie Dickinson in Samuel Fuller's *China Gate.* Dickinson plays a Eurasian in Southeast Asia who guides a

French and South Vietnamese patrol on a mission to destroy a Communist munitions dump. The American demolitionist just happens to be the man who deserted Dickinson and their child. In the end, the Eurasian nobly sets off the explosion and dies, following in the footsteps of Anna May Wong. Twenty-nine years earlier, in *The Toll of the Sea,* she walked into the surf after she and her biracial child were spurned by American in-laws.

Noticeably lacking is the portrayal of love relationships between Asian women and Asian men, particularly as lead characters. Instead, as in Machiko Kyo's case in *Teahouse,* the man often loves from afar, but runs a distant second to the tall, handsome American. Asian men usually have problems with interracial affairs too—quite often they are cast as rapists or love-struck losers.

The 1984 version of the blonde-crazy Asian male in the teen feature *Sixteen Candles* shows how Hollywood dresses up age-old stereotypes in contemporary rags. This time a sex-starved Chinese exchange student dresses in samurai garb and yells "Banzai!" in his libidinous pursuits. So much for normalization.

Generally Asian male roles reflect the state of U.S.–Asia relations at the time a movie is made. Thus, during the Yellow Menace period of the early 1900s, World War II, and the McCarthy years, the number of Asian lechers lusting after white women on the screen increased appreciably. During the early 1950s the prototypical, sex-starved Chinese was the Communist commander in *Shanghai Story,* quite a bit more malevolent than the exchange student in *Sixteen Candles.*

The post-Gandhi interest in India, which earned a cover story in *Vanity Fair,* has managed to dredge up more than one tired cinematic motif. The BBC series "Jewel in the Crown," which aired on American public television, and David Lean's *A Passage to India* represent the height of what critic Salman Rushdie dubbed "Raj revisionism"—the Brit's neocolonial catharsis replete with brown rapists lusting after white female victims.

Neither has the made-up Asian been retired. In 1984 Amy Irving appeared in DRAG (Downright Retrograde Asian Get-up) as the Indian princess of "The Far Pavillions," one of television's more embarrassing moments, produced by Home Box Office. Even mainstream critics had to chuckle at the brown shoepolish make-up and exaggerated boldface eyeliner worn by Irving.

One film that stands out as an exception because it was cast with Asian people for Asian characters is *Flower Drum Song* (1961), set in San Francisco's Chinatown. Unfortunately the film did little more than temporarily take a number of talented Asian American actresses and actors off the unemployment lines. It also gave birth for awhile to a new generation of stereotypes—gum-chewing Little Leaguers, enterprising businessmen, and all-American tomboys—variations on the then new model minority myth. *Flower Drum Song* hinted that the assimilated, hyphenated Asian American might be much more successful in American society than the Japanese of the 1940s and the Chinese and Koreans of the 1950s, granted they keep to the task of being white American first.

The women of *Flower Drum Song* maintain their earlier image with few modernizations. Miyoshi Umeki is still a picture bride. And in *Suzie Wong* actress Nancy Kwan is a hipper, Americanized version of the Hong Kong bar girl without the pidgin English. But updated clothes and setting do not change the essence of these images.

In 1985 director Michael Cimino cloned Suzie Wong to TV news anchor Connie Chung and created another anchor, Tracy Tzu (Arianne), in the disastrous exploitation film *Year of the Dragon*. In it Tzu is ostensibly the only positive Asian American character in a film that villifies the people of New York's Chinatown. The Tzu character is a success in spite of her ethnicity. Just as she would rather eat Italian than Chinese, she'd rather sleep with white men than Chinese men. (She is ultimately raped by three "Chinese boys.") Neither does she bat an eye at the barrage of racial slurs fired off by her lover, lead Stanley White, the Vietnam vet and New York City cop played by Mickey Rourke.

At the outset Tzu is the picture of professionalism and sophistication, engaged in classic screen love/hate banter with White. The turning point comes early in the picture when their flirtatious sparring in a Chinese restaurant is interrupted by a gangland slaughter. While White pursues the culprits, Tzu totters on her high heels into a phone booth where she cowers, sobbing, until White comes to the rescue.

The standard of beauty for Asian women that is set in the movies deserves mention. Caucasian women are often used for Asian roles, which contributes to a case of aesthetic imperialism for Asian women. When Asian actresses are chosen they invariably have large eyes, high cheekbones, and other Caucasian-like characteristics when they appear on the silver screen. As Judy Chu of the University of California, Los Angeles, has pointed out, much of Anna May Wong's appeal was due to her Western looks. Chu unearthed this passage from the June 1924 *Photoplay* which refers to actress Wong, but sounds a lot like a description of Eurasian model/actress Arianne: "Her deep brown eyes, while the slant is not pronounced, are typically oriental. But her Manchu mother has given her a height and poise of figure that Chinese maidens seldom have."

Invisibility

There is yet another important and pervasive characteristic of Asian women on the screen, invisibility. The number of roles in the Oriental flower and Dragon Lady categories have been few, and generally only supporting parts. But otherwise Asian women are absent. Asian women do not appear in films as union organizers, or divorced mothers fighting for the custody of their children, or fading movie stars, or spunky trial lawyers, or farm women fighting bank foreclosures; Asian women are not portrayed as ordinary people.

Then there is the kind of invisibility that occurs when individual personalities and separate identities become indistinguishable from one another. Some memorable Asian masses are the islanders fleeing exploding volcanoes in *Krakatoa: East of Java* (1969) and the Vietnamese villagers fleeing Coppola's airborne weaponry in various scenes from *Apocalypse Now* (1979). Asian women populate these hordes or have groupings of their own, usually in some type of harem situation. In *Cry for Happy* (1961), Glenn Ford is cast as an American GI who stumbles into what turns out to be the best little geisha house in Japan.

Network television has given Asian women even more opportunities to paper the walls, so to speak. They are background characters in "Hawaii 5-0," "Magnum PI," and other series that transverse the Pacific.

I've seen a cheongsam-clad maid in the soap "One Life to Live," and assorted Chinatown types surface whenever the cops and robbers shows revive scripts about the Chinatown Tong wars.

The most stunning exceptions to television's abuse of Asian images is the phenomenon of news anchors: Connie Chung (CBS) and Sasha Foo (CNN) have national spots, and Tritia Toyota (Los Angeles), Wendy Tokuda (San Francisco), Kaity Tong (New York), Sandra Yep (Sacramento), and others are reporters in large cities. All of them cover hard news, long the province of middle-aged white men with authoritative voices. Toyota and Yep have been able to parlay their positions so that there is more coverage of Asian American stories at their stations. Because of their presence on screen—and ironically, perhaps because of the celebrity status of today's newscasters—these anchors wield much power in rectifying Asian women's intellectual integrity in the media. (One hopes *Year of the Dragon*'s Tracy Tzu hasn't canceled their positive effect.)

Undoubtedly the influence of these visible reporters is fortified by the existence of highly organized Asian American journalists. The West Coast–based Asian American Journalists Association has lobbied for affirmative action in the print and broadcast media. In film and video, the same type of political initiatives have spurred a new movement of independently produced works made by and about Asian Americans.

Small Gems From Independents

The independent film movement emerged during the 1960s as an alternative to the Hollywood mill. In a broad sense it has had little direct impact in reversing the distorted images of Asian women, although some gems have been produced. One example is Allie Light and Irving Saraf's documentary portrait *Mitsuye and Nellie*, about two contemporary poets Mitsuye Yamada and Nellie Wong. The biggest disappointment has probably been *Nightsongs*, produced by Marva Nabili and Thomas Fucci for public television's "American Playhouse" series. The lead character is a delicate Vietnamese refugee who speaks barely a word, except for her rather breathy recitations of rather syrupy poems.

But now Asian American independents, many of whom are women, have consciously set out to bury sixty years of Lotus Blossoms who do not

bleed and Mama-sans who do not struggle. These women filmmakers—
most of whom began their careers only since the 1970s—often draw
from deeply personal perspectives in their work: Virginia Hashii's *Jenny*
portrays a young Japanese American girl who explores her own Nikkei
heritage for the first time; Christine Choy's *From Spikes to Spindles* (1976)
documents the lives of women in New York's Chinatown; Felicia Lowe's
China: Land of My Father (1979) is a film diary of the filmmaker's own
first reunion with her grandmother in China; Renee Cho's *The New Wife*
(1978) dramatizes the arrival of an immigrant bride to America; and
Lana Pih Jokel's *Chiang Ching: A Dance Journey* traces the life of dancer-
actress-teacher Chiang. All these films were produced during the 1970s
and together account for only a little more than two hours of screen time.
Most are first works with the same rough-edged quality that characterized early Asian American film efforts.

Women producers have maintained a strong presence during the
1980s, although their work does not always focus on women's issues.
And when it does, the films vary in style, approach, and quality. *With
Silk Wings*, a videotape directed by Loni Ding and produced by San
Francisco's Asian Women United, contains profiles of Asian American
women in various nontraditional jobs. In 1981 the Asian Women
United group in New York collaborated with director Jon Wing Lum to
create *Ourselves*, an introspective study of young activists within the
group. (Wing managed to edit the hour-long piece with only forty cuts.)

Also in this decade veteran filmmakers Emiko Omori and Christine
Choy have produced their first dramatic efforts. Omori's *The Departure* is
the story of a Japanese girl who must give up her beloved traditional
dolls in pre-World War II California. Unfortunately it feels incomplete
at approximately fourteen minutes in length and leaves one wanting more. In *Fei Tien: Goddess in Flight*, Choy tries to adapt a nonlin-
ear cinematic structure to Genny Lim's play *Pigeons*, which explores
the relationship between a Chinese American yuppie and a Chinatown
"bird lady."

Perhaps the strongest work made thus far has been directed by a male
filmmaker, Arthur Dong. *Sewing Woman* is a small, but beautifully
crafted portrait of Dong's mother, Zem Ping. It chronicles her life from

war-torn China to San Francisco's garment factories. Other films and tapes by Asian men include Michael Uno's *Emi* (1978), a portrait of the Japanese American writer and former concentration camp internee, Emi Tonooka; the Yonemoto brothers' neonarrative *Green Card,* a soap-style saga of a Japanese immigrant artist seeking truth, love, and permanent residency in Southern California; and Steve Okazaki's *Survivors,* a documentary focusing on the women survivors of the atomic blasts over Hiroshima and Nagasaki. All these filmmakers are American-born Japanese. *Orientations,* by Asian Canadian Richard Fung, is the first work I've seen that provides an in-depth look at the Asian gay community, and it devotes a good amount of time to Asian Canadian lesbians.

Our Own Image

These film and videomakers, women and men, face a challenge far beyond creating entertainment and art. Several generations of Asian women have been raised with racist and sexist celluloid images. The models for passivity and servility in these films and television programs fit neatly into the myths imposed on us, and contrast sharply with the more liberating ideals of independence and activism. Generations of other Americans have also grown up with these images. And their acceptance of the dehumanization implicit in the stereotypes of expendability and invisibility is frightening.

Old images of Asian women in the mainstream media will likely remain stagnant for awhile. After sixty years, there have been few signs of progress. However there is hope because of the growing number of filmmakers emerging from our own communities. Wayne Wang in 1985 completed *Dim Sum,* a beautifully crafted feature film about the relationship between a mother and daughter in San Francisco's Chinatown. *Dim Sum,* released through a commercial distributor, could be the first truly sensitive film portrayal of Asian American women to reach a substantial national audience. In quality and numbers, Asian American filmmakers may soon constitute a critical mass out of which we will see a body of work that gives us a new image, our own image.

The Business of Selling Mail-Order Brides

VENNY VILLAPANDO

The phenomenon is far from new. Certainly in the Old West and in other frontier situations such as the labor camps at the sugar farms in Hawaii, the colonization of Australia, or even in the early Irish settlements of New York, there were always lonely men who would write to their homeland for a bride. These women would come on the next train or on the next boat to meet their husbands for the very first time.

For Japanese immigrants traditional marriages were arranged in Japan between relatives of the man and the prospective bride. Information was exchanged between the two families about the potential union, and photographs were exchanged between the couple. If both parties agreed, then the marriage was legalized in the home country, and the bride came to America.

While these marriages occurred in less than ideal situations, a number of them were successful. For example the Japanese sugar worker who once waited at the Honolulu pier for the arrival of his picture bride, today enjoys the company of a family clan that spans at least two generations. That is indeed an achievement considering the picture bride of yesteryear, just like the contemporary mail-order bride, has always been at a disadvantage. She comes to the marriage from far away, without the nearby support of her family or a familiar culture. The distance that she has traveled is measured not so much in nautical as in emotional miles. She is not quite the happy bride who has been courted and wooed, freely choosing her groom and her destiny.

Today's mail-order brides are products of a very complex set of situations and contradictions. They are confronted by far more complicated conditions than the picture brides of years past. They do not quite fit the simple pattern of a marriage between a lonely man stranded in a foreign land and a woman who accepts him sight unseen.

In the present matches brides-to-be are generally Asian and husbands-to-be are Caucasians, mostly American, Australian, and Canadian. A majority of the women are poor and because of economic desperation become mail-order brides. Racial, as well as economic, factors define the marriage however. The new wife is relegated to a more inferior position than her picture bride counterpart. Plus the inequity of the partnership is further complicated by the mail-order bride's immigrant status. Consequently she is a foreigner not only to the culture, language, and society, but to her husband's race and nationality as well.

Why Men Choose Mail-Order Brides

"These men want women who will feel totally dependent on them," writes Dr. Gladys L. Symons of the University of Calgary. "They want women who are submissive and less intimidating." Aged between thirty and forty, these men grew up most likely before the rise of the feminist movement, adds Symons. She partially attributes the resurgence of the mail-order bride to a backlash against the 1980s high-pressure style of dating.[1]

Dr. Davor Jedlicka, a sociology professor from the University of Texas, notes in his study of 265 subscribers of mail-order bride catalogues that "very many of them had extremely bitter experiences with divorce or breakups or engagements." His research also shows the median income of these men to be higher than average—65 percent of them had incomes of over $20,000. According to Jedlicka, the average age was thirty-seven, average height five feet seven inches, and most were college educated. Only five percent never finished high school.[2]

The Japanese American Citizens League, a national civil rights group, confirms this general profile of the typical male client and adds other findings. According to its recent position paper on mail-order brides, the group found that the men tend to be white, much older than the bride they choose, politically conservative, frustrated by the women's movement, and socially alienated. They experience feelings of personal inadequacy and find the traditional Asian value of deference to men reassuring.[3]

In her interview in the *Alberta Report,* Symons points out that the men are also attracted to the idea of buying a wife, since all immigration, transportation, and other costs run to only about two thousand dollars. "We're a consumer society," says Symons. "People become translated into commodities easily."[4] And commodities they are.

Gold at the End of the Rainbow

Contemporary traders in the Asian bride business publish lists sold for twenty dollars for a catalogue order form to twenty thousand dollars for a deluxe videotaped presentation. Perhaps the most successful company is Rainbow Ridge Consultants run by John Broussard and his wife Kelly Pomeroy. They use a post office box in Honakaa, Hawaii. Explains Broussard:

> Basically, we just sell addresses. . . . We operate as a pen pal club, not a front for the slave trade, although some people get the wrong idea. We're not a Sears catalogue from which you buy a wife. You have to write and win the heart of the woman you desire.[5]

For providing this service, Broussard and Pomeroy reported a net profit in 1983 of twenty-five thousand dollars, which catapulted to sixty-five thousand in 1984.

Rainbow Ridge Consultants distribute three different publications, of which the top two are *Cherry Blossoms* and *Lotus Blossoms*. These differ from the Sears catalogue only because an issue is only twenty-eight pages long, not several hundred, and photos are black and white, not glossy color. A typical entry reads: "If you like 'em tall, Alice is 5'9", Filipina, social work grad, average looks, wants to hear from men 25–40. $4." For the stated dollar amount, interested men can procure an address and a copy of her biographical data.

Broussard and Pomeroy's sister publication *Lotus Blossoms* has twice the number of names, but Broussard admits that *Lotus* is a "second string" brochure, offering pictures of women who do not have the same looks as those in *Cherry Blossoms*.[6]

Six months of subscription to the complete catalogues of Rainbow Ridge will cost the wife-seeker $250. A special service will engage Broussard and Pomeroy in a wife hunt at the rate of $50 per hour and includes handling all details, even writing letters and purchasing gifts when necessary. Should the match succeed, the business pockets another fee of $1,000.

Kurt Kirstein of Blanca, Colorado, runs Philippine-American Life Partners, which offers one thousand pictures of Filipino women looking for American men. Louis Florence of the American Asian Worldwide Service in Orcutt, California, provides men with a similar catalogue for $25; another $630 will permit the bride-seeker to correspond with twenty-four women, of whom any fifteen will be thoroughly investigated by the service. The California business reports an annual gross income of $250,000.

Selling Asian women is a thriving enterprise because the number of American men who seek Asian brides continues to grow. Broussard estimates the total number of daily inquiries is five hundred. In 1984 the Gannett News Service reported that seven thousand Filipino women married Australians, Europeans, and Americans. The *Wall Street Journal* noted that in 1970, only 34 Asians were issued fiancée-petitioned visas; while in 1983, the figure jumped dramatically to 3,428.[7]

Broussard says that he receives one hundred letters a day from Asian and other women. He publishes about seven hundred pictures every other month in his catalogues. Still, Broussard reports that the chances of a man finding a wife through his service is only about one in twenty.

When he receives a letter and the appropriate fees from a prospective groom, Broussard sends off a catalogue. One of his correspondents describes the process: "I selected fourteen ladies to send introductory letters to. To my amazement, I received fourteen replies and am still corresponding with twelve of them."[8] One of the reasons why letters so often succeed is the detailed coaching both parties receive. For instance Broussard and Pomeroy publish a 130-page pamphlet entitled "How to Write to Oriental Ladies." There is also one for women called "The Way to an American Male's Heart."

The Japanese American Citizens League points out the disadvantage to women in these arrangements because of the inequality of information disseminated. Under the traditional arranged marriage system, family investigation and involvement insured equal access to information and

mutual consent. Now only the women must fill out a personality evaluation which asks very intimate details about their life style and history,
and is then shared with the men. Prospective grooms do not have to
submit similar information about themselves. Some companies, in fact,
even discourage their male clients from disclosing certain types of personal facts in their correspondence, including such potentially negative
characteristics as being black or having physical disabilities.[9]

The Economics of Romance

Coaching or no coaching, the mail-order brides business succeeds partly
because it takes advantage of the economic deprivation faced by women
in underdeveloped Asian countries. The Broussard brochure categori-
cally states:

> We hear lots of stories about dishonest, selfish and immature women
> on both sides of the Pacific. Perhaps women raised in poverty will have
> lower material expectations and will be grateful to whoever rescues
> them and offers a better life.

One Caucasian man who met his wife through the mail says: "They
don't have a whole lot of things, so what they do have they appreciate
very much. They appreciate things more than what the average American woman would." In other words, they are properly grateful for whatever the superior male partner bestows on them.

"Filipinas come because their standard of living is so low," asserts
Pomeroy. In 1984 the per capita income in the Philippines was $640.
"Most of the women make no secret of why they want to marry an
American: money."[10] An Australian reporter who has studied the influx
of Filipino mail-order brides to her country agrees: "Most Filipinas are
escaping from grinding poverty."[11] Indeed most Asian governments
that are saddled with chronic unemployment, spiraling cost of living,
malnutrition, and political turmoil, are faced with the problem of emigration and a diminishing labor force. In contrast, Japan, the economic
and technological leader of Asia, has very few women listed in mail-
order catalogues.

The *Chicago Sun-Times* describes Bruce Moore's visit to the family home of his mail-order bride, Rosie, in Cebu, Philippines:

'All of a sudden, we were driving through the jungle. There was nothing but little huts. I really started worrying about what I got myself into.' . . . The house turned out to be an unpainted concrete building with no doors, plumbing or electricity. . . . Rosie had worked in a factory, eight hours a day, making 75 to 80 cents a day. [12]

Because the Filipinas who avail themselves of mail-order bride service may not have much, Broussard's instructional brochures advise men to use caution in describing their financial status. The woman may turn out to be "a con artist after your money or easy entry into the United States." [13] Despite the poverty, though, many of the women are truly sincere in their responses. The Broussard customer who is still writing to twelve of the fourteen women who wrote him notes:

They all appeared genuine, and not one has asked me for money or anything else. In fact, in two instances, I offered to help with postage, and in both cases, it was declined. One of the ladies said she could not accept postal assistance, as that would lessen the pleasure she felt in the correspondence. [14]

Regardless of the sincerity of the parties involved, one women's rights group in the Philippines has denounced the promotion of relationships through "commerce, industry, negotiation or investment." Their protests, however, do not seem to affect the business. [15]

Racial Images and Romance

Added to economic exploitation, a major cornerstone of the mail-order bride business, is the prevalence of racial stereotypes. They have a widespread effect on the treatment of women and influence why so many men are attracted to mail-order romance. "These men believe the stereotypes that describe Oriental women as docile, compliant and submissive," says Jedlicka. His 1983 survey showed that 80 percent of the respondents accept this image as true.

One Canadian male, who asked not to be identified, was quoted as saying: "Asian girls are not as liberated as North American or Canadian girls. They're more family-oriented and less interested in working. They're old-fashioned. I like that." [16]

The California-based American Asian Worldwide Service perpetuates the stereotypes when it says in its brochure: "Asian ladies are faithful and devoted to their husbands. When it comes to sex, they are not demonstrative, however, they are inhibited. They love to do things to make their husbands happy." [17]

This company began after owner Louis Florence began his search for a second wife. He says that friends had touted how their Asian wives "love to make their men happy" and finally convinced him to find a wife from Asia.

Another mail-order pitch describes Asian women as "faithful, devoted, unspoiled and loving." [18] Broussard confirms this popular misconception by saying these women are "raised to be servants for men in many Oriental countries." Referring to the Malaysian and Indonesian women who have recently joined his list of registrants, Broussard insists: "Like the Filipinas, they are raised to respect and defer to the male. . . . The young Oriental woman . . . derives her basic satisfaction from serving and pleasing her husband." [19]

Virginity is a highly sought virtue in women. Tom Fletcher, a night worker in Ottawa, Canada, who dislikes North American women because they "want to get out [of the house] and work and that leads to break-ups," is especially appreciative of this sign of purity. "These women's virginity was a gift to their husbands and a sign of faithfulness and trust." One mail-order service unabashedly advertises virginity in a brochure with photos, home addresses, and descriptions of Filipino women, some of whom are as young as seventeen. "Most, if not all are very feminine, loyal, loving . . . and virgins!" its literature reads. [20]

Many of the Asian countries affected by the revived mail-order bride business have a history of U.S. military involvement. Troops have either fought battles or been stationed in Korea, the Philippines, and countries in Southeast Asia. During their stays, the soldiers have often developed strong perceptions of Asian women as prostitutes, bargirls, and geishas. Then they erroneously conclude that Asian American women must fit those images, too. Consequently the stereotype of women servicing and serving men is perpetuated.

The Japanese American Citizens League objects to the mail-order bride trade for that very reason. "The marketing techniques used by the catalogue bride companies reinforce negative sexual and racial stereotypes of Asian women in the U.S. The negative attitude toward Asian women affects all Asians in the country." Further, the treatment of women as "commodities" adds to the "non-human and negative perception of all Asians." [21]

Romance on the Rocks

A marriage made via the mail-order bride system is naturally beset by a whole range of problems. In her testimony before the U.S. Commission on Civil Rights, professor Bok-Lim Kim, then with the University of Illinois, noted that negative reactions and attitudes toward foreign Asian wives "exacerbates marital problems," which result in incidences of spouse abuse, desertion, separation, and divorce. [22] In addition, writes an Australian journalist, most of the men they marry are social misfits. "Many of them drink too much; some beat their wives and treat them little better than slaves." [23]

The Japanese American Citizens League asserts:

Individually, there may be many cases of couples meeting and marrying through these arrangements with positive results. We believe, however, that for the women, there are many more instances in which the impetus for leaving their home countries and families, and the resulting marriage relationships, have roots and end results which are less than positive. [24]

Many of the Caucasian men who marry what they believe are stereotypical women may be in for some surprises. Psychiatry professor Joe Yamamoto of the University of California at Los Angeles says: "I've found many Asian women acculturate rather quickly. These American men may get a surprise in a few years if their wives pick up liberated ways." [25]

One legally blind and hard-of-hearing American, married to a Korean woman, was eventually bothered by the same problems that plague other couples: in-laws and lack of money. "She gets frustrated because I don't hear her," complains the man about his soft-spoken Asian wife. In response, she says, "The main problem is [his] parents. I can't adapt to American culture. I was going to devote my life for him, but I can't." [26]

Another area which specifically affects foreign-born brides is their immigrant status. According to the Japanese American Citizens League, "these foreign women are at a disadvantage." This civil rights group targets the women's unfamiliarity with the U.S. immigration laws as one of the most disturbing aspects of the business. "As a result [of the ignorance], they may miss an opportunity to become a naturalized citizen, forfeit rights as a legal spouse, or live under an unwarranted fear of deportation which may be fostered by their spouse as a means of control." [27]

Conclusion

Despite the constant stream of criticism, the mail-order bride system will prevail as long as there are consumers and profit, and as long as underdeveloped countries continue failing to meet the economic, political, and social needs of their people. Indications show the business is not about to collapse now.

Erroneous ideas continue to thrive. An Asian woman dreams she will meet and marry someone rich and powerful, someone to rescue her and free her from poverty-stricken bondage. She hopes to live the rest of her life in a land of plenty. An American man dreams he will meet and marry someone passive, obedient, nonthreatening, and virginal, someone to devote her entire life to him, serving him and making no demands. Only a strong women's movement, one tied to the exploited underdeveloped country's struggle for liberation and independence, can challenge these ideas and channel the aspirations and ambitions of both men and women in a more positive and realistic direction.

Domestic Violence among Pacific Asians

NILDA RIMONTE

This essay presents an overview of the phenomenon of domestic violence in the Pacific Asian community of Los Angeles.[1] Who are the women involved? Why do they get battered? Why do they stay? When do they leave? And how, if at all, do they differ from battered women of other races, other groups?

The typical Pacific Asian battered woman exhibits a wide range of characteristics. She may be a first-generation immigrant or a refugee. She may speak fluent English or any of the forty different Pacific Asian languages and dialects that are represented in Los Angeles County.[2] She may be highly educated or preliterate, have an income of $22,050 or make less than the legal minimum hourly wage. She may have arrived here legally or "creatively"; lived in the United States for years or be an imported bride of barely three months. Such a woman will in time also exhibit the characteristics of someone so badly abused that she feels helpless; so diminished in self-esteem that she feels she deserves nothing more; and so lacking in a sense of self that she is almost invisible to herself as well as to her family and community.[3]

Of the approximately three thousand Pacific Asian clients served by the Center for the Pacific Asian Family in Los Angeles between 1978 and 1985, one-third were Korean, one-third Southeast Asians (mostly Vietnamese), and the last third distributed among Chinese, Filipinos, Japanese, South Asians, Thais, Samoans, and others.[4] It should be noted that this breakdown reflects to some degree the presence of staff from, and their outreach to, specific ethnic groups. For instance, having Korean-speaking workers at the center from the start has resulted in more response from that community.[5]

During one recent two-year period, the residential caseload averaged about four hundred women and children annually. Of this number, about 120 are Korean, with approximately one-half being adult Korean women. This means that among Koreans more than one woman each week is so severely abused by her husband that she seeks the safety of shelter outside of her home. Only the severely abused seek shelter. Some women just call the hotline for help. Therefore the actual number of women who suffer from varying levels of abuse is probably much greater than these figures indicate.

Why Domestic Violence Occurs

Domestic violence, or wife abuse, occurs among Pacific Asians as often as it does in the dominant community, in approximately one out of every two marital relationships. Factors contributing to this fact include the Pacific Asian family's traditionally patriarchal system and the attendant belief in the supremacy of the male; the socialization goals and processes which favor the family and community over the individual; the cultural emphasis on silent suffering versus open communication of needs and feelings; and the enormous adjustment pressures which test the limits of immigrants' and refugees' survival skills. Cultural norms and values directly or indirectly sanction abuse against women and tend to minimize it as a problem in the community.

Traditionally Pacific Asians conceal and deny problems that threaten group pride and may bring on shame. Because of the strong emphasis on obligations to the family, a Pacific Asian woman will often remain silent rather than admit to a problem that might disgrace her family. If domestic violence is made public, the topic is given short shrift. Community leaders prefer to view it chiefly—if not entirely—as the result of economic and social adjustment pressures. In short, if the cause of stress was removed from the environment, abuse of women would cease.

This is an over-simplified explanation of domestic violence. Pacific Asian women are truly at great risk because their families are unusually vulnerable. Despite their financially successful image, many Pacific Asian families can survive only on the combined incomes of husband and wife, who are often overworked by an average of six hours per week.[6] This need for both spouses to work creates changes in the family and sex role system. These changes are perceived as liberating by the woman, but extremely threatening by the man. Often he will describe these changes as the Americanization of his Asian wife.

To be American, from the Pacific Asian perspective, is to enjoy individual freedom, be self-determined, and be self-defined. Pushed by economic needs, and then exposed to the Western ideals of independence and self-reliance, the Pacific Asian woman does change. She begins by demanding changes in the home itself, particularly in areas that by culture and habit have been exclusively hers—housework and childcare, for instance.

Already humbled by his lack of control in the new and alien world, and perhaps also feeling a sense of failure, the Pacific Asian man resists the change. He insists on his accustomed privileges and esteemed place: she mustn't change; she mustn't turn her back on her ethnic culture; she mustn't become Americanized. She mustn't, that is, abandon him.

Such dependency is made clear in the desperate efforts of abusive husbands to retrieve women whom they have abused and who have fled for their lives. This dependent relationship is more than just the anxious attachment of the insecure and the psychologically impaired. It is the "relentless reciprocity"—Sartre's phrase—that exists between the oppressor and the oppressed. Because one's identity and status is derived from the other, if one person ceases to exist, so does the other.

The community's earlier explanation of domestic violence, blaming the circumstances, is only denying the problem. It also denies the victims the right to look for alternatives and ignores their need to seek help. It also does not question the man's assumed right to beat women during times of stress, or the woman's assumed obligation to respect that right.

Thus a woman is first brutalized, and then pressured to conceal her victimization. Fear, guilt, and shame are the means by which pressure is applied. Hence the community shelters the inequality between women and men and nurtures the ancient patriarchal family structure.

A healthy family by Western standards has an open structure. Members are allowed to be individuals and to communicate their feelings freely.[7] This ideal contrasts starkly with the controlled, conforming style of Pacific Asians, in which a high value is placed on one's strict accountability to the family. The Pacific Asian family has a closed structure. Communication is restricted and decision making is vertical. Power in the marriage is hierarchical. Even in extended families power belongs to the most senior male, often the woman's father-in-law.[8]

Studies have shown that the more closed the system is, the more disordered and dysfunctional the family becomes.[9] They also show that men's limited ability to express their feelings results in a continual state of explosiveness and possible violence.[10]

This does not mean that the Pacific Asian family is by nature dysfunctional; it is merely more responsive to the needs of men than to those of women. The Pacific Asian family has been the traditional source of support and nurturance to its members. The emotional and economic security that the individual finds within the bosom of her family are seen to compensate for the harsh restrictions and de-emphasis on individuality. Even the achievements of individual Asians are generally laid at the doorstep of a highly supportive family which throws the full weight of all its resources behind the aspiring individual—albeit for the glory and future economic well-being of the family itself.

Nevertheless, this system, which is propped up by traditional sex roles, that is, male dominance, results in a power imbalance. Wherever that imbalance exists—especially without the mediating presence of elders—there is always at least the potential for violence.

Seeking Shelter

It is still true, for the most part, that the family remains the major source of support for Pacific Asian individuals. Tradition requires the individual to turn first to her immediate family and then beyond in widening concentric circles: to the extended family, to the community, and last to an agency that is perceived as culturally hospitable and linguistically accessible.

However, even if this support system remains intact outside the homeland—which is questionable because of changes in the structure due to immigration—the Pacific Asian woman faces betrayal. First, her attacker comes from the very group to which she has been taught to turn. Second, when relatives are available, they often discourage her from taking steps toward safety and rescue because they too believe in the traditional role of women. Even when they recognize her need to risk family disapproval for the sake of survival, they often are in no position economically to provide significant assistance. Third, community gate-keepers are interested in maintaining the status quo in order to preserve the culture. Church leaders, for example, preach the acceptance of private suffering for the sake of peace. In any case, the Pacific Asian woman is often ineluctably alone.

A shelter away from relatives and the community becomes for the woman her first, if not only, alternative for both support and refuge. This is particularly true if she is fleeing physical as well as emotional abuse.

Studies in the dominant culture indicate that women stay in abusive relationships for both economic and psychological reasons.[11] Women know that escape may mean greater poverty for themselves and their children. This has been called in various studies the "feminization of poverty."

The process is particularly prevalent with battered Pacific Asian women. This is true because they often have few marketable skills, limited English, and neither the knowledge of how to get around the city nor the means to do so. So for them the prospect of suddenly becoming the single head of an impoverished household can be extremely daunting. Given the threat of the unfamiliar and having been socialized to function well only within the home, they often lack the self-confidence to leave. They may prefer the security of the predictable—even if the predictable includes the certainty of abuse.

If a woman does leave, she must face the possible loss of control over her children. If she is a first-generation immigrant, she may be bewildered by her children, who grow up in America embracing Western values and behaviors and who are in turn bewildered by her values. She often says the children's need for a father as a source of control is one of her major reasons for staying in the abusive relationship.

There is also the matter of coping with loneliness and the often unspecified need for sexual companionship. Because discussion of this subject is taboo for many Pacific Asians, it is frequently glossed over if not actually ignored. Only when a counselor encourages an open discussion of sexual needs do women freely acknowledge this as another reason for either staying with or returning to an abusive partner.[12]

Choosing to Leave, Return, or Be Independent

Some women do manage to leave the abusive relationship, even if only temporarily. And given the Pacific Asian culture and the psychodynamics of abuse, this act is an extraordinary gesture of self-assertion.

The most frequently cited reason for seeking shelter is a woman's fear for her own life and for that of her children. This is especially true when one or more of the children has already been physically or sexually abused, or inadvertently injured during a domestic fight. The reason cited second is a woman's desire to leave while she is still young enough to rebuild her life, preferably with another partner. Thus, her flight from home represents a paradox of hopelessness about her ability to manage an abusive relationship and hopefulness about the possibility of life without violence.

The woman who chooses to leave suffers from intense conflicts. She comes from a culture where the ideals of personal independence and individual freedom are alien. Instead the ideals of mutual obligation and family interdependence are valued. So, first of all, she feels guilt about having chosen herself and her goals over those of her family; she feels she has betrayed her ethnic values. She also experiences shame about her failure to live up to community-prescribed roles and behaviors; she is deeply concerned about what the community might think of her. Finally, her children—depending on their ages and on the relationship with their father—bring pressures to bear on her decision to stay away or return.

Sometimes the pressures are too great and the woman returns to the abusive relationship, often for very much the same reasons that originally compelled her to leave. She is the woman whose conflicts remain unresolved despite a stay at a shelter. She is not uncommon. Since her respite at the shelter is brief compared to the years of exposure she has had to traditional Pacific Asian values, she is inclined to return to her husband. [13]

Let us emphasize again that given her background and limited resources, the woman who chooses to leave an abusive situation, however temporarily, has taken extraordinary action. The woman who chooses to be independent after her stay at the shelter is even more unusual. Choosing not to be a victim a woman strikes out for herself and goes against the tradition in which she was raised and by which she defines herself. For a woman raised in a conformist and other-directed culture, this choice requires immense courage. It also requires mobilization of resources and support from others to maintain that independence.

Strategies for Intervention

The strategies that can help battered Pacific Asian women before, during, and after their stay at a shelter are many. Intervention must be well coordinated and sufficiently comprehensive in response to their multifarious and complex needs. The words "mobilization of resources" are most apt, for not only does the woman have to gather up her internal and personal resources, but the shelter and community must also orchestrate their resources.

Though the woman who returns to an abusive relationship, the woman who chooses independence, and the woman who stays but reaches out for help, all have their own particular needs, they all share some common ones as well. They need practical assistance, such as housing, food, work, financial help, legal aid, childcare, transportation, police protection. More than those things, however, they need to be taught to see for themselves, and then to make decisions based on their own perceptions and priorities.

The first steps for the battered woman are to see herself as a victim, how she became one, and that she has a choice not to be one any longer. Understanding how victimization takes place and how to avoid it not only helps in her immediate situation, but also in the larger contexts of culture and society.

Next, she must learn to speak. It is alarming how so many Pacific Asian women still rely on silence as a way of communicating their feelings—particularly hurt and anger. They rely on silence to keep the family intact.

Finally, she must learn to act. But on what will she act? She will decide among the various alternatives she is assisted to explore, once armed with accurate information about property and child custody laws, immigration laws, and domestic violence laws. In short, she will act when she knows her rights and obligations. This is particularly urgent for the battered woman who was brought to the United States by a green card holder (a permanent resident), or who came hoping to become one herself via marriage.[14] What happens next depends on which course the woman selects.

If she chooses independence and becomes a single parent, single parenting education will be tremendously important. She will also need practical help, that is, respite care, childcare, and emotional support for the difficult task of managing a separated family.

If she returns to her husband, the challenge could be even greater. For if she is to avoid abuse, or better yet, eliminate it altogether, her family environment must change. Counseling for the abused and the abuser alike is needed because the woman who leaves and then returns is not the same person she was before. Now at the very least she knows there are other women in much the same position as she; that she has a right not to be abused; that there are people with resources willing to help; and that life without violence is possible.

Battered Women Immigrants: A Special Class

Immigrants and refugees all confront loss. What is lost is the security which comes with the familiar; in its place is a whole set of new and unfamiliar demands and expectations. This unfamiliarity coupled with rejection in the new community creates enormous feelings of social incompetence, confusion, isolation, and cultural alienation.[15]

In order to cope in the new country, immigrants are forced to accept change, but the change involves still another kind of loss. This time the loss is of traditional beliefs, attitudes, roles, and lifestyles.[16] For instance, to ask an unemployed Pacific Asian man to modify his expectation of his working wife is to ask him to accept diminution of his status, to risk losing face before his own family and community. To suggest to a battered Pacific Asian woman that she can choose not to be a victim is to challenge the view by which she has always lived, to wit, that as an individual she does not count for very much and that only her roles and functions within the family have any value.

Both of these examples are extreme, involving the uprooting of individuals from the cultural values on which their identity is based. Tension between the demands of the new environment and an individual's ability to conform can breed illness and sometimes violence.[17]

Asian Pacific cultures allow a certain amount of violence as a behavior-shaping tool and a way of venting frustrations. Nonetheless such violence seems acceptable only when directed at women and children and other social inferiors.

Acknowledging that the use of violence as a form of power and control is rooted in and sanctioned by a culture does not mean, however, that the culture is itself the problem. The problem is still the battering. Shifting responsibility for battering from the abuser to the cultural system means that the individual is not held responsible. If this is true, then there is no victimizer and consequently no victim. Without a victim, no law has been broken, and therefore there is no crime. An additional problem results from blaming the culture: Because the system of beliefs, values, and norms is difficult to alter, those working for the abolition of violence against women and children could feel paralyzed by the enormity of their task.

Children of Violent Homes

Throughout most of this essay domestic violence has been discussed as if it meant only abuse against women. This is because women have always been perceived as the primary victims. The reality, of course, is much broader. Children who accompany abused mothers to shelters have sometimes been abused themselves. At the Center for the Pacific Asian Family, for example, two-thirds of the population in the shelter are children. One-fourth of them have been abused; the remaining three-fourths are at risk of abuse by both the father and the mother.[18]

All the children who have witnessed abuse and violence in their homes have been traumatized. Children of violent homes are "terrified, at a loss of what to do, feeling responsible and guilty for the violence and for their mother's having to leave the home. . . . Moreover, these children are passive and withdrawn, use aggressive behavior to handle situations, and have impaired peer relations." [19] They also suffer from "pseudo-maturity, resulting from their having been made to play an adult role, encouraged by parents who are themselves emotionally immature." [20]

The children at the Pacific Asian shelter exhibit all these symptoms. But because they are the offspring of immigrant mothers, they have the added burden of playing mediator between the home and the outside world. They are equipped to do so because as children they acquire a facility with English more quickly than their elders. All this causes a role reversal of monumental proportions.

Aside from the emotional difficulties, children who witness or suffer abuse learn to use violence as a way of coping and a means of communicating. Because they see violence as a normal way of living, they become predisposed to marrying abusers or becoming abusers themselves. Thus, "children suffer simply because they live in a battering household." [21] Without doing anything else, before even stepping out of their homes, their futures are already compromised.

Any intervention strategy must necessarily include the treatment of all children of violent homes. Preferably, such treatment is done in conjunction with the treatment of mothers at the shelter, with a follow-up program when they leave to return home or become independent. One object of such treatment must be to change the mothers' and children's behavior to one without verbal abuse or physical violence.

Conclusion

The use of violence as a means of coping and of getting what one wants is a learned behavior; it is a choice that the abuser makes. Fortunately, it can be unlearned. An abuser needs to choose again, this time deciding to acquire nonviolent interpersonal skills. Indispensable to this first step is taking responsibility for one's actions.

For the abused woman, a willingness to commit to change and the courage to confront all the difficulties is required. This commitment is also required of the community.

Pacific Asians have always been proud of the role of the family in their cultural and economic survival. It is time for Pacific Asians to reevaluate this role. Does it have meaning for Pacific Asians living in a Western setting? If not, what does, and what can?

It would be ironic if the cultural concept of a strong family should become the very force that would cause the family to disintegrate. Perhaps the approach to changing culture and institutions is to change individuals. In articulating the mission and philosophy of the Center for the Pacific Asian Family I wrote in 1979 that "adaptability is the hallmark of the survivor species." I believe this to be true of the Pacific Asian.

Matchmaking in the Classifieds of the Immigrant Indian Press

RASHMI LUTHRA

Immigrant communities are usually caught between the cultural mores of their home country and their adopted country. For Indians in the United States, the conflict of values is apparent when it comes to marriage. In India most marriages are arranged by the parents of the young man and woman. The American environment, though, stresses independence of choice and romantic love as the basis for marriage. Caught in this dilemma, different types of Indian families in the United States respond in distinct ways.

Families who have come to this country with children over eight years old (by which time their values are relatively anchored in Indian society), tend to maintain the tradition of arranged marriage. By contrast, families whose children are born in America are forced to be more flexible in their views on marriage, allowing their children to have a much greater say in the choice of a spouse.

More than forty years ago, an interesting development took place in India among the elite classes in urban areas. Matrimonial advertisements in newspapers began to supplement matchmakers who had operated solely through personal networks. Several factors may have contributed to this change in the mode of matchmaking. People of similar geographical origins had become widely dispersed, and rules of endogamy (marrying within a designated grouping) had been relaxed gradually in regard to subcastes. These factors, along with several others, made it possible, and even desirable, for parents to cast a wide net for a spouse through the mass media.

Indian families in the United States who persist in arranging the marriages of their children felicitously use this marital aide. Matrimonial advertisements in U.S. newspapers are important for these immigrants, whose distance from appropriate potential spouses is greater and personal networks weaker than when they were in India. Indeed, marriage ads are flourishing in this fertile ground. The classified advertisement section of *India West* carries about three columns of marriage ads in each issue, and *India Abroad* carries five to six columns in each issue.[1]

Family Background

After the Vedic times, marriages in India began to be arranged by the parents of the bride and groom, often both still quite young. The elders occasionally asked the boy for his consent, but the girl was expected to acquiesce to her parents' choice.[2] In this arrangement, the economic and social status of the families were the primary criteria for selection. Superficial personal qualities related to social status, such as height and skin color were also rated.[3] A girl's beauty—indicated by color, facial features, and her figure—earned her high points in vying for eligibles within her economic and social reach. But family background was the supreme criterion, since marriage was an alliance not between individuals but between families.

By and large, the advertisements in the American papers reflect the same concern with family background. A fairly representative ad from the female's side is: "Respectable family invites correspondence from educated, good family background, vegetarian Gujarati[4] men for their attractive, educated girl, 28 . . ." Sometimes, family background is indicated through the caste or subcaste of the family: "Father invites correspondence from suitable professionals for North Indian Kayastha[5] postgraduate daughter in early 30's/162.5 cm, slim, and beautiful. Please send particulars with photo. Reply to . . ."

In accordance with Indian tradition, the woman is in the custody of her parents until she is "given" to the husband, at which point she becomes the charge of the husband. It is notable here that the father is inviting correspondence not from the parents of the professionals, but from the professionals themselves. In this father's eyes, at least, it is all right for the man to assert himself independently and make his life choices, but it would hardly be respectable for his daughter to solicit proposals for marriage independently.

Also of note is the use of the word "suitable" in this context. This probably alludes to an adequate level of education, but also implies that men of North Indian Kayastha origins have a distinct advantage over all other aspirers. Ads from the woman's side predominantly state the caste or subcaste and regional origins (North Indian, Punjabi, Bengali) of the woman, and then sometimes suggest that prospectives must also belong to the same groupings. A few are overt about their caste requirements, as is the one that follows: "Correspondence invited from Tamil Brahmin[6] men (age 28 to 32) for a well educated, beautiful girl. Brother U.S. citizen . . ."

From the man's side the caste requirements are stated in a similar fashion, with one difference. Ads from the male side more often state explicitly, "caste no bar" or "no bar" than ads from the female side. This echoes the finding from an analysis of ads in Indian papers; it probably reflects the Indian tradition of hypergamy, or marrying into a higher status.[7] Women, in some sense, take on the caste of the husband with the family name. Therefore, when a Brahmin man marries a non-Brahmin woman, the woman becomes a bit more Brahmin, and the man's caste remains intact. But when a Brahmin woman marries a non-Brahmin man, she takes a step down the caste ladder, and the man retains his lower caste.[8]

The man's family is more liberal regarding intercaste marriages (with the possibility of marrying into a lower caste) than the woman's family. But even the indication "no caste bar" points to the survival of the caste institution among Indians living in the United States. To what extent caste determines the destinies of individual Indians in this country is difficult to ascertain. It is not possible to maintain the occupational segregation between castes in the United States, as still exists to a large extent in India. But social mores, among them marriage customs, are more difficult and slow to change. Therefore, although caste restrictions on marriage have been substantially relaxed here, some communities still maintain old taboos. Almost all communities still find it necessary to retain "caste" as an important category in the dialogue about marital arrangements, whether or not it is a criterion of eligibility in any given case.

The significance of intercaste marriages in the United States is diminished as compared with in India. In India intercaste marriages are still frowned upon, and there is active resistance against marriages between harijan (members of the lowest caste) and non-harijans. Since the continuation of the caste hierarchy and the power it represents are highly dependent on maintaining endogamy within castes, intercaste marriages—especially between harijans and non-harijans—threaten the caste system itself. But in the United States, the structures supporting the Indian caste system do not exist. The system is already being weakened by the various social forces in the American environment. Therefore, intercaste marriages do no more than deal an extra blow to an already disintegrating institution.

Along with caste, religion appears in a majority of the advertisements. The woman's family looks for these, and for the career of the man first. The man or his family look for caste and religion often, and generally prefer women with a high level of education. Again this concurs with earlier research.[9]

Home and Career

Often the woman's family indicates that their daughter possesses what seems to be a winning combination of traits: highly educated and "homeloving." The following advertisement illustrates this: "Doctor brothers and well established parents invite correspondence from highly qualified Jains/Agarwals[10] for homeloving university educated girl, 27,

5' 1". Canadian citizen, pure vegetarian from traditional North Indian Jain family."

The man's family often asks for a combination of education and "homeliness" (by which they mean not that she be ugly but that she be devoted to domestic duties). The popularity of this combination of traits suggests that women's education should equip them to be superior wives and mothers rather than career women.

But there are also a number of ads from both the man's and woman's side that specify the professional qualification of the woman, suggesting that earning power is often an asset for the woman. Doctors' families are a case in point. Whether the advertiser is a male or female doctor, the families usually expect the match to be a doctor as well. One system analyst male seeking a beautiful Punjabi woman even specified "computer professional preferred."

Some men are especially demanding: "American trained ambitious dentist, tall, fair, with modest habit invites proposals from home loving professional ladies in 30's from tristate area. . . ." This suggests that the "lady" is not only expected to retain responsibility for the housework, but also contribute to family income. Economic aspiration leads to the acceptance of the working woman, but tradition anchors her firmly to the home.

Women are affected by the double burden of domestic work and outside work in different ways, depending upon their particular circumstances. Some women manage to strike a happy medium between a fairly satisfying part-time job and home care. Others resent the burden they are forced to carry, especially if because they need the money they have to work at a tedious job during the day, and then pick up after their husband and children in the evenings. Some women in the latter situation suffer silently, taught by tradition to be patient and compromising. But still others demand better treatment. This can lead to tensions which may affect the marriage. The different possible outcomes depend on several factors such as the socialization of the wife and husband, as well as their awareness of and ability to change.

Special Circumstances

A number of matrimonial ads indicate the attitudes of the Indian community on divorce, such as: "Doctor brother invites correspondence for good looking, homeloving, charming sister, 32, immigrant, innocently divorced, has 4 year old son. . . ." And, "Matrimonial alliance invited for handsome Punjabi Khatri,[11] 40, well settled business man. Innocently divorced with two children. Returnable photograph appreciated."

Judging from the number of such ads, it appears that remarriage is now acceptable in the U.S. Indian community. Yet the term "innocently divorced" suggests that guilt feelings still surround divorce. Families of divorcees feel obliged to say that their son or daughter was not the cause of the divorce, and therefore should still be considered marriageable.

The very act of stating that the man or woman is divorced points to the honesty of advertisers. Especially where personal networks of family and friends are weak, and a period of courtship between the man and woman is not allowed, such honesty minimizes the considerable risks involved in arranging marriages through marital advertisements. If one party withholds crucial information about the family background or individual's history, the other party incurs a great risk. What makes matters worse is the difficulty of proving such fraud.

Also, if one party's primary motivation for marriage is material gain, the other party incurs a risk. In the United States this can happen when one party seeks to gain permanent resident status (by acquiring a green card) through the other.[12] Sometimes, this person (usually a male), obtains a divorce when the purpose is achieved and legal requirements of time duration have been satisfied.

For reasons just outlined the following ad should evoke caution in discerning parties who read it: "Houston relative invites correspondence for 26 years Charotar (Navali) Patel[13] youth working executive Nairobi from citizen or Green Card girls. Contact . . ." And here is an example of a person cheated by a green card seeker: "25 year old Bengali[14] female law student, American citizen, innocent victim of marriage for greencard. Marriage lasted only a few months. Invites correspondence from Indian young men already in the U.S.A. for correspondence and friendship." This Bengali woman has learned she would like to know the person before she commits herself again to marriage. A period of courtship or friendship may help to reduce the risks involved.

Another type of mercenary activity prevalent in India is dowry seeking by the man's family. Veiled references to a dowry also appear in the U.S. ads. The woman's family often offers the promise of a "decent marriage." Matrimonial advertisers in India say that a "decent marriage" implies that the bride's parents alone will pay for all wedding arrangements and that a dowry will probably be included. Is it a surprise that along with arranged marriage and matrimonial advertising, dowries also survived the Indians' passage to America? [15]

Exceptions to the Rule

Some ads stand out because of their entirely different tone and others because they express completely different expectations of marriage than the norm. Two examples of such exceptional ads are:

Punjabi clean shaven Sikh 29, 5' 9", fair, handsome, MBA/MS computer science, well settled in California, innocently divorced (marriage lasted very shortly), invites correspondence from serious minded, cultured, preferably professional, and independent ladies. Returnable picture appreciated.

An attractive 30 year old medical professional seeks an interesting, exciting, attractive, well educated, well cultivated man, with a sense of humor and lots of hobbies, seeking a sincere relationship to end in marriage.

Both these advertisements seem to be placed by independent, self-assured, realistic persons who think of marriage as a partnership rather than an economic and social convenience or necessity.

Last but not the least, there is the incurable romantic:

Highly educated accomplished entrepreneur. U.S. resident for over 20 yrs, affectionate, romantic, vulnerable and caring. Loves laughter, masterpiece theater, movies, Indian and western music/culture, walks, reading, family, friends. Interests: Yoga, tantra, zen, world affairs/trade, economy, photography, architecture and women's fashions. Frequent business traveller to Europe, India, Far East. Much younger looking than 51. Divorced, no children. Nonsmoker, non-drinker, business family. Seeking a soulmate, any nationality/religion for wife with similar/compatible interests, highly attractive, bright, energetic, lively and yet mild-mannered, affectionate woman, 25-35 yrs 5' 3" or taller with positive, cheerful outlook. Sense of humor. Send letter, bio, returnable photo, phone.

Conclusion

It is impossible to gauge their impact by looking at the ads themselves. So through informal interviews, I learn that both the way in which the ads are used and their consequences for the users vary greatly. Usually the ads are merely the initial means of introduction or contact. If one or more responses appear suitable, the advertiser requests further correspondence, sometimes inquiring about specific facets of the family and the eligible man or woman. Often references are asked for recommendations about the person in question. Interpersonal and organizational networks are used by some to verify facts and obtain yet further information. Such systems of verification allow both parties to reduce the risk of being cheated and to gain substantial confidence in the suitability of the match.

Marriages arranged through the help of marital advertisements can be ordinary and healthy, or they can be tragic. Verification helps to achieve a positive outcome. Involvement of the woman or man in the selection process can also help to avoid undesirable consequences. For Indians whose children are first-generation Americans, this combination of parental guidance, individual choice, and marital ads, may be the most viable option. It is possible that the woman and man will more often place their own ads in the future, and that these ads will reflect different attitudes towards marriage than now exist. Although the complexion of the ads may change, the continual immigration of Indians to the United States, the increasing dispersion of Indian professionals to different and sometimes remote rural areas of the country, and the desire of substantial numbers of Indians to marry within their ethnic community, all help to ensure the survival of the advertisement system of matchmaking. [16]

PART SEVEN

Making Waves:
Activism

Introduction

Asian American women have fought actively against racial stereotyping. And throughout their history they have struggled for what they believed was the best for their families, their communities, and their own survival. Sometimes Asian culture—with its traditional relegation of women to inferior status—has contributed to the difficulties of this struggle. The dominant culture magnified this characteristic in its own stereotypes and came to expect Asian immigrants to accept, not resist, injustices.

The growth of the civil rights movement to its apex in the late 1960s and early 1970s spurred some Asian American women to become involved with the struggle for racial and ethnic equality. For others, the catalyst was the women's movement that followed. Asian women's participation in the U.S. women's movement has historically been relatively small. Esther Chow, in "The Feminist Movement: Where Are All the Asian American Women?" provides insight into that question. Her findings take into account their status as racial minorities and as women.

Many other issues inspire Asian American women to action. "From Homemaker to Housing Advocate," by Nancy Diao, follows the life of one immigrant woman who went against cultural and familial expectations to work for better housing for low-income persons. Janice Mirikitani's "In Remembrance" recounts the story of her uncle, whose life was disrupted by the U.S. internment during World War II. His experience, as well as that of thousands of other Japanese Americans, helped spur on a movement toward redressing this historic wrong. The women in "Dust and Dishes," by Patricia Lee and Yoichi Shimatsu, have succeeded in making changes through group action, particularly through unions representing hotel and restaurant workers. Jyotsna Vaid, in "Seeing a Voice," echoes the effectiveness of the collective approach among South

Asian women in America. Many of the women she interviewed have also organized local responses to injustices facing women in India.

Those who fought to change society and to open up equal opportunities for all people soon learned that they had to examine their personal lives and commitments as well. "Growing Up, 1968–1985" by Juanita Tamayo Lott introduces some of the women who struggled with this question. As more of them took on new jobs, married, and became parents, many of the women began to refocus their priorities and struggled to maintain their principles in light of the new demands on their lives.

The close ties that many immigrants have with the land of their birth have inspired action supporting social and political issues in Asia. Valorie Bejarano's "Firetree" was written to commemorate the death of Benigno Aquino, one of the leaders who opposed the regime of former Philippines president Ferdinand Marcos. Since this piece was written, Corazon Aquino succeeded Marcos as president of the Pacific island nation.

The number of Asian American women turning to mainstream politics as a way of having an impact on their communities is also growing. In her essay "Asian Pacific American Women in Mainstream Politics," Judy Chu interviews many of the women who have either run for office or work in politics. In the political arena women not only have to compete with an opponent, but also with the sometimes less than encouraging expectations of society and their own communities.

Asian American women grow stronger with the support of their communities and other activist movements. In the end, though, no one else can speak for them. They, like all of us, must speak for themselves. We can expect no one else to fight our battles; we must fight them ourselves. We must make our own waves.

In Remembrance

JANICE MIRIKITANI

For Uncle Minoru, died January, 1984

We gather at your coffin,
Uncle Minoru.
Mother, with her hands like gardenias,
touches your sleeves.
We whisper of how well you look
peaceful in your utter silence.
How much we remember.
Why so much now, at death?
    Your kindnesses, Uncle,
as you crafted paper monkeys,
multicolored birds
to climb and jerk on a stick
to amuse children who gathered
at your innocent dark eyes,
always slightly moist.
We would jump on your back, riding you
like a silent horse,
as you lumbered on your hands and knees
from room to room.
    How much we remember . . .
We rode your shoulders,
knotted with hurt,
dressed in faded denim, smelling like
laundry soap and fish.
You never complained of it
only through those dark moist eyes,
and your smile that drew
living animals to you, even wild birds.

Obachan said they could smell
the wounds hiding in your throat,
the wound in your heart
pierced by unjust punishment, racism, and rejection
sharp as blades.
     When did you vow silence, Minoru?
After the camps,
after you buried a daughter?
You slumped into a light
of your own and let life ride you.
Your daughter thrown broken
on the road by a drunk driver
who mumbled she flew from nowhere like a dumb chicken,
stretched out $200, not one apology,
and said we were safer in the camps.
     Was there nothing left to say, Minoru,
as you slapped away his hot white hand?
     How much we remember . . .
When they took you to Amache Gate
locked us up like herded horses,
your dark innocent eyes, moist
with disbelief at charges of
sabotage, espionage,
your shoulders staggered from the lies.
Fear like a cold finger
pressed at your heart.
The sky scummed over with clouds
and punishment without crime
stabbed between the blades of your back.
     Was there nothing left to say?
Minoru, the children who rode you
have tongues like birds.
We chatter. We remember
the mounds of hurt at your shoulders.
Could we but massage them to soothe

the pain, but death
makes our regrets scattered as apologies.
We did not expect them
to rip the coat of pride from your bones
nor the melody from your throat.
      Yes, there is much to say.
We will not leave your memory
as a silent rancid rose.
Our tongues become livid with history and
demands for reparations.
Crimes are revealed like the bloody lashes
of a fallen whip:
      the falsehoods, deletions, the conspiracy
      to legalize mass imprisonment.
No, we will not forget
      Amache Gate, Rohwer, Poston, Heart Mountain,
      Minidoka, Jerome, Gila River, Manzanar, Topaz,
      Tule Lake.
Our tongues are sharp like blades.
We overturn furrows of secrecy.
      Yes, we will harvest justice.
And Uncle, perhaps
your spirit will return
alive in a horse, or a bird,
riding free in the wind
life surging through
the sinews of your strong shoulders.
      And yes,
the struggle continues on
with our stampede of voices.

For the Poets of "Firetree" on the Second Anniversary of the Death of Benigno Aquino

VALORIE BEJARANO

Ang bayan ko
Sweet Motherland of my birth
I hear you wailing in the midnight of your despair
Beating your breast with bloodied fists
Your rage and your pain
Strangles me in my sleep.
For whom do you mourn?
Is it the children of Tondo?
Of Smokey Mountain?
Born in filth, poverty and disease
Dying in the shadows of the Holiday Inn
Is it for twelve-year-old prostitutes in Alongapo?
Selling their soft silkening flesh
The first blush of puberty
Traded for a sailor's price
There is no shame, Mother.
Shame is a dear price to pay
When a chicken is forty pesos
Ask yourself why they sell, Mother.
Then ask why the buyers buy
And who lacks morality.
Are your tears for the dead and the dying?
Salvaged bodies in shallow graves
Or those who wait
In stinking cells, laid bare to the horrors
That deny any shred of human decency
Detained
Such a polite word for savage behavior.
Do you weep for yourself, Mother?

You who have been raped by greed
Beaten bloody by oppression
Held for ransom by the hollow eyes and swollen bellies
Of the babies who die at your dried teat.
Sack cloth and ashes
For the bearer of the dream
Dead before he touched you
The voice of reason
Silenced by assassins of truth
While the sin eaters in the palace
Nodded.
Hush now Mother, the dream isn't over
And there is still a light in this darkness
A burning in this darkness
I see a firetree on the horizon
Flaming with the light of freedom
Fueled by the souls of thousands of lost lives.
Listen, Mother
I hear their voices chanting a new song
Strong and demanding
Take my hand now and we will join them
Never mind the miles, I'm not far away
Isn't it your blood that runs in my veins?
Isn't it your voice that shouts from my throat
LABAN

Growing Up, 1968–1985

JUANITA TAMAYO LOTT

It is an ice-cold February evening when car doors freeze and human breath hangs in the air. Pungent reds, greens, and pinks simmer on the stove. Miniature lava flows of broth spit up evergreen okra. Authentic shrimp gumbo from the family recipe of my sansei friend's southern belle, Jewish mother-in-law, spices the air. White, glutinous rice steams in the Panasonic rice cooker. Moments later, we sit in leisure and warmth, savoring each bite. Between spoonfuls, we stop to share white wine and bits and pieces of our lives as Asian American women with a friend, a young, black woman—young, she was in the third grade when Martin Luther King was assassinated in 1968. It strikes me that vivid reality too soon becomes impersonal history.

The Awakening

Many things happened in 1968 that stirred the awakening of an Asian American woman's identity, events that stimulated my and others' personal and political growth. Martin Luther King, Jr., and Robert F. Kennedy were assassinated. Caesar Chavez and a host of farm workers called to public attention the iniquities of laborers who harvested the nation's crops. Americans began to demonstrate visibly against U.S. involvement in the Vietnamese civil war. Richard M. Nixon was elected president of the United States. On college campuses young men and women of every color protested against the war, called for affirmative action policies, and demanded ethnic studies curricula.

The term "Asian American" kept surfacing among Chinese, Japanese, and Filipinos in their communities. I watched and oftentimes joined young Asian American women, particularly on campus, walk picket lines, march in demonstrations, take notes at meetings, run duplicating machines, make coffee, support Asian American men, and then remain silent as the men departed with non-Asian women.

By 1970 American involvement in the Vietnam War had expanded to Cambodia and Laos. The class of 1970 faced grim prospects: to support or resist the war; to do business as usual or develop a counterculture; to choose between acts of living or those of dying. This was a difficult and challenging time to be young. Draft resisters went to jail, performed alternate community services, or fled to Canada or other sympathetic countries. From around the world, the class of 1970 was bombarded with headlines about Janis Joplin, Jimi Hendrix, and Jim Morrison— young, successful Americans, found dead.

Amidst this gloom, I found myself among several Asian American women graduating from college or taking leaves of absence from school. We went to our motherlands and other countries to find a more hopeful view of society and our future. A few of us traveled to Southeast Asia and even the People's Republic of China. We learned from our counterparts in Asia and other lands the varying meaning of "woman"—child, daughter, sister, wife, mother, mistress, chattel, partner, colleague, comrade, soldier.

Nineteen seventy-two was a presidential election year. The war in Indochina still dominated the front page, but other events occurred to compete with the coverage of Vietnam. Two events in particular influenced the shape and direction of the newly asserted identity of Asian American women. In 1972 the United Nations recognized China and Nixon visited there to sign the Shanghai Accord. This feat served to turn attention away, even if momentarily, from the waste and destruction in the Southeast Asian countries of Laos, Cambodia, and South and North Vietnam. People began to look to the untapped, long-term, social, economic, and political potentials of China and other Asian and Pacific nations. The other event in 1972 of great importance to Asian American and other women was twofold: passage of Title IX of the Education Amendments, which prohibits discrimination on the basis of sex in all federally supported educational programs, and inclusion by Congress of sex discrimination in the jurisdiction of the U.S. Commission on Civil Rights.

But in the personal lives of Asian American women like myself, these events went utterly unnoticed. We were too busy moving from the familiar, comfortable world of undergraduates (many of us the first college graduates in our immigrant families) to the unknown role of "the graduate." Some of us went directly into the labor force, primarily in traditional female and Asian occupations: clerical, domestic, service, nurturing, and technical fields. Others stayed on campuses around the country to enter graduate and professional schools, including law and business, not necessarily realizing that policies like Title IX and other civil rights statutes were at least indirectly responsible for our presence in higher education.

Some of us continued our college days' extracurricular activities of making music and dance, performing plays and poetry, and organizing around community issues. We got involved in local organizations and public agencies, getting funds and staff to run grassroots programs. A few of us immersed ourselves in the first national Pan Asian organization, the Pacific Asian Coalition (PAC). This group was funded through the early and mid-seventies by the National Institute of Mental Health to provide grassroots services for Pan Asian communities and to conduct research on their needs. Through PAC and other nationally oriented organizations, Asian American women became visible leaders conversant with national issues. As this development occurred, the ups and downs of our relationships with the men in our lives continued. Some of us even began our own families.

In 1973 two events pervasively affected the American nation, Watergate and the Supreme Court decision *Roe v. Wade.* The political and moral consequences of Watergate have been and will continue to be discussed by analysts, historians, and philosophers for years to come. For women of color, the poignant point of Watergate was that it revealed the power structure of American society as a very closed, elite, white male-dominated province. The drama of Watergate was noteworthy for the virtual absence of women and minorities.

With respect to *Roe v. Wade,* the Supreme Court stated that abortion in a woman's first trimester of pregnancy was the decision of each individual woman and her physician, unfettered by governmental interference. This ruling was interpreted by women's rights groups as affirmation of a woman's right to reproductive choice and control of her body.

As individuals many women, including young Asian American women, rejoiced in this decision. We celebrated this freedom, perhaps overindulged. Then we watched the generation of young women after us assume reproductive choice, and later held their hands as they rebounded from harsh legislative, judicial, and civilian attempts to restrict abortion and other contraceptive options.

As a group we expressed dismay at the potentially high level of abusive family planning practices for poor and minority women, specifically forced sterilization and cultural, if not physical, genocide. After all, optimal number of children; virginity of brides; and working mothers, especially mothers of young children, are valued differently in each culture.

Watershed Years

Nineteen seventy-four can be viewed as a watershed for the political development of Asian American women at the national level because "race and sex," that is racism and sexism, were being linked verbally and visibly. This link, even if only superficial at times, was articulated continually and consistently by the growing 1970s feminist movement in the United States. It was also a common theme in the various departments offering Ethnic Studies or Women's Studies on various college campuses. Furthermore, it strengthened civil rights legislation, including but not limited to Title IX.

In 1974 Congress passed the Women's Educational Equity Act Program (WEEAP) to provide grants to individuals and organizations across the nation to promote educational equity between women and men. One of the major sponsors of that legislation was a Pan Asian woman, then Representative Patsy Mink of Hawaii. Women's organizations developed and flourished at grassroots, regional, and national levels. While a great portion of WEEAP monies funded mainstream projects, minority women's projects also developed and for several years have been a WEEAP funding priority.

In the executive branch, 1974 was when the U.S. Bureau of the Census began serious planning for the 1980 decennial census. The plan was to enumerate more accurately the country's racial and ethnic populations. Three years later the federal government formally designated five racial/ethnic categories for reporting requirements: American Indian or Alaska Native, Asian or Pacific Islander, Black, Hispanic, and White.

These new names, revised categories, additional identities, and combined possibilities (I could be counted as a woman and a minority), left other Asian American women and me elated and perplexed. Elated because our difference was formally recognized. No longer would we be placed conveniently in the "Other" category. We were further elated because issues dear to us were also gaining public attention. Our minds, our bodies, childbirth, childcare, sexuality, rape, child and spousal abuse, juggling outside work with home work, peace, clean air, education, and employment were getting attention through various channels—intimate talks, structured discussions, creative outpourings, scholarly writings, music, drama, film, radio, television, newspapers, legislation, and litigation.

Yet at the same time we were perplexed at becoming tokens or spokespersons for minority women in general and Asian American women in particular. Oftentimes we found ourselves alone and isolated in our workplace. Many of us were exhibited as model employees, and model minorities who don't rock the boat. Some of us joined majority women's organizations and experienced similar feelings of loneliness. Comparing notes with other women of color, we found ourselves asked to speak and work, almost exclusively, on minority women's issues, regardless of our interests and expertise. Among ourselves, we spoke of our perplexed and elated feelings, but only in snatches on lunch dates or during breaks at conferences when we discussed the other pieces of our lives.

Nineteen seventy-five brought even more attention to Asians in America. The federal government withdrew from the war in Southeast Asia—not with pomp or circumstance, or even a subdued but civil manner, but with haste, disorganization, and panic. The first, and perhaps most lasting, memory of that departure is of a handful of armed, combat-green Marines clinging to a U.S. helicopter hovering above the American embassy in Saigon. Below them the waves of brown faces in black pajamas rose and fell. Immediately everyone needed figures. How many refugees were fleeing? How many were coming to the United States? Who were they? When would they stop coming?

We did not have the answers. At the beginning, no one had. Yet Asian American women like myself began to be identified with the refugees, the newest U.S. immigrants. More innocuous methods of association included being asked to translate Vietnamese or Laotian, or to explain Asian preferences for diet and living arrangements. Less kindly means of identification were intimations or humor about being girlfriends of U.S. servicemen. It was not comfortable but we viewed the error as an extension of the series of questions and comments flung at us since childhood such as "You speak English very well," or "You don't look Filipino," or "Where are you from?"

Bicentennial year 1976 came in massive displays of red, white, and blue fireworks. Everyone was ready to party and celebrate the nation's two-hundredth birthday. We had survived many wars—the Civil War, the world wars, wars in Asia. We had emerged from other tragedies—presidential assassinations, Watergate. We had gone to the moon and beyond.

On the global level, 1976 marked the start of the United Nation's Decade for Women. From all over the world women and supportive men gathered in Mexico City in 1977 to celebrate this historic and joyous occasion.

In our own ways, Asian American women joined other women in celebration of our abilities to endure, persevere, and be recognized. We rejoiced with Maxine Hong Kingston and all women warriors. No longer were we talking about what we felt and thought as women just in passing conversations. We blocked out vast portions of our time for regular, intensive meetings and workshops to develop organizations and support individuals who would advocate specifically for our concerns. We formed a range of local Asian American women's groups and national organizations such as the Organization of Chinese American Women and the Organization of Pan Asian American Women, both headquartered in Washington, D.C. We encouraged women to run for elected and appointed offices at every level. We had great expectations for each other. Some of us worked to exhaustion and today continue to kill ourselves by expecting and doing the most work with the most minimal resources.

Reality Sets In

In contrast to the jubilant bicentennial year, the years between 1978 and 1981 were grim, uneasy ones for the United States. Inflation had replaced war in media headlines. The Equal Rights Amendment failed to be ratified, even with a three-year extension. Following the disgrace of

Vietnam, Americans were greeted by the fall of a U.S.-supported Iran. They watched in frustration as hostages in the American embassy were evacuated under tense circumstances. The dollar barely held its own on the international market. The almighty dollar and Big Brother America were losing ground.

Interestingly, as the macho super power image of the United States came into question, and indeed began to wane, American women including Asian Americans continued to expand their horizons beyond traditional women's issues. Through vehicles such as the President's Advisory Committee for Women, they sought inclusion in the decision-making processes of war and peace, international issues, and the federal budget. They demanded a place beside men in religion, in the political arena, and throughout the labor force. Swiftly and often severely, they were reprimanded by church and state officials, including a bishop and a president.

Not surprisingly, Asian American as well as other women had mixed feelings of hope and despair. Growing up to face political realities was not an easy process. We learned we saw only the tip of the iceberg. Realizing that our strength came from unity and numbers, five hundred of us convened in Washington, D.C., on a hot August weekend in 1980 to delineate national issues in relationship to Asian American women. We met other Pan Asian women, older women, younger women, women who did not grow up in the United States in the 1960s but who shared similar hopes and dreams. We all realized the overwhelming magnitude of tasks we had chosen to tackle whether health, education, employment, sex roles, or international relations.

On the personal side, we also faced sobering moments. We had to make difficult, adult decisions. For mere girls who had marched in the sixties, time was marching by. Our biological clocks ticked away in the new decade of the eighties. We were forced to make decisions about long-term commitments, being homeowners, locking one's self into a career or vocation, juggling home and outside responsibilities. Time management and coping with stress were prime topics of discussion. We discovered that as we gave overtime to one dimension of our lives (whether career, family, community, or extracurricular activity), we were taking time away from the rest of our lives. We also learned that the energies of a woman in her thirties were quite finite, especially when compared to her twenty-year-old sister.

The last five years, 1981–1985, were five more years of painful maturity for the nation. The overriding issues of the day were the budget deficit, the trade deficit, the horrors of unvictorious wars in Lebanon, Nicaragua, South Africa, and elsewhere, and nationwide famines around the world. During this time, the United States also witnessed the unraveling of a major political party. Of equal, if not greater historical significance, were the 1984 events of increased voter participation by minorities and women, the inclusion of a black presidential candidate, and the nomination of a female for vice-president. Closer to home, many people remained unemployed; the rewards of reduced inflation benefited only the wealthy; the number of families with two employed parents increased; one-fifth of all children lived with just one parent; more children than ever were being cared for by non-family members or themselves.

A New Definition

In contrast to these realities, advertisements portray an affluent, peaceful, contented life style. The particular image for the majority of baby boomers (including Asian Americans) is the "yuppie" life style, dressed and housed for success in an antiseptic, high-tech environment.

Especially for those of us with advanced degrees and professions, the yuppie image is consistent with the prevailing stereotype of Asian American women. We live and work in respectable, even choice, neighborhoods. Judging from those of us in the media, we at least sound, and almost look, like mainstream Americans. Some of us, perhaps a growing number of us, are married to men outside our ethnic groups. But beyond the surface, the impressions, and the stereotypes, we cling to and maintain the strengths of our Asian American heritage while we also welcome and incorporate what is good in the larger world. We define our own Asian American womanhood. We are not here to accept or bow to existing standards for ourselves and others, but to strive for standards that acknowledge our bond and responsibility to those who came before us and those yet to come.

We applaud the trilogy of black Japanese playwright Velina Hasu Houston, which is about her life and the lives of her mother and friends—World War II war brides married to U.S. servicemen who were black, white, Latino, and Japanese Americans. We demonstrate against apartheid, war, and budget cuts for human services. We register voters and throw fundraisers for one another. We continue to support grass-roots organizations. We sit on boards of directors for profit and nonprofit organizations. We give to charities that promote consumer issues and humane public policies. We select stocks from corporations who show social responsibility. We join in coalition with other women and men from different walks of life to work within and improve the system.

This is the recollection of seventeen years that my sansei friend, our black friend, and I shared that snowy February evening. By the time the tale was told, our wine glasses were drained, our tea cups empty. Each of us parted with a little more understanding of each other and other women. We walked away from each other with warm hearts to love the men and women in our lives, and to nurture our children who are every color of the rainbow.

The Feminist Movement: Where Are All the Asian American Women?

ESTHER NGAN-LING CHOW

From its inception the feminist movement in the United States has been predominantly white and middle class. Like blacks, Hispanics, and other women of color, Asian American women have not joined white women and, thus far, have not made a great impact on the movement.[1] Since the late 1960s, Asian Americans have begun to organize themselves and build bonds with other women's groups to advocate for their civil rights as a racial minority and as women. Their relative lack of political activism stems from cultural, psychological, and social oppressions which historically discouraged them from organizing. This resulted in their apparent political invisibility and powerlessness.

Political Organizing of Asian American Women: An Overview

Following the civil rights movement in the 1950s, and the feminist movement in the 1960s, Asian American women began to organize formally and informally to address various sources of discontent and social inequities, and to work towards improving conditions for themselves and the Asian American communities. However, political organizing among Asian American women has been slow and limited in many respects. Their political invisibility is related partly to their small numbers in the U.S. population, a result of past restrictive U.S. immigration policies toward Asians. As of the 1980 census, Asian Americans comprise 1.6 percent (3.5 million) of the total U.S. population. Slightly over half of the Asian American population is female. In addition, ethnic diversity among Asian Americans and geographic dispersion make it difficult for them to organize and be perceived as a significant group with political force.

To some extent, political participation may be a class privilege for women who have the luxury of time, money, and energy. Slightly more than half of the Asian women in the United States are immigrants and they are generally preoccupied with balancing responsibilities at home, in the workplace, and in the community. Like their white counterparts, well-to-do or better-educated Asian American women formed the early women's groups, such as church organizations, social service centers, and women's professional societies.[2]

Few in number and with little institutionalized leadership, these groups have been traditional and conservative in nature, frequently serving as auxiliaries to male organizations that tend to support the male status quo. Only to a very limited extent have they functioned to advance the cause of women's liberation. While there have been efforts to organize Asian American women around specific issues and concerns (e.g., the unavailability or high cost of basic goods, preservation of history and poetry of the Angel Island Immigration Station, World

War II internment camps), these attempts have generally lacked conti-
nuity and support, thus limiting the emergence of Asian American
women as a formalized force.[3] However, these initial efforts of organizing served as a forum where women acquired leadership skills and political experience helpful in future organizing.

The civil rights and feminist movements guide Asian American
women in many ways. They help them to become aware of their doubly
disadvantaged positions as members of a racial minority and as females,
to learn about the structural sources of their deprivation and social
inequalities, and to acknowledge the need to resolve their unique
problems.[4]

Following the lead of blacks, many Asian American organizations
were created to combat racism and to work toward unity with other
racial minorities. The women who joined these organizations are mostly
middle-class, U.S.-born, college-educated, professional, and relatively
established, and many are strong and active participants. Many others
are aware they occupy subservient positions and are relegated to traditional women's functions. They know this prevents them from developing their potential or from holding leadership positions, but their ethnic
pride and loyalty frequently keep them from revolt.[5]

More recently, Asian American women have recognized that some of
these organizations have not been responsive to their particular needs
and concerns. These members also protest that their intense involvement has not, and will not, result in equal participation and leadership
development as long as the traditional sex-role relationship between
Asian men and women remains unchanged. Despite their efforts at sen-
sitizing Asian men about their attitudes towards, and treatment of,
women, some Asian women have opted for a separate organization to
deal with their specific issues and problems and to maximize their
participation.[6]

Since the late 1960s, several Asian American women's groups have been
established in local communities across the country. These include
women's courses sponsored by college-level Asian American studies
programs, community education programs, social service programs,
women's unions, physical and mental health projects, and political inter-

est groups. Many of these groups were short-lived because they lacked funding, leadership, grassroots support, membership, or strong networking. Susie Ling and Sucheta Mazumdar recently pointed out that a lack of momentum and direction also plagued many of the organizations.[7]

Contrary to the common belief about the passivity of Asian American women, they tend to be more actively involved in women's groups of their respective ethnic backgrounds and in Asian groups than in white feminist organizations. Many of them (e.g., National Organization of Pan Asian Women, Asian American Women United, Vietnamese Women's Association, Filipino American Women Network, and Cambodian Women for Progress, Inc.) are organized at the regional level and are in the process of expanding their influence and building networks from the grassroots level to a national one. For example, the Organization of Chinese American Women is nationally based, with over one thousand members throughout the United States. And the National Network of Asian and Pacific Women consists of many regional groups working to build a visible political force.

Like their white counterparts, the Asian women participants in the feminist movement are not homogeneous, but can be classified into two main types: the radical group and women's rights support group.[8] Many participants in the radical group joined the civil rights movement in the 1960s.[9] Subscribing to radical politics, some of these Asian women organized small study groups. They did research to analyze the circumstances and events causing the subordinate position of women, explored new ways of thinking to alter or revolutionize the social conditions of Asian American women, and sought collective action to end all forms of oppression, including sexism.[10]

The second group, the women's rights support group, consists of those who have gained confidence, leadership skills, and experience through women's groups within the Asian communities and have become active in various women's organizations of the larger society.[11] Some of its members witnessed or suffered from gender oppression within the Asian American communities and the society at large and then sought to organize women's groups with this and other specific women's concerns as their top priorities.

The radical group and women's rights support group differ more in their ideological positions than in their strategies and actions. The goals of the women's rights group are to combat sexism and racism, to achieve social equality and justice in society, and to increase the social participation of women at all levels. The goal of the radical group is to build a classless society, for its members believe that once the class struggle is over, sexism and racism will be resolved.[12] While the women's rights group subscribes to a reform ideology attempting to make more limited and gradual change within the social system, the radical group adheres to a radical ideology advocating large-scale revolutionary change that would eliminate structural barriers based on gender, race, class, and culture and lead to social equality and human liberation.

In other words, the women's rights group maintains a certain commitment to the basic structure of the system viewing it as either essentially just or at least acceptable. Hence, their efforts are aimed at making specific improvements within the system. The radical group is, however, critical of the American system, which they see as never intending to include Asian Americans, nonwhites, or even the majority of working-class Americans.[13] Building a class movement and/or supporting the civil rights movement are primary concerns for some members of this group rather than actively joining the feminist movement in the larger society.

However, different as their political ideologies are, the two groups share many common tactics and strategies, such as consciousness-raising, education and training, peaceful demonstration and rallies, establishment of counter-institutions for women, active lobbying and negotiation for policy changes, and other program interventions.

Barriers to Political Activism

In order to become and remain politically active, Asian American women must overcome many barriers at various levels: in individuals, in racial relations, in the cultural system, in the class structure, in gender-role stratification, and in the legal-political system. These constitute the main sources of multiple oppression faced by this group of minority women and can be classified into two major types: internal and external barriers.

The former refers to those factors that are specifically inherent to Asian American women as a group, including psychological constraints, cultural restrictions, and patriarchy and structural impediments. The latter refers to those elements existing primarily in American society at large that have kept them from full involvement in the women's liberation movement, including legal-political barriers, racial insensitivity and unreceptivity, and class cleavage. External barriers are more invidious and harder for Asian American women to overcome than internal ones. These two types of barrier may be dialectical in nature, providing stability as well as contradiction in the life experience of many Asian American women. [14]

Internal Barriers

Psychological constraints. Because of their dual status, Asian American women derive their identification and self-esteem from both ethnicity and gender. [15] Although Asian American women may benefit from and contribute significantly to the feminist movement, joining such a movement seems to be a double bind for them because it pits ethnic identity against gender identity. It could also lead to absorption or cooptation into the larger society, resulting in an eventual loss of ethnic identity. In any case, Asian American women must deal with this identity crisis. The key issue here is how to balance one's ethnic and sexual or gender identification in order to develop a healthy self-concept.

Research has indicated that gender-role stereotypes are psychologically and socially detrimental to the personality and achievement of women. [16] And Asian American women suffer from racial stereotypes as well. All stereotypes, whether positive or negative, serve as self-fulfilling prophecies when contending with them gradually leads to internalizing them as part of an illusionary reality. Being perceived generally as subservient, obedient, passive, hard working, and exotic, Asian American women themselves become convinced that they should behave in accordance with these stereotyped expectations. But if they act accordingly, they are then criticized for doing so, becoming victims of the stereotypes imposed by others.[17] For Asian American women to develop their political potential, they must develop a positive self-concept and maintain psychological well-being.

Cultural restrictions. Although certain Asian values emphasizing education, achievement, and diligence account for the high level of aspiration and success of some Asian American women, other values hinder active political participation. Such cultural limitation is further compounded by the adjustment to American culture, which is often in conflict and contradiction with their ethnic one.

Four cultural dilemmas frequently face Asian American women: (1) obedience vs. independence; (2) collective (or familial) vs. individual interest; (3) fatalism vs. change; and (4) self-control vs. self-expression or spontaneity.[18] On the one hand, adherence to Asian values, that is, obedience, familial interest, fatalism, and self control, tends to foster submissiveness, passivity, pessimism, timidness, inhibition, and adaptiveness, which are not necessarily conducive to political activism. On the other hand, acceptance of the American values of independence, individualism, mastery of one's environment through change, and self-expression generates self-interest, aggressiveness, initiative, and expressive spontaneity. All these traits tend to encourage political activism, but at the same time are incompatible with the family upbringing of most Asian American women. The key problem here is how to maintain a bicultural existence by selecting appropriate elements of both cultural worlds to make the best adaptation according to the demands of social circumstances.

Among Asian Americans, apathy and avoidance are common reactions to unpleasant and stressful situations, particularly when others are trying to involve them in political activity. Because one of the major reasons Asians immigrate to this country is to seek political refuge and escape the political purges and turmoils of their homelands,[19] this avoidance is not surprising. For example, generally and historically women in China have been socialized to be politically apathetic and now as immigrants are still discouraged from participating in organizations that challenge the status quo.

Unfamiliarity with the language is another factor that hinders the acculturation and political participation of Asian immigrant women. This barrier limits the extent to which Asian American women can express themselves, reduces their ability to make demands, restricts their access to many types of information, curtails the flow and scope of communication with others, and eventually limits the development of political efficacy in America. Although the English proficiency level of many Asian American women of foreign birth is generally adequate for functioning well in the workplace and in social circles, language remains a handicap for some. These women tend to prefer speaking in their native tongue, feel inhibited from engaging in open dialogue with others in English, and subsequently increase their political powerlessness and decrease their ability to influence others. The American-born are better able to overcome this communication difficulty and thereby can participate readily in the larger society. However, their physical features still remind others of their foreign backgrounds, thus presumably limiting full acceptance by others in the larger society. The integration of Asian American women of diverse backgrounds and generations into both the Asian American communities and the larger feminist movement remains key for their future political activism.

Patriarchy and structural impediments. As long as patriarchy persists, the social institutions that encompass Asian American women will continue to perpetuate the devaluation and subjugation of women. School, family, workplace, and other social institutions within and outside the Asian communities all reinforce this gender-role conditioning. The education system has frequently failed to provide women with knowledge of their legal rights. The doctrine of three obediences for a Chinese woman to her father, husband, and son well illustrates her subservient roles. The male is still perceived as major breadwinner and the woman as homemaker. For many employed Asian American women, managing multiple roles is a significant problem. Those with young children are more likely than their white counterparts to stay at home.[20] Overburdened with family and work, and without much support and cooperation from their spouses and sometimes from other family members, Asian American women find political participation beyond their own ethnic group difficult, if not impossible.[21]

Although many Asian American women do engage in political

organizing within ethnic communities, their activity in white feminist organizations is often perceived by their male partners and even their female peers as a move toward separatism. They are warned that the consequences of separation will threaten the male ego, damage working relationships between Asian men and women, and dilute efforts and resources for the Asian American cause. All these forces have impeded Asian American women from more active participation in the larger feminist movement.

External Barriers

Legal-political barriers. Historically, structural receptivity to Asian Americans, men and women alike, has been low in the United States. Legal and political barriers deeply rooted in the social system can be documented from the first immigration of Asians to this country. For example, fourteen pieces of legislation were written by state and federal governments to discriminate against the Chinese in America and to strip them of their rights as lawful members of society.[22] The economic exploitation and deprivation that frequently go hand in hand with legal exclusion under political dominance are strongly evident in the century-old history of Asian Americans.[23]

To prevent Asian Americans from forming a strong coalition and political force, U.S. immigration policies emphasized the importance of cheap labor and discouraged the formation of family unity by setting up restrictive quotas for women and children of Asian laborers. The virtual absence of Asian women until the 1950s and the enforcement of anti-miscegenation laws made it difficult for these laborers to find mates in this country. As a result, bachelor communities consisting mainly of single males became characteristic of many Asian ethnic groups.

Although many of these discriminatory laws have been revoked, the community still bears the long-term effects of cultural, socioeconomic, and political exploitation and oppression. Institutional discrimination and deprivation continue, but in new forms, such as the Immigration Reform and Control Act of 1986, which disproportionately affects people of color, including Asians, and exclusion elsewhere of Asian

Americans as minorities entitled to special services and opportunities. As long as Asian Americans are not treated as full citizens of this country, their political participation and contribution will remain limited.

Racial insensitivity and unreceptivity. Along with other women of color, some Asian American women criticize the role that white women, in partnership with white men, play in defending and perpetuating racism.[24] The capitalist patriarchy has differential effects on white women and Asian American women. While white women experience sexism, Asian American women suffer from both racism and sexism. For example, sexual stereotypes compounded with racial stereotypes continue to degrade the self-image of Asian American women. White supremacy and male dominance, both individually and in combination, have detrimental effects on the political functioning of Asian American women. For this reason, white women are seen as partly responsible for perpetuating racial prejudice and discriminatory practices.

More specifically, Asian American women who are committed to fighting both sexism and racism feel that white feminists are not aware of or sympathetic to the differences in concerns and priorities of Asian American women. Although Asian American women share many common issues and concerns with white feminists, many tend to place a higher priority on eradicating racism than sexism. They prefer to join groups that advocate improved conditions for people of their own ethnic background rather than groups oriented toward women's issues only. They advocate for multiculturally sensitive programs, not ones just aimed at reforming gender inequality. For instance, they prefer multilingual childcare programs and counseling services that bridge communication gaps and promote cultural understanding.

Some white feminists may accept Asian American women and other women of color as an integral part of the movement in the abstract. But entrance into the predominantly white feminist organizations has not been extended to include them in actuality. The open-door policy allows Asian American women as members, but closed attitudes limit their efforts to work on issues and problems concerning Asian American women, to build coalitions, and to influence decision making. Without understanding the history and culture of Asian American women, some white feminists are impatient with the relatively low level of consciousness and apparent slow progress made by Asian American women in organizing. Their token presence indicates the superficial nature of the invitation to join. The same frustrations of voicelessness, namelessness, and powerlessness run parallel to the experience of white women trying to break into a male-dominated system, the "old-boy" network.[25] While white feminists belong to the center of the movement, Asian American women and women of color remain on its margin.[26]

Class cleavage. In addition to racial insensitivity, the typical middle- and upper-class composition of the feminist movement repels many Asian American women who feel more concern about working-class women.[27] The economic class structure has unfortunately created social barriers between working-class women and middle- or upper-class women. While affluent white women, because of their class entitlement, have more resources, extra time, and the personal energy for political organizing, working-class Asian American women struggle to survive and have little time to question the economic structure. They may not therefore fully understand how the class structure of America limits their aspirations and achievements. Furthermore, greater acceptance of traditional sex-typed ideology by Asian American women and their perception of the feminist movement as alien, radical, and irrelevant to their needs also account for their lack of participation. As a result, it is difficult for them to relate their own economic issues to other women's concerns and place them in a larger sociopolitical context.

Class cleavage exists not only in the larger feminist movement, but also among Asian American women as well. While Asian American working-class women tend to see economic survival as a primary concern, those with high levels of education, social status, and income tend to be more concerned with job advancement, professional licensing requirements, and career development. Regardless of occupational levels, the immigrant status of Asian American women and their families does not enable them to adapt easily to current demands and requirements of the American labor market. Many experience tremendous status and financial losses as the result of immigration.

Ethnicity, however, cuts across all the class sectors, and provides a form of identification and social bonding among Asian American women from different classes. Limited efforts, such as providing tutoring, social, legal, and health services, women's shelters, counseling, job-training programs, and outreach, are helping bridge the gap between class groups. Class barriers are thus much easier to overcome among Asian American women than between the white feminists and Asian American women from working-class backgrounds.

Implications and Conclusion

Asian American women confront problems on multiple fronts. Thus no social movement that addresses only one of the problem areas can adequately resolve their multiple oppressions sexually, racially, legally, economically, and culturally. The feminist movement is not an exception to this, for the specific concerns of Asian American women are often not those of white feminists. Without recognizing these multiple oppressions, political participation in the larger movement will be incompatible with the definition, goals, and interests of the Asian American cause. In this case, the concept of feminism needs to be broadly defined to address the interconnectedness of sex, gender, race, class, and culture so that its defining character and meaning are grounded in the experience of various kinds of women, including Asian American women. Broadening feminism implies that sisterhood is inclusive regardless of one's race, class background, national origin, sexual preference, physical condition, and life-style. Then strategies of collective action are needed to address the specific needs of Asian American women, to overcome the barriers that block their political participation, and to strengthen their relationship with others in the feminist movement as well as human liberation as a whole.

If Asian American women participate in the larger feminist movement, they can benefit from as well as contribute to it. By and large, the movement has provided an impetus for the organizing and political activism of Asian American women. For some, working with white feminists has inspired critical examination of their subordinate status and limited role. They have been prompted to develop themselves fully as contributing members of the family, their ethnic community, and society, thus raising their level of consciousness. Through support from the movement, a number of Asian American women have established their own organizations and have gained skills in language, assertiveness, leadership, coalition building, and negotiation. Thus they are now able to communicate effectively with others and to build strong networks with groups of white women and women of color in the larger society.

In return, Asian American women can also contribute to the movement in unique ways. The presence of Asian American women and other women of color in feminist organizations and activities has sensitized white women to their ethnocentric views, broadened their concerns, and challenged the existing social structure that has persistently defined and perpetuated sexist and racist values. As advocates for the civil rights, social equality, and human liberation of all people, Asian American women have shown support for feminist issues by participating in political activities (e.g., marches in support of the Equal Rights Amendment), forming coalitions with feminists on common issues (e.g., voter registration projects in the 1984 and 1988 elections), sharing resources for important causes, and providing leaders as representatives to women's meetings. They have also enlightened women in the larger movement concerning the uniqueness of their social and cultural backgrounds, the experience of the combined effects of sexism and racism, and the pressing needs of working-class women.

The increased involvement of Asian American women in the feminist movement will enhance the Asian American cause by broadening the perspective of their political struggle; by identifying more resources, channels, and opportunities existing in the larger society; and by gaining support through the formation of networks with diverse groups. Asian American women involved in both Asian American activism and the larger feminist movement have played an important role in decreasing sex and racial discrimination, in providing leadership and role models for others to emulate, and in paving the way for Asian American political visibility and efficacy in the society at large. As Rita Elway remarks, "Asian and Pacific women in elective office have, for the most part, introduced more community people to the political process; they have responded to a broader range of concerns both inside and outside of the community; they have advocated for civil rights on behalf of all ethnic minorities and women." [28]

Therefore, it is important that Asian American women should increase their political participation in the Asian American community as well as in society at large. Although some Asian American women have been actively involved in their communities, their accomplishments are not less than those of white feminists in the larger society. Because the origins of many of the barriers encountered by Asian American women are beyond their control and are deeply embedded in the social structure, collective efforts are needed to solve these structural problems. Asian American women should join forces with others to increase their political clout and to work for lasting social change. Thus political activism is the first step toward becoming visible, eradicating the stereotype of passivity, and challenging the condition of namelessness. Political participation is also necessary to help overcome voicelessness as Asian American women, to gain power in making demands on their own behalf, and to address the pressing needs and problems of disadvantaged people. It is through political participation that Asian American women will be able to establish networks with other women's groups and to empower themselves in the struggle for equality, justice, and liberation for all people.

To effect their political course of action Asian American women must develop strategies and programs to overcome internal and external barriers. When developing appropriate courses of action, the differences in their historical pasts, the uniqueness of their subculture, and structural arrangements within the Asian American communities and in the larger society must be taken into account. What has successfully advanced the cause of other women's groups cannot be simply imposed on Asian American women.

Five major suggestions are outlined here. First, strategies targeted to overcome psychological barriers may include consciousness-raising techniques to deal directly with identity crises and conflicting loyalties resulting from the double status as women and as members of a racial minority group. Asian American women might develop a transcendent type of gender consciousness that encompasses concern for all forms of multiple oppression.[29] Education is one of the necessary ingredients for increasing political awareness and the power of Asian American women. The women need to develop leadership and organizational skills in order to become active in the political arena. They may identify outstanding women leaders as role models to emulate. Networking and coalition building would provide them mutual support and contact with other women's groups. Programs designed to overcome language difficulties and to improve communication skills and image management are also needed. The goal is to develop a healthy self-concept, positive in outlook, assertive in behavior, and androgynous in style.

Second, self-awareness and cultural programs aimed toward cultural pluralism may be designed to educate Asian American women. They can learn what past conditions and ineffectual activities have led to their current plight. These programs will assist them in seeking cultural resolutions by combining the parts of the Asian and American cultures that are compatible with one another and most appropriate given the demands of current social circumstances. By exposing Asian American women to a wide range of life options, they will learn to demand self-determination, to explore ways of self-expression, and to seek strategies for self-empowerment. They will realize that they can change the course of their life by their own actions.

Third, the role of males in the life struggle of Asian American women is a critical but unanswered question to be explored. As long as patriarchy persists, male dominance will exist inside and outside Asian American communities. While some Asian American women are willing to work with men in partnership for happiness and success, others may opt for independence from males politically and/or sexually. The issue here is that freedom of choice must be available to women if they are to be totally liberated.[30] Whatever choices Asian American women make, others, whoever they are, have to accept these women's definition of gender relationship and respect their choice of self-determination.

Fourth, white feminists and Asian American women should work to build a foundation for feminist solidarity and deal together with racism and classism. White feminists must first critically examine their attitudes and behavior toward women of color and different classes. They need to demonstrate consistency in attitudes and behavior when relating to Asian American women. They need to show sensitivity toward Asians and place the eradication of racism and classism as the top priority in the larger feminist movement. They should take responsibility for educating the general public about cultural and ethnic differences and join Asian American women in protesting and stopping actions that reinforce racism and classism.

Finally, Asian American women must unite with other women of color who, for the most part, share similar life circumstances, experience multiple oppression, and struggle for common goals. Unless the whole social structure is uprooted, many institutional barriers in law, housing, education, employment, economics, and politics that are deeply embedded in the system will remain unchanged. Only when different groups work effectively and strategically together as a political force will all women achieve a new political consciousness and gain collective strength, to supersede the race, gender, sexual, class, and cultural differences that now divide them.

From Homemaker to Housing Advocate: An Interview with Mrs. Chang Jok Lee

NANCY DIAO

I first met Mrs. Lee in 1976 at a rally in front of the International Hotel and then again in 1985 in the midst of a financial crisis in the San Francisco Housing Authority. The agency was more than $9 million in debt, and its executive director Carl Williams had been asked to resign by Mayor Diane Feinstein. During this time, the Ping Yuen Residents Improvement Association (PYRIA) remained the best organized and most effective tenant association in the city.[1] Much of its strength was due to the consistent participation of Mrs. Lee. She had been the backbone of a monumental effort to protect the rights of low-income tenants in San Francisco's Chinatown. This is an unusual role for an immigrant woman whose Chinese tradition frowns upon women activists.

What struck me was Mrs. Lee's dedication to working for social change, an unusual choice for a woman her age. Instead of playing mah-jongg with her contemporaries, she prefers to attend community meetings, testify at city hearings, and help fellow tenants settle disputes. Mrs. Lee is in her late fifties, but looks much younger. With glasses and short black hair, permed and fashionably kept, she is always well groomed and impeccably dressed. For a Chinese woman, she is rather big-framed, but looks sturdy and confident. She speaks her mind freely, from telling stories about her favorite granddaughter to tales about growth pains with the tenant association or gossip in the Chinese community. Though she speaks a combination of Chinese dialects, with a mixture of some English words, she looks you straight in the eye when she talks. You can't help but notice her sincerity and passion.

Growing Up in Japan

In a 1985 interview, Mrs. Lee told of how poverty and discrimination have plagued her since her childhood in Japan. Born in 1927, in Kobe, she was the third of eight children, and the second girl. Her family suffered the hard life of Chinese immigrants in Japan, and she remembers growing up poor, segregated from the Japanese.

> My family was very poor when I was born. We didn't even have money to buy soy sauce. When I was two years old, my father got a job as a chef in the Egyptian Embassy, so our entire family lived in the servants' quarters of the embassy. My mother helped out with the house-cleaning and ironing.
>
> We didn't have much contact with the Japanese except when we went shopping. In Kobe, the Chinese operated pastry, coffee, tailoring, and other shops and had two Chinese schools. I went to the Mandarin school until the sixth grade, but we didn't have enough money for me to continue; my sister went only to night school.

The heavy responsibilities she assumed as a girl helped to groom her for her later leadership role in the Chinatown tenants' group. When her family returned to the Zhongshan district in southeastern China during the Sino-Japanese War, and while her father and older brother remained in Japan, Mrs. Lee had to bear the bulk of caring for the family though she was only eleven years old. This responsibility continued even after the family reunited in Japan one year later. More aggressive and verbal than her older, frail sister, Mrs. Lee represented the family at air raid exercises and in food ration lines. After the sixth grade, she worked in a Taiwanese-owned shoe factory and then in a candy factory to help with the family income.

Along with other Chinese in Japan, she and her family were subjected to many forms of discrimination because Japan and China were on opposite sides of a war.

> Some pharmacies would use slogans like "Can even kill the Nanking Bloodsuckers" as advertisements for the effectiveness of pesticides.[2] In many Japanese shops we would have to wait until the Japanese customers were served first. We were also discriminated against in employment and were only able to get lower class jobs regardless of our education, skills, and abilities. This situation forced many of us to start our own small businesses such as cafe/restaurants, tailor shops, and painting stores.

When the United States began bombing Kobe in 1944, life became even harsher for Mrs. Lee's family.

> Whole families died in air raid shelters, smothered by smoke. When the planes came, everyone in my family went into caves or shelters; only my older brother and I stayed behind to watch our house. One time our house was firebombed, and I tried to put out the fire by stomping, but in vain. My brother went looking for me all over the place, but the fire and smoke had spread so fast that he couldn't see anything. Fortunately I had escaped, and he did thereafter. We lost our house, and our family split up. I was sent to live with a family friend who came from the Fukien province.

Romance Leads to America

While living with the Fukienese family and working for them to earn her keep, Mrs. Lee met her future husband, George, through her first boyfriend. George was a Chinese American GI who was stationed in

Yokohama after the surrender of the Japanese government at the end of World War II. When asked how she met George, Mrs. Lee giggled. Her face lit up and she blushed. Then her eyes softened with a watery glow. Compared to her first boyfriend, who treated her like a "good little workhorse," George was considerate and romantic, though they didn't talk much in those days.

> George always treated me with kindness and respect, very different from my first boyfriend. He always saved me a seat on the bus and gave me little gifts, whereas my boyfriend never showed any appreciation. [For instance], when my boyfriend's family's house was bombed, and he lost all of his belongings, I stayed up all night to knit him a sweater. He never even said "thank you."

Mrs. Lee and George married in 1946, and their first son was born one year later. When the son was just six months old, George returned to the United States while Mrs. Lee remained in Japan with her parents till her husband came back to get her. They arrived in San Francisco in 1950, and in two years moved into one of the Ping Yuen public housing apartments in Chinatown. She remembers her life being full, but also one of poverty.

> We were so poor that most of the time we didn't even have a penny in the house, but I wasn't scared or worried. We raised eight children, four boys and four girls, and from them I learned some English.

When the children were small, Mrs. Lee spent all of her time raising them; but as they grew older, she found more time to think about her own needs and interests. She began to become more active in the community, beginning first with just singing and socializing, and then onto more serious work.

> When the children were all grown up, I started learning Mandarin and singing songs at the Asian Community Center.[3] Since I went to a Mandarin school in Japan, I wanted to keep it up. While I was learning Mandarin, I had the opportunity to read a lot of newspapers and books, and went to May Day celebrations with George. Ever since George got disabled from a car accident in 1972, he has had a lot of free time to get involved in community issues.

Confrontation with Housing Issues

The Asian Community Center was a commercial tenant of the International Hotel block, which soon became the focal point of the early conflict of interests between low-income tenants and land developers.[4] Mrs. Lee's association with the center eventually led to her involvement with community housing issues.

In 1977, when my youngest daughters, Sylvia, Patricia, and Teresa, were twenty-one, nineteen, and ten, I became involved in the International Hotel struggle. I would take my youngest daughter, Teresa, to meetings and classes with me. Because I knew some of the tenants who lived in the International Hotel, I got upset when I saw leaflets about the possibility of them being evicted; I did not want to see them homeless. The young people at the Asian Community Center encouraged me to go to meetings on the third floor of the I-Hotel. It took me a while to get used to meetings and rallies, but eventually I even spoke with bullhorns at demonstrations.

On August 3, 1977, the night of the eviction, George, Teresa, Patricia, and I were there. It was a warm night; there were four hundred policemen on horses, in addition to the tactical squad. The I-Hotel was surrounded by thousands of people—Asian, white, black, young and old, including many from Reverend Jim Jones's church who came in busloads. It seemed that we all stood on the sidewalk for hours. Suddenly the horses charged. I screamed, and everywhere there was yelling, screaming, and crying. We wanted the horses to stop charging, but the tactical squad used their billy clubs to hold us back on the sidewalk. As the horses rushed and trampled, the human chain around the hotel broke. People fell down. Tears poured out of my eyes as I heard Hongisto (then chief of police) breaking down the door to the I-Hotel. We stayed in front of the I-Hotel until three in the morning—watching every tenant being either dragged out or carried out of the hotel; then we went to Portsmouth Square.

Even as Mrs. Lee's support of the I-Hotel continued, she transferred more energy toward improving living conditions in Ping Yuen. In 1977 all the pipes in Ping Yuen were rotting, but in spite of repeated calls to the San Francisco Housing Authority, nothing was being done to fix the problem. Eventually George and some members of the tenant association initiated a massive petition drive to get the plumbing repaired. At the end of 1977, the housing authority finally repaired all of the pipes and painted the exterior walls of half of the buildings. And George was elected president of the association.

A year later, when the housing authority proved unresponsive in meeting the tenants' demands for better security, Mrs. Lee participated in the Ping Yuen tenants' first rent strike. The action was instigated by the brutal rape and murder of tenant Judy Wong.[5] It was an intense period for Mrs. Lee.

> I remember passing out leaflets door to door, talking to the tenants, attending lots of meetings, and collecting rent for fifteen days of each month at the association office on Pacific Avenue. The strike lasted for four months, with numerous press conferences and tedious negotiations with the housing authority, at the end of which we got our security guards.

The second strike followed at the end of 1979, when housing authority groundskeepers and office workers struck for higher pay. The city-wide Public Housing Tenants Association (PHTA) wanted to strike in support, but only the Ping Yuen tenants actually did. When the city employees went back to work, the Public Housing Tenants Association withdrew their support. But the Ping Yuen group continued the strike for maintenance issues, such as fixing apartment interiors and elevators, repairing floors, and painting. It was a long and drawn-out fight, but the tenants' persistence brought them victory.

> We started with eighty households, but some tenants discontinued their strike support for fear of eviction. We held many meetings and visited people door to door. We also had membership drives and sponsored activities to keep the striking tenants together. Since I was the treasurer, I collected the rent, put it in escrow, and kept the books. After two years, we finally got our demands met.

At the end of the strike, most of the tenants chose to donate 50 percent of the escrow interest, about ten thousand dollars, to PYRIA for a color television in the community room and a banquet at Asia Garden. At the banquet the tenants surprised Mrs. Lee and George with two round-trip tickets to Japan to show their appreciation for the couple's efforts in the strike.

During her husband's term as president of the improvement association, from 1979 to 1981, Mrs. Lee worked on two major projects that brought additional benefits to the Ping Yuen tenants. In 1979, at the request of the tenant population, Mrs. Lee went door to door at least two hours a day to sign up enough tenants to pressure Cablevision to install cable television services. Second, Mrs. Lee took over the coordination of the vegetable garden and established new rules: each member had an opportunity to have a garden and the size of all the lots was made equal. She thereby abolished all favoritism in the distribution of garden plots.

Reactions to Activism

Though Mrs. Lee can now act fearlessly, this was not so when she first became active in the community.

> At first I was scared, or rather, kind of embarrassed. I didn't speak English and was not used to speaking in front of people. But after a while, I got used to it. As long as I am fighting for a just cause, then I am not scared.

Since Mrs. Lee's own family has remained in Japan, and George is also alone in the United States, neither has had to face pressure and criticism from relatives, who traditionally might have frowned on women's activism. She and her husband have, however, had some run-ins with the more conservative element of the community.

> I didn't really get much reaction from getting involved in I-Hotel, but when I became active in the business of the association, I started getting a lot of harassment. The wall near our apartment was often spray painted with the word "commies!" with a black arrow pointing to our apartment. Everytime we challenged the previous PYRIA administration's way of doing things, we were called "commies." There were also flyers and posters attacking us.

Neither have her relationships with other tenants always been smooth. Some have criticized her for "doing too much." Take, for example, the laundromat project.[6]

> One of the officers of the association says that I am stupid to sweep the floors of the laundryroom. But when the laundryroom is dirty, I just can't stand it. It took so much out of us to get this project done; I feel like it's my own. So, when people don't clean up after themselves and youths abuse the furniture and write on walls, it really hurts me. But what hurts me more is when other officers nag at me for "doing too much." If they do some and if everybody does something, then I wouldn't have to do so much. Sometimes I squeeze in the sweeping when the baby is taking a nap.

After a recent officers' meeting, Mrs. Lee went home crying. The stress brought her a few sleepless nights and some additional white hair. At times like these, she wonders about whether her efforts are worth all the headaches and talks about quitting, but she stays. She remains undaunted about making Ping Yuen a better place to live and confident about the tenants' overall good feelings towards her.

> Deep down, I know a lot of tenants really like me. They respect me and support George. The maintenance worker, Mr. Wong, complains about the youths not listening to him, but I don't have any problems with them. I just tell them to get out [of the laundryrooms] and they do. Most of the tenants listen to me, and whenever there is something bothering them, they always either ask me questions or ask me to help them.

Sometimes even her children scold her for "wasting her time." Yet other times they have helped out by protecting her at demonstrations or doing errands.

> Some of my children get down on me for doing so much volunteer work. They say that I am crazy for spending so much time on the association when I don't get paid. They don't really understand me. I am happier when I am active, though there is nothing material to gain. It keeps me young. I don't have much white hair or wrinkles [she points to her head], do I?

Sylvia doesn't get down on me for doing so much. She just doesn't want me and George to be taken advantage of; she helps me out a lot. She is the one who taught me how to do books, how to do a membership drive, and keep a membership list. Her husband took off work a couple of times to take care of their daughter whom I watch [five days a week], so that I could be freed up to go to the public hearings on the Orangeland Project at the City Planning Commission.[7]

Teresa . . . knows that I am happier when I am active. She doesn't complain when I am not home to cook dinner, and sometimes she even translates for me.

Conclusion: Balancing Life's Demands

When asked if it has been hard to balance all the demands in her life— being a wife, mother of eight, grandmother of eleven now (eight when she was interviewed), and a housing activist—she laughed:

From these activities, I learned that there is nothing to fear. I feel alive when I come out to do things. But I do take a lot of abuse from people—gripes, complaints, blames, and a lot of headaches. Even George and I have differences sometimes, and he is very stubborn. But basically we are alike, so things don't get too bad at home. At least he doesn't bug me about housework or cooking; sometimes we just go out to eat. . . .

In the past a lot of the community leaders courted George and me. They always invited us to events and asked us to help. Now no one comes. I guess they realize that they can't just use us anymore. I try to keep up with the issues. Sometimes I get upset about association business, and I can't sleep at night. But most of the time, being active keeps me alive. I don't play mah-jongg or go to Reno, so I take care of my granddaughter, and I go to meetings.

On 10 July 1985, Mrs. Chang Jok Lee was honored for her dedication and hard work with the Ping Yuen Residents Improvement Association at the eighth anniversary celebration of the Chinatown Neighborhood Improvement Resources Center, which has spearheaded much of the effort to retain housing in San Francisco's Chinatown. In front of 550 people, she said in Chinese, "I don't really deserve this, but I know that if we all work together, anything can be done." Then, the fifty-eight-year-old grandmother smiled and curtsied.

Dust and Dishes: Organizing Workers

YOICHI SHIMATSU AND PATRICIA LEE

On Nob Hill the Christmas holidays are a fancy affair. Limousines glide past antique cable cars to deliver partygoers to grand hotels. Inside, the pastry chefs have constructed a life-sized gingerbread house for the children.

The resplendence comforts even the busiest minds as thoughts of oilfields and mergers, inheritances and mining rights are soon forgotten. Sprinkled throughout the lobby, foreign tourists and Midwestern couples pop flashbulbs in the glamorous setting of the recent television series "Hotel." Even the staff at the front desk and in the dining rooms strongly resemble the wholesome cast of the show.

Behind the scenes, however, Asians and other immigrants carry on the more mundane work of operating a major hotel. Every morning at sunrise, Asian workers trudge up the steep grade from neighboring Chinatown or nearby bus stops to clock in at employee entrances. Inside cavernous kitchens, cooks fire up ovens and start the coffee while buspersons prepare table settings of china, flowers, and real silverware. Room cleaners push their carts by linen stations to pick up fresh sheets and towels. Before any of the guests wake up, another workday has begun.

Nob Hill owes its reputation for opulent wealth to an earlier generation of Asian workers. On this hill above San Francisco Bay, the railroad barons built their mansions after amassing a fortune from the steel track laid by Chinese contract laborers. A century later the jetliner has surpassed the transcontinental railroad, and luxury hotels have replaced the old mansions. Asian immigrants, however, continue to fill the ranks of labor.

Unsuk Perry, a Korean American room cleaner, recalled her first day on the job at a downtown hotel. "I had never been employed before, so I was ready for anything. I didn't expect the work to be so hard physically, especially turning over the mattresses. It took a long time to get used to such work. The other employees were friendly and helped me along. Most of them were immigrants, too, so they understood how I felt." [1]

Perry had married an American employed in South Korea and came with her husband to San Francisco in 1963. After nine years at the Hilton, she transferred to the Fairmont Hotel's housekeeping department. As a union shop steward, she frequently translates for her Korean co-workers. "During lunch breaks, I explain to them our union's medical and dental plan for their families. It takes about five years for the newer non-English-speaking women to fully adjust to their jobs and fit in with the rest of the employees," she noted. Perry's ability to help her colleagues stems not only from her years of experience, but also from leadership training and counseling that she received from a community-based group which helps Asian immigrant women working in entry-level jobs. [2]

Historical Animosity

Though Perry is active with her union, Asians have not always felt welcome among the groups representing workers' interests. This tension has its roots in the anti-Chinese agitation of over a century ago. [3] With the completion of the railroad, Chinese laborers scattered throughout the West in search of other employment. Their willingness to take jobs shunned by others led to the perception of the white working class that they were cheap foreign competition undercutting wages in a limited market. The image then led to hostility, beatings, arson, and even murder. Populist labor organizations, such as the Workingmen's Party, made opposition to Asian immigration its central rallying point. The Federation of Organized Trades (forerunner of the American Federation of Labor) provided the driving force behind the Chinese Exclusion Act of 1882, which severely curtailed immigration from China.

To their credit, however, some of the early California union leaders spoke out against the anti-Asian policies. The San Francisco culinary unions, for example, opened their membership to Asians at a time when most other labor organizations excluded Asians. During the 1920s and 1930s Waiters Union president Hugo Ernst, himself an immigrant, often spoke out as the lone voice against the anti-Asian bias in the Central Labor Council. In return, during the 1934 San Francisco general strike, all 150 Chinese union members, including female elevator operators, walked the picket lines.[4] All this transpired before the International Union convention finally eliminated its official "color line" in 1936.[5]

Hotel and Restaurant Workers

Employment patterns within the hotel business are similar to those of other industries. Job categories are basically divided into two tracks: the "back of the house" or less visible, lower paying positions, such as room cleaner, buspersons, and dishwashers; and the "front of the house" or high visibility, tipped jobs and skilled crafts, including bartenders, food and cocktail servers, and chefs. The wage gap between the two tracks can be extremely wide, with chefs earning double the pay of room cleaners. There exists a corresponding hierarchy in social status where white Americans and Europeans are clustered in the higher ranking positions.

The inequity in wages and social status was the main cause of the organizing movement among San Francisco Asian and Latina room cleaners in the late 1970s. Although physically isolated from each other on the job, the room cleaners maintained a high level of camaraderie at impromptu meetings in the employees' cafeteria and women's locker room.

Though the women hoped the union would confront their employers, their hopes were stifled by an entrenched local union leadership which had failed to keep up with the rapidly changing ethnic composition of the work force. Comprising over 30 percent of the total local membership by 1980, Asians had special problems of language, immigration status, and discrimination, all of which the union was unwilling to address.

Following the merger of five craft unions, the International Union imposed a trusteeship in 1978 to control dissent in the unified local. Hotel room cleaners played a major role in the rank and file movement which eventually resulted in a court order overturning the trusteeship and returning control to the local members. The defeat of the old-line leadership opened the way to a new round of negotiations.

During the two-year period of arbitration and contract negotiation from 1978 to 1980, the Asian and Latina room cleaners won a series of victories, including an unprecedented 44 percent wage increase, a reduction of workload by one room per day, free meals, a grievance procedure, and a shop steward system. One main problem remained: what the women workers felt to be the management's overbearing attitude towards them. The local press described the 1980 hotel strike which followed as a fight for "dignity and respect."[6] After the month-long strike, the room cleaners returned to work with an improved sense of worth and self-esteem, and with hopes that they would never again be discounted by either the management or the union.

Other Asian women in the hotels have also developed affirmative action strategies to challenge sex and race barriers. Behind a gleaming stainless steel counter, Filipina American cook Lina Abellan decorates trays of small cakes with floral designs of whipped cream and chocolate frosting. As a *garde manger,* or garnish chef, she applies her artistry to fancy relishes, ice carvings, and other ornamental arrangements.

She is also fighting for fair promotions at her downtown hotel. "Hotel management has this mistaken idea that it's classier to have European or white American chefs. Whenever there's an opening for a sous chef's position, managers will usually pass up a qualified minority applicant even if they have to hire from the outside," she explained. "Other minority cooks and I have applied unsuccessfully for a chef's position, myself five times. Frankly, we are getting tired of training inexperienced outsiders who were supposed to supervise us."

A black shop steward advised her to file a complaint with the state Fair Employment and Housing Commission. After reviewing her case, the commission authorized her to initiate a civil lawsuit under Title VII of the Civil Rights Act, which prohibits employment discrimination.

With the assistance of an Asian American community legal group, Abellan and her co-workers are preparing a class action suit. "Filipino and other minority cooks don't really want to 'rock the boat,' but sometimes you don't have any other choice. Whatever it takes—in the union or in court—we must make sure that everyone is treated fairly and equally," she said.

Abellan has demonstrated the same level of commitment and leadership within her union. In early 1985 she successfully ran for the executive board with a multi-ethnic reform slate which was attempting to dislodge the incumbent administration. "The election campaign was very difficult since the rank and file were divided. In only a few months time we had to build a campaign organization, raise money, publish literature, and hold meetings. Without any outside help or full-time staff, we ran a strong race and positioned ourselves for the future. If you don't try, you'll never learn," said the garnish chef.

One of just a handful of Asian American women union leaders, Abellan admits she still has much to learn. "Parliamentary procedure, financial matters, policy issues . . . these are all very new to me. It's a big responsibility to represent such a large membership. Now I can appreciate the importance of support from the rank and file." Since Local 2 of the Hotel and Restaurant Workers Union is the city's largest labor organization, with thirteen thousand members, her leadership role has a direct influence on the future of many San Francisco–area working women.

Department Store Activists

"Coming from a business background, I never dreamed that I would ever become involved in a union," mused Eiko Mizuhara, who for most of her life was a middle-class housewife married to the owner of a San Francisco drugstore. Planning to return to college, Mizuhara found a part-time job at San Francisco's Emporium-Capwell department store in order to pay her tuition. A retail clerk at the cosmetics counter, she handled a wide selection of colognes and perfumes.

"Then one day, it happened. My colleague, another sales clerk, was detained by a security guard for over four hours. She wasn't even allowed to make a phone call. Whatever she might have done, her civil rights were clearly violated." Mizuhara instinctively took action in defense of the detained woman by gathering signatures of her co-workers on a petition to the management. She presented copies of the petition to the company's board of directors, several managers, and to her union, the Department Store Employees' Local 1100.

"I often wondered why I reacted so forcefully. Looking back, I think that my camp experience had a lot to do with my present involvement." Mizuhara was seven years old when she was relocated with her family to an internment camp in Poston, Arizona, and later at Tule Lake, California. At the outbreak of World War II, her father, the manager of Otagiri import/export company, was forced to close the prosperous business and move the family out of their home in Japantown, San Francisco.

"Our sense of justice was just routed. We were incapable of doing anything to protect our rights. Who would have guessed that my feelings would surface forty years later? The main difference between then and now is that I am finally in a position to *do something*," said the clerk.

When the contract expiration date approached in May 1984, Mizuhara joined the rank and file negotiating committee and observed the bargaining process firsthand. "Being from a Japanese American background, I was appalled by the lack of even small courtesies. Since management and labor must depend on each other, I expected there to be a give-and-take attitude on both sides. The pure greed was shocking, especially considering the monumental profits made the previous year."

Departing from an era of labor-management cooperation, the department store negotiators adopted a hard-line stance against the union. Taking their cue from other industries, the store's management proposed a staggering list of "take-aways," including employee contributions toward medical insurance; a lower wage scale for new hirees; and greater management control over rules determining schedules, shifts, and job descriptions.

"When store employees voted to strike Macy's, Emporium-Capwell locked us out. Even though they are fierce competitors, the two companies decided to combine their forces against the union," observed Mizuhara.

During the breaks in the negotiating sessions, Mizuhara and other committee members picketed the downtown stores. "Some of the Asian women clerks would refuse to picket because their husbands thought it was undignified. A few single women continued to work . . . because they had no other source of income. . . . The majority of Asian workers did show up for picket duty. Most of them, however, kept very quiet out of their sense of decorum. In contrast, I tried to be vocal when attempting to convince shoppers not to patronize the store. I was personally very disappointed with Asian American shoppers [who] crossed the picket lines of Asian strikers," she recalled.

Though she felt that the strike generally encouraged many more women to become involved in union activity, Mizuhara also acknowledged that the conditions of the final settlement led to a major crisis for her local. After striking for six weeks, the employees voted to accept many concessions and return to work. As a result of staggering financial losses due to the lengthy strike, the International Union removed the local's popular president.

For the union membership, these unfortunate repercussions underlined the need to reorganize and revitalize their local. "At this point, trade unions must start looking for new directions. With the decline of blue-collar industrial jobs, service-oriented unions are becoming the main base for organized labor," Mizuhara noted. "The labor movement must once again become the social conscience of America, bringing together all the different unions and reaching out to our communities and involving broader constituencies."

Crossing Barriers

For Asian American women, the push into mainstream economy began shortly after World War II. Bertha Chan, a Chinese American retail clerk, has seen much progress over the decades since she first became a union member in the early 1950s. She recalled the lack of employment alternatives for her parents. "Although they were both second-generation Chinese Americans, my father and mother remained farmworkers all their lives. Outside of farm labor or Chinatown's small businesses, there simply weren't many opportunities for Asians."

Chan spent her early childhood in Isleton, California, in the Sacramento River delta region. Her parents followed the harvests on an annual circuit through the orchards and vegetable farms of the San Joaquin and Sacramento Valleys. Asian farmworkers like the Chan family have played a crucial role in developing the vast agricultural economy of the Western states and Hawaii.

Working as a retail clerk in mainstream department stores offered not only better wages but also a new way of life. After her marriage, Chan found a job in a department store packing room to help support her family. "Asians were *not* in retail in those days immediately after the Second World War. Oh, you could find a job in a factory, cafeteria, or a restaurant, but never in a sales position dealing with Caucasian customers. At the department store, we worked out of sight in the back. The Asian women would always have to pack the heavier merchandise like lamps and suitcases. On my first day, I knew there was discrimination when all the Asians were assigned lockers on the very bottom by the floor," she remembered.

Dissatisfied with this blatantly unequal treatment, in the early 1950s she moved on to H. Liebes, a family-owned department store, where she began work as an elevator operator, a job rarely seen anymore. Elevators with manual switches were run by Asian American women dressed in high-collared Chinese silk dresses and white gloves. During the postwar years, this type of service was considered an exotic attraction. "Of course, I wasn't complaining about being stereotyped. A position as an elevator runner was seen as an opportunity to work with the public. From there, Asian women were able to gradually work their way into sales."

Breaking the color line was less traumatic than Chan had expected. White employees and customers, and her new union, Janitors' Local 87, proved generally favorable to the new Asian clerks.

When the Liebes family sold their business six years later, Chan landed a sales position at Livingston's, a large San Francisco–based chain, and transferred over to the Department Store Employees Union. During the 1960s department stores were becoming large corporate-owned entities. "As department stores expanded in size and the number of employees multiplied, it became even more important to belong to a union," asserted Chan. "A lot of times, management would try to cheat you out of overtime pay or holidays. Then it became very important that someone was there to support and protect you."

Even as late as 1980 Chan, in her late fifties, continued her union work, this time serving on the negotiating committee which successfully gained pay raises and an extra holiday for the workers. She hopes that the future will bring unions to unorganized department stores, and she advises younger employees to assume a greater role in the union's decision-making process. "If you're interested in what's going on, get involved! We always expect someone else to do the legwork. If you just criticize and do not attend any meetings, there's only yourself to blame if things don't turn out right."

Conclusion

As the primary institutions representing the interests of workers, unions have been society's trendsetters in the area of working conditions. Benefits include vacations, sick leave, holiday pay and other paid leave, unemployment and disability compensation, and comparable worth. The traditional opponents of labor unions have been employers, but the government is also included in that group now. Tightening economies, changing political policies, and social priorities have contributed to an atmosphere in which many employee-oriented rights and benefits have fallen by the wayside: the government exhibits a reluctance to increase the minimum wage at a rate commensurate with cost-of-living increases and has reduced its enforcement of labor and occupational safety regulations.

The unions face a growing internal challenge, too. As the workforce changes and includes more women and more immigrants, especially at the entry and middle levels, unions find that their survival may be contingent on an ability to adapt programs and priorities to the needs of their new constituents. They must be willing to develop more allies, including the growing immigrant and minority communities. Immigration laws and access to bilingual information may not have been big issues twenty years ago, but they are certainly being discussed now.

Unfortunately, like many bureaucracies, unions can be slow to recognize the need for change. Some may even take positions antithetical to what immigrants express as being in their best interest. This means that Asian American women and other immigrants must be even more willing to participate vigilantly in the unions in order to raise concerns effectively. As Bertha Chan observed, "If we are going to succeed as a group, there has to be more participation by every one of us."

Seeking a Voice: South Asian Women's Groups in North America

JYOTSNA VAID

Although numerous regional associations of immigrants from South Asia exist all across North America, these organizations are largely cultural or religious in their concerns, and tend not to address issues of sociopolitical significance. Even where such issues are beginning to be addressed, there has been a noticeable lack of attention to the particular concerns of women immigrants from the Indian subcontinent. This neglect is especially interesting given the important role that women have played in overseeing the functions of the regional associations, from running language classes to cooking for festivals. Ethnographic studies of South Asian immigrants also do not generally acknowledge the contributions and experiences of South Asian women.[1]

However, over the past decade a number of women, recognizing the need for a separate forum for articulating their unique concerns, have formed autonomous grassroots organizations in different parts of the United States and Canada. More than a dozen of these groups have sprung up. Founded by and composed entirely of women, these groups highlight the experiences, concerns, and contributions of women from the Indian subcontinent. In many cases the concerns of these North American groups have been directly shaped by issues that have mobilized South Asian women thousands of miles away.

Who are these groups? How did they form? What areas have their members determined to most need services? And what internal problems have they encountered at various stages of development? Before turning to these questions, a brief description of Indian immigrant women and their contemporary situation will help provide a context within which to view the concerns of the women's groups.

A Minority within a Minority

Ratna Ghosh points out that some of the problems faced by South Asian women are shared with South Asian men because both groups are part of a visible minority. Some are shared with women in general due to sexist attitudes prevalent in North American society. Others are common to all Asian immigrant women, and several are unique to South Asian women. She notes:

> [These women have] moved from a society which is itself undergoing transition in the economic roles and personal status of women to an industrially advanced society which is also having to cope with somewhat different problems of changing roles and status of women. The conflict and uncertainty of the changing roles subject women to ambiguities both in their personal lives and in their working world. In Canada, additional factors of race, difference in culture, dependent status, absence of close kinship ties, and extreme weather conditions—all interrelate to make their situation rather complex.[2]

The situation described for South Asian women in Canada is not significantly different from that facing those residing in the United States.

One factor that has given rise to several of the problems experienced by South Asian women immigrants derives from the fact that most of them entered North America as "sponsored" relatives. As Tania Dasgupta observes:

> Being sponsored, our dependent status continues while we try to integrate into Canadian society. Given our socioeconomic background and often the inability to speak English, we feel a sense of isolation and alienation. Though more and more of us are entering the paid work force today, we are concentrated in low-paying and traditionally "female" jobs. This is often compounded by the lack of recognition of our previous skills and education and lack of access to English lan-

guage courses. Due to our social dependence, we are vulnerable to oppression at work, outside, and at home. Being visible minority women, we are also subjected to racism in every sphere of life. We are stereotyped as dirty, passive, slow. Thus, we face a triple oppression as women, workers, and as visible minorities.[3]

These sentiments are echoed by Reeta Bhatia, who points out that working-class women, employed largely in service and production occupations, are the target of more overt forms of prejudice and discrimination.[4] These women typically work in labor-intensive industries or in small businesses where they have a very marginal status in the economic structure. They are required to work long hours and are paid the minimal wage without any fringe benefits. Unaware of struggles launched by other women's organizations for improvements in labor laws, maternity benefits, and other reforms, they remain unable to articulate their oppression and demand their rights.

A 1984 survey of foreign-born women in the United States indicated that half as many South Asian women as men (48 percent versus 86 percent) are in the paid labor force. The women tend to be concentrated in service occupations and technical or sales positions, with less than a third (as compared to 72 percent of men) being employed in managerial and professional occupations.[5] This difference may reflect the fact that many middle-class women work part time or interrupt their careers because their own upgrading of skills, recertification, and preparation for qualifying exams must take second place to the similar needs of their husbands.

For South Asian women who work outside the home, there is the additional problem of a double workload, as they are still expected to take full responsibility for household and parenting demands—tasks that their middle-class counterparts in the subcontinent relegate to servants and members of the extended family. In North America, the woman alone oversees domestic and child-rearing duties simply because these do not fit the South Asian man's concept of appropriate work. Problems resulting from this situation have politicized some women.

In the social domain in particular different standards seem to apply for women and men. As Ghosh has noted, the relationship between men and women is fraught with difficulty, affected as it is by perceptions of male honor and female chastity. However liberal a stance South Asian men may take publicly about women's rights, a rather different attitude is revealed when the women from their own family (whether daughters, sisters, or wives) seek these rights. It is thus not uncommon to find young Indian women who came to the United States as children being sent to India for their undergraduate education to safeguard them from the social permissiveness of Western society.[6]

A similar reasoning underlies the preference of first-generation immigrant parents to have their daughters married in traditional arranged marriages. This practice is reflected in the increased number of matrimonial advertisements in the past decade in immigrant newspapers such as *India Abroad,* most of which are placed by family members on behalf of the prospective brides.[7] Since many of these second-generation women are permanent residents or U.S. citizens, their secure legal status makes them particularly attractive to men who regard marriage as an easy means of gaining their own permanent resident status. In many instances, this mercenary intent is revealed only after the wedding has taken place. Cases of this type are increasingly becoming a concern for women's groups.

South Asian women who enter North America through arranged marriages are particularly vulnerable targets of exploitation. Lacking other support systems, they become overly dependent on their spouses— sometimes to the point of tolerating neglect, physical abuse, or infidelity. Because the sanctity of marriage is considered very important, such marriages continue until the stress experienced by the woman leads her to take some action. Many such cases have also come to the attention of South Asian women's groups.

The Rise of South Asian Women's Organizations

The factors just mentioned have prompted the formation of new South Asian women's organizations and have determined many of the groups' services. The eleven groups surveyed for this essay are located across the continent, three in Canada and eight in the United States.[8] The oldest group was founded in 1980, the newest in 1985. The groups are relatively small, ranging in size from just two or three to fifteen core members. All of the members are middle-class women in their mid-twenties to early-fifties. Marital status runs the gamut: unmarried, divorced, widowed, married. Some members are single parents. Some are very recent arrivals, here only a year; others have been here for as long as twenty years. The women tend to be highly educated, most either possessing or pursuing graduate degrees. They work as social scientists, doctors, businesswomen, computer scientists, journalists, filmmakers, lawyers, counselors, librarians, and community social workers. The group's core members include few women who work at home or in working-class occupations.

Most of the group members emigrated from India, although a few of them are from Pakistan, Nepal, Sri Lanka, and Bangladesh. There is little representation of Indian women who have immigrated to North America from countries outside of South Asia, such as Uganda or Trinidad. Some minority groups, such as Ismailis, do not participate in the groups, even though they form sizeable immigrant communities in certain regions of North America. Some women active in these groups are also involved in their ethnic communities. There are also several South Asian women, many of whom are students or professionals, who are members of feminist or progressive organizations but who tend not to join the South Asian groups.

Factors Leading to Group Formation

Although all the groups surveyed are concerned with promoting the status of women, their orientation and priorities—which reflect the factors leading to their formation—differ. For one set of groups, events in the Indian subcontinent, such as dowry-related deaths or the impact of Islamization on women's legal rights, served as the impetus.[9] These groups formed to work with women's groups located in South Asia. A second category includes groups which were mobilized by a desire to address specific problems experienced by South Asian women immigrants, such as domestic violence, unequal social and economic opportunities, or discrimination.[10] The last set of organizations formed because the members wished to establish a visible identity, whether along lines of ethnicity or sexual preference.[11]

A member of New Jersey's group, Manavi, which wanted to establish an ethnic identity, described the conditions leading to the formation of that group:

> A few of us had got together to discuss Kavery Dutta's film project on Asian Indian women. Brainstorming for ideas, we found we had so many ideas to share, so many common concerns, anxieties. The meeting and the conversation sparked off a strong sense of commonality. As immigrant women, we felt there were many issues that were unique to our situation. We felt we should meet more often and for more than just a tête-à-tête. So we met again and created Manavi. We felt there were many Indian groups that organized cultural events and family-oriented activities. We knew that there was a tremendous need for a group to be dedicated to women's issues. Our goal is to work towards social change and create a visible ethnic identity for Asian Indian women.

In response to the question about formation, the members of the lesbian group Anamika, which publishes a newsletter of the same name, said, "The isolation in our lives and the reality of our lives, which was never acknowledged either by groups 'back home' or by South Asian groups here, have propelled us to start the newsletter."

The survey also asked whether the groups perceived themselves as "feminist" groups. Responses to the question were evenly divided.[12] Anamika members stated that although they consider themselves feminists, the women they hope to reach may or may not be so. The woman in Los Angeles who responded on behalf of the Asian Indian Women's Network explained that she would not refer to her group as feminist because the "women are still not ready." It is unclear, however, whether the "women" in this case refers to the group's members or those whom the group hopes to serve. On the other hand, the respondent from the Madison Committee on South Asian Women noted that the term "feminist" is appropriate for her group "because of our concern with the unique situation of women in South Asia and our long-term goal to help improve this situation." In a profile of Manavi, Shamita Das Dasgupta sums up her group's stance:

> Although we deal with problems and concerns of women, as a group we have refrained from declaring ourselves a feminist organization. This decision is a conscious one and taken for pragmatic reasons. We feel that, at present, identifying ourselves as a feminist organization will create hostile societal pressures which may ultimately render our work ineffective.[13]

The services and activities offered reflect what these women feel are the priorities for their community. While the degree of the groups' involvement in these services varies depending on available resources, the activities fall into four general categories: (1) information, referral, and networking; (2) counseling and crisis intervention; (3) direct social services; and (4) advocacy on issues affecting women's rights.

Activities may focus on issues in South Asia or North America. For instance the Committee on South Asian Women has donated books and given small grants to autonomous women's groups in South Asia and sponsored visits by feminists from these groups. Montreal's South Asia Community Center circulated an anti-dowry petition in 1984, which was delivered to the Indian prime minister. On a more local level, the center's members also started a drop-in center and women's cooperative. Along with the South Asian Women's Group of Toronto, they participated in the Canadian government-sponsored workshops on visible minorities and race relations in the workplace. Similarly, the New York–based Association of Asian Indian Women in America took part in a White House briefing on Asian American women.

Many of the groups have used newsletters and other publications to disseminate information about South Asian women from their own perspective. The Committee on South Asian Women has published a monograph containing a bibliography on women's status, a statistical overview, and a directory of organizations and individuals committed to improving the status of women in South Asia. In addition, the group produces an internationally circulated quarterly publication, the *COSAW Bulletin,* which features theme-oriented articles, essays, interviews, book reviews, research index, and reports on the activities of other South Asian women's groups. In 1987 Manavi published a tri-state regional resource directory providing social and legal referrals for Indian women immigrants. As mentioned earlier, Anamika put out the first newsletter on South Asian lesbians. The South Asia Community Center of Montreal produces a community-oriented newsletter in several different South Asian languages. The South Asian Women's Group and the Association of Indian Women in America also circulate newsletters.

Internal Problems

Despite the groups' achievements, members acknowledge that they have met with some problems, ranging from the pragmatic to the ideological. One of the most obvious and most prevalent problems is financial insecurity. Inadequate and unstable sources of income place severe restrictions on what the groups can accomplish. For example only two groups, the South Asia Community Center and the South Asian Women's Group, both in Canada, have their own office space and telephone. The former is perhaps the most established of the groups surveyed; it offers a full range of free services and, in fiscal year 1985–86, responded to 7,200 various requests.

Another obstacle is limited time. The Manavi respondent notes, "Our members are all very committed, but we need to make Manavi a top priority to do what we are targeting for. All our members are fully occupied in their careers . . . so coordinating everybody's busy schedule gets to be quite a task." The time spent on a group activity, such as production of a newsletter, is time that might otherwise be spent on professional pursuits or with family members. Several groups' members experience considerable stress from having to balance these competing demands. The situation is made worse in cases where spouses or other family members do not particularly encourage participation in the women's group.

The respondent from the Asian Indian Women's Network in Los Angeles cited "lack of support from spouses" as one of the most controversial internal problems of her group. In some instances, this lack of support betrays a defensive stance on the part of the South Asian men; in other cases, although disapproval is not overt, it nevertheless appears in the form of skepticism about the value of these groups or indifference toward the problems encountered by the group.

Support, however, also needs to come from the community at large. Here, too, problems have been encountered. These are aptly summed up by the respondent from the Association of Asian Indian Women in America who noted that although the group has become quite visible in New York, "community awareness is 60 percent, community participation is 10 percent."

A related danger is failure of sister groups to recognize the efforts of the women's groups. In one instance, a women's group spent several months preparing a detailed survey to be administered to their clients, only to find that another organization in that city had appropriated the survey without giving them due credit.

Many yet unanswered questions confront the South Asian women's groups. Organizations that have gained some stability must decide whether to develop a more formal structure. While most of the organizations have a written statement of their aims and objectives, decision making follows informal lines and is based on consensus. Many of the policy-related questions are often left to the discretion of the groups' coordinator. There is also the question of whether to expand and, if so, in what direction. Should regional branches be established, or should the groups join existing national women's organizations? Anamika chose to affiliate with an umbrella group, Asian Lesbians of the East Coast, "for reasons of safety," says its respondent. Should special links be forged with autonomous South Asian groups in North America or, perhaps, in South Asia as well? Smaller groups may be able to retain the dedication and solidarity characteristic of many grassroots organizations, but larger groups may be able to accomplish more.

Another problem concerns the position that the group should take on issues that are ostensibly not "women's issues" per se, but on which women are increasingly taking an active stand, such as nuclear disarmament, apartheid, or communal conflicts within South Asia. The question is twofold: where to draw the line between women's issues and other issues and whether such a line even can be drawn. The minutes of three successive meetings of the South Asia Community Center chronicle an internal debate about whether the group should participate in a rally against nuclear weapons. The debate sparked a number of fundamental questions having to do with the group's goals and the most effective ways of achieving them.

Because of the sociopolitical context of most women's issues, one danger that some groups face is that of misconstrued political intent. Allegations have been made, for example, that a particular group is actually a front for a political organization. When key group members also belong to other organizations, the situation becomes even more complicated. To what extent can the group afford to have members with strong political ideologies and still claim to function autonomously? Though some criteria may be used to insure independence, such as refusing donations from other groups, it is difficult to refuse time and other resources.

Last but not least is the difference of opinion about the philosophy of the women's group, a difference that can be characterized as a "struggle versus service" debate. While implicit or explicit feminist principles may have guided the group's formation and initial activities, the subsequent actions of the group may eventually become indistinguishable from those of social services agencies. There is nothing wrong with providing such services if that is the sole and explicit aim of the group. For those who embrace a feminist perspective, however, it becomes a serious problem if their efforts are directed toward providing short-term relief, which only helps their clients adapt to the status quo that keeps them subjugated.[14]

Here, more questions must be faced: what model of social change should be advocated for South Asian women settled abroad, and which solutions offered by which brands of feminism are appropriate or desirable for which South Asian women? In wrestling with these questions, tensions have surfaced between the women's groups that are interested in offering feminist perspectives and solutions and umbrella immigrant organizations that want to steer away from these solutions. These latter organizations are usually dominated by men with considerable clout in the immigrant community. Their endorsement of the women's groups thus becomes important for the groups' effectiveness.

Most groups have not yet resolved all these issues, but increasingly recognize the necessity of periodic self-appraisal. They also agree that to achieve their goals sister organizations need to improve mutual coordination and cooperation.

Conclusion

While the groups discussed in this essay are fairly diverse in their orientations, one shared feature is the women's enthusiastic dedication, as expressed in a report written at the end of the first year of the South Asia Community Center (SACC) in Montreal.

> One of the most striking aspects of SACC as an organization is how organized it in fact is, despite radical changes in its internal structure. . . . One thing that emerges quite clearly is that we are a rather stubborn group of people; we have stubbornly resisted attempts by others to take us into their fold; as well, we have stubbornly kept the idea behind SACC in mind during our periods of inactivity (when other pressures occupied our energies). What accounts for this steadfastness of spirit? No doubt it comes from the strong conviction that something must be done about the situation of women in general, and of our South Asian compatriots in particular. This conviction, coupled with the realization that no one else here has gotten around to doing anything about it has prompted the movement leading to the establishment and development of SACC.[15]

Where this movement will ultimately lead will depend largely on the continued commitment of the women who founded these first few groups and the receptiveness of the society at large to the changes they promote.

Asian Pacific American Women in Mainstream Politics

JUDY CHU

In Oregon, there are only ten Chinese families in a district of eighty thousand, but State Senator Mae Yih's face is a familiar one as she goes door to door to shake the hands of her constituents. Mae Morita waits for the result of her successful school board election in a barnyard in the farming community of Fresno, California. In Anchorage, Alaska, Filipino Thelma Buchholdt is the object of a smear campaign against "foreigners" in her overwhelmingly Caucasian district. But through widespread admiration for her skills and personal integrity she wins a seat in the state legislature, where she serves for eight years. And in the city of San Francisco, where Asians are one-third of the population, Julie Tang triumphs as the number one vote-getter because a coalition of Asians, gays, liberals, and progressive groups supports her election to the presidency of the San Francisco Community College Board.

Whether in Hawaii, California, Washington, Oregon, or Alaska, Asian Pacific American women are steadily making their way into the political mainstream. The stereotype of the passive, servile Asian woman certainly would not be born out by the examples cited here, who typify the growing number of Asian women jumping into the leadership positions of public office. Certainly politics is one of the most difficult frontiers for Asian women to enter. It requires assertiveness and extemporaneous public speaking; it requires a tough skin to weather criticisms; it requires risk-taking to deal with the prospect of defeat. For the highest offices, it requires financial resources and networking with powerful figures, usually male. These are not characteristics usually associated with Asian women, yet there are Asian women who have been able to succeed in their election bids.

Nobody would have dreamed when the first Asian woman set foot in America that 150 years later a Chinese American woman, Secretary of State March Fong Eu, would hold the record for the highest number of votes given a California state official, or that a Japanese American woman, Patsy Mink, would aspire to be governor in her home state of Hawaii. Asian women faced many obstacles that kept them in second-class status. Initially brought to America as slaves/prostitutes, they faced discrimination not only by American society, but by the feudal Asian society. Subsequent numbers of Asian women came as picture brides or war brides; thus, they were always seen as appendages of men, rather than on their own terms. Such cultural values still affect many

Asian women today, especially the large number of recent immigrants. But a few have stepped out of society's molds to be role models and to break the stereotypes.

The focus of this essay is on the experiences of Asian Pacific American women in elected office. Currently they are in the states of California, Hawaii, Oregon, and Washington. However, in order to gain a national perspective, the experiences of women from other states have been included. Amongst these women are a former office holder in Alaska, a political organizer in New York, and a federal appointee in Washington, D.C.

Emerging Numbers

It is not surprising to find that the actual numbers of Asian women in elected office is very small in proportion to their numbers in the general population. Asian women have only in recent years even attempted to run for public office. A look at the number of Asian women officials from just a decade and half ago is revealing. In 1970 there were four Asian women in the nation who held public office. March Fong Eu was in the California State Assembly. In Hawaii, Patsy Takemoto Mink was a U.S. representative; Jean Sadako King and Patricia Saiki were in the state legislature.

The numbers in June 1985 seem exorbitant by comparison. There were forty Asian women elected officials, all in the Western region of the United States. There were twenty in California, seventeen in Hawaii, two in Washington, and one in Oregon.

On the national level, Asian women were glaringly invisible. There was no Asian woman in the U.S. Senate and only one in the House of Representatives, Patricia Saiki. The only other Asian woman ever to have served on the national level was former Representative Mink, who served in the House from 1965 to 1977. On the state level, however, there have been a few breakthroughs. The highest ranking Asian woman currently is Eu, secretary of state for California, who has served in that capacity since 1974, and is continuously elected by a high margin of voters. The highest ranking Asian woman ever to hold state office is Jean

King who was lieutenant governor of Hawaii from 1978 to 1982. As of 1988 there are no Asian women in the 120 seats of the California state legislature, though Asians number 1.25 million, are 6 percent of the population, and are disproportionately high financial contributors. Hawaii is populated by fewer Asians than California at 583,660, but they are a majority of the population at 60.5 percent. Thus, Asian women fare better, with 9 in the state legislature, out of a total 76 seats. Oregon has the distinction of having relatively few Asians, but claiming a state senator, Yih.

On the local level Asian women are beginning to make more of an impact. In 1985 there were eleven Asian women on city or county councils—six in Hawaii, three in California, and two in Washington. Mink chairs the county council of Honolulu. Three women, all in southern California, have served as mayors. Though no longer councilmembers, Carol Kawanami in Villa Park of Orange County was the first Japanese American woman to be a mayor in 1980; Eunice Sato became mayor in Long Beach, its first and only minority and woman; and, in 1983, Lily Chen of Monterey Park became the nation's first Chinese American woman mayor. The current city or county councilwomen outside of Hawaii include Judy Chu (Monterey Park), June Fukawa (Delano in Central California), and Dolores Sibonga and Dana McHenry (from Seattle and Issaquah, Washington, respectively). Three Asian women in California were also elected as city clerks or auditors: Helen Kawagoe (Carson) in 1974, May Doi (Gardena) in 1980, and Norma Lau (Oakland) in 1977.

Considering the fact that Asian culture places much importance on education, and that children have traditionally been under the woman's domain, one would expect a greater proportion of Asian women on school boards. This apparently is not true. In 1985 there were eight women in these seats nationally, six in California and two on the state board in Hawaii. Two of the women were presidents of their boards: Julie Tang, president of the San Francisco Community College Board; and Mae Morita, president in the Central Unified School District in Fresno. Other women on California school boards were Lita David (Sweetwater), Florence Ungab (National City), Eleanor Chow (Montebello), and Julia Wu (Los Angeles Community College). In proportion to the number of Asian students in the California system, Asians were greatly underrepresented. Out of approximately seven thousand school board seats in California, forty-eight were occupied by Asians, which is less than 1 percent. Some areas that are heavily impacted by Asian students, such as the Alhambra School District (45 percent), have never had any Asian school board members whatsoever.

The lack of visibility for Asian women in politics reflects a problem facing Asians in general. Asian Americans, both male and female, can give glaring examples of underrepresentation in politics; for instance, as of 1988 there is not a single Asian American in the California state legislature. Still, Asian males have made some strides, including five members in Congress, one governor of Hawaii, one lieutenant governor in Delaware, and several Washington state representatives. Out of approximately 245 elected positions occupied by Asian Americans nationally in June 1985, only 16 percent of them were held by Asian women who comprise half of the Asian population. There are many examples of this inequity. In 1985, of the 49 Asian American judges nationwide, only 7 of them were women, all in California. Out of the 150 appointments made in Los Angeles in 1984, 15 were given to Asians, but only 2 were women. And even in that stronghold of Asian constituency, Hawaii, only 17 of the 102 Asian elected state/county officials were women, or about 17 percent as of 1985.

Usually, Asian women have fared better in appointed positions, where hard work and competency are more readily rewarded than in the subjective and risky world of electoral politics. Of the twenty-five major state level appointments in California given to Asians in 1984, seventeen were to Asian women. The highest-ranking Asian American in the federal government has been a woman, Julia Chang Bloch, assistant administrator in the Agency for International Development in Washington, D.C., appointed in 1981. The highest ranking Asian American in the California state legislature was a woman, Maeley Tom, chief administrative officer in the state assembly, appointed in 1983; she was the first minority and woman to hold the position. There are many more Asian Pacifics in key staff positions for elected officials, though as Tom says, "There are as many Asian men as women in these positions. Regardless of sex, however, these Asians are not groomed for elected office because of the perception that they are not winnable candidates."

Asian women also lag behind white women in election to public office, though women in general have a long way to go. In 1985 women were only 14.7 percent of state legislators. In the U.S. Congress, they comprised 5 percent: 2 out of 100 senators and 25 out of 435 representatives. This is not much of an increase from 1971, when women were 5 percent of state legislators, and 2 percent of the members of Congress.

As can be expected, most of the Asian women elected officials are of Chinese and Japanese descent; as of 1985, twenty-one were Japanese Americans and ten were Chinese Americans. There were only six Filipinas, Dolores Sibonga, Lita David, Florence Ungab, Velma Santos, Donna Mercado Kim, and Dana McHenry. The highest ranking Filipina ever to hold public office is Thelma Garcia Buchholdt, elected to the Alaska House of Representatives from 1974 to 1983. There is only one elected Korean American woman in the United States, second-generation Eleanor Chow, longtime Montebello school board member. Prospects for electing women from other Asian Pacific groups are increasing. The first Samoan American woman to run on the mainland was June Pouesi, who ran for a city council seat in Carson, California, in 1984. Kanak Dutta, an Asian Indian woman, ran for a seat in the New Jersey Legislative Assembly in 1981. Though both lost their elections, they did well in the returns, and may run again.

Though obstacles could be formidable, being foreign-born has not prevented Asian women from seeking elected office. Among the successful office-holders have been Julie Tang and Mae Yih, both born in Hong Kong; Lily Chen from Taiwan; and Thelma Buchholdt and Lita David from the Philippines. As of 1985, twenty-five of the officials were Democrat, and ten were Republican. Most have sought office after their children graduated from high school, though a more recent generation of officials is deviating from that formula. The youngest successful Asian woman candidate was Ungab, who at the age of nineteen won her first school board seat in National City, near San Diego, and retained it for over a decade.

Why is it so difficult for Asian women to be elected? And what are the factors that made these women win? How do they cope with their non-traditional roles in these elected offices? Through interviews conducted with selected Asian women in elected office and other politically visible positions, one can begin to answer these questions.

Cultural/Societal Factors in Public Office

Asian Pacific American women government officials agree: Asian women are still in the process of emerging when it comes to elected office. In all aspects of public office, from networking to fundraising to public relations, Asian women usually had many obstacles to overcome as they began their bids for office. Many of their stories showed that they had not included seeking public office in their life plans; in fact, many did not dream their life would turn out this way. Few had mentors or role models that encouraged them to run or trained them in dealing with the public. As Chow said about the early days, "Everything I learned the hard way. I had all guts and no brain [in those days]. I'd like to be a mentor to others so they don't have to do it the hard way."

There may, however, be an exception to the rule and that is in the state of Hawaii. Since Asians are the majority of the population, some of the women interviewed could not see Asian women as having any special problem different from that of all women. As King said, "In Hawaii, being an Asian woman is not an impediment since there are quite a number of us. For instance, an Asian woman chairs the Honolulu city council. Ethnicity is just a means of identification, not discrimination." A network of women legislators in Hawaii meets once a month and may coalesce on issues, but does not aggressively pursue the organization of a power base among women.

Elsewhere, the factors precluding Asian women from running are multifaceted—reflecting cultural, racial, and sexual impediments. First and foremost are the cultural values Asian women themselves may have learned. Julia Bloch talked about the socialization of Asian women: we end up "not having our own status as individuals." As Tang said, "In Asian cultures, women take a secondary position to men, which perpetuates low self-esteem. Once you get into the political process, it can be very intimidating because you are fully exposed, and constantly called to task on many issues—on the way you think and the way you act." Tom echoed these sentiments. "What's the most visible way to fail? It's in politics. Asians don't like to take such risks. To fail denotes shame and disgrace, and we are taught to take the safe route."

Several women talked about how Asian women are taught not to be assertive and about the value of being humble. As Sibonga said, "During the campaign, the hardest part for me as a Filipina was to say, 'Vote for me. I've done this and I've done that.' All through school, I'd never vote for myself even when I wanted the position badly. In order to be in politics, you have to speak about your accomplishments and feel good enough about them to have people recognize you."

Breaking with these cultural values may have initially caused conflict with some members of the community. For instance, the pressure to conform to traditional roles created problems for Kawagoe, elected Carson city clerk in 1974 and the first Japanese American woman elected to an office on the mainland. "At that time, there were few other Asians. In the local Asian community, the males said it was arrogant for a woman to run." Doi's election as Gardena city clerk did not receive much support despite the fact that Japanese Americans were 21 percent of that city's population. "I remember the local Japanese newspaper already saying it was too bad I was running since I was a qualified person."

Many of the women referred to an overall lack of experience Asian Americans have in the American political process. It is only recently that Asians have learned the importance of lobbying, networking, and coalitions, especially among the different Asian ethnic groups. Asian Americans have not been taught to be joiners, and as Irene Natividad, chair of the National Women's Political Caucus, said, "Many Asians still need to develop a sense of belonging in the country. Even second- and third-generation Asians don't feel the connection between the political process and their own welfare. And for immigrants, politics may mean what's going on in the country back home." In addition, David said, "Immigrants may be afraid to speak up, especially with the language barrier."

Once an Asian woman decides to be in a leadership position, she must cope with the perceptions that society has about her. Asian women are seen by many in mainstream society as not being leaders or even having such aspirations. David observed, "Because you are a minority, the public may think you will only serve your own ethnic group." Just the uniqueness of their appearance may be ammunition for the opposition. The smear campaign against Buchholdt was not successful; she won despite rumors spread by the opposition that she was not a citizen. But to deal with the mudslinging, she had to overcome her upbringing. "We are very sensitive. At first, you don't want to fight. You think, 'We are more dignified than that. Don't be rude, don't be so obtrusive.'"

Having an accent may initially pose a problem for some. Tang told this story: "Years ago, several of us were working on a campaign for Gordon Lau, who was running for San Francisco county supervisor, and were talking about who should run next. Some were kidding, 'Why not Julie Tang?' Then somebody said, 'Oh, she would never win. She has an accent!' And I thought, 'Oh yeah, he's right.' I accepted it . . . until I ran. Finally, I decided, so what if I have an accent? I can take on issues better than people without an accent. To this day, I hope I will never get rid of my accent so that other Asian women who have accents will see that it is not an impediment to running."

While there are many obstacles for Asian women, there are some advantages and many strengths that they bring to politics. First, their uniqueness may work for them because people remember them. When Eu first ran for a California assembly seat, she was facing "six Anglo males and a black woman who didn't campaign that much. I was the one people remembered most." Second, Asian women may benefit from a positive stereotype. Asian women are perceived by some as being honest, having integrity, and being competent and capable; indeed, such characteristics are the cornerstones of campaigns of women like Fukawa who said, "We have always stuck for the truth. We won't back down." This corroborates the opinion of some officials that the reason Asian women get into office is not ego fulfillment or resume enhancement, but because of an issue, cause, or belief.

Other positive factors reflect the particular interpersonal training of Asian women. Kawanami felt that Asian women are raised to be patient, persevering, and sensitive to the feelings of others. Tom said, "Asian women have learned how to negotiate and compromise, and do it well.

In some ways this is seen as nonthreatening. If people had to choose a nonthreatening minority, they might choose an Asian woman." Overcoming adversity has caused Asian women to realize they must work twice as hard as others. As Tang said, "I think Asian women are extremely strong. Once they fully realize their strength and learn they can exercise it in the community setting, they do a fantastic job because they learned the hard way. They know their limits; they know exactly what to expect."

Considering the obstacles, it might seem that the Asian women who do run would have extraordinary backgrounds, but they don't. Many of the women say they still retain some traditional values. Mink stresses her ordinary upbringing. "We had a very close-knit family. We observed all the family occasions, especially New Year's." Nor is there a common thread in terms of economic background. Some women's fathers ran laundries or businesses; others were in government service or education; still others were domestics, cooks, sharecroppers, longshoremen, gardeners, or electricians. Many of the mothers were housewives; the few who worked outside the home were not in high visibility jobs.

Yet all the women can remember their leadership developing from childhood, leading some to think, as Buchholdt said, "Maybe you have to be born with it." Sometimes it developed because of sibling relationships. Eu, whose parents ran a laundry, recalled, "I brought myself up. As the youngest of four children, I had to fight for survival and hold my place amongst the siblings." As the daughter of a single-parent Korean immigrant woman, Chow remembers, "My mother didn't speak English; we taught her to read and write. I had to translate for the family and to deal with my four brothers' problems at school." Other women remember being active very early in groups such as the Girl Scouts or in church. This led to running for public office in high school or college. Still others were raised in non-Asian areas, so that, as Kawanami recalls, "I didn't know I was supposed to be shy and retiring. Early on I joined groups, learned parliamentary procedure, and found out it was not so risky."

Early experiences with discrimination also gave some women the desire to take leadership in the change process. Chow grew up in Montebello, where there weren't very many Asians. "There was a lot of prejudice in the town. At my intermediate school, I couldn't swim in the eighth grade because they didn't allow non-Anglos in the pool. The main thing that motivated me to politics was to make sure all children would have an equal chance." Fukawa was ten when she and her family lost their farm and were sent to World War II internment camps. "I was so innocent; I didn't even swear. But after camp, I said, 'Hey this is wrong. What did my parents do to deserve this? These injustices must end.'"

Those raised in Asian-majority areas felt they did not have to cope with problems of racial inferiority. As King said about her childhood in Hawaii, "When I was growing up, I was never given the feeling there were things I couldn't do." Chen talked about growing up in Taiwan when Sun Yat-Sen's teachings on the equality of women were influential. David looked to the matriarchal tradition in the Philippines, where she says, "It's different. Men support women in politics." Tang said, "I never faced degradation or racism in Hong Kong where I was born and raised. We grew up in a bilingual/bicultural society where English was fun to learn because it added to our lives, and it was not at the expense of Chinese. I came here when I was eighteen years old and for the first time faced discrimination. I became very angry. I thought, 'Why should I be treated differently?' and became very active in Asian American studies and Asian community voluntary services. I was not afraid to speak out. In fact, people would describe me as very aggressive and gutsy."

In the absence of Asian women leaders, many of the women turned to other significant people in their lives for role models. Some women have very strong and fond memories of their father's encouragement. Chen's father, himself active in politics, made her feel there were no limitations for her as a leader. "He would encourage me to be in speech competitions. He'd sit there and give me a critique. When I graduated from high school, he gave me a huge, life-size mirror. 'After you perfect your speech, then come to me and I'll correct it.'" Bloch developed absolute dedication to hard work and excellence because of her father, who was in public service. He pushed her to achieve and produce, telling her when they immigrated to this country that "you are a minority, and a minority succeeds by being better than average."

Mothers had a more important influence on some of the women.

Though they may not have been in high visibility roles, they were seen by their daughters, as Norma Nomura-Seidel said, as "strong-willed. Being passive is a misnomer." King recognized these qualities in her mother early. "My mother did a very courageous thing when she married my dad. Interracial marriage is common now, but half a century ago it was quite rare. That kind of conviction must have been reflected in her general philosophy." Sibonga too was guided by her mother. "My mother told me you can accomplish anything you can. She encouraged me to go to school and develop a career so that I would be able to take care of myself." Sato concurs, "My mother was a role model. She was an enlightened woman, educated in Japan, active in the church, and always serving the community."

Though all these women exhibited leadership abilities very early, the qualities associated with being a public leader still needed to be developed through involvement in group activities and community issues. Sato talks about being very shy at first. "I remember the first PTA meeting that I chaired. I had to write every word down from 'welcome,' to 'the meeting is called to order,' to 'the motion carried.'" After twenty years of PTA and ten years of public office, she now can talk spontaneously at ceremonies and receptions with ease.

Running for Office

The reasons for Asian women seeking public office seem to be for issues beyond a political career. Many of the women interviewed here were involved in school issues because of their children, and because they wanted to improve education. Women in Hawaii were concerned with special problems facing the state; for Mink, it was fair representation as Hawaii gained statehood, and for King, it was the environment.

For most, participation in community activities was their first priority; they had no intention of running for office. Public office was the culmination of years of involvement during which they proved their leadership skills. However, a crisis was often the actual spark to run. Yih ran after defending a teacher she admired but whom the school board had dismissed. Sato ran when her councilmember was found guilty of perjury. Wasserman was approached to run by non-Asian parents and community members who wanted to oust an inefficient board.

Tenacity and personal contact are major factors for the successful elections of these women. Morita reflected on running for the school board after twenty-five years of involvement—starting from room mother to high school PTA officer. "I never dreamed I would run. But once I filed, I campaigned hard . . . because I didn't want to lose. It was grueling, but exciting, waiting for election returns. I never expected to win but I did." Doing the hard work of precinct canvassing was a way of preventing the shame of failure. Sato walked to 90 percent of the homes in her district, which has forty thousand people and is predominantly Caucasian. Similarly, Yih walked the precincts in her Oregon district of eighty thousand. "The personal contact is important. People got to know me and trust me."

One benefit of the positive stereotype attributed to Asian women is that they don't necessarily require an Asian constituency to win an election. In all the districts Asian women ran in outside of Hawaii, Asians were not the majority. In fact, in Buchholdt's district of thirty thousand, there were only about a dozen Filipino families. In other districts with somewhat larger Asian constituencies, the women had voter support but oftentimes not the kind that was visible, vocal, or organized.

It is only recently that coalition politics have been successfully used by Asians. Prior to her election, Tang had been involved for years in the Chinese American Democratic Club, which had already joined in successful coalitions with gay, progressive, and liberal groups around San Francisco. Through the group, she worked on many election campaigns, and ran successfully herself for a Democratic Party Central Committee seat. When she ran for the community college board in 1980, endorsements were readily mobilized. In the end she got the highest number of votes.

Sibonga also attributes her successful 1980 election to coalition politics in the liberal city of Seattle. However, she says, Asians still need to work on the interethnic differences. "There is a tendency for Asians to be very divisive, to place much higher standards on other Asians. And there is still prejudice that Asians have about other Asians. We need to join together in networks."

Coping with Political Life

Considering the emphasis placed on the Asian woman's role within the family, a public life would seem to create tremendous conflict. The nontraditional role, the time demands, and the various constituent pressures form a potential powder keg. Families inevitably must adjust. Mink recalls, "The first campaign was the most difficult for my parents. It came from the fear of losing; they didn't want to see me humiliated and demolished from defeat. But after I proved I could win, they fully supported my fifteen plus campaigns."

Many of the women found their families were indeed enthusiastic, and that family support was even critical to their success. Often both the candidate and her husband already had an active interest in politics, thus influencing their children. Daughters, sons, and husbands became campaign managers or walked precincts. Chen's husband told her when she was deciding whether to run, "I would never do it myself, but I think you have good qualities. If you want to run, I'll support you." He took six months off his job without pay to help in her campaign.

But there are still difficulties. Husbands must be secure because they face a great deal of peer pressure when they don't fill the traditional role. Mink believes that the pressures facing husbands of politicians are tougher than those facing wives. "The expectations of the public are vastly different with respect to a husband. . . . If you're a woman, you have to do all sorts of things. A wife goes along, and nobody thinks anything of it. For a married woman in elected office, people have expectations that the husband should be around every minute in all the activities. And I think that's a very unfair expectation."

For most of the women who ran during more traditional times, child-rearing took precedence, and so they ran for office after their children were out of high school. Children were enthusiastic and energetic campaigners for their mothers. Wasserman recounted, "When I decided to run, I sat down and explained to my two sons that they might hear negative things about their mother. But both were pleased and proud of me, and it seemed to enhance their views of themselves." Inevitably, children face conflicts as well. Nomura-Seidel felt that her "children felt pressure to set a good example." Chow waited until her children were older, but they still sometimes were lobbied by parents and teachers. As a result, she tried to stay away from the schools they attended.

Many of the pressures have to do with basic time demands. Chen expressed her frustration at not being able to spend enough time with her family. "Take the other night. I went to work early, and had nothing to eat because I had to go straight to the city council meeting which lasted until midnight. I ate at midnight, and then got a call from my daughter at 2:00 A.M., who wanted to talk because of a problem she's having with her boyfriend. I want her to feel free to share, but I just didn't have the time or energy. It's very difficult."

The recent generation of elected officials, however, are experimenting with traditional childrearing roles formerly prescribed them. Tang, for instance, is "doing it all" by having her first child while holding office; he was fifteen months old when she ran for reelection. Though it would seem to be impossible to handle everything, she doesn't see the demands as being all that different from earlier times in her busy life, such as when she first ran for office during law school. Bloch's responsibilities as a federal agency administrator keep her traveling around the world. She and her husband decided they couldn't spend the proper time with them, so they would not have children. She says, "There are certain trade-offs to jobs like this." Wasserman ran for school board while her children were still small. Being an attorney and a school board president did not allow her the time to spend on her first priority, the family. She decided not to seek reelection for a third term, because her sons were entering their adolescence, a period she feels requires more attention.

Not only are there adjustments in relationships with husbands and children but also with friends. Nomura-Seidel emphasized the need to keep up friendships. "When you're in office, it's easy to neglect your friends, but you have to take the time to keep those ties going." Wasserman found that being a politician could be a barrier to making friends. "You are treated differently as a politician. You're recognized at functions. I can't casually compare notes at Little League anymore. Some people feel they have to address me as Mrs. Wasserman." In addition, the lack of privacy can sometimes be difficult, causing families like Sibonga's "to be concerned for my safety."

Asian women inevitably experience many personal changes as they stay in office. Many said they became much stronger and tougher. They have become better able to handle both fair and unfair criticism. However, this scrutiny had made some women become more guarded about what they say in public. Other women appreciated the broadened horizons to which they became exposed. And still others felt that in being responsible to all the constituency, they had become much more sensitive to a variety of people's experiences and concerns.

Many of the women are quite conscious of the responsibility they carry as Asian women; their performance has an impact on how other Asian women are judged by the public. However, they also reported great satisfaction from knowing they have been role models to others. Tang says, "I know that because of me, several other Asian women are involved in politics." As Asian women in visible leadership positions, they have shown through example, "that an Asian American woman can do a job equally as well as a non-Asian man or woman," notes Eu. "I am proudest of the fact that I have changed public perception so that it is favorable to Asian women." Other Asian women are glad they've shown that Asian women can be assertive leaders who represent the interests of all. In fact, Tang jokes that perhaps she has created a new stereotype— that Asian women are aggressive! Though life can be trying, renewed satisfaction for these women comes from making a positive impact on an unrepresentative system. As Chen says, "I found that as a politician you have to give a great deal—much more than you receive, but I get tremendous satisfaction by knowing that I've accomplished something, that I've changed things for the better."

Future Needs

Asian Pacific women still have many avenues to pursue in order to make a stronger impact in mainstream politics. David emphatically states, "We must build networks! We have to get out of our shell. We can't be too polite, or people will step all over us." Mink stressed the all-encompassing nature of the political system. "Asian women have to be interested in the issues and fight for opportunities on all levels of politics. Elected office is only a minutia. Everybody has something to offer. You have to understand political dialogue and believe that one individual can make a difference. You have to understand where you stand in this process and develop a view, a thought, a philosophy . . . and go for it."

The consensus is that Asian women need to develop their interests and be active in a variety of groups. Asian Pacific women must be visible in public interest groups that are both Asian and non-Asian. A milestone was reached in 1985 when Irene Natividad was elected the first Asian American to chair the National Women Political Caucus, a bipartisan organization committed to ensuring the election of women to office. Partisan politics are also important, especially for those seeking top positions in government. Bloch says, "When you get to the highest level, you have to make a choice. I am a Republican. I am a presidential appointee of this administration. You cannot be on the highest level without making a commitment." Tom, founder of the California Asian Democratic Caucus, stresses, "Because of the way the system is set up, party politics are important if Asians are to impact the state and federal government."

Finally, Asian women must go beyond the concept of role models to that of active mentoring. Since Asian women do not have access to the "old-boy network," they must obtain concrete help and guidance from others who empathize with their situation. Mentoring, networking, lobbying, fundraising, and learning the political process are but some of the ways Asian women can become visible until the time comes when Asian women do not have to count numbers, but see themselves, and are seen by society, as a natural part of the political process.

Appendix: A Chronology of Asian American History

JUDY YUNG

1521   Ferdinand Magellan claims the Philippine Islands for Spain and colonial rule begins in 1565.

1587   First "Luzon Indians" (Filipinos) reportedly set foot on the California coast with Spanish explorer Pedro de Unamuno.

1761   The British defeat the French and gain colonial control of India.

1763   "Manilamen" jump ship in New Orleans.

1778   English explorer Captain James Cook chances upon the 200,000 native inhabitants of the Sandwich Islands, now Hawaii.

1785   Three Chinese seamen land in Baltimore.

1790   First known native of India reported in Salem, Massachusetts.

1790   Naturalization Act of 1790 grants to all "free white persons" the right to U.S. citizenship.

1820   The first group of American missionaries from New England arrives in Hawaii, paving the way for U.S. dominance in the future.

1834   Afong Moy, the first known Chinese woman in the United States, put on display in a New York theater.

1839–   Opium War between China and Britain. China forced to sign the
1842   Treaty of Nanking, opening China to foreign penetration by Western and later Japanese powers.

1843   First known Japanese immigrant arrives in the United States.

1848   First Chinese immigrants—two men and one woman—arrive in San Francisco on the American brig, *Eagle*.

1848–   Gold Rush in California. By 1852, 20,000 Chinese arrive to join in
1853   the Gold Rush. Foreign Miners' Tax imposed in 1850 against the Chinese.

1852   180 Chinese indentured laborers brought to Hawaii to work in the sugar plantations.

1853   Commodore Perry forces Japan to open its ports to foreign trade, ending the 250-year isolation policy of the Tokugawa regime.

1854   In *People v. Hall*, the California Supreme Court rules testimony by Chinese, blacks, mulattos, and Native Americans against whites invalid; later repealed in 1872.

424

1858   French troops invade Vietnam; colonial rule imposed throughout Indochina by August 1884.

1866–   Construction of the first transcontinental railroad with largely Chi-
1869   nese labor. Some 2,000 Chinese workers strike for improved working conditions.

1868   148 (141 men, 6 women, and 1 child) Japanese contracted laborers brought to Hawaii to work in the sugar plantations.

1868–   72,000 Japanese participate in 62 strikes and work stoppages on the
1920   sugar plantations in Hawaii.

1870–   The Anti-Chinese Movement. The Chinese, singled out as scapegoats
1885   during a time of labor unrest, become targets of discriminatory laws and racial violence.

1870   The Rev. Otis Gibson organizes Women's Missionary Society in San Francisco for rescuing Chinese prostitutes; Presbyterian Mission Home for Girls established in 1874.

1875   The Page Law bars prostitutes and coolie labor entry to the United States.

1876   Japan forces Korea open to foreign trade.

1880   California Civil Code amended to prohibit the issuance of a marriage license to a white person and a "Negro, Mulatto, or Mongolian"; Filipinos added in 1933; repealed in 1948.

1882   The Chinese Exclusion Act bans immigration of Chinese laborers to the United States and prohibits Chinese from becoming naturalized citizens; repealed in 1943.

1882   United States negotiates first trade treaty with Korea and approximately 100 students and diplomats from Korea enter the country for training.

1885   The Meiji government officially sanctions the emigration of 30,000 Japanese to Hawaii as contract laborers between 1885 and 1894.

1886   Vietnam incorporated into French Indochina, which later includes Cambodia and Laos.

1889   First two Korean women arrive in the United States—Mrs. Lee Wan-yong and Mrs. Lee Chae-yon, both wives of Korean diplomats.

1898   The Spanish-American War ends with the signing of the Treaty of Paris, giving Cuba, Puerto Rico, and the Philippines to the United States. Filipinos declared "wards" and need no visas to travel to the United States. Filipino wives of Spanish-American War veterans allowed to come as war brides.

1898   United States annexes Hawaii.

1903   93 Korean contract laborers arrive in Hawaii to work in the sugar plantations. Approximately 7,000 Koreans (including 637 women) immigrate to Hawaii between 1903 and 1905, when Japan establishes a protectorate over Korea and formally ends emigration.

1903   Pensionado Act allows Filipino students to come to the United States for education.

1904–   6,000 to 15,000 South Asians, the majority of whom are male farmers
1924   originally from the Punjab province of India, immigrate to the Pacific coast of Canada and the United States.

1905   The Asiatic Exclusion League organizes in San Francisco to prevent the immigration of Asians.

1907   White lumber mill workers drive East Indian workers out of Bellingham, Washington.

1907–   Gentlemen's Agreement between United States and Japan. Japan im-
1908   poses limitations on emigration of Japanese and Korean laborers to the United States, and rights of Japanese insured in America. Wives, including picture brides, and family members are exempted.

1907   210 Filipinos (188 men, 20 women, and 2 children) arrive in Hawaii to work in the sugar plantations. From 1907 to 1924, 46,605 men and 7,187 women immigrate to Hawaii.

1908   Hankuk Puin Hoe, the first Korean women's organization, formed in San Francisco to promote Korean language education, church activities, and Korean solidarity.

1910   Japan annexes Korea.

1910   One woman and two girls arrive in San Francisco from India, bringing the total number of Indian women on the West Coast to six.

1912   Sikh Temple established in Stockton, California.

1913   The California Alien Land Act, aimed at Japanese farmers, bars aliens from owning land; further restrictions are added in 1921 and 1923; repealed in 1948.

1913   Gadar Party ("Party of Rebellion"), founded on Pacific coast by Indian political activists and immigrants, establishes headquarters in San Francisco, and begins publishing weekly newspaper *Hindustan Gadar*.

1914   Padma Chandra becomes first Indian woman to enroll at the University of California, Berkeley.

1916   Kanta Gupta becomes the first Indian woman to apply for U.S. citizenship.

1916   The San Francisco Chinese Young Women's Christian Association (YMCA) is established.

1917   United States enters World War I, three years after its outbreak. In the aftermath of the war, United States, Britain, and Japan become main contenders for control of China, and the Communist movement in Asia is inaugurated.

1917	The 1917 Immigration Act establishes "barred zones" to prohibit immigration of laborers from virtually all of Asia except for Japan.
1918	Act of 9 May 1918, extends the right of naturalization, regardless of race, to one who enlisted and served in the U.S. armed forces.
1918	The Japanese women's monthly *Zaibei Fujin no Tomo* (*Women's Companion in America*) begins publication in Los Angeles.
1919	Korean Americans support the Korean independence movement; Korean Women's Patriotic League in California and Korean Women's Relief Society of Hawaii formed for this purpose.
1920	Japanese and Filipino plantation workers demand an end to race discrimination in pay scales and paid maternity leave for female workers.
1921	The Japanese government voluntarily prohibits female emigration to the United States because of American hostility to picture brides.
1922	*Ozawa v. United States* interprets Japanese aliens as ineligible for U.S. citizenship through naturalization.
1922	The Cable Act provides that woman citizens will lose their U.S. citizenship if they marry aliens ineligible for citizenship; unlike white women, Asian American women cannot regain their U.S. citizenship through naturalization; repealed in 1931.
1923	*United States v. Thind* rules aliens from India ineligible for American citizenship.
1924	Approximately 1,600 Filipino workers go on an eight-month strike, one of the bloodiest strikes up to that time in Hawaii.
1924	Immigration Quota Act excludes all aliens ineligible for citizenship (all Asians except Hawaiians and Filipinos) and allows entry of alien wives of Chinese merchants, but not alien wives of U.S. citizens until 1930, when Public Law 349 admits wives married before 26 May 1924.
1929	Race riots break out around Watsonville, California, against Filipino agricultural laborers.
1931	Filipinos who served in the U.S. armed forces now eligible for U.S. citizenship.
1934	*Morrison v. California* holds Filipinos ineligible for citizenship.
1934	Tydings-McDuffie Act promises independence to the Philippines in ten years and assigns an annual quota of fifty Filipino immigrants.
1935	Congress passes Repatriation Bill to encourage Filipinos to return to their homeland. Only 2,000 Filipinos leave.
1935	Public Law 162 authorizes naturalization of certain resident alien World War I veterans, despite not being white or of African descent.
1938	150 Chinese women garment workers strike for thirteen weeks against

the National Dollar Stores chain and form the first Chinese chapter of the International Ladies' Garment Workers Union (ILGWU).

1938   CIO cannery unions enroll over 1,000 Japanese women members.

1941   Japan attacks Pearl Harbor and the Philippines; United States declares war on Japan.

1942   Executive Order 9066 authorizes the military to prescribe military zones from which persons may be excluded; 112,000 Japanese Americans are incarcerated in ten relocation centers as a result.

1943   Congress repeals Chinese exclusion acts, removes racial bar to naturalization of Chinese aliens, and establishes annual quota of 105 for Chinese immigration to the United States.

1945   The United States drops the atomic bomb on Hiroshima and Nagasaki; Emperor Hirohito submits to unconditional surrender; Korea gains independence.

1945   War Brides Act, GI Fiancees Act, and Act of 9 August 1946 facilitate entrance of Asian war brides, fiancees, and children. An estimated 200,000 Asian war brides immigrate to the United States after World War II.

1946   United States declares the Philippines independent, sets annual immigration quota of 100 for Filipinos and Asian Indians, and grants them the right of naturalization. Manuel Roxas elected president in the Philippines.

1946   Philippine Trade Act grants nonquota immigrant status to Philippine citizens, their spouses, and children who have resided in the United States for a continuous period of three years prior to 30 November 1941.

1947   The British, in granting independence, creates the two nations of India and Pakistan.

1948   The Republic of Korea is formed in the south under Syngman Rhee and the People's Republic of Korea in the north under Kim Il-sung.

1949   The People's Republic of China under Chairman Mao Tse-tung established; Nationalist government of Chiang Kai-shek driven to the island of Taiwan. In subsequent years, Refugee Acts passed to encourage immigration of politically persecuted, highly skilled, and relatives of U.S. citizens.

1950–   Korean Conflict occurs at the 38th parallel border and concludes with
1953   the ratification of the Mutual Defense Treaty, reestablishing the status quo along the 38th parallel.

1950   Act of 19 August 1950 gives spouses and minor children of members of the American armed forces nonquota immigration status if married before 19 March 1952, aiding primarily aliens of Japanese and Korean ancestry. As a result, between 1950 and 1965, 6,423 war brides arrive in the United States.

1952   The McCarran-Walter Act upholds the national-origin quota based on the 1920 U.S. Census but retains the same quotas for Asia-Pacific triangle countries of the 1924 Immigration Act; aliens previously ineligible to citizenship are allowed naturalization rights.

1954   Viet Minh victory at Dien Bien Phu ends the First Indochina War. The Geneva Agreement divides Vietnam into North and South at the 17th parallel. Laos and Cambodia gain independence from France.

1955   Republic of South Vietnam established with Ngo Dinh Diem as president.

1956   Dalip S. Saund of California becomes the first Asian American to be elected to the U.S. Congress.

1964   U.S. involvement in the Vietnam War escalates with the North Vietnamese bombing of two U.S. intelligence ships in the Gulf of Tonkin.

1964   Civil Rights Acts of 1964 and 1965 passed to legislate against racial discrimination.

1965   The Immigration and Naturalization Act of 1965 abolishes the national-origin quotas and substitutes hemispheric quotas; eastern hemisphere quota set at 170,000, with a limit of 20,000 per country.

1965   Voting Rights Act guarantees all citizens equal access to electoral politics.

1965   The Filipino Agricultural Workers Organizing Committee launches strike against thirty-three grape growers near Delano, California, and is later joined by Cesar Chavez's National Farm Workers Association.

1965   Ferdinand Marcos elected president in the Philippines.

1966   President Lyndon Johnson orders the bombing of Hanoi, and the anti-war movement mounts.

1967   The U.S. Supreme Court rules that states cannot outlaw inter-marriages by race.

1968–   Third World student strikes at San Francisco State College and the
1969   University of California, Berkeley, successfully call attention to the need for ethnic studies in the college curriculum; Asian American Studies is inaugurated as a result.

1968   North Vietnam launches Tet offensive. Richard Nixon is elected president and promises to end the war. U.S. troop withdrawals from Vietnam begin in 1969.

1971   Sub-Title II of the McCarran Act, which provides for detention camps, repealed by Congress.

1971   East Pakistan becomes independent nation of Bangladesh.

1972   President Marcos declares martial law in the Philippines, as does President Park in South Korea.

1972   The Shanghai Communique, jointly issued by President Richard Nixon and Premier Chou En-lai, advocates normalization of relations between China and the United States; however, normalization does not take place until 1979.

1972   North-South Korea Peace Agreement announces joint efforts towards peaceful unification of the country without outside interferences.

1972   Title VII of the Civil Rights Act bans discrimination against employees on the basis of race, color, religion, sex, or national origin. Title IX of the Education Amendments forbids sex discrimination in all federally assisted education programs.

1973   A Vietnam peace agreement reached, and direct U.S. military intervention in Indochina ends.

1974   *Lau v. Nichols* rules that school districts must provide children who speak little or no English with special language programs to give them an equal opportunity to education.

1974   Women's Educational Equity Act authorizes funding for model educational programs that overcome sex stereotyping and achieves educational equity for all women.

1975   The Khmer Rouge attacks Phnom Penh, capital city of Cambodia, and a new government is established under Pol Pot. Over one million Cambodians are killed in a reign of terror.

1975   North Vietnam violates the Paris Agreement and attacks South Vietnam, which falls in April. American forces withdraw from Vietnam and Congress passes Public Law 94-23, authorizing the resettlement of 130,000 Southeast Asian refugees under the Indochinese Refugee Assistance Program.

1975–   United Nations' Decade of Women. Asian American delegates partici-
1985   pate in three international conferences to discuss women's issues on a global level.

1976   President Gerald Ford rescinds Executive Order 9066, which authorized the relocation of Japanese Americans from the Pacific coast.

1976   Vietnam proclaims its unification as the Socialist Republic of Vietnam.

1976–   762,100 Southeast Asian refugees, including many who fled by boat,
1985   are resettled in the United States.

1976   *Wong v. Hampton* opens federal jobs to resident aliens.

1977   Iva Ikuko Toguri d'Aquino, alias "Tokyo Rose" and convicted of treason in 1948, pardoned.

1979   President Park assassinated by the chief of KCIA in South Korea; General Chun Doo Hwan seizes control of the government in a military coup and is elected president in 1981.

1979   The Orderly Departure Program set up by the Vietnamese government and United Nations High Commissioner for Refugees to provide a legal alternative for persons desirous of leaving Vietnam.

1980   First national Asian Pacific American women's conference on educational equity held in Washington, D.C.

1980   Asian immigrant women participate in a successful month-long hotel workers' strike in San Francisco.

1980   Commission on Wartime Relocation and Internment of Civilians formed to investigate the justification for the internment of Japanese Americans during World War II. Later findings conclude there was no military necessity for internment.

1981   Martial law lifted in the Philippines; President Marcos elected to a new six-year term.

1982   10,000 Asian garment workers in New York go on a strike that results in an improved union contract.

1982   Twenty-seven-year-old Vincent Chin clubbed to death with a baseball bat after an argument with two white men in a Detroit bar. American Citizens for Justice organizes Asian Americans nationally to protest the light sentences of three years probation and a fine of $3,780 each. After a federal grand jury investigation, Ronald Ebens is sentenced to twenty-five years imprisonment and Michael Nitz is acquitted in 1984. Ebens is later acquitted by the Court of Appeals in Cincinnati in 1986.

1982   President Ronald Reagan establishes a 1982 ceiling of 10,000 Southeast Asian admissions.

1982   Congress passes Public Law 97-359 (American Immigration Act), offering top priority for immigration to children in Korea, Vietnam, Laos, Cambodia, or Thailand known to have been fathered by a U.S. citizen.

1982   The Coalition Government of Democratic Kampuchea formally proclaimed by Prince Norodom Sihanouk.

1983   Benigno Aquino assassinated upon his return to the Philippines.

1983   National Committee for Japanese American Redress files federal lawsuit on behalf of an estimated 120,000 internees, asking for monetary redress.

1983   Fred Korematsu, Minoru Yasui, and Gordon Hirabayashi file federal petitions to reverse their wartime convictions for defying government curfew and internment orders. All convictions subsequently overturned.

1985   Attorney General Edwin Meese proposes amendment to Executive Order 11246 that would prohibit use of goals and timetables by federal contractors in the hiring and promotion of minorities and women.

1986   The Marcos regime in the Philippines falls; Corazon Aquino elected president.

1986   U.S. Civil Rights Commission issues a draft report on the rise of anti-Asian violence—its history, causes, and recommendation that all Americans work together to resolve the problem.

1986   California passes initiative declaring English as the official state language.

1987   Congress passes Simpson-Rodino Immigration Bill, which penalizes employers who knowingly hire illegal aliens and provides amnesty for illegal aliens in the United States since before 1982.

1987   The admissions policy of the University of California at Berkeley under attack as discriminating against Asian American students.

1988   Congress passes bill publicly apologizing for the internment of Japanese Americans during World War II and paying $20,000 to each eligible former internee.

About the Contributors

MEENA ALEXANDER: Alexander was born in India and currently lives and works in New York City. Her poems have appeared in the United States in journals such as *Chelsea, Ikon, Ironwood,* and *New Letters.* Her volume of poems and short prose pieces, *House of a Thousand Doors,* has just been published by Three Continents Press; her long poem *The Storm* is forthcoming from Red Dust Press. Her book *Women in Romanticism* is forthcoming from Macmillan, London. In the spring of 1988 she was poet-in-residence at the Center for American Culture at Columbia University. She is assistant professor of English at Hunter College, CUNY.

VALORIE BEJARANO (NAKAMA): Bejarano was born Valorie Slaughter in Cebu in 1950 and grew up in Los Angeles' Filipino community in everything from Queen contests to the Coalition Against the Marcos Dictatorship. A "Temple Street brat," she attended Virgil, Belmont, and UCLA and has been performing her work for over fifteen years. Her work has been published in *Urthkin, Electrum Misc. Magazine,* and *Ang Katipunan.* While a member of Poets Gathering in Los Angeles she wrote two chapbooks, *Ladies First* and *Before the Sun Comes Up* and co-wrote and produced two poetry shows: *Voices from the Other Side of the Wall* and *Lovers Make the Worst Ex-Husbands.*

CECILIA MANGUERRA BRAINARD: Born and raised in Cebu, Philippines, Brainard migrated to the United States as a graduate student at UCLA. A columnist for the Los Angeles-based *Philippine American News,* she has published essays and stories in the Philippines and the United States. Her short story collection, *Woman With Horns And Other Stories,* was released by New Day Publishers in 1988. Married to a former Philippine Peace Corp Volunteer, Brainard resides with her husband and three sons in Santa Monica, California.

VIRGINIA CERENIO: "I am a second-generation Filipino American and first in the family to be born in the United States. I work at a management consulting firm, where I am a project manager in diverse areas such as social services to the elderly and disabled, bilingual education, and assisting nonprofit organizations. The rest of the time I maintain my soul by writing poetry. Most recently, some of my poems have appeared in *Without Names: A Collection of Poems* (San

434

Francisco: Kearny Street Workshop Press, 1985) and *East Wind Magazine*. I am a member of Kearny Street Workshop and Bay Area Filipino American Writers."

SUCHENG CHAN: Professor of history and director of Asian American Studies at the University of California at Santa Barbara, Chan is the author of *This Bittersweet Soil: The Chinese in California Agriculture, 1860–1910*, which won the 1986 Theodore Saloutos Award in Agricultural History, the 1987 American Historical Association Pacific Coast Branch Book Award, and the 1988 Association for Asian American Studies Book Award. She has also edited four other volumes in ethnic studies and held a Guggenheim Fellowship for 1988–89.

ESTHER NGAN-LING CHOW: Professor of sociology at the American University, Washington, D.C., Chow is a feminist scholar and researcher who has conducted several studies on Asian American women and has published articles on Chinese women, Asian American women, and women of color. In addition to serving as a commissioner of the Montgomery County (Maryland) Commission for Women, Chow is also a community activist who has promoted social services in Chinatown and has been active in developing training models, career and family education, leadership building, and life/stress management for Chinese and Asian American women. She received an Outstanding Women of Color Award from the National Institute of Women of Color in 1984 and an Outstanding Achievement Award from the Organization of Chinese American Women in 1986.

JUDY CHU: Chu holds a doctorate in clinical psychology and now teaches at California State University, Los Angeles, in Asian American studies/sociology and at East Los Angeles College in psychology. She has written numerous articles on Asian American women and co-authored a book, *Linking Our Lives: Chinese American Women in Los Angeles*. She was named by the *Los Angeles Times* as one of the "88 for 1988," one of the rising leaders in Los Angeles County. Active in many community organizations, she founded and chairs the Asian Task Force, United Way. In 1985 she was elected to the Board of Education in the Garvey School District, Los Angeles County. In 1988 she was elected to the City Council of Monterey Park with the highest number of votes.

DOROTHY CORDOVA: A Seattle-born-and-raised mother of eight and grandmother of seven, Cordova heads the Demonstration Project for Asian Americans, a research organization in Seattle. The project collects oral histories and photos documenting the story of Asian immigration to and settlement in America. She produced the photo exhibit "Filipino Women in America, 1860–1985," and also edited the book *Filipino: Forgotten Asian Americans*, by

Fred Cordova. She and her husband are active in the Filipino American community and have worked extensively with youths across the country.

KARTAR DHILLON: Born in Ventura County, California, Dhillon is the daughter of pioneering Sikh émigrés from India. Her father arrived in the United States in 1899; her mother came in 1910. She modestly states, "Other than my origins, there is nothing particularly remarkable about my history."

NANCY DIAO: An immigrant from Beijing, China, Diao became active in the antiwar and Asian American movements during her undergraduate years. After receiving her B.A. in East Asian studies from Princeton in 1975, she entered the University of California, Berkeley, and studied comparative literature. While teaching English as a Second Language in Oakland's Chinatown, and getting involved in community issues, she became disillusioned with academia and left Berkeley for ten years of community organizing and advocacy. She now lives in Oakland with her husband and two children.

PAMELA H.: A native sansei of Los Angeles, Pam loves women, literature, dogs, and sports—especially basketball and racquetball. On sunny days she can be found bicycling on Venice Beach. For the past few years she has been affiliated with Asian/Pacific Lesbians and Gays in Los Angeles and San Francisco Asian lesbian groups. In 1983 she received her B.A. in English literature and women's studies; and in 1986, she graduated from the University of California, Los Angeles, School of Law. She now practices law in Los Angeles.

DENNIS HAYASHI: A Los Angeles native and an attorney with the Asian Law Caucus in California since 1979, Hayashi specializes in labor law. He was one of the lead attorneys in the T & W Fashions Inc. case and also served as an advisor for a videotape on immigrant garment and hotel workers. In addition Hayashi was on the legal team for Fred Korematsu in his successful effort to overturn a World War II conviction for violating the Japanese American relocation and exclusion laws.

K. KAM: Hong Kong-born Kam immigrated to the United States at age two with her parents. She spent her childhood in Colorado and California and graduated from the University of California, Davis, in 1982. After writing "The Hopeland," she toured China extensively and was able to visit her parents' ancestral villages in Chungsan. Having worked in the education and social services fields for three years, she pursued a master's degree in journalism in Syracuse, New York, and is now editor for *California Tomorrow*.

CHUNGMI KIM: An immigrant from Korea, Kim now lives in the Los Angeles area. Her book of poetry, *Chungmi,* was published by Korean Pioneer Press in Los Angeles.

ELAINE H. KIM: Born in New York City, Kim earned her bachelor's degree from the University of Pennsylvania, a master's from Columbia, and a doctorate from the University of California, Berkeley. She is an associate professor of Asian American studies at Berkeley, has chaired the Student Affirmative Action Advisory Committee, and is a member of both the Graduate and Professional Student Affirmative Action Committee and Faculty against Apartheid. Kim is author of *Asian American Literature: An Introduction to the Writings and Their Social Context* (1982). She also was Asian Women United project director for *With Silk Wings,* and helped establish the Korean Community Center in Oakland, Asian Immigrant Women Advocates, and Asian Women United. She lives in Berkeley with her son Oliver.

EVELYN LEE: Lee is on the faculty of the Department of Psychiatry, University of California, San Francisco. She is also chief program director in the Department of Psychiatry at San Francisco General Hospital. Formerly an executive and administrator in Asia as well as in the United States, Lee has over twenty-five years of clinical experience in the treatment of Asian families and has led workshops, made national presentations, and written papers on family therapy, mental health, women in management, and cross-cultural communication.

PATRICIA LEE: Lee is a union representative in San Francisco for the Hotel Employees and Restaurant Employees Union, Local 2. Her labor activism began in 1973 with an organizing drive at an Oakland electronics factory where she was employed as an assembler. In 1975 she started working as a hotel room cleaner, a job category dominated by immigrant and minority women, and was soon elected as shop steward and local executive board member. Serving on the boards of several community organizations, Lee has been an advocate for women workers and immigrant rights in the United States and against sexual exploitation in the Asian tourism industry. The daughter of Toisanese immigrant farmworkers, Lee was raised in Marysville, California.

ANGELA LOBO-COBB: Lobo-Cobb is a poet and fellow at the Women Studies Research Center of the University of Wisconsin-Madison. Her works include *Roots and Rootlessness: Poems of Indian History, Change and Migratory Experience,* published by the Writers Workshop (Calcutta, India, 1983). She works as the editor of The Poetics of Colors series, which includes works such as *A Confluence of Colors: The First Anthology of Wisconsin Minority Poets* (Madison: Blue Reed Arts, 1984) and *Winter Nest: A Poetry Anthology of Midwestern Women Poets of Color* (Madison: Blue Reed Arts, 1987). As a poet, she has geared her efforts toward artistic sharing and a cultural appreciation of the fine arts.

JUANITA TAMAYO LOTT: Lott, who grew up in San Francisco's Japantown and Haight-Ashbury areas, has worked for two decades on policy issues. She is published in social science journals, college texts, and creative writing anthologies. She also chaired San Francisco State College's Pilipino Studies Program (1969), directed the Department of Health, Education, and Welfare's Asian American Affairs Division (1974–1977), and worked for the U.S. Commission on Civil Rights as deputy director of the Women's Rights Program Unit and director of the Program Analysis Division (1978–1982). She is a public policy consultant in Silver Spring, Maryland.

FELICIA LOWE: Lowe is project director of *Carved in Silence,* a documentary on the Angel Island Immigration Station and was producer/director/writer of *China: Land of My Father,* an award-winning documentary filmed in the People's Republic of China. She formerly worked at commercial and public television stations as a broadcast journalist and public affairs program producer.

RASHMI LUTHRA: "I was born in New Delhi, India, on October 29, 1959. Most of my schooling was done in the Philippines. I returned to India and obtained a bachelor's in English literature from Delhi University, received my master's in journalism and mass communication from the University of Wisconsin, Madison, and am continuing at the same school to obtain a doctorate. My research and journalistic writing are geared towards the understanding and transformation of oppressive situations. My major interests include women and the media and feminist approaches to communication and development."

VAN B. LUU: Luu came to the United States at the age of twelve and has lived largely in the Bay Area ever since. After earning a bachelor's degree at the University of California, Berkeley, she spent the fall of 1986 in China, where she researched Chinese economics and development. She notes, "I am also interested in issues within the Asian American society, particularly the lack of information on Vietnamese women."

VALERIE MATSUMOTO: "I was born in the Imperial Valley of California and grew up in Nogales, an Arizona-Mexico border town. Recently I completed a doctorate in U.S. History at Stanford University. My dissertation, 'The Cortez Colony: Family, Farm and Community among Japanese Americans, 1919–1982,' is a study of three generations in a Central California agricultural settlement."

SUCHETA MAZUMDAR: Born in India, Mazumdar obtained her doctorate in Chinese history from the University of California, Los Angeles, and recently joined the faculty of the State University of New York, Albany. Awarded a

438

fellowship at Harvard University, Mazumdar is writing a book on China's economic history. She has also published works about Asian immigration history and Asian women. She and her husband, Vasant Kaiwar, helped establish and still publish the *South Asia Bulletin*. On the board of Everywoman's Shelter, Los Angeles, she feels her experience as an activist helped alter her self-identity from that of a foreigner to that of an Asian American.

JANICE MIRIKITANI: Mirikitani, a sansei, or third-generation Japanese American, is a poet, choreographer, teacher, and community organizer. She is program director and president of the Corporation at Glide Church/Urban Center. In her work as writer and editor for the past fifteen years, she has edited several anthologies, including *Aion Magazine, Third World Women, Time to Greez: Incantations from the Third World,* and *Ayumi: Four Generations of Japanese in America.* Mirikitani's first book of poetry and prose, *Awake in the River* (Isthmus Press) is in its third printing. Her latest book is *Shedding Silence: Poetry and Prose* (Celestial Arts Publishing, 1987).

KESAYA E. NODA: A sansei writer born in California, Noda was raised in rural New Hampshire. She learned Japanese after graduating from high school, when she spent nearly two years living and studying in Japan. Following college, she researched and wrote *The Yamato Colony,* a history of the California community where her grandparents settled and her parents were raised. She then returned to Japan for a year of work and travel. Noda has received a master's degree from Harvard Divinity School and is now working at Lesley College, in the Boston area.

GAIL M. NOMURA: Nomura is director of the Asian/Pacific American Studies Program and holds a joint appointment with the Department of Comparative American Cultures and the Department of History at Washington State University. She holds a Ph.D. in history from the University of Hawaii. She has published articles on Hawaii and Pacific Northwest Asian American history in *Amerasia Journal, The Journal of Ethnic Studies, Women's Studies: An Interdisciplinary Journal,* and several anthologies. A sansei born in Hawaii, she is married to another Hawaiian sansei and academic, Stephen H. Sumida. The birth of their daughter, Emi, in 1984 has done much to teach Nomura the realities of working women's history.

GLORIA OBERST: Oberst holds a master's degree in social work and is at present on the staff of Kaiser Permanente Mideical Center, San Francisco.

MYRNA PEÑA-REYES: Filipina poet Peña-Reyes lives in Eugene, Oregon. She was born and raised in the Philippines. She came to the United States for graduate studies and earned an M.F.A. in creative writing from the University of Oregon. She has taught creative writing and literature in the Philippines and the United States and has been published in both countries. She is married to William T. Sweet, also a poet, whom she met in graduate school.

BARBARA M. POSADAS: Posadas, the daughter of a Filipino father and a Polish American mother, was born and raised in Chicago. She is a specialist in U.S. urban/social history and holds a doctorate from Northwestern University. Since 1974 she has been a member of the history department at Northern Illinois University. She is director of the department's M.A. Option in Historical Administration and a former member of the Illinois Historic Sites Advisory Council. Her articles on Chicago suburbanization and the Filipino old-timer community have appeared in *Labor History, Amerasia Journal, Chicago History,* and the *Illinois Historical Journal.* In 1982 she held a Senior Fulbright Research Grant for research in the Philippines. She is married to Roland L. Guyotte, also a U.S. historian.

JONNY SULLIVAN PRICE: Born in Yokohama, Japan, of a Japanese mother and American GI father, Price was raised and educated in the United States. She earned her B.A. degree in drama and theater from the University of Hawaii and an M.F.A. in writing from Sarah Lawrence College, where she studied with Jean Valentine and Galway Kinnell. Price lives with her husband and three children in Ohio.

NILDA RIMONTE: In 1978 Rimonte founded the Pacific-Asian Rape and Battering Line, which later became the Center for the Pacific-Asian Family. She then established the first shelter for Pacific Asians in the United States and Women Entrepreneurs, a self-employment and business development program for women. In 1985 she developed the first child abuse treatment and prevention program for Pacific Asians in Los Angeles. Rimonte was born and raised in the Philippines.

SAKAE S. ROBERSON: Roberson writes for garnets, sapphires, and "other jewels we call our mothers, our sisters, our lovers." A graduate of Mills College and the University of Southern California, she is from a multicultural, multiracial heritage and defines herself as a "communicator who hopes to transcend race, ethnicity, economic and social class differences" through her work.

R. A. SASAKI: Sasaki grew up in the Richmond District of San Francisco. She has a master's degree in creative writing from San Francisco State University and her fiction has been published in *Transfer* magazine and the *Short Story Review.* "The Loom" won the American Japanese National Literary Award in 1983.

YOICHI SHIMATSU: Shimatsu is a freelance writer and researcher who has contributed to several film and book projects on Asian America. He is a consultant to the Pacific and Asian American Center for Theology and Strategies in Berkeley, directing publications production and coordinating the immigrant counseling program for ethnic churches.

BEHEROZE F. SHROFF: Born in India, Shroff studied for her bachelor's and master's degrees in English literature at St. Xavier College in Bombay. After teaching English in Bombay and acting with a Gujerati-language theater company, she came to the United States in 1975 and changed from English studies to film and television production. An independent filmmaker in Los Angeles, Shroff directed *Sweet Jail: The Sikhs of Yuba City,* a documentary on the East Indian/Sikh immigrant community of Northern California. She has continued to write poetry while working on her films.

CATHY SONG: Song was born in 1955 in Honolulu, Hawaii. She received a B.A. from Wellesley College and an M.A. from Boston University. Her first book, *Picture Bride* (1983), won the Yale Series of Younger Poets Award and was nominated for a National Book Critics Circle Award. She currently lives in Denver, Colorado.

BRENDA PAIK SUNOO: Sunoo, a third-generation Korean American, is a human rights advocate, lecturer, and journalist. In June 1984 she was a member of the first Korean American delegation to visit the Democratic People's Republic of Korea. She and her husband, Jan, have two sons, David and Tommy. Sunoo is currently a copy editor with the *Korea Times* (English section) in Los Angeles.

RENEE E. TAJIMA: Tajima is the producer of a public television documentary "Adopted Son: The Death of Vincent Chin." She is a free-lance writer and associate editor of *The Independent Film and Video Monthly* and runs the Film News Now Foundation with filmmaker Christine Choy. Formerly editor of *Bridge: Asian American Perspectives,* and director of Asian Cine-Vision, where she founded the first Asian American International Video Festival, Tajima has written for *American Film,* edited *Journey Across Three Continents: Black and African Films, Anthology: Asian American Film and Video,* and is editing the second edition of *Reel Change: Guide to Social Issue Media.*

KITTY TSUI: "I was born in the City of Nine Dragons in the Year of the Dragon, spent my childhood in England and Hong Kong, and immigrated to Gold Mountain in 1969. I am a competitive bodybuilder, a writer, artist, actor, and the author of *The Words of a Woman Who Breathes Fire* (San Francisco: Spinsters Ink, 1983)."

JYOTSNA VAID: Vaid received her Ph.D. in experimental psychology from McGill University in 1982 and has done postdoctoral research in psycholinguistics at the University of California, San Diego, and the Salk Institute for Biological Studies. She has also edited a quarterly newsletter, *The Committee on South Asian Women Bulletin,* which is circulated internationally, and in 1984 coedited a monograph *South Asian Women at Home and Abroad: A Guide to Resources,* with Barbara Miller and Janice Hyde. She is currently on the faculty at Texas A & M University.

CHEA VILLANUEVA: Villanueva's father was born in the Philippines (Luzon); her mother is an American of Irish descent. Villanueva enjoys karate and art. She was born in Philadelphia and moved to New York in 1982 to pursue her writing career. A lesbian feminist, she is the author of *Girlfriends* and *The Things I Never Told You.*

VENNY VILLAPANDO: Villapando received his journalism degree from the University of the Philippines and a master's in ethnic studies from Goddard University. He works full time as editor of the *Hawaii Laborer,* a monthly union publication, and writes for the *Honolulu Star Bulletin* on a free-lance basis. He also produces and hosts a weekly local Filipino television program which is broadcast throughout Hawaii. He resides in Honolulu with his wife, Jessica, and son, Norman.

REBECCA VILLONES: Villones has been active in community politics for many years. An educator and formerly a member of the Human Relations Commission of Santa Clara County, she is active in Philippine support work and has worked for four years with the United Electrical Worker Organizing Committee in its attempts to organize electronics workers.

MARCELLE WILLIAMS: Williams was born and raised in Stanislaus County, California. She received her bachelor's and master's degrees in cultural anthropology from the University of California, Berkeley, where she is also working towards the completion of a doctoral degree. She plans to compare the rural California Sikhs with her own ethnic group—"Okies"—who worked, and often continue to work, in the same fields and factories.

DIANE YEN-MEI WONG: A lawyer, journalist, and community activist, Wong is the national executive director of the Asian American Journalists Association and was director of Asian Women United. She has also edited a Bay Area Asian American newspaper and written two books of questions and answers for Asian American girls. Originally from Seattle, she practiced law and served as director of the State Commission on Asian American Affairs. Wong and her husband, sansei attorney Dale Minami, live in Oakland, California, with their two cats.

KATHY WONG: "I was born in San Francisco and raised in Chinatown on Stockton Street, the North Beach in Paw Paw's Prescott Court flat, and the Sunset District in Hing's Hand Laundry. I now live in Seattle and work as director of the Denise Louie Child Care center in the International District, the only Asian multilingual, multicultural early childhood education program in the city. When I'm not slugging and confronting heads of Seattle for more services for minority children, you'll find me slugging softballs and fast-breaking down court. I authored *Don't Put Vinegar in the Copper,* a bilingual children's book, and a second children's book will soon be published."

NELLIE WONG: "Born in the Year of the Dog, committed to the struggles of my Toisanese forbears, I am a socialist feminist poet/writer/activist who's published two collections of poetry, *Dreams in Harrison Railroad Park* and *The Death of Long Steam Lady* (West End Press, 1986). Politics and art inform my commitment to radical social change via Radical Women and the Freedom Socialist Party. Falling like confetti on New Year's night, the *sze yip* voices of my fore-mothers form the words and images which imprint themselves on that precious invention: paper."

DEBORAH WOO: Woo is an assistant professor at the University of California, Santa Cruz. Her research interests include the politics of culture and cross-cultural issues in mental health. She earned her doctorate in Sociology from the University of California, Berkeley.

WAKAKO YAMAUCHI: A resident of Gardena, California, Yamauchi simply states, "I write short stories and plays." Her works have appeared in ethnic journals and papers and in several anthologies. Among her plays are "And the Soul Shall Dance," "The Music Lessons," "12-1-A," and "Memento."

SUN BIN YIM: A visiting scholar at the Asian American Studies Center of the University of California, Los Angeles, Yim has participated in several Asian American and Korean American studies conferences and published several papers on Korean women in America. Born in Korea, she earned her B.A. degree from Ehwa Women's University and completed her graduate work in sociology at the University of California, Santa Barbara and Los Angeles. In 1974 she received a Rockefeller Foundation Research Fellowship and in 1975 a Ford Foundation Teaching Fellowship.

CONNIE YOUNG YU: Historian and writer Yu has contributed to numerous publications. Her work on Chinese American history and Asian America have appeared in the *Civil Rights Digest, Amerasia,* and a women's anthology, *Working It Out.* She wrote *Profiles in Excellence* (Stanford Area Chinese Club, 1986), a collection of biographies of Chinese Americans, and produced a videotape on domestic violence with the Asian Law Alliance. She is active in the Angel Island Immigration Station Advisory Committee. Married and a mother of three, she also writes poetry and fiction.

JUDY YUNG: Born and raised in San Francisco, Yung is a librarian, historian, and writer with a special interest in Chinese American history. She is the author of *Chinese Women of America: A Pictorial History* (Seattle: University of Washington Press, 1986) and co-author of *Island: Poetry and History of Chinese Immigrants on Angel Island, 1910–1940* (San Francisco: Chinese Culture Foundation, 1980). She was the project director for *Making Waves* and is now doing doctorate work in ethnic studies at the University of California, Berkeley.

Notes

General Introduction: A Woman-Centered Perspective on
Asian American History/Sucheta Mazumdar

1. See also Emma Gee et al., eds., *Asian Women* (Berkeley, University of California Press, 1971); Elaine Kim et al., *With Silk Wings* (San Francisco: Asian Women United, 1983). I would also like to thank friends and colleagues at the Bunting Institute (1986–87) for their comments at the presentation on Asian American women.
2. The section title here uses Ruthanne Lum McCunn, *Thousand Pieces of Gold* (Boston: Beacon Press, 1989). A biographical novel about a Chinese woman pioneer in Idaho.
3. Mary Coolidge, *Chinese Immigration* (Tapei: Ch'eng-Wen, 1968), 502 (reprint).
4. Walter Bean, *California: An Interpretive History* (New York: McGraw Hill, 1973), 168.
5. Thomas Chinn et al., *A History of the Chinese in California* (San Francisco: Chinese Historical Society of America, 1975), 61.
6. Rosalyn Baxandall et al., eds., *America's Working Women* (New York: Vintage Books, 1976), 93.
7. Curt Gentry, *The Madames of San Francisco* (Garden City, N.Y.: Doubleday, 1964), 57.
8. Lucie Cheng, "Chinese Immigrant Women in Nineteenth Century California," in *Asian and Pacific American Experiences: Women's Perspectives*, ed. Nobuya Tsuchida (Minneapolis: Asian/Pacific American Learning Resource Center, 1982), 39.
9. Joan Hori, "Japanese Prostitution in Hawaii during the Immigration Period," in *Asian and Pacific American Experiences*, 56–65.
10. In Eureka a Chinese woman was beaten and blinded by an angry white man. See Judy Yung, *Chinese Women of America: A Pictorial History* (Seattle: University of Washington Press, 1986), 25.
11. See Leonore Davidoff, "Class and Gender in Victorian England," in Judith Newton et al., eds., *Sex and Class in Women's History* (London: Routledge and Kegan Paul, 1983).

446

12. See essay by Renee Tajima in this volume.

13. Heizer and Almquist, *The Other Californians* (Berkeley: University of California Press, 1977), 164.

14. Chinn, *History of the Chinese,* 27.

15. The section title here uses Fumiko Enchi, *The Waiting Years,* trans. John Bester (Tokyo: Kodansha International, 1971). A novel depicting the discrimination and oppression of women in Meiji Japan.

16. Maxine Hong Kingston, *Woman Warrior* (New York: Vintage Books, 1975), 4–8.

17. Coolidge, *Chinese Immigration,* 19.

18. Marlon Kau Hom, "Some Cantonese Folksongs on the American Experience," in *Western Folklore* (1983), 130.

19. Miriam Sharma, "Labor Migration and Class Formation among Filipinas in Hawaii, 1906–1946" in Lucie Cheng and Edna Bonacich, eds., *Labor Immigration under Capitalism* (Berkeley: University of California Press, 1984), 583. See also essay by Gail Nomura in this volume.

20. Jovina Navarro, "Immigration of Filipino Women to America" in *Asian American Women* (Palo Alto: Stanford University, May 1976), 19–20.

21. Karen Leonard, "Marriage and Family Life among Early Asian Indian Immigrants" in *From India to America,* S. Chandrasekar, ed. (La Jolla: Population Review Publications, 1982), 67.

22. Jane Singh, oral history, South and Southeast Asian Studies Center, University of California, Berkeley, Gadhar Archives.

23. Him Mark Lai et al., trans., *Island: Poetry and History of Angel Island 1910–1940* (San Francisco: Hoc Doi, 1980), 38.

24. Emma Gee, "Issei Women," in Emma Gee et al., eds., *Counterpoint* (Los Angeles: Asian American Studies Center, UCLA, 1976), 359.

25. John Liu, "Asian Labor in Hawaii 1850 to 1900," in Cheng and Bonacich, *Labor Immigration,* 195.

26. Ronald Takaki, *Pau Hana* (Honolulu: University of Hawaii Press, 1983), 26.

27. Linda Pomerantz, "The Background of Korean Emigration," in Cheng and Bonacich, *Labor Immigration,* 300.

28. Gee, "Issei Women," 361.

29. Harold H. Sunoo and Sonia S. Sunoo, "The Heritage of the First Korean Women Immigrants in the United States, 1903–1929," in *Koreans in America* 2, Korean Christian scholars journal (1976), 149.

30. The subtitle here combines the titles of two important sources: Akemi Kikumura, *Through Harsh Winters: The Life of a Japanese Immigrant Woman* (Novato, Calif.: Chandler and Sharp Publishers, 1981), a study of her mother's life and struggles; and *Land of Sunshine,* a California journal of the

1890s that published the work of Amerasian Sui Sin Far (Edith Eaton), who wrote about the lives of early Chinese immigrant women in San Francisco. Far's best known collection is *Mrs. Spring Fragrance* (Chicago: A. C. McClurg and Co., 1912).

31. Cheng, "Chinese Immigrant Women," 49.

32. Brett Melendy, *Asians in America: Filipinos, Koreans, and East Indians* (Boston: Twayne Publishers, 1981), 162.

33. Sunoo and Sunoo, "First Korean Women," 154.

34. Evelyn Nakano Glenn, "The Dialectics of Wage Work: Japanese American Women and Domestic Service, 1905–1940," *Feminist Studies* 6, no. 3 (Fall 1980): 443.

35. Section subtitle in Baxandall, *America's Working Women*, 153, which provides an overview of American agriculture.

36. Kikumura, *Through Harsh Winters*, 30–32.

37. Cheng, "Chinese Immigrant Women," 46–47.

38. Takaki, *Pau Hana*, 77–78.

39. Bong-Youn Choy, *Koreans in America* (Chicago: Nelson Hall, 1979), 321.

40. Yamato Ichihashi, *Japanese in the United States* (New York: Arno Press and the *New York Times*, 1969), 280.

41. Gail Nomura, "Tsugiki, A Grafting," *Women's Studies: An Interdisciplinary Journal* (Summer 1987): 20–21.

42. Michi Weglyn, *Years of Infamy* (New York: William Morrow, 1976), 77.

43. Janice Mirikitani, ed., *Ayumi: A Japanese American Anthology: Poetry from the American Relocation Camp Experience* (San Francisco: The Japanese American Anthology Committee, 1980), 87.

44. Baxandall, *America's Working Women*, 284.

45. Judy Chu and Susie Ling in *Linking Our Lives* (Chinese Historical Society of Southern California, 1984).

46. Until 1948 California was one of thirty-nine states which forbade the marriage of whites with nonwhites, including Chinese, Filipino, Japanese, Korean, and South Asians. See Jesse Quinsaat et al., eds., *Letters in Exile: An Introductory Reader on the History of Pilipinos in America* (Los Angeles: Asian American Studies Center, UCLA, 1976), 41; Chinn, *History of the Chinese*, 27; Ichihashi, *Japanese in the United States*, 216–217; and Leonard, "Marriage and Family Life," 65.

47. Interview with author, 1986.

48. Interview with author, 1986.

49. The term "yellow peril," reflective of the prewar hostility directed towards Asian Americans, was a term widely used to support discriminatory legislation against Asians.

50. William L. Tung, *The Chinese in America, 1870–1973: A Chronology and Fact Book* (Dobbs Ferry, N.Y.: Oceana Publications, 1974), 82.

51. Juanita Tamayo Lott, *Beyond Stereotypes and Statistics: Emergence of Asian and Pacific American Women* (Washington, D.C.: Organization of Pan Asian American Women, 1979), 2.

52. Victor Nee and Brett deBary Nee, *Longtime Californ': A Documentary Study of an American Chinatown* (Boston: Houghton Mifflin, 1974), xxiii.

53. Nee and Nee, *Longtime Californ'*, 300–301.

54. Ibid., 313–314. Union activists in Chinatown have had a difficult time organizing workers. The anticommunist mood of the 1950s had placed labor organizers under government scrutiny and suspicion. The prevailing conservative political climate allowed the anti-unionism of the employers to be interpreted as righteous anticommunism. Even today, the fear of being branded a political undesirable hampers the many immigrant women in the garment and restaurant industries from asserting their rights. See Peter Kwong, *Chinatown: New York Labor and Politics, 1930–1950* (New York: Monthly Review Press, 1979), 140–147.

55. See Judy Yung, oral history collection; and Kikumura, *Through Harsh Winters*, 15–19.

56. Kim, *With Silk Wings*, 124.

57. Proshanta K. Nandi, "The World of an Invisible Minority: Pakistanis in America," *California Sociologist* 3, no. 2 (Summer 1980): 159.

58. Shamita Das Dasgupta, "Marching to a Different Drummer? Sex Role Orientation of Indian Women in the U.S.," *Committee on South Asian Women Bulletin* (1985), 15–17.

59. See Kikumura, *Through Harsh Winters*, 134; and Eui Young Yu et al., eds., *Koreans in Los Angeles: Prospects and Promises* (Los Angeles: Center for Korean American and Korean Studies, California State University, 1982), 146.

60. Nee and Nee, *Longtime Californ'*, 278.

61. "Immigrants," *Time*, 8 July 1985, 42.

62. Chu and Ling, *Linking Our Lives*, 84.

63. Robert Seto Quan, *Lotus among Magnolias: Mississippi Chinese* (Jackson: University Press of Mississippi, 1982), 18.

64. Yu, *Koreans in Los Angeles*, 54–55. This type of self-employed venture has become the single largest job category for Korean women. Nearly one in eight Korean Americans is self-employed, the highest level for any ethnic group, though the success story of Korean entrepreneurs pales somewhat when one considers the sheer number of unpaid labor hours that go into the operation of such businesses. See "Immigrants," *Time*, 41–42.

65. Suvarna Thaker, "The Quality of Life of Asian Indian Women in the Motel Industry," *South Asia Bulletin* II, no. 1 (1982): 68–73.

66. Sun Bin Yim, *Korean Women in America* (Seoul, Korea: Ehwa University, 1978).

67. Nee and Nee, 314.

68. *Sewing Woman*, title of Arthur Dong's film portrayal of the life of a Chinese immigrant garment worker.

69. Chu and Ling, *Linking Our Lives*, 88.

70. Belinda Aquino, "Occupational Mobility of Filipino Women Workers in Hawaii," *Journal of Asian Pacific and World Perspectives* 4, no. 1 (1980): 33.

71. Rachel Grossman, "Changing Role of South East Asian Women," *South East Asia Chronicle and Pacific Resource*, 66 (January–February 1979).

72. An initial glance shows impressive gains; a second glance reveals a more dismal picture. In the early 1970s less than 4 percent of the nation's lawyers were women (all races); a decade later the figure rose to 16 percent, but only about 5 percent of female lawyers are partners at the more prestigious law firms. In 1960 women made up less than 7 percent of the nation's doctors; the number now exceeds 13 percent, but 47 percent of all female doctors (compared to only 24 percent of male doctors) work in hospital-based positions, which are salaried and have limited mobility. Middle management women with M.B.A. degrees working in manufacturing earn as much as $18,000 *less* a year than men with equal qualifications a decade after entering at equal pay levels. See Mary Ann Devanna, Interview and abstract of forthcoming study, *San Francisco Chronicle*, 23 July 1985.

73. Pauline Fong and Amado Cabezas, *Selected Statistics on Asian American Women* (San Francisco: Asian Inc., 1976).

74. Nobuko Miyamoto, "Ballad" (presented at the performance art program "Immigrants and Survivors," by Suzanne Lacy, Los Angeles, 1983); see also *Los Angeles Times*, 23 June 1983, 5:22.

75. See for example an interview quoted in Nee and Nee, *Longtime Californ'*, 163; second incident described in Jean Wakatsuki Houston and James D. Houston, *Farewell to Manzanar* (Boston: Houghton Mifflin, 1973).

76. See Linda Wong, "The Esther Lau Trial: A Case of Oppression and Sexism," *Amerasia* 3, no. 1 (1975): 16–26; Kim, *With Silk Wings*, 93; and Redress and Reparation Hearings, *Amerasia* 8, no. 2 (1981): 53–105; *India West*, 29 May 1987.

77. See Kim, *With Silk Wings*, 125; and Alice Chai, "Korean Women in Hawaii, 1903–1945," in *Asian and Pacific American Experiences*, 82.

78. Kala Bagai, oral history recorded by author, 1978.

79. In New Jersey and New York in particular racial violence against visible minorities has escalated in recent years. In addition to Howard Beach and the murder of black men by white youths, there have been several incidents targeting Asian Indians. (See *New York Times,* 12 October 1987 and 26 June 1988.) A group calling itself the "Dotbusters" (referring to the dot on the forehead that Hindu women wear as a symbol of marriage) has attacked Indian women repeatedly. There have been several severe beatings of men and women; a man died from one such attack.

The World of Our Grandmothers/Connie Young Yu

1. B. E. Lloyd, *Lights and Shades in San Francisco* (San Francisco: San Francisco Press, 1878).
2. Under the Chinese Exclusion Act of 1882, Chinese laborers could no longer immigrate to America. Until the act was repealed in 1943, only merchants, diplomats, students, and visitors were allowed to enter.
3. Between 1910 and 1940 Chinese immigrants arriving in the port of San Francisco were detained at the Angel Island Immigration Station to await physical examinations and interrogation to determine their right to enter this country. Prior to 1910 immigrants were detained in a building on the wharf known as "the shed."
4. Chinese pastries.
5. The Immigration Act of 1924 affected all Asians who sought to immigrate to the United States. Congress repealed the law as to Chinese in 1943, and then in 1952 through the McCarran-Walter Act as to other Asian ethnic groups.

Voices from the Past: Why They Came/Dorothy Cordova

1. The "First Wave" (1763–1906) of Filipino immigrants were primarily "seafaring exiles and working sojourners" who settled in the United States, including Alaska and Hawaii. See Fred Cordova, *Filipinos: Forgotten Asian Americans* (Dubuque, Iowa: Kendall-Hunt, 1983), 10, 14–15.
2. Ibid., 23.
3. Ibid., 20.
4. Ibid., 153.

Korean Immigrant Women in
Twentieth-Century America/Sun Bin Yim

1. Unlike the early Chinese and Japanese female immigration, there did not appear to be a phase of "prostitute migration" for Koreans. For the period

1906 to 1924 the *New Korea* newspaper, published weekly out of San Francisco, contained only one story referring to prostitutes and the identity of these prostitutes was not revealed. In 1907 Koreans in Sacramento passed a regulation that "prohibited Koreans from going to the Chinese area because they could learn immoral behavior," suggesting that Koreans had been in Chinese-owned brothels. See *New Korea*, 12 May 1906 and 27 September 1907. The *New Korea* (*Shinhan-Minbo*) was established in 1905 and contained accounts in Korean about community affairs, marriages, births, and deaths. The author translated pertinent articles for this essay. See also Lucie Cheng, "Free, Indentured, Enslaved: Chinese Prostitutes in Nineteenth-Century America," in Lucie Cheng and Edna Bonacich, eds., *Labor Immigration Under Capitalism* (Berkeley: University of California Press, 1984), 402–434; and Yuji Ichioka, "Japanese Prostitutes in Nineteenth-Century America," *Amerasia Journal* 4:1 (1977): 1–21.

2. The primary source for this study was a series of personal interviews in Korean with eight early Korean immigrant women. The interviews were conducted in California in 1978.

3. In 1922 the age category was changed from zero to thirteen to zero to fourteen.

4. Kyoo Whan Hyun, *A History of Korean Wanderers and Emigrants* (Korea: Samwha Publishers, 1976).

5. U.S. Commissioner General of Immigration, *Annual Reports* (Washington, D.C., 1899–1925). See also U.S. Immigration Commission, *Statistical Review of Immigration 1820–1910* (Washington, D.C., 1911).

6. U.S. Bureau of the Census, "Statistics by Subject," *Fifteenth Census of the United States, 1930: Population* (Washington, D.C., 1933); and *Fifteenth Census of the United States, 1930: Outlying Territories and Possessions* (Washington, D.C., 1932). In Hawaii the number of Korean men to 100 women dropped from 241 in 1920 to 162 in 1930. In California the ratio declined from 261 in 1920 to 168 in 1930.

7. For example, see *New Korea*, 5 July 1911, 15 August 1913, 12 March 1914, and 18 December 1917.

8. *New Korea*, 23 July 1914.

9. U.S. Bureau of the Census, *Fifteenth Census, 1930: Population;* and *1930: Outlying Territories and Possessions*.

10. Ibid.

11. Two of the eight women interviewed were not picture brides.

12. *New Korea*, 3 June 1908.

13. *New Korea*, 18 April 1918. It is also interesting to note that there were no

editorial comments decrying the divorce, presumably because it was an interracial marriage.

14. See Sonia Sunoo, "Korean Women Pioneers of the Pacific Northwest," *Oregon Historical Quarterly* (Spring 1978): 51–63; and *New Korea*, 18 September 1909.
15. *New Korea*, 4 February 1915.
16. High fertility of the Korean population in 1914 was mentioned in the *New Korea* (22 October 1914), but no evidence was presented. Birth rates derived from data on age and marital status in the 1930 U.S. census, however, do support the claim. In Hawaii the ratio of children under five years old per 1,000 married women fifteen years of age and older increased from 892 in 1910 to 1,135 in 1920. Mainland data are not sufficient to draw conclusions.
17. *New Korea*, 9 November 1910.
18. Ibid., 22 January 1908.
19. Sun Bin Yim, "The Social Structure of Korean Communities in California, 1903–1920," in Cheng and Bonacich, *Labor Immigration*, 515–548.
20. U.S. Immigration Commission Reports, *Immigrants in Industries* (Washington, D.C., 1911). While it is questionable whether the overall figures reflect accurately the number of Korean farm laborers, the reported ratio of women to men is fairly accurate.
21. Sun Bin Yim, "The Social Structure of Korean Communities in California."
22. Sunoo, "Korean Women Pioneers."

The Hardships of Escape for Vietnamese Women/Van Luu

1. U.S. Committee for Refugees, *Vietnamese Boat People: Pirates' Vulnerable Prey* (Washington, D.C., February 1984), 1.
2. Lani Davidson, "Women Refugees: Special Needs and Programs," *Journal of Refugee Resettlement* 1 (1981): 17.
3. Kasumi Hirayama, "Effects of the Employment of Vietnamese Refugee Wives on Their Family Roles and Mental Health" (Ph.D. diss., University of Pennsylvania, 1980), 156.
4. Lynelle Burmark-Parasurman, *Interfacing Two Cultures: Vietnamese and Americans* (California: Alameda County, 1982), 58.
5. Burmark-Parasurman, *Interfacing Two Cultures*, 58.
6. Bill Soiffer, "Viet Mental Health Project in a Bind," *San Francisco Chronicle*, 14 January 1980, 7.
7. Scott Stone and John McGowan, *Wrapped in the Wind Shawl: Refugees of Southeast Asia and the Western World* (San Rafael: Presidio Press, 1980), 39.

8. Bruce Grant, *The Boat People: An Age Investigation of Bruce Grant* (New York: Penguin Books, 1979), 80.

9. Ibid., 63–64.

10. Ibid., 65.

11. Nhat Tien, Thuy Vu, and Duong Phuc, "Report on the Kro-Kra Trial" (Unpublished report compiled by the Boat People S.O.S. Committee, San Diego, 1980).

12. This and subsequent interviews were conducted in Vietnamese by the author in 1985.

13. Barry Wain, *The Refused: the Agony of the Indochina Refugees* (New York: Simon and Schuster, 1981), 71.

14. Eve Burton, "Surviving the Flight of Horror: The Story of Refugee Women," *Indochina Issue* (February 1982), 1.

15. U.S. Committee for Refugees, *Vietnamese Boat People*, 6.

16. Burton, "Flight of Horror," 2.

17. Ibid., 1.

18. Hirayama, "Effects of Employment," 4.

19. Ibid., 13.

20. Gia Thuy Vuong, *Getting to Know the Vietnamese and Their Culture* (New York: Frederick Ungar Publishing Co., 1976), 23.

21. Daniel Dinh Phuoc Le, "Vietnamese Refugees' Perceptions and Methods for Coping with Mental Illness" (Ph.D. diss., United States International University, 1979), 41.

22. Davidson, "Women Refugees," 17.

23. John Hubner and Carol Rafferty, "After the Storm," *San Jose Mercury News*, 17 October 1982.

24. Davidson, "Women Refugees," 18.

25. Hirayama, "Effects of Employment," 144.

Nisei Women and Resettlement
during World War II/Valerie Matsumoto

1. This essay is excerpted from a fuller treatment of the World War II experiences of nisei women, "Japanese American Women during World War II," in *Frontiers* 8, no. 1 (1984): 6–14. Recent works examining the wartime experiences of nisei women include Yoshiko Uchida's *Desert Exile: The Uprooting of a Japanese American Family* (Seattle: University of Washington Press, 1982) and Joy Kogawa's novel dealing with the experiences of the Canadian Japanese, *Obasan* (Boston: David Godine, 1982).

2. The personal letters, which comprise a major portion of my research, were

written in English by nisei women in their late teens and twenties. Their writing reflects the experience and concerns of their age group. It is important, however, to remember that they wrote these letters to Caucasian friends and sponsors during a time of great insecurity and psychological and economic hardship. In their struggle to be accepted as American citizens, the evacuated Japanese Americans were likely to minimize their suffering in the camps and to try to project a positive image of their adjustment to the traumatic conditions.

3. Sources on evacuation: Robert A. Wilson and Bill Hosokawa, *East to America: A History of the Japanese in the United States* (New York: William Morrow, 1980); Audrie Girdner and Anne Loftis, *The Great Betrayal: The Evacuation of the Japanese Americans during World War II* (Toronto: Macmillan, 1969); Michi Weglyn, *Years of Infamy: The Untold Story of America's Concentration Camps* (New York: William Morrow, 1976); Daisuke Kitagawa, *Issei and Nisei: The Internment Years* (New York: Seabury Press, 1967); Roger Daniels, *The Decision to Relocate the Japanese Americans* (Philadelphia: J. B. Lippincott, 1975).

4. Susan M. Hartmann, *The Home Front and Beyond: American Women in the 1940s* (Boston: Twayne Publishers, 1982), 125.

5. Many Japanese community leaders were arrested by the FBI before the evacuation and interned in special all-male camps in North Dakota, Louisiana, and New Mexico. Some Japanese Americans living outside the perimeter of the western defense zone, in such states as Arizona and Utah, were not interned. For an account of Latin American Japanese who were seized and interned in secret camps in the United States, see C. Harvey Gardiner, *Pawns in a Triangle of Hate: The Peruvian Japanese and the United States* (Seattle: University of Washington Press, 1981).

6. In the relocation camps, doctors, teachers, and other professionals were at the top of the low pay scale, earning nineteen dollars per month. The majority of workers received sixteen dollars and apprentices earned twelve dollars.

7. Until 1948 California's antimiscegenation law prohibited marriage between Caucasians and persons of Asian and Mexican descent. For detailed discussion, see Megumi Dick Osumi, "Asians and California's Anti-Miscegenation Laws," Nobuya Tsuchida, ed., *Asian and Pacific American Experiences: Women's Perspectives* (Minneapolis: Asian/Pacific American Learning Resource Center and General College, University of Minnesota, 1982), 1–37.

8. May Nakamoto to Mrs. Jack Shoup, 20 November 1943, Mrs. Jack Shoup Collection, Hoover Institution Archives (hereafter referred to as HIA).

9. Shizuko Horiuchi to Henriette Von Blon, 27 December 1942, Henriette Von Blon Collection, HIA.

10. From 1942 to the end of 1945, the Council allocated about $240,000 in scholarships, most of which were provided through the donations of churches and the World Student Service Fund. The average grant per student was $156.73, which in that era was a major contribution toward the cost of higher education. See National Japanese American Student Relocation Council, Minutes of the Executive Committee Meeting, Philadelphia, Pennsylvania, 19 December 1945.

11. Robert O'Brien, *The College Nisei* (Palo Alto: Pacific Books, 1949), 73–74.

12. Toshiko Imada to Margaret Cosgrave Sowers, 16 January 1943, Margaret Cosgrave Sowers Collection, HIA.

13. Ayako Kanemura, personal interview, Glendale, Ariz., 24 March 1978.

14. Kathy Ishikawa to Mrs. Jack Shoup, 14 June 1942, Mrs. Jack Shoup Collection, HIA.

15. Anonymous nisei nurse in Poston Camp to Margaret Finley, 5 May 1943, Margaret Finley Collection, HIA.

16. Mine Okubo, *Citizen 13660* (New York: Columbia University Press, 1946), 139.

17. *Topaz Times,* 24 October 1942, 3.

18. Masako Ono to Atsuko Ono, 28 September 1942, Margaret Cosgrave Sowers Collection, HIA. Prior to the war, few nisei had college experience: the 1940 census lists 674 second-generation women and 1,507 men who had attended or were attending college.

19. Lillian Ota, "Campus Report," *Trek* (February 1943), 33.

20. Ibid., 33–34.

21. Marii Kyogoku, "a la mode," *Trek* (February 1943), 39.

22. O'Brien, *The College Nisei,* 73–74.

23. Ibid., 85–86.

24. Grace Tanabe to Josephine Duveneck, 16 February 1944, Conard-Duveneck Collection, HIA.

25. In 1943 the War Relocation Authority tried to expedite the clearance procedure by broadening an army registration program originally aimed at nisei males to include all adults. With this policy change, the migration from the camps steadily increased. The disastrous consequences of this poorly conceived clearance procedure have been examined by Wilson and Hosokawa, *East to America,* 226–227; and Girdner and Loftis, *The Great Betrayal,* 342–343.

26. Advisory Committee for Evacuees, *Resettlement Bulletin* (April 1943), 2.

27. Leonard Broom (Bloom) and Ruth Riemer, *Removal and Return: The Socio-*

Economic Effects of the War on Japanese Americans (Berkeley: University of California Press, 1949), 36.

28. Evelyn Nakano Glenn, "The Dialectics of Wage Work: Japanese-American Women and Domestic Service, 1905–1940," *Feminist Studies* 6, no. 3 (Fall 1980): 432.

29. Advisory Committee for Evacuees, *Resettlement Bulletin* (July 1943), 3.

30. U.S. Bureau of the Census, *Special Report, 1950* (Washington, D.C.).

31. Marii Kyogoku, *Resettlement Bulletin* (July 1943), 5.

32. Kyogoku, "a la mode," 39.

33. *Poston Chronicle*, 23 May 1943, 1.

34. *Poston Chronicle*, 23 May 1943, 1.

35. Dorcas Asano to Josephine Duveneck, 22 January 1944, Conard-Duveneck Collection, HIA.

36. Mine Okubo, *An American Experience*, exhibition catalog (Oakland: Oakland Museum, 1972), 41.

37. Ayako Kanemura, personal interview, Glendale, Ariz., 24 March 1978.

38. Elizabeth Ogata to Mrs. Jack Shoup, 1 October 1944, Mrs. Jack Shoup Collection, HIA.

39. Hartmann, *The Home Front*, 126. There is some debate regarding the origins of the assessment of evacuee losses at $400 million. However, a recent study by the Commission on Wartime Relocation and Internment of Civilians has estimated that the Japanese Americans lost between $149 million and $370 million in 1945 dollars, the equivalent of between $810 million and $2 billion in 1983 dollars. See the *San Francisco Chronicle*, 16 June 1983, 12. In 1988 Congress enacted H.R. 442, a bill which authorizes $20,000 for each survivor of the internment camps and establishes a trust fund to support educational efforts that will prevent similar acts from happening again in America.

Issei Working Women in Hawaii/Gail M. Nomura

1. The first group of Japanese immigrants to Hawaii arrived in 1868. They were called the *gannenmono*, or first year people, because they arrived in the first year of the reign of the new emperor of Japan, which marked the fall of the old Tokugawa government and the start of a new Meiji era of modernization. There were 141 men, 6 women, and 1 child. Due to laborers' complaints of brutal treatment and low pay and planters' complaints about the unsuitability of Japanese as plantation labor there was no further emigration until 1885. Only one woman of this first group remained in Hawaii. See Masaji Marumoto, "'First Year' Immigrants to Hawaii and Eu-

gene Van Reed," in Hilary Conroy and T. Scott Miyakawa, eds., *East Across the Pacific* (Santa Barbara, Calif.: American Bibliographical Center/ Clio Press, 1972), 5–39.

2. R. W. Irwin to Charles T. Gulick, 12 September 1884, Interior/Miscellaneous, Immigration-Japanese, R. W. Irwin–Correspondence, 1884–1886, State Archives of Hawaii, Honolulu, Hawaii (hereafter referred to as SAH).

3. R. W. Irwin to Walter Murray Gibson, 13 September 1884, Interior/ Misc., Immigration-Japanese, R. W. Irwin–Correspondence, 1884–1886, SAH.

4. Francis Hilary Conroy, "The Japanese Expansion into Hawaii, 1868–1898" (Ph.D. diss., University of California, 1949; published ed. San Francisco: R and E Research Associates, 1973), 219–220.

5. R. W. Irwin to Charles T. Gulick, 10 March 1886, Interior/Misc., Immigration-Japanese, R. W. Irwin–Correspondence, 1884–1886, SAH.

6. L. A. Thurston to H. Hackfeld and Co., 19 January 1889, Bureau of Immigration, Letters, 1888–1889, No. 5, SAH. (Also sent to C. Brewer and Co., W. G. Irwin and Co., F. A. Schaefer and Co., and Castle and Cooke.)

7. R. W. Irwin to L. A. Thurston, 30 March 1889, Interior/Misc., Immigration-Japanese, R. W. Irwin–Correspondence, Jan.–Sept. 1889, SAH.

8. Hawaii (Kingdom), Interior Office, Bureau of Immigration, *Report of the President of the Bureau of Immigration to the Legislative Assembly, 1886,* 239.

9. W. M. Gibson to R. W. Irwin, 25 September 1884, Japanese Diplomatic and Miscellaneous, No. 12, SAH.

10. Minutes of the Meeting of the Board of Immigration held 29 June 1887, Board of Immigration Minutes, 1879–1891, SAH.

11. R. W. Irwin to L. A. Thurston, 8 September 1887, Interior/Misc., Immigration-Japanese, R. W. Irwin–Correspondence, 1887, SAH.

12. R. W. Irwin to L. A. Thurston, 16 December 1887, Interior/Misc., Immigration-Japanese, R. W. Irwin–Correspondence, 1887, SAH.

13. R. W. Irwin to L. A. Thurston, 18 February 1889; R. W. Irwin to L. A. Thurston, 18 September 1889; and R. W. Irwin to L. A. Thurston, 19 March 1890, Interior/Misc., Immigration-Japanese, R. W. Irwin–Correspondence, Jan.–Sept. 1889, and R. W. Irwin–Correspondence, 1890, SAH.

14. Hawaii (Kingdom), Bureau of Public Instruction, *Report of the General Superintendent of the Census, 1890,* 22.

15. Ibid., 30.

16. Ibid., 66–67.
17. Oral history interview with Kiku Yoshida in Charlotte H. Tanji, *Eight Life Stories: Japanese Senior Citizens of Waipahu* (Waipahu, Hawaii: Friends of the Waipahu Cultural Garden Park, 1984), 30–31.
18. Oral history interview with Kaku Kumasaka in Tanji, *Eight Life Stories*, 48–49.
19. Yoshida interview, ibid., 24.
20. Kumasaka interview, ibid., 48.
21. J. S. B. Pratt, Jr., "The Duty of Labor," *The Hawaiian Planters' Record* 29 (January to December 1925): 9.
22. U.S. Department of Labor, Office of the Commissioner, *Report of the Commissioner of Labor on Hawaii, 1902*, 71.
23. Oral history interview with Sagami Shinozawa in Tanji, *Eight Life Stories*, 21.
24. Kumasaka interview, ibid., 46.
25. Frances Blascoer, *The Industrial Condition of Women and Girls in Honolulu: A Social Study* (Honolulu: Board of Trustees of the Kaiulani Home for Young Women and Girls, 1912), 45.
26. U.S. Department of Labor, *Report of the Commissioner of Labor on Hawaii, 1901*, 107.
27. U.S. Department of Labor, *Labor Conditions in Hawaii, 1915*, Table 3, 18; U.S. Department of Labor, Bureau of Immigration, *Industrial Conditions in Hawaiian Islands, 1913*, 7; and U.S. Department of Labor, *Labor Conditions in Hawaii, 1915*, Table 7, 22.
28. U.S. Department of Commerce and Labor, Bureau of Labor, *Third Report of Commissioner of Labor on Hawaii, 1905*, 108.
29. U.S. Bureau of the Census, *Chinese and Japanese of the United States, 1910*, E. A. Goldenweiser and Daniel Folkmar, Bulletin 127 (Washington, D.C., 1914), 23.
30. U.S. Bureau of the Census, *Fourteenth Census of the United States, 1920: Population*, 4:1272, 1278.
31. See Hawaii (Kingdom), *Report of the President of the Bureau of Immigration to the Legislative Assembly, 1886* for a history of Hawaii's attempts at importing laborers.
32. Conroy, "Japanese Expansion," 219–220.
33. Hawaii, *Census, 1890*, 20, 26, 43.
34. Ibid., 43.
35. U.S. Department of Labor, *Report, 1901*, 102.
36. U.S. Department of Labor, *Report, 1902*, 109.
37. Blascoer, *Industrial Condition of Women*, 45.
38. In a 1913 industrial conditions report a "prominent planter" is reported to

have desired a return to the days of the penal contract system when "women had worked all day in the field with infants strapped to their backs, and if either men or women refused to obey orders they were arrested and the court would fix the penalty—a fine or imprisonment. . . ." See U.S. Department of Labor, *Industrial Conditions, 1913*, 8.

39. Oral history interview with Kame Iwatani in Ethnic Studies Oral History Project, *Women Workers in Hawaii's Pineapple Industry*, III (Honolulu: Ethnic Studies Oral History Project, 1979), 845.

40. The 1900 report for the Waialua Agricultural Company lists an expenditure of $243.97 for a "Kindergarten," Waialua Agricultural Company, Ltd., *Second Report of the Waialua Agricultural Company, Ltd., for the Fifteen Months Ending December 31, 1900* (Waialua, Oahu, Hawaii: Waialua Agricultural Company, Ltd., 1901), 16. The 1901 report lists $1,370.95 expended for the kindergarten, *Third Report of the Waialua Agricultural Company, Ltd., for the Twelve Months Ending December 31, 1901* (Waialua, Oahu, Hawaii: Waialua Agricultural Company, Ltd., 1902), 8. In 1902, $813.15 was expended for the kindergarten, including $771.94 for labor and $41.21 for materials and sundries, *Fourth Annual Report of the Waialua Agricultural Company, Ltd., for the Twelve Months Ending December 31, 1902* (Waialua, Oahu, Hawaii: Waialua Agricultural Company, Ltd., 1903), 13.

41. Franklin Odo and Kazuko Sinoto, *A Pictorial History of the Japanese in Hawaii, 1885–1924* (Honolulu: Bishop Museum Press, 1985), 55.

42. Shinozawa interview in Tanji, *Eight Life Stories*, 21.

43. Yoshida interview, ibid., 36.

44. Interview with issei senior citizen women, Ewa, Hawaii, 8 August 1980.

45. Kumasaka interview in Tanji, *Eight Life Stories*, 42–43.

46. Ibid.

47. Annette Shiramizu, "Various Aspects of Plantation Life among the Japanese of Hanamaulu, Kauai in the Early 1900s," (Unpublished manuscript, 1970, Hawaii-Pacific Collection, University of Hawaii, Honolulu, Hawaii). See also Shinozawa and Yoshida interviews in Tanji, *Eight Life Stories*, 21, 36.

48. Iwatani interview in Ethnic Studies Oral History Project, *Women Workers*, 859–860.

49. Ibid., 872–877.

50. Kumasaka interview in Tanji, *Eight Life Stories*, 42.

51. Iwatani interview in Ethnic Studies Oral History Project, *Women Workers*, 867.

52. U.S. Department of Commerce and Labor, *Report, 1910*, 51.

53. Blascoer, *Industrial Condition of Women*, 44.

54. Ibid., 69.

55. U.S. Department of Labor, *Report, 1901*, 112.

56. U.S. Department of Commerce and Labor, Bureau of Labor, *Fourth Report of the Commissioner of Labor on Hawaii*, 1910, 80–81.

57. Letter from Higher Wage Association to the Manager of Oahu Sugar Co. in Waipahu dated 12 May 1909 in U.S. Department of Labor, *Report, 1910*, 80–81.

58. Ernest K. Wakukawa, *A History of the Japanese People in Hawaii* (Honolulu: The Toyo Shoin, 1938), 243.

59. U.S. Department of Labor, Bureau of Labor Statistics, *Labor Conditions in the Territory of Hawaii*, 1929–1930, Table, 3.

60. Ibid.

61. U.S. Bureau of the Census, *Fifteenth Census of the United States, 1930: Outlying Territories and Possessions; Number and Distribution of Inhabitants, Composition and Character of the Population, Occupation, Unemployment and Agriculture*, 90.

62. U.S. Department of Labor, *Labor Conditions in Hawaii*, 1915, 45, 134, 169.

63. U.S. Department of Commerce, *Census, 1920*, 1278. In two pineapple plantations Japanese women were reported to represent 80.4 percent of the average number of employees in 1929. See U.S. Department of Labor, *Labor Conditions*, 1929–1930, Table 36, 79.

64. U.S. Department of Labor, *Labor Conditions in Hawaii*, 1915, 45.

65. U.S. Department of Labor, Women's Bureau, *The Employment of Women in the Pineapple Canneries of Hawaii*, Caroline Manning, Bulletin of the Women's Bureau, no. 82 (1930), 6–7.

66. U.S. Department of Labor, *Labor Conditions in Hawaii*, 1915, 45, 169, 171.

67. U.S. Bureau of the Census, *Census, 1930*, 90.

68. Jane Dranga, "Racial Factors in the Employment of Women," *Social Process in Hawaii* 2 (May 1936): 11; and U.S. Department of Labor, Women's Bureau, *Earnings and Hours in Hawaii Woman-Employing Industries*, Ethel Erickson, Bulletin of the Women's Bureau, No. 177 (Washington, D.C., 1940), 50.

69. U.S. Bureau of the Census, *Census, 1930*, 90.

70. Yukiko Kimura, "Honolulu Barber Girls—A Study of Culture Conflict," *Social Process in Hawaii* 5 (June 1939): 22.

71. Erickson, Bulletin of the Women's Bureau, 53.

72. Ibid., 2.

73. Kumasaka interview in Tanji, *Eight Life Stories*, 42.

Ladies on the Line: Punjabi Cannery Workers in
Central California / Marcelle Williams

1. During spring 1985, I conducted several interviews with South Asian immigrants residing and working in Stanislaus County, California. Most of the Asian Indian immigrants that I interviewed are involved in agribusiness, often both as small-scale farmers and as waged laborers in food-processing canneries and factories. Since most of these Asian Indian immigrants are Punjabi Sikhs—immigrants from the Punjab area of north India who follow the religious doctrine of Sikhism—I decided to focus on this group. To protect the privacy of the family that I present in the essay, I have changed their name and any other distinguishing characteristics.

2. Pratibha Parmar, "Gender, Race and Class: Asian Women in Resistance," *The Empire Strikes Back: Race and Racism in 70s Britain* (London: Centre for Contemporary Cultural Studies, 1982), 250. There are very few studies of Asian Indian immigrant women in the United States. One that addresses these women, their work, and family is Suvarna Thakar's "Quality of Life of Asian Indian Women in the Motel Industry," *South Asian Bulletin* 2 (1982): 68–73. Even one of the most recent surveys of Asian Indians in the United States fails to discuss the women other than to say that they usually stay in the domestic, "private" domain. See Paratma Saran and Edwin Eames, eds., *The New Ethnics: Indians in the United States* (New York: Praeger, 1980). Most literature on South Asian immigrant women has concentrated on Britain as the host country. See for example Zaynab Dahya, "Pakistani Wives in Britain," *Race* 6 (1965), which depicts the women as homebound, passive, and dependent; on the other hand, Barbro Hoel, "Contemporary Clothing 'Sweatshops,' Asian Female Labour and Collective Organization," in Jackie West, ed., *Work, Women, and the Labour Market* (London: Routledge & Kegan Paul, 1983), 80–98, looks at the women as active participants in waged work.

3. Joan Jensen, "East Indians," in Stephen Thernstrom, ed., *The Harvard Encyclopedia of American Ethnic Groups* (Cambridge: Harvard University Press, 1980), 296. For historical studies of Punjabi Sikh immigrants in California, see for example Harold Jacoby, "Some Demographic and Social Aspects of Early East Indian Life in the United States," in Mark Juergensmeyer and Gerald Barrier, eds., *Sikh Studies: Comparative Perspectives on a Changing Tradition* (Berkeley: Berkeley Religious Studies Series, 1979), 159–171; Bruce LaBrack, "The Sikhs in California: A Socio-Historical Study" (Ph.D. diss., Syracuse University, 1980); and Sucheta Mazumdar, "Punjabi Agricultural Workers in California, 1904–1945,"

in Lucie Cheng and Edna Bonacich, eds., *Labor Immigration Under Capitalism* (Berkeley: University of California, 1984), 549–578.

4. Bruce LaBrack, "Occupational Specialization among the Rural California Sikhs: The Interplay of Culture and Economics," *Amerasia* 9 (1982): 29–56. My thanks to Gary Kawaguchi, graduate student in the Ethnic Studies Program at the University of California at Berkeley, who searched the U.S. census of 1980 data (STF4B tapes) for statistics on Asian Indians in California. See also Jayashree Ramakrishna, "Health Behavior and Practices of the Sikh Community of the Yuba City Area of California" (Ph.D. diss., University of California, Berkeley, 1979), 50. Ramakrishna noticed that Sikhs in the Marysville–Yuba City area also tended to live on small farms outside the city limits.

5. See Stanislaus County Farm Bureau, "Fact Sheet: Agriculture—A Growing Industry" (Mimeographed, Modesto, California, 1984); and Kathie Smith, "Changing of the Guard at Tri/Valley," *Modesto Bee,* 3 June 1985. According to literature published by Tri/Valley Growers, Inc., Plant 7 consists of twenty buildings covering a space of forty-four acres on a 120-acre site in Modesto, California. Plant 7 is capable of producing five million cans of fruit and vegetables a day at peak season. After a series of mergers, Tri/Valley's brands now include S & W, Libby, Sacramento Olives, and Oberti Olives.

6. Interview with Tri/Valley public relations representative, Michael J. Miller, Modesto, California, 23 May 1985.

7. Ramakrishna, "Health Behavior and Practices," 55, states that most Sikh women work in the canneries because of poor English skills, and that, through their word-of-mouth networks, large numbers work together in the same plants.

8. Patricia Zavella, "Women, Work, and Family in the Chicano Community: Cannery Workers of the Santa Clara Valley" (Ph.D. diss., University of California, Berkeley, 1982), 157, 175. Reference to the "canned finger" legend, which almost every cannery belt worker knows, appears in Shirley Hom, "Working in a Cannery," *Asian Women's Journal* (Berkeley: University of California, 1971), 94.

9. Statistics from Tri/Valley Growers, Inc. composite records on minority group employment for 1984; Zavella, "Women, Work, and Family," 1.

Behind Unmarked Doors: Developments in the Garment Industry/
Diane Yen-Mei Wong with Dennis Hayashi

1. "Labor Department Sues T & W Fashions," *Asian Law Caucus Reporter* 6, nos. 3–4 (June–Dec. 1984).

2. Shiree Teng, interview with author, 27 March 1985, provided the smaller figure. Kraig Peck, "Why Sweatshops Remain in King County," *International Examiner*, Seattle, January/February 1978, stated the larger figure would be needed to "set up an adequate shop."

3. "Garment Workers Laid Off," *International Examiner*, Seattle, May 1980. Article discusses the layoff of about 100 workers by the Thaw Corporation in Seattle.

4. Kathleen Pai, "Korean Immigrant Women and the Garment Industry" (Senior thesis, University of California, Berkeley, 1984), 26.

5. Chalsa Loo and Paul Ong, "Slaying a Dragon with a Sewing Needle," *Berkeley Journal of Sociology* 27 (1982): 81.

6. Bernice Tom, interview with author, 22 April 1985.

7. Harold Paul Dygert III and David Shibata, "Chinatown Sweatshops: Wages and Law Violations in the Garment Industry," *University of California at Davis Law Review* 8 (1975): 66.

8. The center began in 1982 to implement a pretrial diversion plan for garment workers charged by the state with unemployment insurance fraud; it has since closed.

9. Norman Fong, interview with author, 17 March 1985; and "Garment Workers Project: Justice, Equality, Empowerment," *Asian Law Caucus* (pamphlet).

10. Shin interview with author, 15 April 1985. The center for which Shin works, Asian Immigrant Women Advocates, provides job training, vocational English classes, leadership training, and advocacy workshops for Korean, Chinese, Vietnamese, and Filipino women working in the garment, hotel, restaurant, electronics and nursing home industries.

11. Clothing for the thirty-seven National Dollar Stores on the West Coast was manufactured in one Chinatown factory. At the workers' request, the ILGWU obtained an agreement with National Dollar in January 1938 to negotiate with the newly formed Chinese local, but the manufacturer sold its manufacturing arm to the Golden Gate Manufacturing Company— many of whose officers and representatives had been employed by National Dollar—and retained only its retailing function. Employees charged that Golden Gate refused to meet with the union and thus voted to strike on 28 February. See Patricia M. Fong, "The 1938 National Dollar Store Strike," *Asian American Review* 2, no. 1 (1975): 183–196.

12. "Labor Board Still Seeks to Find Forty Former Jung Sai Workers," *East/West*, San Francisco, 4 January 1984.

13. Richard Moore, "Workers Rock Chinatown," *In These Times*, 25 August 1982, 6. (Summarized from a 1985 working paper by Yoichi Shimatsu and Pat Lee entitled "A Stitch in Time.")

464

14. Dygert and Shibata, "Chinatown Sweatshops," 69–70; and Fong interview. See also the Jennie Low case in Victor and Brett de Bary Nee, *Longtime Californ'* (New York: Pantheon, 1972).

15. See "Labor Department Sues T & W Fashions," 1; "Labor Department Sues Manufacturer for Violation of Minimum Wage Law"; and C. W. Chang and Ben Chang, "Garment Workers at T & W Fashions Speak Out about Their Workplace," *East/West,* 10 October 1984.

16. See "Labor Department Sues Manufacturer for Violation of Minimum Wage Law"; C. W. Chang and Ben Chang, "Garment Workers at T & W Fashions Speak Out about Their Workplace"; and "Dept. of Labor Lawsuit Pleases Garment Workers' Attorney," *East/West,* 10 October 1984.

17. Dennis Hayashi, interview with author, 3 August 1987.

18. Eugene Moriguchi, interview with author, 17 June 1985.

19. Comments made by Leonard Joseph, executive director of San Francisco Fashion Industries, an association of Northern California garment manufacturers and by Randy Shiroi, Sacramento Human Rights/Fair Housing Commission in Ted Bell, "Immigrants Face Long Hours, Hard Work, Low Pay," *Sacramento Bee,* 10 February 1985. See also *Asian Law Caucus Reporter* 6, no. 3–4 (June–Dec. 1984).

20. Ted Bell, "Shops Grew," *Sacramento Bee,* 13 February 1985, and Teng interview.

21. Bell, ibid.

22. Under California law, employees can apply for partial unemployment compensation in seasonal businesses, including the garment industry. (The women's attorneys also challenged the criminal action as racially discriminatory because only Chinatown factories had been investigated.)

23. Clement Kong, interview with author, 20 June 1984.

24. Norman Fong, interview with author, 5 March 1985.

25. Jan Gilbrecht, interview with author, 9 May 1985. (Gilbrecht headed the Plant Closures Project of Oakland, a program designed to respond to the shutdown of major local factories.) Sierra Designs wanted to use subcontractors in Hong Kong, Taiwan, China, and Mexico.

26. Gilbrecht, "Letter to the Editor: End of the Rainbow," *San Francisco Chronicle/Examiner,* 1 June 1986.

27. See Laura Henze, "Analysis of Problems at Rainbow Workers Cooperative," Report to Industrial Cooperative Association Revolving Loan Fund, Inc., 15 May 1986; and Maureen Fenlon, "Overview and Analysis of the Rainbow Workers Cooperative," report to Adrian Dominican Sisters Portfolio Advisory Board, August 1986.

28. Fong interview, 17 March 1985.

29. Shin interview.

30. Moriguchi interview.
31. Teng interview. Though currently with the San Francisco local, Teng worked in the research department of the New York ILGWU from 1982 to 1984. Union membership has been changing in ethnic make-up, but this trend has yet to be reflected in the leadership.
32. Shin interview.

Women in the Silicon Valley/Rebecca Villones

1. Michael Eisenscher, *Digest of Electronic Data* (San Jose, 1984).
2. Interviews by author with workers and union organizers.
3. Eisenscher, *Electronic Data*.
4. Interviews by author with workers and union organizers.
5. Pat Sacco, United Electrical Workers Organizing Committee, San Jose, Calif., interview with author.
6. Dave Bacon, United Electrical Workers Organizing Committee, San Jose, Calif., interview with author.
7. Interviews by author with electronic workers and union organizers.
8. Eisenscher, *Electronic Data*.
9. Interviews by author with electronic workers, *San Jose Mercury News*.
10. Statement by Pat Namborn, director of the Santa Clara County Committee on Safety and Health.
11. Interviews by author with electronic workers and union organizers.
12. Dr. Mark Sapir, M.D., San Jose, Calif., interview with author.
13. Dave Bacon interview.
14. Interviews by author with union organizers, *San Jose Mercury News*.

The Gap between Striving and Achieving:
The Case of Asian American Women/Deborah Woo

1. Ted Bell, "Quiet Loyalty Keeps Shops Running," *Sacramento Bee*, 11 February 1985.
2. Amado Y. Cabezas and Pauline L. Fong, "Employment Status of Asian-Pacific Women" (Background paper; San Francisco: ASIAN, Inc., 1976).
3. U.S. Bureau of the Census, *Race of the Population by States* (Washington, D.C., 1980). According to the census, 40 percent of all Chinese in America live in California, as well as 46 percent of all Filipinos, and 37 percent of all Japanese. New York ranks second for the number of Chinese residing there, and Hawaii is the second most populated state for Filipinos and Japanese.
4. Tricia Knoll, *Becoming Americans: Asian Sojourners, Immigrants, and Refu-*

gees in the Western United States (Portland, Oreg.: Coast to Coast Books, 1982), 152.

5. U.S. Commission on Civil Rights, *Social Indicators of Equality for Minorities and Women* (Washington, D.C., 1978), 24, 50, 54, 58, 62.

6. David M. Moulton, "The Socioeconomic Status of Asian American Families in Five Major SMSAs" (Paper prepared for the Conference of Pacific and Asian American Families and HEW-related Issues, San Francisco, 1978). No comparative data were available on blacks for the fifth SMSA, Honolulu.

7. James E. Blackwell, *Mainstreaming Outsiders* (New York: General Hall, Inc., 1981), 306; and Commission on Civil Rights, *Social Indicators,* 9.

8. California Advisory Committee, "A Dream Unfulfilled: Korean and Pilipino Health Professionals in California" (Report prepared for submission to U.S. Commission on Civil Rights, May 1975), iii.

9. See Amado Y. Cabezas, "A View of Poor Linkages between Education, Occupation and Earnings for Asian Americans" (Paper presented at the Third National Forum on Education and Work, San Francisco, 1977), 17; and Census of Population, PUS, 1980.

10. Census of the Population, PUS, 1970, 1980.

11. A 1977 report on California families showed that an average of 9.3 percent of Japanese, Chinese, and Filipino families were below the poverty level, but that only 5.4 percent of these families received public assistance. The corresponding figures for Anglos were 6.3 percent and 5.9 percent. From Harold T. Yee, "The General Level of Well-Being of Asian Americans" (Paper presented to U.S. government officials in partial response to Justice Department amicus).

12. Moulton, "Socioeconomic Status," 70–71.

13. Commission on Civil Rights, *Social Indicators,* 54.

14. The few exceptions occur in Honolulu with women who had more than a high school education and in Chicago with women who had a high school education or three years of college. Even these women fared poorly when compared to men, however.

15. Bob H. Suzuki, "Education and the Socialization of Asian Americans: A Revisionist Analysis of the 'Model Minority' Thesis," *Amerasia Journal* 4:2 (1977): 43. See also Fong and Cabezas, "Economic and Employment Status," 48–49; and Commission on Civil Rights, *Social Indicators,* 97–98.

16. U.S. Commission on Civil Rights, "Education Issues" in *Civil Rights Issues of Asian and Pacific Americans: Myths and Realities* (Washington, D.C., 1979), 370–376. This material was presented by Ling-chi Wang, University of California, Berkeley.

17. Illsoo Kim, *New Urban Immigrants: The Korean Community in New York* (Princeton, N.J.: Princeton University Press, 1981).
18. For further discussion of the model minority myth and interpretation of census data, see Deborah Woo, "The Socioeconomic Status of Asian American Women in the Labor Force: An Alternative View," *Sociological Perspectives* 28:3 (July 1985): 307–338.

Growing Up Asian in America/Kesaya E. Noda

1. Patia R. Isaku, *Mountain Storm, Pine Breeze: Folk Song in Japan* (Tucson, Ariz.: University of Arizona Press, 1981), 41.

Mestiza Girlhood: Interracial Families in Chicago's Filipino American Community since 1925/Barbara M. Posadas

1. An extended treatment of Filipino-white intermarriage is in Barbara M. Posadas, "Crossed Boundaries in Interracial Chicago: Filipino American Families since 1925," *Amerasia Journal* 8:2 (1981): 31–52. Illinois did not bar interracial marriage between Filipinos and white women. The material for this study, part of a forthcoming book on the Filipino old-timers' generation in Chicago, is derived almost exclusively from oral interviews conducted with a dozen elderly Filipinos and their families. See also Posadas, "The Hierarchy of Color and Psychological Adjustment in an Industrial Environment: Filipinos, the Pullman Company and the Brotherhood of Sleeping Car Porters," *Labor History* 23:3 (Summer 1982): 349–373; and Posadas and Roland L. Guyotte, "From Student Community to Immigrant Community: Chicago's Filipinos before World War II" (Paper delivered at the Philippine Studies Conference, Ohio University, Athens, Ohio, August 1983).
2. *Associated Filipino Press*, VI, no. 2, 30 December 1934, cited in Bessie Louise Pierce Notes, Chicago Historical Society.
3. H. Brett Melendy, *Asians in America: Filipinos, Koreans, and East Asians* (Boston: Twayne, 1977), 251. Melendy's seven chapters on Filipinos in America constitute the best survey of this subject. For material on the Chicago community, see Albert W. Palmer, *Orientals in American Life* (New York: Friendship Press, 1934), 94–102; Paul G. Cressey, *The Taxi-Dance Hall: A Sociological Study in Commercialized Recreation and City Life* (Chicago: University of Chicago Press, 1932), 145–174; and Benny F. Feria, *Filipino Son* (Boston, Meader, 1954).
4. U.S. Bureau of the Census, *1940 Census of Population: Characteristics of the*

468

Nonwhite Population by Race (Washington, D.C., 1943), 109–110. See also, Posadas, "Crossed Boundaries."

5. U.S. Bureau of the Census, 1940, 109.

6. U.S. Bureau of the Census, 1950 Census of Population. Vol. II: Characteristics of the Population. Part 13; Illinois (Washington, D.C., 1952); U.S. Bureau of the Census, 1960 Census of Population. Vol. I: Characteristics of the Population Part 15: Illinois (Washington, D.C., 1963), 15–58; U.S. Bureau of the Census, 1970 Census of Population, Subject Reports: Japanese, Chinese, and Filipinos in the United States (Washington, D.C., 1973), 140; U.S. Bureau of the Census, 1980 Census of Population. Race of the Population by States: 1980 (Washington, D.C., 1981), 13.

7. Benicio T. Catapusan, "Filipino Intermarriage Problems in the United States," Sociology and Social Research 22 (January–February 1938), 269–270.

8. Catapusan, "The Social Adjustment of Filipinos in the United States" (Ph.D. diss., University of Southern California, 1940), 86; and Severino F. Corpus, "Second Generation Filipinos in Los Angeles," Sociology and Social Research 22 (May–June 1938), 450.

9. Alfredo N. Munoz, The Filipinos in America (Los Angeles: Mountainview, 1971), 119.

10. Edwin B. Almirol, "Ethnic Identity and Social Negotiation: A Study of a Filipino Community in California" (Ph.D. diss., University of Illinois, Urbana-Champaign, 1977), 169.

11. As a group, the Chicago Filipinos were more educated than their California contemporaries. Median years of schooling for the Chicagoans stood at 12.2 in 1940; for Californians, the figure was 6.8. See Posadas, "Crossed Boundaries," 34.

12. See Posadas, "The Hierarchy of Color."

13. See for example Humbert S. Nelli, Italians in Chicago, 1880–1930 (New York: Oxford University Press, 1970); and Allan Spear, Black Chicago: The Making of a Negro Ghetto, 1890–1920 (Chicago: University of Chicago Press, 1967).

14. In contrast, on black-white intermarriages in Chicago, see St. Clair Drake and Horace R. Cayton, Black Metropolis: A Study of Negro Life in a Northern City (New York: Harcourt, Brace & World, 1962 [1945]), 129–159.

15. Lois W. Banner, Women in Modern America: A Brief History (New York: Harcourt Brace Jovanovich, 1974), 191–196.

16. Posadas, "Crossed Boundaries," 35, 40; and Posadas and Guyotte, "From Student Community to Immigrant Community."

17. Encarnacion Alzona, A History of Education in the Philippines, 1565–1930 (Manila: University of the Philippines Press, 1932), 240–337; and Dor-

othy L. Cordova, "Educational Alternatives for Asian-Pacific Women," in U.S. Dept. of Education, National Institute of Education, *Conference on the Educational and Occupational Needs of Asian-Pacific American Women* (Washington, D.C., 1980), 143.

18. Carl N. Degler, *At Odds: Women and the Family in America from the Revolution to the Present* (Oxford: Oxford University Press, 1980), 418–435.

19. Christopher Jencks and David Riesman, *The Academic Revolution* (New York: Doubleday, 1968); and Roland L. Guyotte, "Liberal Education and the American Dream: Public Attitudes and the Emergence of Mass Higher Education, 1920–1950" (Ph.D. diss., Northwestern University, 1980).

Mosquitoes in the Main Room/Meena Alexander

1. Draupadi, a pawn in the dice match between the Panvas and the Kauravas, discovers to her horror that she is lost, dishonored, when suddenly her flesh is sheathed in a miraculous, unending sari that male hands cannot tear away. The tale is in the Hindu epic *Mahabharata*.

The Business of Selling Mail-Order Brides/Venny Villapando

1. Interview with Calgary sociologist Gladys L. Symons in "Mail-Order Marriage Boom: Submissive Foreign Women Are Just Dying to Meet Albertans," *Alberta Report*, 18 December 1981.

2. "Mates by Mail: This Couple Catalogs Affairs of the Heart," *Chicago Sun-Times*, 12 August 1984. Statistics based on a 1983 survey ("American Men in Search of Oriental Brides") of 265 American men "actively seeking a partner from the 'Orient.'"

3. Japanese American Citizens League (JACL), "Mail-Order Asian Women Catalogues" (Report issued by the Japanese American Citizens League, Spring 1985), 4.

4. *Alberta Report*, 18 December 1981.

5. John Broussard and Kelly Pomeroy, telephone interview with author, 1985.

6. Hugh Paterson, "Brides Jump from Pages of Pamphlet," *The Citizen*, Ottawa, Canada, 3 March 1982.

7. Karen Peterson, "Mail-Order Brides from the Unliberated East," Gannett News Service; Raymond A. Joseph, "American Men Find Asian Brides Fill the Unliberated Bill: Mail-Order Firms Help Them Look for the Ideal Women They Didn't Find at Home," *Wall Street Journal*, 25 January 1984.

8. Letter to Broussard and Pomeroy from *Cherry Blossoms* customer who asked to remain anonymous, 27 December 1984.

9. See JACL, "Mail-Order" (Questions and Answers section), 1–2.
10. Rita Calvano, "Mail-Order Marriages Blossom: Western Men Turn to Catalog Listing Oriental Women," *The Tribune,* San Diego, 6 September 1984; and Jack Lessenberry, "Brides to Go: Mail-Order Service Aids Hunt for Good Wives," *The Detroit News,* 8 July 1984.
11. Lloyd Shearer, "Mail-Order Brides," *Parade,* 10 October 1982.
12. Pat Tremmel, "Mates by Mail: Love Letters Spell Trouble," *Chicago Sun-Times,* 12 August 1984.
13. Calvano, *The Tribune,* 6 September 1984.
14. Letter to Broussard and Pomeroy from *Cherry Blossoms* customer, 27 December 1984.
15. Peterson, Gannett News Service.
16. Paterson, *The Citizen,* 3 March 1982.
17. American Asian Worldwide Service brochure quoted in JACL, "Mail-Order," 2.
18. Peterson, Gannett News Service.
19. Paterson, *The Citizen,* 3 March 1982; and Shearer, *Parade,* 10 October 1982.
20. Paterson, ibid.; and JACL, "Mail-Order," 2. Many women listed in the catalogues include virginity as one of their positive traits, writing, "I am still a virgin." See *Cherry Blossoms,* September/October 1981.
21. JACL, "Mail-Order," (Questions and Answers), 3.
22. Quoted in JACL, "Mail-Order," 5.
23. Shearer, *Parade,* 10 October 1982.
24. JACL, "Mail-Order," 4.
25. Peterson, Gannett News Service.
26. Calvano, *The Tribune,* 6 September 1984.
27. JACL, "Mail-Order," 3.

Domestic Violence among Pacific Asians/Nilda Rimonte

1. "Pacific Asian" is defined here as those persons from the Asian and Pacific regions who retain their native languages and whose worldview remains essentially Asian despite varying levels of Western acculturation.
2. The main languages, however, are Chinese, Japanese, Tagalog, Korean, Vietnamese, Cambodian, Hindustani, Thai, and less often Samoan.
3. This essay is based on my observations as executive director of the Los Angeles–based nonprofit Center for the Pacific Asian Family, which I founded in 1978. It began with a rape victim assistance hotline and has grown to a four-pronged program including a battered women's shelter, a child abuse treatment and prevention program and a self-employment

program called "Women Entrepreneurs." Some of my conclusions are also drawn from tentative studies I conducted to determine the concrete needs of our clients.

4. Pacific Asians now represent 85 percent of the caseload at the center. From 1982 to 1985, 90 percent of the resident clients were battered women and their children; the remaining 10 percent were rape victims or child sexual assault cases.

5. There has always been a direct correlation between the presence of ethnic workers and the number of clients from that particular ethnic group. One reason for this include the traditional help seeking behavior of Pacific Asians starting with the immediate family, relatives, community resources, and then to agencies such as the Center. Another has to do with the Center's policy of doing outreach only to those communities that are represented by either paid or volunteer staff.

6. *Los Angeles Times*, 1983.

7. Manocchio and Petit, *Families Under Stress* (Routledge & Kegan Paul: London, 1975), 103.

8. One consequence of this extended family configuration is that a Pacific Asian woman may be abused by her husband as well as by other relatives, male and female, including brothers, uncles, cousins, and mothers-in-law. The traditional power structure does not necessarily apply in families where older parents are brought to America by adult children; these parents become dependents of their grown children.

9. Manocchio and Petit, *Families Under Stress*.

10. Leonore Walker, *The Battered Women*, 1978.

11. Walker, *The Battered Women;* and Fleming, *Stopping Wife Abuse*.

12. In 1982 a counselor at the center reported that 80 percent of the women she interviewed mentioned the need for sexual companionship as a reason for returning to an abusive partner when she introduced the subject.

13. The residents at the center can stay for fourteen days as a general rule, but when language and resources are at issue, a longer stay (sometimes considerably longer) is possible.

14. Many battered women stay in abusive relationships because of the very real fear that they will lose immigration status if divorced. If her husband wants to get rid of her because he has become involved with another woman or for the price of a green card, as we see more and more at the shelter, she may be forced to endure the humiliation and the difficulties of being discarded without resources and without status.

15. Totman, *Social Causes of Illness* (London, 1979).

16. Wolfe, 1974.

17. Totman, *Social Causes of Illness*.

18. Figures in Los Angeles County indicate that child abuse is 129 percent more prevalent in homes with spousal abuse (Statement by Lt. Richard Willey, Los Angeles County Sheriff's Department, 2 March 1983).

19. Alessio and Hearns, "Group Treatment of Children in Shelters for Battered Women," in Roberts, ed., *Battered Women and Their Families* (New York: Springer Series, 1984).

20. Myers and Wright, 1980; Pizzey, 1977.

21. Del Martin.

Matchmaking in the Classifieds of the Immigrant Indian Press/Rashmi Luthra

I obtained very useful insights for this article from Devi Bhargava, an immigrant who lives in Madison, Wisconsin. She was president of the Madison Chapter of the Association of Indians in America for one year, and is well acquainted with the Indian community and its particular situation.

1. For the present analysis, I looked primarily at advertisements from *India Abroad*. By its own proclamation in each issue, this is "the oldest Indian newspaper in North America and the largest outside India." It is published weekly in four regional editions—Eastern, Midwestern, Western, and Canadian. I carefully perused all advertisements contained in one issue each month from October 1984 to July 1985 of the Eastern edition. I did not conduct a formal content analysis. Rather, I examined all the advertisements separately, then conjointly, to assess them qualitatively, noting both the typical and the exceptional in my account. Although *India West* was not included in the analysis, it also carries matrimonial ads. It is a large weekly newspaper published in Western United States, and caters primarily to Indians living in the West.

2. In Pratima Bhatia's "Shorter Notes," *The Eastern Anthropologist* 26:3 (July–September 1973), 271–277, she briefly traces matchmaking patterns in Indian history. In her account, during Vedic times the girl was free to choose her husband. After the Muslim invasion and subsequent spread of the Purdah system—which existed in India on a smaller scale before the Muslims came—mates were selected by the father alone. During the feudal age and time of the zamindars, the Barber (Nai) pleaded to one party on behalf of the other. Friends and relatives were also used as intermediaries.

3. In India fair skin and tall stature are considered to be very positive, the former being especially beneficial for the girl and the latter for the boy.

4. Gujarat is a state in West Central India. Gujarati is the language spoken in this region.

5. Kayastha is an important Hindu subcaste of northern India. Although subcaste endogamy has been greatly relaxed in India, some communities are still particular about marrying within the subcaste. This appears to be the case in the United States as well.

6. Tamil is one of the major languages in South India, spoken predominantly in the state of Tamil Nadu. The Brahmin caste is the highest in the caste hierarchy and originally was composed of priests. The advertisement says that suitors must fulfill both the language and caste requirements.

7. For an illuminating, fairly detailed analysis of marital advertisements in selected Indian newspapers, see Arthur Niehoff, "A Study of Matrimonial Advertisements in North India," *The Eastern Anthropologist* 12:2 (December 1958–February 1959), 73–86.

8. J. H. Hutton suggests that the offspring of a low-caste mother and high-caste father has some chance of acquiring the higher caste in the course of a few generations, but the offspring of a low-caste father and a high-caste mother has no such chance. Also in connection with hypergamy, Hutton notes that "one result of hypergamy is to put a price on bridegrooms instead of on brides, and it is significant that while a high price for bridegrooms is paid where hypergamy prevails, hypogamy, on the other hand, is associated with a bride-price." See J. H. Hutton, *Caste in India: Its Nature, Functions, and Origins* (London: Oxford University Press, 1961), 55.

9. Bhatia, "Shorter Notes," 274. Bhatia conjectures that the education of men is not considered as important as their job status, and is therefore not specified by the girl's family.

10. These refer to clans or family groups connected through ritual/worship to a common patriarch. Jain could also refer to the members of a particular religion practiced in India called Jainism.

11. Punjab is a state in Northwest India, and Khatri is a clan grouping of the Kayasthas found in Punjab and Uttar Pradesh.

12. The Immigration and Naturalization Service issues a document, commonly referred to as a green card, which signifies permanent resident status and allows the holder to stay and work in the United States indefinitely. Obtainment of a green card is greatly facilitated by marrying someone who already possesses one or who is a U.S. citizen. For some people, this type of marriage is the only possible legal means by which to obtain immigrant status in the United States.

13. A subcaste affiliation.

14. West Bengal is a state in Northeast India. A Bengali is a person from the region and who would normally speak the Bengali language.

15. Bhatia, "Shorter Notes," 277. Only Hindus of North India were interviewed about this.

16. For other analysis of matrimonial advertisements, see K. Anand, "An Analysis of Matrimonial Advertisements," *Sociological Bulletin* 14:1 (1965), 59–71; Noel P. Gist, "Mate Selection and Mass Communication in India," *Public Opinion Quarterly* 17:4 (Winter 1953–54), 481–495; and Amelia Reyes-Hockings, "The Newspaper as Surrogate Marriage Broker in India," *Sociological Bulletin* 15:1 (1966), 25–39.

The Feminist Movement: Where Are All the Asian American Women?/Esther Ngan-Ling Chow

1. The term "Asian American" is used to refer to major Asian groups as well as Pacific Islanders. Because of the dearth and uneven information about different groups of Asians and Pacific Islanders, most of the discussion and observations are drawn primarily from the five largest Asian groups: Chinese, Japanese, Korean, Filipinos, and Vietnamese Americans.

2. Germaine Q. Wong, "Impediments to Asian-Pacific-American Women Organizing," in *Conference on the Educational and Occupational Needs of Asian-Pacific-American Women* (Washington, D.C.: National Institute of Education, Department of Health, Education, and Welfare, 1980), 89–103.

3. Ibid.

4. Esther Ngan-Ling Chow, "The Development of Feminist Consciousness among Asian American Women," *Gender and Society* 1, 284–299.

5. Wong, "Impediments to Organizing."

6. Black, Hispanic, and Asian American women alike seem to share some common experiences in conflicting loyalty and identity based on race and gender in the early stage of their respective movements. The Organization of Chinese American Women, which recently separated itself from the Organization of Chinese Americans, is a prime example of this gender struggle.

7. Susie Ling and Sucheta Mazumdar, "Editorial: Asian American Feminism," *Cross Currents* 6, 3–5.

8. Identification with these two major types is mainly for analytical purposes. It neither denies that other factions may exist among different groups of Asian American women nor that a mixed type of the two is possible. Two interviews with Asian American feminists, Sunni and Aurora, reflect these alternative viewpoints about the Asian American women's involvement in the feminist movement. See G. M. Lee, "One in Sisterhood," in *Asian*

Women, ed. Editorial staff (Berkeley: University of California Press, 1971), 119–21.

9. Wong, "Impediments to Organizing."

10. See Jeanne Quan, "Congresswoman Patsy Takemoto Mink," 116–118; Cindy Takemoto, "Pat Sumi: Off the Pedestal," 107–111; Grace Lee Boggs, "The Future: Politics as End and as Means," 112–115; Yuriko Payton-Miyazaki, "Three Steps Behind and Three Steps Ahead," 116–118, all in *Asian Women.* See also Nellie Wong, Merle Woo, and Mitsuye Yamada, *Three Asian American Writers Speak Out on Feminism* (San Francisco: San Francisco Radical Women, 1979), and Wong, "Impediments to Organizing."

11. Juanita Lott and Canta Pian, *Beyond Stereotypes and Statistics: Emergence of Asian and Pacific American Women* (Washington, D.C.: Organization of Pan Asian American women, 1979).

12. See Boggs, "The Future: Politics as Ends and Means," and Lucie Cheng, "Social Mobility of Asian American Women in America: A Critical Review," in *Conference of the Educational and Occupational Needs of Asian-Pacific-American Women,* 323–341.

13. Quan, "Patsy Takemoto Mink."

14. Patricia Madoo Lengermann and Jill Niebrugge-Brantley, "Contemporary Feminist Theory," in *Contemporary Sociological Theories,* ed. George Ritzer (New York: Alfred A. Knopf, 1988), 430–432.

15. Esther Ngan-Ling Chow, *Acculturation of Asian American Professional Women,* research monograph (Washington, D.C.: National Institute of Mental Health, Department of Health and Human Services, 1982); Chow, "Acculturation Experience of the Asian American Woman," in *Beyond Sex Roles,* ed. Alice Sargent (St. Paul: West, 1985), 238–251.

16. Inge K. Broverman, Susan Raymond Vogel, Donald M. Broverman et al., "Sex-Role Stereotypes: A Current Appraisal," *Journal of Social Issues* 28 (1972), 59–78, and Susan A. Basow, *Gender Stereotypes: Traditions and Alternatives,* 2d ed. (Monterey, Calif.: Brooks/Cole, 1986).

17. Esther Ngan-Ling Chow, "The Politics of Racial and Sexual Stereotypes at Work," paper presented at the annual meeting of the society for the Study of Social Problems, San Francisco, 1982.

18. Few significant variations were found among different subgroups in their adherence to Asian values and acceptance of American values in two survey samples of Asian American women on both the East and West Coasts. See Chow, *Acculturation of Professional Women.*

19. See Bok-Lim Kim and M. E. Condon, *A Study of Asian Americans in Chicago: Their Socio-Economic Characteristics, Problems and Service Needs* (Wash-

ington, D.C.: National Institute of Mental Health, Department of Health, Education, and Welfare, 1975); and Canta Pian, "Immigration of Asian Women and the Status of Recent Asian Women Immigrants," in *Conference on the Educational and Occupational Needs,* 181–210.

20. Pauline Fong and Amado Y. Cabezas, "Employment of Asian-Pacific-American Women," in *Conference on the Educational and Occupational Needs,* 255–321.

21. Esther Ngan-Ling Chow, "Job Decision, Household Work and Gender Relations in Asian American Families," paper presented at the annual meeting of the American Sociological Association, Chicago, 1987.

22. Major legislation passed to ban and discriminate against Asians in America includes the 1850 Anti-Prostitution Law, the Naturalization Act of 1870, the Chinese Exclusion Act of 1882, the 1906 California Anti-Miscegenation Law, the California Alien Land Acts of 1913 and 1920, the Cabel Act of 1922, the Exclusion Act of 1924, and Executive Order 9066 in 1942–45, which put 112,000 Japanese Americans in concentration camps.

23. American history is filled with examples of such injustice, including anti-Chinese riots and massacres that forced the relocation of Chinese communities in many cities, mass internment and relocation of Japanese Americans during World War II, and land invasions and colonization in the Pacific Islands. See Judy Yung, *Chinese Women in America: A Pictorial History* (Seattle: University of Washington Press, 1986).

24. Chalso Loo and Paul Ong, "Slaying Demons with a Sewing Needle: Feminist Issues for Chinatown Women," *Berkeley Journal of Sociology* 27 (1982), 77–88; and Esther Ngan-Ling Chow, "Development of Feminist Consciousness."

25. Rosabeth Moss Kanter, *Men and Women of the Corporation* (New York: Basic Books, 1977).

26. Bell Hooks, *Feminist Theory: From Margin to Center* (Boston: South End Press, 1984) and *Ain't I a Woman: Black Women and Feminism* (Boston: South End Press, 1981).

27. Mitsuye Yamada, "Asian Pacific American Women and Feminism," in *This Bridge Called My Back: Writings by Radical Women of Color,* ed. C. Morage and G. Anzaldus (Watertown, Mass.: Persephone, 1981), 71–75; Loo and Ong, "Slaying Demons"; Chow, "Development of Feminist Consciousness"; and Cheng, "Social Mobility of Asian Women."

28. Rita Fujiki Elway, "Strategies for Political Participation of Asian/Pacific Women," in *Civil Rights Issues of Asian and Pacific Americans: Myths and Realities* (Washington, D.C.: U.S. Commission on Civil Rights, 1979), 133–139.

29. Chow, "Development of Feminist Consciousness."
30. See Alice Jardine and Paul Smith, eds., *Men in Feminism* (New York: Methuen, 1987).

From Homemaker to Housing Advocate: An Interview with
Mrs. Chang Jok Lee/Nancy Diao

1. The Ping Yuen Residents Improvement Association (PYRIA), formed in 1966, serves as the official representative of 430 households of mostly monolingual Chinese public housing tenants in San Francisco's Chinatown. The Pings, as the four buildings are commonly called, constitute 15 percent of the low-income housing in Chinatown, have a waiting list with more than two thousand names, and a waiting period of five to ten years.
2. Nanking (Namking) is a city in the southern part of China. Nanking bloodsuckers are particularly poisonous and vicious worms from the area.
3. The Asian Community Center was a volunteer community service and advocacy organization which provided English, Mandarin, and singing lessons for community people. The center is now closed.
4. The International Hotel, or I-Hotel, was a San Francisco residential hotel in the last foothold of Manilatown and on the edge of Chinatown. In 1965 Four Seas Corporation, owned by real estate investors from Thailand, bought the hotel with plans to demolish the building and convert the space into mixed-use development, including offices. It became the rallying point for a concerted community-wide effort to stem the loss of low-income housing in the area.
5. Judy Wong was raped and murdered in North Ping Yuen in 1978. The elevators had not been functioning for six months, forcing Wong to use the stairs, where she was attacked.
6. In 1983 PYRIA received city funds to renovate the Ping Yuen laundromats.
7. The Orangeland Project was designed to include both low-income housing and mixed-use commercial development. But its construction would have involved the dislocation of 195 elderly and family tenants residing on the site and fourteen commercial and neighborhood shops. The Ping Yuen tenants supported the Orangeland tenants' efforts to keep their homes. With communitywide support, the Orangeland tenants were able to stay in their homes, and the original development project was relocated to another site.

Dust and Dishes: Organizing Workers/
Yoichi Shimatsu and Patricia Lee

1. Interviews for this article were conducted by the authors in 1986.
2. The group, based in Oakland, California, is called Asian Immigrant Women Advocates. Executive director Young Shin explained that the project teaches women how to use the resources of their workplace, union, and community agencies. Sometimes learning different communication skills can help defuse tense situations. "If there's a problem of communication with their employers, we try to assist by translating and by helping managers become more sensitive to cultural differences. A good case in point is the longstanding tension between Asian room cleaners and their supervisors, most of whom are European or Latin American. The supervisors communicate in a typically Western style—blunt and straightforward. The Asian women, however, expect their superiors to act with politeness, to *ask* rather than *tell* them what to do."
3. See Him Mark Lai, "Blood and Sweat in the Golden Mountains," *East/ West News*, 1 January 1976; and Alexander Saxton, *The Indispensable Enemy: Labor and the Anti-Chinese Movement* (Berkeley: University of California, 1971), 171–177.
4. *Chinese Working People in America* (San Francisco: United Front Press, 1974), 227.
5. Matthew Josephson, *Union House, Union Bar* (New York: Random House, 1956), 227.
6. See Paul Shinoff, "Local 2 Trustee's Rough Day," *San Francisco Examiner*, 15 November 1978; and "Maids Hail a Victory at St. Francis," 17 April 1980.

Seeking a Voice: South Asian Women's Groups
in North America/Jyotsna Vaid

1. Paramatma Saran, *The Asian Indian Experience in the United States* (Cambridge: Schenckman, 1985).
2. Ratna Ghosh, "Sarees and the Maple Leaf," in G. Kurien and R. Srivastave, eds., *Overseas Indians: A Study in Adaptation* (Delhi: Vikas, 1983).
3. South Asian Women's Group, "Memorandum commemorating International Women's Day," Toronto, 8 March 1985.
4. Reeta Bhatia, "South Asian Community Center: Its Background and Objectives" (Paper presented at panel on South Asian Women at Home and

Abroad, during Twelfth Annual Meeting of the South Asia Conference, University of Wisconsin, Madison, 1983).

5. Amaru Bachu, "South Asian Immigrant Women in the United States: A Statistical Overview," in J. Vaid, B. Miller, and J. Hyde, eds., *South Asian Women at Home and Abroad: A Guide to Resources* (Syracuse: Metropolitan Studies Program, Syracuse University, 1984), 8–14.

6. See, for example, Vasu Varadhan's personal account, "The Double-bind of Culture: An Indian Woman in America," in special issue on immigrant women, *COSAW Bulletin* 5 nos. 1–2 (1987), 4–7.

7. Ramdas Menon & Jyotsna Vaid, "The Ideal Mate: An Analysis of Matrimonial Advertisements in the Indian Immigrant Press" (Paper presented at panel on Dual Universes: Perspectives on the Female Immigrant Experience, during Fifteenth Annual Meeting of the South Asia Conference, University of Wisconsin, Madison, 1987). See also essay by Rashmi Luthra in this volume.

8. My observations are based on a detailed survey circulated in 1985 to eleven of the sixteen exclusively South Asian women's groups in North America. The groups include: Anamika, New York City; Asian Indian Women's Network, Los Angeles, California; Association of Asian Indian Women in America, New York City; Committee on South Asian Women, formed in East Lansing, Michigan, and now based in College Station, Texas; Committee on South Asian Women, Madison, Wisconsin; Indian Women's Association, Pullman, Washington; Manavi, New Jersey; Samaanta, Vancouver, British Columbia (since disbanded); South Asia Community Center, Montreal, Quebec; South Asian Women's Group, Toronto, Ontario; and Women from the Indian Subcontinent in Michigan, Ann Arbor, Michigan (no longer in existence). The groups not surveyed were the Cercle de Femmes du Quebec d'Origine Indienne, Montreal, Quebec; the Club of Indian Women, Chicago; the Indian Women's Club, Houston; Diva, Toronto; and the International Sikh Women's Organization, New York City. I also relied on newsletters and telephone interviews.

9. Organizations that fall into this South Asia–oriented category include the Committee on South Asian Women in Texas and its branch in Madison, Wisconsin.

10. Samaanta in Vancouver, British Columbia, focused on domestic violence against South Asian women. Two other Canadian organizations—South Asia Community Center of Montreal, Quebec, and South Asian Women's Group of Toronto, Ontario—started in an attempt to foster social and economic integration. New York's Association of Asian Indian Women in America and Los Angeles' Asian Indian Women's Network had similar integration objectives.

11. The Asian Indian Women's Network and New Jersey's Manavi are examples of groups that wished to establish an ethnic identity; Anamika formed to establish a sexual preference identity.
12. The Committee on South Asian Women and Manavi responded affirmatively. The Asian Indian Women's Network and Asian Indian Women in America both said no, they are not feminist.
13. Shamita Das Dasgupta, "Manavi: A Profile," in special issue on immigrant women, *COSAW Bulletin* 5 nos. 1–2 (1987), 22–24.
14. On the ideological level, some of the problems encountered by immigrant women's groups are shared by groups based in South Asia. In a newsletter from the Bombay Women's Center, for instance, activist Vibhuti Patel described various concerns of members of women's groups across India. One basic question each group confronted at the outset was whether to be a small group with a common understanding or a mass organization of women. Another question is related to the actual role of the activist—is it one of consciousness raising or solving personal problems? Finally, how could consciousness be raised if the group's perception of the importance of certain activities differed from that of most women? See Vibhuti Patel, "Introspection by Indian Feminists," *Women's Center Newsletter* 2(1), 1985.
15. Jyotsna Vaid, "South Asia Community Center: A Report of the First Year" (Montreal, 1982).

Asian Pacific American Women in Mainstream Politics / Judy Chu

Sources

Fritz, Sara. "Women Find Bias along Campaign Trail." *Los Angeles Times,* 11 September 1984.
Nakanishi, Don T. and LaForteza, Bernie C. *National Asian Pacific Roster: 1984.* Los Angeles: Asian American Studies Center, UCLA, 1984.
Natividad, Irene. *A Directory of Asian/Pacific Elected Officials at the Federal, State, County and City Levels.* New York: Asian/Pacific Caucus of National Women's Political Caucus, April 1982.

Acknowledgments

Thanks to the following for consenting to be interviewed for this essay: Julia Chang Bloch, Assistant Administrator, Agency for International Development, Washington, D.C.; Thelma Garcia Buchholdt, former State Representative, Anchorage, Alaska; Lily Chen, former Mayor, Monterey Park, California; Eleanor Chow, Montebello Unified School Board, Los Angeles County,

California; Lita David, Sweetwater Unified School Board, San Diego County, California; May Doi, City Clerk, Gardena, California; March Fong Eu, Secretary of State, California; June Fukawa, City Council, Delano, Central California; Helen Kawagoe, City Clerk, Carson, California; Carol Kawanami, former Mayor, Villa Park, California; Jean Sadako King, former Lieutenant Governor, Hawaii; Norma Lau, City Auditor, Oakland, California; Dana McHenry, City Council, Issaquah, Washington; Patsy Takemoto Mink, Chair, County Council, Honolulu, Hawaii; Mae Morita, Central Unified School Board, Fresno, California; Irene Natividad, Chair, National Women's Political Caucus; Norma Nomura-Seidel, former City Council member, La Palma, California; June Pouesi, Regional Director, Office of Samoan Affairs, Carson, Los Angeles County, California; Eunice Sato, former Mayor, Long Beach, California; Dolores Sibonga, City Council, Seattle, Washington; Julie Tang, San Francisco Community College Board, California; Maeley Tom, Director, State Senate Office of Asian Pacific Affairs; Judge Fumiko Hachiya Wasserman, former member Torrance Unified School Board, California; Mae Yih, State Senator, Oregon.

Thanks also for the assistance of Kanak Dutta, Irene Hirano, Don Nakanishi, and Mae Takahashi.

ASIAN WOMEN UNITED OF CALIFORNIA is a nonprofit organization founded in 1976 to promote the social, economic, and general welfare of Asian American women. In addition to *Making Waves*, Asian Women United has published three other books—*With Silk Wings: Asian American Women at Work*; *Dear Diane: Questions and Answers for Asian American Women*; and *Dear Diane: Letters from Our Daughters*.